THE IDEA OF SOCIAL STRUCTURE

Dr. George Park, a former journalist, studied literature and philosophy at Yale. He received his M.A. degree in the social sciences (1951) and a Ph.D. degree in anthropology (1958) from the University of Chicago. He did postdoctoral work in archaeology and African ethnography at Cambridge University and has carried out field studies in East Africa and Norway. At present Dr. Park is professor of social anthropology at the Memorial University of Newfoundland.

THE IDEA OF SOCIAL STRUCTURE

GEORGE PARK

ANCHOR BOOKS
ANCHOR PRESS/DOUBLEDAY
GARDEN CITY, NEW YORK
1974

ISBN: 0-385-01158-x
Library of Congress Catalog Card Number 73-9043

Printed in the United States of America
First edition

To Derrick Stenning
Sunt aliquid manes

CONTENTS

PART ONE

SOCIAL STRUCTURE AND MOTIVATION

SECTION ONE

HUMAN CONCERNS AND THEIR SOCIAL FRAMEWORK

HUMAN NATURE

Thomas Hobbes
Leviathan 1651

The word Person is latine: instead whereof the Greeks have *prosopon,* which signifies the *Face* as *Persona* in latine signifies the *disguise,* or *outward appearance* of a man, counterfeited on the Stage; and sometimes more particularly that part of it, which disguiseth the face, as a Mask or Visard: And from the Stage, hath been translated to any Representer of speech and action, as well in Tribunalls, as Theaters. So that a *Person,* is the same that an *Actor* is, both on the Stage and in common Conversation.

N INITIAL ASSUMPTION

The idea of social structure has evolved over the last two r three generations in anthropology and sociology. In one ay or another, structural conceptions inform most current nalyses of institutions. But the evolution of the ideas has not een without struggle, and controversy is still with us. Ideas bout the anatomy of human society underlie our best hopes and worst fears for the future of the world. As the ideas of social science begin to affect the behavior of governments, will the conditions of social change and survival be altered? To find an answer it is not enough to describe societies as they are and have been; we must derive from those descriptions a theoretical understanding of the relation of social structure to the balance of tradition and reform. A problem which can't be avoided is the relation of social structure to cultural difference and change: can the same political formula work for East and West, twentieth and twenty-first centuries?

If you were asked to draw a diagram of a modern, urban-industrial society, you would probably sketch a model showing distinct social classes ranked in vertical relation to one another. You might incorporate regional, ethnic, or racial cleavages as well. If you were then asked to sketch an ideal society of the future, wouldn't you try to reform your model society by altering its basic structure? That implies setting aside approaches to reform through religious revival, a deep revolution of the spirit, or an awakening to new cultural values. There is an underlying assumption that religion, culture, and the state of the human soul can't be radically changed without a redistribution of access to power, property, and the main chance—that is, structural change.

There is no community without structure, and there can be no human community without culture. Man's social structures are a good deal more variable than those of other species, but not as variable as his cultures: there are not as many ways of building with blocks as there are ways of painting designs on them. There are not as many workable kinship systems as there are kinship terminologies, not as many kinds of power as there are names for it. This means that structural phenomena are relatively open to analysis, and gives hope for tangible conclusions. Try to imagine a society of "all chiefs and no Indians" or of "all Indians and no chiefs." The study of social structure should make clear why neither of those conditions has ever prevailed, why the human condition is inseparable from structure, and where the limits of equality and of freedom lie.

HOBBES ON THE NATURE OF MAN AND SOCIETY

I began with a passage by Thomas Hobbes, written three centuries ago, at a time in English history which provoked a famous literature on man and his relation to political society. There is good reason for starting with a seventeenth-century writer. The language of the social sciences was new then; it was a great age of discovery. The implications of the idea of culture had not been worked out. Psychology and the idea of personality formation were not known, although men surely had many practical theories about the formation of *character*. The idea of social structure was unformulated. But the problems of social and political institutions were seen, if only because it was a time when old solutions were failing. By pausing to consider the way ideas of social structure were discussed when they were new to our intellectual tradition, we may gain a fresh view for ourselves.

The section of *Leviathan* I have cited concerns the distinction between natural and artificial persons, which is very close to the distinction we make today between persons and social roles. The book was an attempt to ground a comprehensive prescription for civil order upon a scientific base. Man was, for Hobbes, by nature quarrelsome, but also inclined through fear of death and cupidity to the wary use of reason. The problem of maintaining peace and order in political society was one of taking advantage of man's limited inclination to be reasonable.

Leviathan is the book of an exile. As an outspoken monarchist, Hobbes fled to Paris in 1640, and the book was composed in the ensuing decade; it was not a time in which peace could be taken for granted or attributed to nature or to the will of a benign God. Hobbes none the less wanted to show that the conditions for a stable peace could be attained, though with difficulty. The simplest way of accounting for order in human life, the idea that it is merely handed to each generation by the one before, was closed. Hobbes found that men, taken by themselves, will "appeale from custome to reason, and from reason to custome, as it serves their turn; receding from custome when their interest requires it, and setting themselves against reason, as oft as reason is against them."[1] There are not many students of society today who would claim that Hobbes found a real solution to the problems he saw—even his fellow monarchists were not quite pleased with the book at the time, for it was not facile and it challenged every sort of facile assumption on which less thoughtful men would have relied. If Custom was not fit to be king, neither was Reason; and that position was taken by the person we now consider the most eminent English philosopher of his time, at mid-century in what we still call the Age of Reason. His position is today the position a social scientist must take, though we may sometimes use *culture* for Custom and *rationally oriented action* (or *goal orientation*, or the like) for Reason.

But the main challenge to received thinking is the proposition that you can't deal with the action of men in an institutional setting as though the motivation of each act could be said to spring from the life history of the individual as a natural person. The psychology of the person is not the same as the psychology of the social role. It is a tribute to Hobbes that, although he was disposed to be a mechanist, he was not consistent to the point of excluding wholly the humane conception of man which was his original philosophical heritage. And in the idea of the artificial person he enormously complicates the problem of deriving the conditions of social order and stability from a knowledge of human nature. In so far as I am a creature falling within the order of nature, my behavior is predictable. If you understand my nature, and have power at your disposal, you should find it easy to keep me in my place. A mechanistic view of human society is not difficult to build out upon such presuppositions. The principle of order is manipulative—the whole society is *managed*. To be sure, you need a sort of superman at the top, the unmanaged manager; but if Hobbes had been content with the facile doctrine of divine kingship (by which God becomes the king's manager, and hence

[1] Hobbes, p. 84.

through the royal-aristocratic hierarchy the Provider for all men), he could have offered a simple apology for monarchic authoritarianism, instead of the difficult political philosophy which he did work out, and which gave only dubious comfort to his king. Hobbes did not believe in the essential freedom of the human will—in that he was an uncompromising modern, as we may see him in retrospect (and an atheist, as he was seen by his opponents then). But neither did Hobbes attempt to derive the critical institutional structure of society from a deterministic model of human nature. And in that he was the more radically modern.

We have to consider here three models of human society. There is first the idea that, since man's will is unpredictable, you can't reason from a knowledge of his nature toward knowledge of his ways. Few men would take the position that ants are free, or that the social structures of ant colonies are essentially more than the spelling out of coded messages embedded in formic nature. But, granting the point for ants, not many men are prepared to take the same view of their own condition. Approached in this way, the extreme free-will position seems to imply that a science of human society is impossible, since there is no necessary order in our lives.

The other two positions may be regarded as attempts to retrieve the possibility of a social science. Human institutions are neither so uniform nor so stable as their counterparts in the anthill, but can be shown to possess important regularities. Why not attribute those regularities to human nature? Aren't the coded messages in our genes like those of ants, except for the degree of specificity entailed? For example, isn't marriage patterned everywhere, though manners vary, and isn't marriage then a predictable consequence of man's nature? With care, such reasoning can be applied to the round of human institutions and made plausible: not only marriage but divorce, not only punishment but crime, not only peace and religion but war and witchcraft can be made to seem inevitable consequences of our genes. This second model of human society suggests that a social science, though difficult, is possible; and that the task of such a science is to trace connections between man's biologically given nature and the pattern of his social life.

The *Leviathan* of Hobbes, on a superficial reading, seems to have been predicated on that model, since it starts with a theory of human nature and works through it to a theory of orderly society. But we've seen that man's nature is, for Hobbes, no guarantee of order. And the special interest he showed in the conditions of political stability suggests a further point of logic. I think you can defend the view that political systems "derive" from human nature, even where you suppose that the state of nature would be a war of all against all. In terms current today you could argue that man needs repression. Is there naturally ungovernable greed? It will beget a system of government, as crime begets a system of punishment. But if order derives from a tendency to disorder, then wealth derives from poverty and illness from health, good from evil and evil from good. It might be fun to argue for each of those propositions, but I think the argument would be irrelevant to the concerns of a social science. Of what use is it to show that the conditions of political stability can be derived from the conditions of instability? If man's nature bears the seeds of both civilization and decay, order and chaos, and I wish to explain how men may move from one condition to the other, I must look for a set of intervening variables. That step of logic leads to the third sort of model of human society, based in the recognition that there may be elements of necessary order in human affairs which presuppose but do not derive from the nature of man as an individual organism.

For Hobbes, as his biblical title suggests, the well-ordered society was like a huge organism. The great Leviathan, the state, was artificial—it was made and maintained by intelligent effort, and would collapse without it. Nonetheless, the form was *like* one of the forms of nature, and deserved the same sort of objective study that physical and biological forms require. Man, left to *his* nature, could only create an ungoverned war of all against all. The reason that he did not always live so was therefore not to be found in the order of nature but must be derived from the qualities of Leviathan. Only a strong sovereign authority could draw men to agreement on certain "convenient Articles of Peace" which they would find reasonable.[2] We can liken those articles, which Hobbes regarded as natural laws, to the architectural principles by which a society must be built. We should grant that it is easier to insist that such principles have to exist than it is to give them exact formulation. We make the same admission, after all, about man the biopsychic organism: we are quite certain that he has a nature which can't be gainsaid, though we find it hard to formulate. Symmetrically, let us admit that society also is governed by laws not of its own making—laws logically prior to the existence of any particular human society, as the laws governing human nature are logically prior to your existence or mine. That is to adopt the third model of human society, of the three we have considered. We grant that society has a nature of its own, and we must therefore conceive the study of social structure as a direct approach to it. We are not bound to see society as a giant organism, an inanimate machine, or an anthill: those are mere analogues. Our task is to see human society as a thing in itself, radically unlike any other. How do we proceed?

WHAT SHOULD WE ASSUME ABOUT HUMAN NATURE?

We can't form a clear idea of social structure without first considering to what extent it is at odds with common sense. One view is that human nature is the central puzzle for students of man—that territoriality and war, depressions, scientific progress, and the current rate of divorce are all somehow to be understood as perennial expressions of the human condition, unalterable as our natures. But if the structural principle which keeps an igloo from collapse will apply to blocks of stone as well as of ice, then you can't reduce the explanation of an igloo to the description of its parts. Following the same reasoning in relation to human affairs, the idea of social structure does not all come down to human nature but requires independent consideration. There are no nonhuman societies in the known cosmos which are suffi-

[2] Hobbes, p. 106.

ciently like our own to operate on the same set of principles. If we should discover one, would the creatures have to be bipedal? viviparous? sexually dimorphic? Would their blood be red? What, in short, is the necessary relationship between the kind of societies men can make and their nature as it has evolved?

Part of the answer can be reasoned out. The structure of human societies we know is always focused on such tasks as rearing and educating children, combining sexual and domestic roles, devising a sexual division of labor, exercising authority, and handling life crises. Only a culture-bearing creature could proliferate communities structurally like man's. But what about quadrupeds? Would a creature without free hands and tools have enough use for language to evolve the faculties of articulate speech? What is the relation of life span and maturation to psyche and social life? The puzzle deepens as the questions pick at finer points: how far could man's sense organs be changed without affecting social structure? how far does society depend upon the fact of our mammalian guts and emotionality, and how far upon the symmetry, or the ridden asymmetries, of the brain? A good deal less is known than is submerged. What theories of man's nature can we reject out of hand?

Some of the questions call for better microscopes, but some are of another sort, and all of them sprawl across the borderline that separates the realms of natural and social science. Is language part of nature? emotion to be known without an introspective sense? or will the structure of the brain be understood without logical models, analogy to computer circuitry, and the testing of behavioral hypotheses in mazes? The condition of man is so profoundly affected by artifice, and has been for a million years or more so closely identified with educated experience, that one is tempted to ask how far human life is natural at all.

For the study of social structure, the spongy quality of human nature presents a special danger. If the sight of an igloo does not immediately evoke reflection on the principles of Newtonian mechanics, the sight of a human group is no more likely to evoke the idea of social structure. We can't understand war without structural analysis of the group relation it expresses. But my students find no important variables between war and human nature: war comes of "aggression" (and that comes, I hear, of "repression"—which, some say, derives from the suppression of aggression). Does this help predict when wars will occur? Ideas of human nature have common currency, and that currency alone could make them imprecise. When they are stretched to cover all the ground of explanation in the social sciences, they can only be misleading.

What should we assume about human nature? If we assume as little as we can, without denying how much there is to know, we may succeed in reversing the flow of speculation. For it is time that we began in earnest reasoning from the evidence of the social sciences, carefully considered, toward a more precise appreciation of man's nature. We would then be reasoning inductively from regularities found in actual behavior toward a generalized model of man, rather than deductively deriving the behavior from some doctrinaire conception of the unseen, inner workings of men. The science of man proceeds, after all, by successive steps of demythologization; and that begins with the attitude of skepticism. Whenever you find yourself believing that man by nature is good or bad, rapacious or magnanimous, authoritarian or democratic, sex-ridden or reasonable, consider all the disconfirming evidence as well as what confirms your view. There will always be plenty of both.

Technical terms can be useful for distinguishing the perennial questions about human nature from problems of social structure. Conceiving an individual as a biopsychic system, we can think of groups as sociocultural systems. The gain in so demarcating boundaries is that we can at least restrict human nature to one side of the field; intimacy, submission, authority, competition, and such variables then fall on the other side and aren't sponged up into the master category of commonsense psychology. We set aside the one package, the better to get at the other. The interconnections between body and mind are subtle and many, justifying curiosity, but those between social structure and culture are no less so.

CULTURE AND STRUCTURE

CULTURAL DETERMINISM

There are questions about man and history which in one form or another must recur in each generation, so long as man is curious. They are questions about life and death, peace and war, man and woman, youth and age, we and they. Each generation asks them in a characteristic form and answers accordingly. For the generation of North American anthropologists writing in the nineteen-twenties and thirties the master category for the phrasing of question and answer was culture. A generation before the category had perhaps been progress. Why were the Australian Aborigines still paleolithic hunters ten thousand years after the Europeans had transcended that way of life? At the start of this century, the answer was isolation, which accounted for backwardness. By the time of the Great Depression the question was sometimes being put a little more humbly: Why, after prolonged exposure to European example, did the surviving Aborigines continue to prefer their own life? The answer lay in the relativity of cultures conceived as systems of value, and the immersion of man from birth onward in the culture of his fathers. Willing or unwilling, the anthropologist found he had a mission to the world, because although it was rapidly shrinking, few other scholars were truly aware of the range of difference, in culturally sponsored beliefs and values, among the world's peoples. What explanation of these differences would put all cultural groups, great or small, on an equal plane?

The simplest and often the most effective answer was to paint a picture of the omnipotence of culture. There were popular doctrines bearing on all the perennial questions. To confront the racist or the environmental determinist (or the biologist who announced that war, homosexuality, and crime were all glandular), anthropologists were led to an extreme position of their own, cultural determinism. The time is past for erecting a structural determinism in its place. The two ideas represent disparate but indispensable frames of reference. Perhaps we should see them as two dimensions of all social space, since you can be close to another person either culturally or structurally—you can marry a person of different culture, and a stranger may prove to be culturally very close. Structural ties are often strongest where the two parties are quite different, as when a farmer and a fisherman have a trading relationship. Cultural ties depend on homogeneity, the sharing of values.

In one respect cultural determinism parallels the historical determinism of Karl Marx. Both assume that society can be explained as a product of historical process, and that human nature doesn't appreciably limit that process. Both positions assume and stress the educability of man. Marx was the first modern writer to offer a comprehensive view of history within the frame of social structure. His dialectical materialism was patterned on and opposed to the dialectic of Hegel, which discussed the movement of world history within what we would now call a cultural frame. Marx and Hegel both pretended to understand the meaning of the past and the direction of change of the future world. But the anthropologists' claims were almost diametrically opposite. Rejecting cultural evolutionism, they rejected the unity of history, assuming the radical individuality of every age and each human culture.

On the political scene Marxism became synonymous with radicalism; but on a philosophical plane cultural determinism was a more radical departure. Marxism readily became an ideology, a system of belief and practice, because it claimed to show how a human society could transcend historically relative teachings and found itself on everlasting truths. But anthropology suggested that no society—and anthropologists had to be acquainted with hundreds of them, mainly classless—could possess truth and ethical perfection. In their ethical emphases all societies were equally arbitrary, and people were "shaped to the form of their culture." Ruth Benedict's statement is from a famous book, in which (as in *Leviathan*) the whole problem of the relation between human nature and social order was reconsidered:

Ruth Benedict
Patterns of Culture 1934

We have seen that any society selects some segment of the arc of possible human behaviour, and in so far as it achieves integration its institutions tend to further the expression of its selected segment and to inhibit opposite expressions. . . .

The vast proportion of all individuals who are born into any society always and whatever the idiosyncrasies of its institutions, assume, as we have seen, the behaviour dictated by that society. This fact is always interpreted by the carriers of that culture as being due to the fact that their particular institutions reflect an ultimate and universal sanity. The actual reason is quite different. Most people are shaped to the form of their culture because of the enormous malleability of their original endowment. They are plastic to the moulding force of the society into which they are born.

It is largely because of the traditional acceptance of a conflict between society and the individual, that emphasis upon cultural behavior is so often interpreted as denial of the autonomy of the individual. . . . Anthropology is often believed to be a counsel of despair which makes untenable a beneficent human illusion. But no anthropologist with a background of experience of other cultures has ever believed that individuals were automatons, mechanically carrying out the decrees of their civilization. No culture yet observed has been able to eradicate the difference in the temperaments of the persons who compose it. . . . It is not possible to discuss patterns of culture without considering specifically their relation to individual psychology.

What is the "beneficent human illusion" which this philosopher-anthropologist was afraid we might lose? We may say, the individuality or perhaps the originality of the person. In relation to politics, we are especially apt to think of the dignity of the individual; in the more general context of humane discussion, Benedict's illusion has at once no name and a thousand names: if it were not everywhere assumed, the discussions would have no point. Benedict argued that the findings of anthropology did not threaten that assumption, or in any way deny "the autonomy of the individual." But how good is her argument, and how much comfort can the humanist safely take from it? Her doctrine of the "enormous malleability" of human nature is precisely the counter-doctrine to a racist or other genetic determinism.

Compare the Benedict of 1934 with the Hobbes of 1651, asking in each case what aspects of human behavior seem to be predetermined by our natures. For Benedict, temperament was inborn, and each of us had one; but in most cases it was "plastic to the moulding force" of our culture, as clay is plastic to the sculptor's hand.

A few of us, in the scheme of history and the human condition which Benedict sketched, were predestined to suffer as deviants, unable to adjust to the specific demands of our culture, because the demands of temperament were opposite and equal—nature had not suited us to the one way of life which history had dealt. It's easy enough to imagine the plight of an ascetic born into a licentious society, a sensualist among Puritans, an Othello in a society of Iagos, or a Milquetoast among wolves. For Benedict, such persons were the unfortunate but inevitable sports of history, product of the occasional clash between an extreme variant of natural temperament and an opposite emphasis in the dictates of a particular culture. But most persons adhered to a cultural standard, with only minor tokens of their individuality remaining.

For Hobbes in the seventeenth century the problem of human nature was not a problem of individuality or its absence. Self-centered, self-interested man aspired to his own ends; originality was basic, resulting from the tendency of the human passions to set one man against another as each indulged his appetites. Hobbes assumes a world of Pistols and Falstaffs—can it be that there *were* so many more in his day than we see in ours?

Though the two models of man and society have been juxtaposed, they do not meet. Nature, for Hobbes, gives rise to reason, and reason in the right circumstances will give rise to society. Always that society is maintained in a fragile balance above the tide which would wash it away; the social conventions have no secure purchase *in the character of the individuals* composing any human community. But the idea of culture, in the scheme of anthropological theory which Benedict best presented, presupposed just such a purchase of social convention within the individual. For the person, as we have seen, was from the start "shaped to the form" of his culture. And in that measure, it follows, his culture resided in him.

THE VOICES OF CULTURE

The difference between Hobbes and Benedict, seventeenth century and twentieth, is the difference between the idea of custom and the idea of culture. Hobbes had but to look about him to see men everywhere appealing "from custome to reason, and from reason to custome, as it serves their turn." Benedict, impressed by the diversity of cultures, the evidently arbitrary nature of their emphases, and their apparent conservatism, found she must fall back on the notion of inborn temperamental differences to keep alive the illusion of personal originality, which accords with our ordinary experience. The ideas of custom and of culture coincide in giving us a picture of a body of external dictates to which an individual should conform. But the idea of culture is bolder—it adds to that picture another, of the person who *is* little more than the creature his culture is disposed to produce.

In working out a strategy for the study of social structure, trying to eliminate major contradictions, we found that we should regard man as one natural system and society as another system, of comparable importance in the explanation of behavior. But now we confront the possibility that *within* man there is much that is not natural but derives directly from his participation in society. Should we take back "culture" and put it in "human nature," not in "society"? Evidently, that would be no solution. Culture is an antithesis to nature. Culture is quite particular, derivative of the historical process; nature is universal, logically prior to any historical process. The cultural process, even when it replicates an item in manifold copies and maintains it over great reaches of time, produces things that are time- and space-bound; while whatever is true of nature is timelessly true; ultimately, nature repeats. But if these considerations are well founded, then culture can't comfortably be ascribed to either man or society, if the former is a natural system and if we wish to conceive of the latter as a like-natural system. The struggle with words has brought us to an impasse.

The boldest way out may lie in reforming or expanding our ideas of nature, but I will not take that path here. A proximate solution will suffice, which lies in wrestling loose from the tyranny of words. The capacity for culture—for example, the ability to acquire a language—is built into human nature. Similarly, society requires culture (language) for its existence. It is then in the nature of man to require some language as a condition of normal association, and it is in the nature of societies to require *some* language, in order to exist. That is, a culture bridges the distance from the raw man to the orderly social group. To say man is a cultural animal is to say he has and depends on a protean capacity for making and keeping orderly structures. His two main types of structure are technical (including language, music, and law as well as machines) and social.

We have not resolved all the contradictions, but I think we have wrestled free enough to dare turn our backs on those that remain. Where do culture and social structure meet, not on the plane of abstractions but in fact? We can best settle that by turning to a case study. The following scene is from an account of a woman who, in a crisis of her marriage, wanted help from others. In the end, when it was offered, she refused; and it will profit us to ask why.

J. H. M. Beattie
A Nyoro Case Study 1953
Africa XXXV: 3 (July 1965) p. 259

The place is:

Bunyoro kingdom, Uganda, East Africa, in the 1940s: in a hut. The writer is a young Nyoro assistant to Dr. Beattie, and the account is retrospective.

The persons are:

Nyangoma, *a woman whose husband has taken a second and younger wife.*

A diviner and medicine man, a traveller. His name is Rukara.

The writer, *who was a boy when the incident occurred.*

Time:

In the nineteen-forties.

Nyangoma said: "And what am I to do?" Rukara threw the cowries down again and said: "If you don't take care your co-wife will succeed in killing you. Look, she has already begun visiting various doctor-diviners to look for medicine to kill you with. You are going to die."

I could see Nyangoma's eyes, and see, they started to fill with tears, and she began to look very distressed. Rukara said: "Bear up, she won't kill you: the matter will be settled. I want to give you medicine to kill your co-wife with." But Nyangoma replied: "No: I am not able to do this thing of killing my co-wife; let her herself give up using medicine for killing people."

At this point I said to that woman Nyangoma: "But haven't you understood that that 'sister' of yours is wanting to kill you? Do you forgive a person who wishes to kill you?" She did not reply to this, but Rukara said to me: "Child, you will be a man!" And when I saw that Rukara agreed with what I said, I went on and said more to her. Bur she was indeed a good and loving woman; look, even though I and Rukara advised her that she should kill her co-wife in order to save herself, she completely refused to agree. She said: "Better I should die than that I should kill anybody."

It would not be easy to say what are the cultural dictates of Nyoro society, as they apply to Nyangoma. At the time, the men advised her to take the way of aggression; but in retrospect one man admired her refusal; and the advice of the other was scarcely disinterested: Rukara had medicine to sell. Also the boy took his clues from the impressive doctor-diviner, and so could not speak without prejudice the dictates of his culture.

But is not divination an institution of Nyoro society? and is not the role of doctor-diviner well established in Nyoro social structure? And is Nyangoma, then, a cultural deviant who will not accept the definition of her situation, which is socially established? Evidently, Nyoro are expected to cope with personal problems through aggressive assertion of the self, couched in the idiom of sorcery. Is Nyangoma one whose natural endowment, as Ruth Benedict would have put it, simply did not suit her to holding her own in Nyoro culture? I think we can understand Nyangoma's case without such special pleading. Is it likely, after all, that either Nyangoma or any other Nyoro woman in her place would be aware of any dictate of the culture which made the decision an easy one? As she squats there in a hut with an itinerant diviner, Nyangoma is aware that there are many different minds to which her situation is known, each with its own grasp of the matter and most with some advice. We can predict that if Nyangoma knew beyond doubt that all would advise her to buy the killing medicine, she would do it: then there *would* be a pertinent dictate. But usually the voices of one's culture are many and indistinct. That is only the more likely in a trouble case, where emotions conflict and men move secretly.

Our conclusion is that culture has many voices, seldom wholly in concert. Here the idea of culture and the idea of social structure meet. Who speaks to me or to Nyangoma for my culture or hers? To answer, you will need models of the two societies, showing my structural position and hers. A culture has no impersonal voice but dwells in particular persons, emerging only in the peculiar forms which actual situations elicit. It is to such situations that we must turn for the empirical meaning of the two complementary abstractions, culture and social structure.

MY BROTHER'S KEEPER: THE IDEA OF RECIPROCITY

Though we have rejected the idea of an omnipotent culture, we have learned from Ruth Benedict and from the anthropology of her day to be wary how much we will assume about a man before we are acquainted with his culture. If human nature is not so plastic as it was thought to be, and culture not the demiurge she would have had it, we still can't go back to the model of Hobbes, in which the passionate interests of man spring full-blown from his nature. If at times culture seems to be little more than a veneer and an idiom through which the self-regarding, rationally calculating natural man is visible, there are other times when the springs of human action don't seem to lie in nature at all but in ideas or ideals of man's own distinctive invention. We reject the plastic theory of man in extreme form, though we know that you can't move easily from animal nature to adult behavior, or make inferences back from behavior to nature, in the case of man, as you can for beasts less dependent on learning. But if there is no omnipotent culture to keep us in line, what prevents men "receding from custome when their interest requires it, and setting themselves against reason"?

Hobbes took for granted the human family; he took it to be natural. But Hobbes never married and so could escape discovering that a family is, like the polity of a nation, maintained by unremitting effort. It is the same with social groups of any size, each of which exhibits the style of its culture. If we can explain why that is so, have we not explained why societies and their cultures tend to persist? Isn't it mainly a matter of living up to the direct demands people put on us?

This is to say that the problem of the persistence of societies and ways of life will yield to the same principles that explain the persistence of small groups, a convenient working assumption. The idea of reciprocity really implies personal relations; it applies to the relationships of large groups insofar as they behave in the manner of persons. Men are less inclined to live up to an impersonal ideal or norm than they are to meet the legitimate personal demands of their fellows. I may be a great one for cursing out in the garage where I am left alone; but I shall be more restrained before guests in the living room, even when equally frustrated. The policeman is of course very conscious of the law, but he decides for himself when to obey it. That would be more often if his colleagues were inclined to arrest him as readily as you or me.

I don't champion the idea of reciprocity to the exclusion of the idea of culture. I argue that culture has many voices; that is, it is embodied in the living demands on you of other persons, who are in position to put an effective hand on your shoulder. The question, What persons are in position to sanction which of your activities? is about the same as the question, What is your position in the social structure of your group? A culture is, after all, a living thing. Medieval Europe has left many remains, from which we can get a sense of its culture. Closer at hand, we can reconstruct the cultures of Nazi Germany or of Tsarist Russia, and still interview men who were agents of those cultures. But Nazism is alive only where there are survivors who have formed themselves into exclusive social groups, in which fascistic values are maintained. If Hitler had survived, as Eichmann did, his cross-examination would have produced no less weird a picture; for a culture is nowhere—in no book and in no man's head—neatly packaged and formulated. The many voices *are* the culture, and it is unambiguous only when its thinking agents are unanimous.

The idea of reciprocity is more general and more elemental than the idea of contract. A family could be regarded as a structure composed of informal, dyadic contracts, securing benefits to the members and committing them to services. With two parties, there is one contract; with three members, there are three; but with four members there would be six contracts, and so on—such a model soon becomes unmanageable. It is easier and more realistic to conceive that each person occupies a particular *status* in the family, and that the others recognize what that status implies—what claims the person has upon them, and they upon him. In the case of a contract, we assume that the benefits to each side are equivalent because we suppose that the parties are free and self-interested. But realistically, a contract is a special sort of human relationship, and an artificial one. We are not assured of equivalence in any formal sense; rather, we are accorded a status of more or less importance, and we are prepared in a rough way to settle for that. Where the lord can claim substantial and regular services, the serf has protection in return; but the question of equivalence is a subtle and subjective one which we had best not try to settle. If a man accepts the status of serf he will be bound to play the part, and the system will persist as long as men do that. Yet a serf on a medieval manor farm was not free to isolate his contract with the lord from all the rest of his network of social ties; if he would break with the lord he must break away entirely. Evidently, he was usually willing to settle for the benefits and obligations which his status on the farm implied. Reciprocity in its most pervasive form is for each person a one-many relationship, a constraining net, not a dyadic contract. Yet reciprocity implies, as does a contract, a rough balance of rights and duties, claims and counterclaims. I am my brother's keeper and he is mine; and I am held to my tasks not by his claims alone but by those of all with whom we are connected. For my brother it is the same.

The differences between the two ideas of contract and structural reciprocity can be seen in relation to the problem of sanctions. Contract presupposes an external sanctioning power to which you can appeal if I default. But structural reciprocity exists only where that reserve sanctioning power is built into our relationship, such that I jeopardize an important social status if I default in meeting your legitimate claims upon me. Instead of a simple dyadic relationship, there is a network of ties in which we both are implicated; neither can default upon the other without public knowledge and status loss; and, indeed, our relation to one another *is* one of status, not of contract. That is, we have not freely decided what our mutual claims shall be; we have fallen into a role relationship, ready-made, for which the pattern of mutual claims is socially defined and sanctioned.

THE PUZZLE OF MOTIVATION

FUNCTION AND SURVIVAL

The name most closely associated with the idea of reciprocity is that of Bronislaw Malinowski (1884–1942), who also championed functionalism over the doctrine of survivals. Malinowski argued that human institutions survived because they worked, that a culture was not an exhibition of a people's history but of its sociology and psychology. This means that although we can discover clues to the past in the usages of today, if a church, a political constitution, a peculiar ceremonial dance, or a bit of garden magic is a living facet of your culture it is not mainly because grandfather had a use for it but because you do.

Functionalism in this sense is a sound position to take, since a society whose culture was heavily laden with useless survivals of the customs of bygone generations would itself be unfit to survive. There must be a mechanism by which a society is able to adapt through its institutions to the needs of the time, uncluttering itself of its ethical and ideological deadwood.

The problem that arises next is specifying what sorts of functions an institution might have; and, having done that, we want to find out how important each sort of function is, in connection with particular types of institutions, in particular types of human society. The second question is a program for at least another century of work, but the first can be fairly simply answered. We can sort the statements anthropologists have made, attributing functions to human institutions, into the following types;

(a) Statements that the institution serves the biopsychic needs inherent in man's nature and therefore general to all men and all societies.

(b) Statements that the institution answers to deep personality needs prevalent in the particular society concerned, and functions in the satisfaction of those needs.

(c) Statements that the institution serves to maintain the particular system of beliefs and values characteristic of the culture concerned.

(d) Statements that the institution has the function of maintaining order through lending support to existing social arrangements—*i.e.*, structural-functional statements.

Malinowski associated himself for the most part with statements of type (a). A varied group of anthropologists, psychologists, and psychiatrists, using one or another theory of developmental psychology, have constituted the culture and personality approach associated with statements of type (b). Ruth Benedict and many other North American anthropologists of her generation gave us interpretations of whole cultures which rested firmly on statements of type (c). But the association between an institution (church, state, school) and the values it fosters (religion, civil order, docility) is one very nearly of identity—we often say the church *embodies* religion. For that reason, the functional character of such analysis has often not been noted. Perhaps the most explicit statement of type (c) is one of the earliest, by A. R. Radcliffe-Brown in *The Andaman Islanders* (1922), where he argues that the function of ceremony and myth is to maintain the "appropriate sentiments" and the "social values" according to which behavior is regulated in a particular society. But, rightly or not, Radcliffe-Brown is best known for his functional analyses of structural arrangements; and it is clear that statements of type (d) should be our main concern in this book: we are primarily concerned with the way social structures work.

Structural-functional theory has contributed more controversy to anthropology than any of the other types, including even the various psychoanalytic approaches to culture and personality. The reason is not far to seek. If an institution has the function, not of serving my needs but, as an end in itself, of turning the wheels of the social system, why do I and why does anyone else *support* the institution? Where institutions are regarded as centering in beliefs and values, that question does not arise, because men may have all sorts of reasons for accepting and dedicating themselves to the beliefs and values current in their society. If one could only find ways of explaining all social behavior in propositions of type (a), type (b), and type (c)—if one could do without structural-functional statements—one could avoid a good many problems. Who does not prefer a monism ("It all goes back to human nature") to the dualistic position which is forced on us by structural-functional theory? You can't hope to explain the character of human institutions without a model of human nature. But if you must add to that a model of *society's* nature, then you're faced with a theoretical problem reminiscent of the old mind-body dualism. If there are two separate systems, what sort of magic keeps them yoked in parallel? If changes in the one are not the cause of changes in the other, how can they be linked?

It will help to take up examples and follow out the analogy between this new problem of dualism and the old. The mind-body problem manifested itself as a puzzle of consciousness; the present one can be called the puzzle of motivation.

As long as the mind-body problem is not confused with the question of a supernatural soul, psychologists have been inclined to regard the puzzle as solved, however much we may yet have to learn about both body and mind. Instead of regarding man as a tentative and not quite natural compound of physical and (somehow) nonphysical events, today we find it easy to conceive of consciousness as an inseparable attribute of human mental activity. You can't credit the reality of unconscious, subconscious, or preconscious mental processes if you don't believe that mind and body are intimately joined. The difference between wrong and right reasoning can't be stated in biological terms, but it can be discussed in the language of cybernetics; the difference between anguish and elation can be stated in biological terms, yet who would say they are, in cause and consequence, essentially biological phenomena? On the whole, we are content to work today toward what has here been called a biopsychic model of man, though we are perhaps more aware than ever of the danger in failing to distinguish psychological from somatic symptoms and treatments.

The social-structural puzzle of motivation is destined to be treated in much the same way as the puzzle of consciousness. The mystery of human awareness and conscious thought is connected with the uniqueness of intelligent experience, and will not be dispelled by an analytical science of mind. But while the scientist no longer tries to build either a materialist or an idealist model of man, he has gradually been able to lay the foundations for a monism which will include mind and body, psyche and soma, as autonomous systems interacting in a single field—or even as subsystems within an integral model of man. Before we had some firm understanding of the causal interconnections between psychic and somatic processes, their qualitative distinctness seemed to be all-important; so that if both processes were considered real, dualism couldn't be avoided. Today, the interconnections have come to seem just as real. Our task in preparing the way for a study of social structure is similar to that which was done for psychology during the first half of the twentieth century, except that we are now moving on from the level of individual experience to that of the collective social life of man. We assume that social structures are real and therefore subject to the laws imposed by their nature. But we seek to show also that the interconnections to psychology are perfectly real.

It is the problem of those interconnections that lies at the heart of the puzzle of motivation. Let us consider an example.

Jules Henry
Jungle People 1964 (1941)
New York: Vintage Books, pp. 194–97

The place is:

Highland Brazil, a government reservation in the state of Santa Catarina, where dwell one hundred-odd Kaingang, remnants of a more numerous hunting people.

The time is:

1932–34

NOTE:

Here and there the original text has been reworded to avoid the use of difficult native terms.

THE CEREMONY OF THE PLACENTA AND UMBILICAL CORD

When the child is born the placenta and the piece of the umbilical cord that was attached to the child are wrapped in medicinal herbs, placed in a little basket, and sunk in a stream, and a sharpened stick is forced through the basket to keep it from floating away. This is called by the term which means to steal or to conceal, and it is done most usually by a brother of the mother and his wife. Through the series of rites that begin with the sinking of his umbilical cord the child is bound to his father's affinal relatives.

THE BABY-BLACKENING

This was the most joyful ceremony of the Kaingang. Every few years, whenever there were enough children to warrant a baby-blackening, a large number of the people of one extended family used to come together in a big camp. While the men with children to blacken went out with their brothers and first cousins to get honey for beer, the others made dance ornaments and hunted. The Kaingang cannot restrain themselves as the day of the festa draws near, and night after night as the beer ferments the men walk back and forth across the camp circle carrying their babies on their backs and singing. When at last the beer is ready the women paint their husbands with a black mixture made of charcoal and the sticky sap of a tree and stick feathers in it, and the men put little square hats of embira bark on their heads and wide bark belts around their waists, with bark tassels hanging down. Some of the belts are painted with black paint or animals' blood in crude designs that represent nothing at all. Now some men and women pass around the beer while the men stand or sit and sing, beating time by pounding on the ground with their clubs and lances. When the men have been singing awhile their wives come and stand or sit behind them, moving their arms slowly up and down in time to the music. Everyone sings as he chooses and as loud as he can, while clusters of young men stand around the older ones to try to learn the songs. There is no attempt to achieve harmony—everyone sings a different song, self-centered, musically oblivious to his surroundings. As they stand shaking their rattles or pounding their weapons on the ground—dancing, the Kaingang call it—they stop from time to time to drink the beer. All day long and until late at night they drink while the women now stand, now sit, behind them, drinking beer, nursing babies, cooking food, eating, mourning, singing, quarreling. Every once in a while a group of men and women break out of the circle and walk across and around the dance circle in a confused singing knot, drunk, intense, and unsteady. This staggering around the circle is called dancing but bears not the slightest resemblance to the rhythmic artistic form usually called dancing. The Kaingang make no effort to execute a formalized dance step. All they do is walk; yet their word for it is dancing, and they use the same term for the Brazilian polkas. What the word really means is something like "motion on foot while singing." Little children of five or more are not excluded from the festa but drink their beer, try to sing, and march around with the others. Sometimes two or three little boys will take a gourd of beer and go off by themselves and drink it, shaking rattles and singing.

At some time during this festa the children's lips are pierced. I saw only one child pierced—a boy about two. While Chantagn, its mother, held it on her lap, its grandmother forced beer into its mouth by pressing her lips against the child's and squirting while it wriggled and bawled to high heaven. This was to make the child sleep. Now while the child's mother, aunt, and some other women wept, the child was bathed in beer, wrapped in a blanket, screaming all the while, and laid down on a small heap of blankets. While the child was lying down it was coaxed to nurse to quiet it, even as its *kokla* (ceremonial father) sat by swinging the little piercing knife in time to his own song. "They sing," say the Kaingang, "so that the child will become frightened and go to sleep." While we may credit the Kaingang with deep knowledge of infantile behavior under stress, it was clear that in this case the infant was completely unaware of just what was going to happen to him; for in spite of the beer and the nursing he was wide awake when his lower lip was marked with three parallel black lines and his upper with one. These were centering lines made so that the piercing would be precisely in the middle of the child's lower lip just under the red part.

Now as the completely terrorized infant is held down by a number of people, while its mother and other women around it weep and the loud singing goes on, the *kokla* thrusts his fingers into the child's mouth, distends the lip, and thrusts home with the knife. The child wriggles and screams, seizes the knife, and tries to pull it out as its mouth fills with blood and saliva. Now that the knife is extracted they try to insert the tiny lip plug, pushing and twisting and turning while the baby howls and the blood streams from its lip until at last the plug breaks in an ugly splintery end. Evidently the hole is not properly made. Again the *kokla* distends the little lip and thrusts again with the knife. This time must be the last, so he twists and twists the knife until he is sure at last that the hole is big enough. When the plug is successfully inserted it is bound around on the outside with a bit of fiber to prevent its slipping back. Then one of the men takes water in his mouth and squirts it over the wound.

The piercing over, the *kokla* picks up the baby, slings it in a blanket on his back, and begins to walk back and forth across the circle singing. Then he and the rest of the men stop and shout, "This is your [the infant's] making."

INTERPRETATION

When the beer is gone the camp breaks up.

Although the Kaingang do not say so, it is clear that the ceremonies have the purpose of giving the child a ceremonial father and mother, usually brothers or sisters of the mother. They perform the first formal act after the child is born by putting the umbilical cord, the symbol of its birth, in the water; and at last they "make the child" at the ceremony of baby-blackening. On this occasion they receive presents along with the other affinal relatives of the parents, but they are especially rewarded for their services in the lip-piercing.

How is it that the anthropologist is able to state with confidence the "purpose" of the ceremonies, though "the Kaingang do not say so"? Presumably, if you asked a Kaingang person, he would say that the object of the first ceremony is to provide safe disposal of a set of very dangerous bits of human flesh; and the object of the second is to "make the child." Clearly, the anthropologist wants to go further. Although the explanation he did offer was a structural-functional statement, he might well have offered functional statements of the other three types also. As the "most joyful ceremony of the Kaingang" the baby-blackening obviously serves some of the biopsychic needs of the people, which they share with all mankind—a statement of type (a). Further, when we note how irregular and confused is the dancing we gain some insight into the typical personality of the Kaingang: where another people would demand a strong rhythm and a clear patterning of the dance, this community shows a radically egoistic personal style. Accordingly, we can frame statements of either type (b) or type (c): dancing and drinking in that style helps to satisfy needs rooted deeply in the Kaingang way of life, and helps to reinforce its values.

But Jules Henry was probably right in sensing that the distinctive function of these ceremonies, which sets them apart om others among the same people, is that of "giving the ild a ceremonial father and mother." Theirs was a society which life was terribly insecure; their communities were rn by enmities which marriage in some measure could itigate; the ties between a child and his mother's people ere especially important. Could the making of such ties, en, have been the *explicit* purpose of the ceremonies? I ink the answer is that by making such a purpose explicit e Kaingang would have weakened the force of the cere- ony to the point that the new ties would have had little no structural significance. The Kaingang believe that the aking of the birth waste and the lip-piercing are essential a baby's welfare; accordingly, the ceremonial parents have, performing real services for the child, committed them- lves to caring for its welfare. But if there were some other otive for their actions, then the caring motive would *not* ave been demonstrated in the ceremonial procedures. Ties reciprocity everywhere depend on the same paradoxical rinciple. The structural function is never the explicit motive a customary act; there is a clean disjunction between the nction (which is the *raison d'être* of the act *as custom*) ıd the purpose or motive (which is the *raison d'être* of the ct, considered as the deed of an individual). We have to eal with that discontinuity, which we earlier recognized, etween the motivation of the role and that of the person; ut we have also to go further, and recognize that the *otivation* of the role may be apparently discontinuous with s *function.*

Applying those lessons to the Kaingang case, we can say at the major function of many of their ceremonies and ther institutions as well is that of building up and reinforc- g social ties upon which a person can depend when at- cked or otherwise in need; but that the Kaingang them- lves do not know that, and do what they do for quite ifferent reasons. The structure—the social system—is there; ut there seems to be no valid psychological explanation for . There seem to be no tangible interconnections between e biopsychic system and the social system, the psychologi- al level and the sociological.

The difference between civilization and the (hypothetical) state of nature is likely to come down to the questio of whether or not you can depend on help when you ar attacked or wrongfully oppressed. Human survival depend on the maintenance of social ties. One way or another, al major institutions *must* have structural functions. The puzzl is to understand how it can be brought about that the need of the social system and the requirements of a coherentl motivated, autonomous individual are simultaneously met If we can't simply fall back on an omnipotent Custom (o Society) which dictates men's actions so that they don' think or want for themselves, then we are faced with th task of finding an alternative explanation for man's con ventionality, and the usefulness to "Society" of his conven tions.

CHARACTER AND ROLE

Confronted with the evidence that societies can be scale as ranging between a pole you could call conservative o traditional to one you could call progressive or digressive some observers have been content with a rather simple psy chological explanation. They hold that the traditional societ is such because its citizens are tradition-oriented, while socie ties that can be scaled toward the other end of the continuum must be composed of persons otherwise disposed. As an ex planation of social stability, the idea of tradition orientatio has little to recommend it; it amounts to saying some societie are conservative because they are societies of conservative people. That is a bit like saying the difference between chairs and tables is explained by the fact that chairs are made of chair parts and tables of table parts. No doubt, conventionality is an attribute of life in a very stable society; in fact, conventionality is characteristic of all orderly socie ties, whether stable or changing; a culture, like a language, *is* a great complex of conventions. What makes one such complex traditional and the other not?

The question raises afresh the problem of the relation between psychology and sociology, reminding us that thei subjects are associated in part-whole relationships. A group of very conservative people, earnestly devoted to an unworkable set of conventions, will not constitute a workable society; a group of very progressive people, earnestly trying to build an unworkable utopia, will not build it. The lessons for us are two: first, that character (or orientation) and social structure go together, as chair parts go with chairs, table parts with tables; second, that the solution to our new problem of duality apparently lies in finding out *why* character and social structure, where you find them, usually are well suited. More than any other single thinker, Freud trampled over the old mind-body dualism, supplying us with a glimpse of the mechanisms by which the two systems were joined. What, in the new context, are the mechanisms by which biopsychic and social systems are integrated?

The idea of *social role* is neither unfamiliar nor difficult. Hobbes was hardly the first, nor was Shakespeare, to see that ordinary social life could be regarded as a sort of show with an internal audience, like a workshop drama done for its own sake. We only notice the element of make-believe, perhaps, when we are new to a role: the first dates of courtship, the first weeks of marriage, the first months of parenthood. After the initial insecurities, when we must take care not to fall out of character, we are usually able to make the role our own, if it puts no demands upon us which we are not equipped to meet. When we are perfectly comfortable in a social role it does not seem artificial; and nothing could make us step out of character. One of the mechanisms by which the social system is motivated lies just there: an established social role is a well-beaten path where the going is easier, far less risky than going it alone and depending on your own sense of direction.

Correlative to social role is the idea of *character*, which is at least as familiar but, whether in the analysis of drama or the analysis of ordinary life, slips much more easily away from us. On the one hand, *character* is closer in current English usage than *personality* to the *Persona* of Hobbes, which "signifies the *disguise*, or *outward appearance* of a man." I can step in and out of character, but I am bound by my personality. On the other hand, my *character* is something I know intimately, as no one else could. *Per-*

sonality has become a technical term. Men submit patiently to study, hoping that expert advice will help them cope with their own intransigent personalities. But when you think of someone talking about your character you don't usually think of a dispassionate and "clinical" analysis, nor would you usually be willing to pay for it. My character is as close to my heart as my personality is not. A second mechanism by which the social system is motivated lies just here: for my character, which is so visible, so outward, is also a way into me, a sort of inward-reaching wire which touches where my motives are. Wherever I go, however I may despise it I will be "given a character"; in every encounter, however I may disguise it, I betray my judgment of someone else.

We have seen that the idea of culture calls for an amendment to the view of man and society which one finds in Hobbes and in many writers of his time. As we move from infancy toward adulthood we become both social (socialized) and cultural (enculturated). We don't readily lose ability to move from one cultural group to another, even though the styles of life be very different. Nonetheless, the customs of a particular society do have some secure purchase in the character of the individuals composing it; just as linguistic conventions (English, French, Urdu . . .) are rooted in a group, though they need not bind individuals, so with other idioms and so with that whole complex of conventions, the culture. As I can't invent my own grammar and yet be understood, so I can't invent the rules by which my character is judged.

The phenomena of shame and guilt, social danger and risk, ignominy and glory, flattery, pomposity and "impression-management," hero-worship and identification, envy and emulation and infatuation—these are some of the mechanisms which relate psyche and social structure. They are common to all social systems on the human level and distinctive of that level; some writers have identified them with human nature itself. They will serve here to suggest the stuff of which characters are made. As a preliminary formulation of the relationship we have seen between man and society, by which the individual career and the social structure are brought into a common field, let us conclude that *character is the vehicle of conventional motivation.* We understand that character in that formula has both an ethical and a dramatic meaning, and that conventional motivation would have a somewhat different face in each different social role, corresponding to a distinct position in the social structure.

SECTION TWO

CASE STUDIES IN SOCIAL CONTROL

KIOWA OF THE NORTH AMERICAN PRAIRIES

Jane Richardson
Law and Status Among the Kiowa Indians
19th Century Retrospect Cases 16, 13, 17, 84, 14, 6

CASE I: MURDER OF A WIFE

The persons are:

H (=*Husband*): *Twkoide, a lesser headman, Ten Medicine Keeper. Of middle rank*

W (=*Wife*): *one of three.* Onde-*born–that is, aristocratic rank.*

C (=*Co-respondent*): *a young man of middle rank. Member of Adltoyui military society.*

Time:
About 1865

He was a "mean," "not very good," man. He was a war chief. Sometimes he would steal women by force from other men. He had three wives, whom he whipped a great deal because he was very jealous. One day while H and W were both in the tipi a woman opened the flap of the tipi and peeped in. When she saw them both there, she left. She came again and left immediately without saying anything. He suspected that she was being sent by a young man who was trying to establish a liaison with his wife. He went out to spy on them. He saw the woman go inside his tipi and then come out with W, both carrying ropes with canvas (for wood carrying). They walked toward the timber. From the other end of the camp he saw a young man follow in the same direction. H picked up a knife and followed them. When he got into the timber he saw C and the two women sitting talking together. He rushed up, stabbed his wife several times and killed her instantaneously. The other woman and C ran off. The parents of the onde girl were angry, but "when they heard that she had been caught in the act they cooled off."

C went into hiding. C was a member of Adltoyui. The society heard about his troubles. They sang an Adltoyui war song: "Adltoyui are calling me, I shall go there." Then they called to H to come if he wanted trouble, made fun of him, and followed him to his camp, where his Ten Medicine Bundle was. H's own camp was against him; he left his Medicine and hid out while the Adltoyui were looking for him. Then the Adltoyui went to another Keeper of the Ten Medicines and paid him to bring the pipe to H's brother so that peace could be made. The Keeper presented the pipe to the brother of H and named whom he was representing. In this case he was representing C's society that was intervening in behalf of one of its members. He told what the society was willing to give if the H would not take revenge. Each member of the society chipped in blankets, ponies, etc., and revenge was forestalled. The Adltoyui were assisted by C's relatives. They gave W's relatives some gifts. They afterwards composed a song about the event. However, because of the murder, "after this H's heart became poor like a pet dog, and it became taido and had no power." He kept his Ten Medicine, but he was no longer topadok'i. "For killing his wife, H was reduced from second rank to third in people's eyes. While he was in third rank he cut off the nose of one of his remaining wives thereby being reduced to an even lower place in the third rank because he was cruel to women. C had been in second rank before the affair and his rank was not affected."

Another version relates that H inherited his Medicine Bundle after the event, and by virtue of it, was raised to the second rank. However, continued disorderly conduct toward wives reduced him again.

CASE II: EXECUTION OF A WIFE

Back in the time when the Kiowa were at war with the Comanche a man and his wife were out hunting. It was winter and they went into a cave for shelter from a blizzard. During the night a man came in for shelter. In the morning they saw that he was a young and handsome Comanche. As the Kiowa man was going out of the cave the Comanche jumped on him. They struggled and the Kiowa called to his wife to take the Comanche's knife and kill him. The woman got the knife but the Comanche pleaded so eloquently with his eyes and was so handsome that she did not want to kill him. The husband told her again to kill the Comanche but she did not. Finally, after a terrific struggle the Kiowa killed the Comanche without his wife's help, and scalped him.

When they returned the husband told the story in the smoking tipi. The wife's older brother asked: "Why didn't you kill her then?" The husband answered that he was afraid that her family would not believe the story. Then the brother left the tipi, got his bow and went to his sister's tipi. He called her out, and as she came through the door, shot her dead.

CASE III: FATHER AND SON: A SHAMELESS ACT

The persons are:

H (=Husband): the same Twkoide, with two wives.
G (=Girl): an Arapaho girl, without kin to defend her.
S (=Son): the son of Twkoide.

Time:

After 1885

S was courting an Arapaho girl. When H saw her he began to flirt with her. S went on a war party, and while he was gone H married her. When S returned he heard about it. He called his mother and asked her why H had done this. She told him she had tried to prevent it, but H was stubborn and hot-headed. He had given two horses, some arrows and other gifts for her. S spoke to his father. "What are you doing married to this woman? You are not going to live with this woman and keep her here as your wife." "What's the matter?" said H. "She is my wife. Why shouldn't I live with her? Are you going to fight with me over her? You know my record as a brave warrior. Are you going to fight me?" "Yes, father, I have always heard that you were a chief and a brave man. Are you a chief today?" "Yes!" "All right, chief, here is something for you." S struck his father across the face with his whip and went for his gun. H grabbed the woman with one hand and his knife with the other. He stuck the knife into her stomach, cut her side wide open and killed her. "All right, here is your woman. Take her." S started to shoot but some men took the gun away from him. So he beat his father with his whip. S swore to kill his father. Four men were present. They grabbed S and kept him from acting; made him give his word to do nothing more.

Case IV: JUSTICE BY SHAMING

There was a widow of a prominent family who had to take care of her own horses. One day she was out looking for her horses a long way from camp. On her way she met a man and asked him whether he had seen her horses. He told her that he had seen them in a wood some distance away. He pulled her off the horse and raped her. When he finished he said, "Women of your class are good to rape." The woman rode back to the camp and reported the incident to her mother who was living with her. The mother was enraged. She sharpened her knife and cried out, "Where is this man? I'm good too." She cut up his tipi, shields, tipi poles, etc. The culprit's family was humiliated. They stood by and didn't interfere while the woman destroyed their property. The man to escape his shame ran away.

CASE V: PURSUIT BY JEALOUSY AND SHAME

The persons are:

H (=Husband): Iapa, a son of Twkoide.

W (=Wife): Ak bai, daughter of the chief officer of the tribe.

Time:

1876–77

H was a doctor. One day he happened into a tipi in which a sick young woman lay. She said: "I've heard you are a good medicine man. If you cure me, I'll marry you." Since she was good looking, he did his best and cured her. She was then his wife.

However, he was uncontrollably jealous and whipped her often and severely. Once in the presence of her two brothers he struck her on the head with something heavy so that she was unconscious for a long time. This made the brothers very angry. They took her away to their home. "They had the right to do so." The husband was afraid to take her back from the protection of her brothers by force, so he went to them and begged them to let her return. H wrongly imagined she was in love with another man.

H kept track of her and once saw her when he camped at Fort Sill. She had started with another woman through the woods late in the evening along the trail that led to the slaughter house. H followed them and stopped them. The other woman spoke up and said, "What do you mean by stopping us?" H: "Go on ahead. This is my wife." He asked his wife to come home but she refused. H: "Why won't you come? You are my wife. I cured you. You promised to live with me." W: "I'm not going with you." H: "Why?" W: "I'm through. I quit." He asked her a second time and she refused, so he brandished a butcher knife at her. H: "If you don't come with me I'll kill you. You are my wife." W: "I won't come." Other woman: "What do you mean?" H: "You go on. This is my wife." He asked a third time, but she refused. H: "What's the reason?" W: "I'm not going back." H: "I'll ask you once more, and this will be the final time. If you don't come, I'll kill you. Are you coming with me? You'd better come, and everything will be all right." W: "I'm not coming." H pulled out his butcher knife and grabbed his wife by the hair and stabbed her in the breast. The other woman screamed and ran to the camp and told the others. W's two brothers then got their guns and set out to kill H, but they couldn't find him because H ran away and hid way under the driftwood in the timber with his body under water. He sat on a log, with only his head above the water. When the people came the wife was dead. It was too late for a doctor.

H stayed hidden until after dark, then came out and went to his brother's tipi. His brother asked him why he fled. B said that since he had killed the woman he should be a man and not run off. H should get his gun and die like a man—but if he was going to run away, he didn't know where he could go unless it was to a certain mountain. If he died like a man the people wouldn't talk about him so much. H said he would go there to the mountain and hide. It was midnight, and he called his mother to fix something to eat as he had no supper. He ate in the darkness. They gave him dry clothes and some food to take along, and his brother set off with him on horseback to the mountains south of Mt. Sheridan. They took a complete outfit: matches, quilts, etc., and found a rocky place where H could hide. His brother brought food to a certain place at night every four or five days. H stayed there about a month until it began to get cold.

Meanwhile, the case was reported to the authorities at Fort Sill. The agent said the murder was a terrible crime. Kiowa chiefs were called and asked to take action. They said they would do anything the agent said, kill him if necessary. They said he was young and foolish and ignorant of white laws, however, so asked that his life be spared if possible. Scouts were sent out. The brother who brought him food advised him to surrender. (Another version states that he was apprehended near Lawton.) So H came at daybreak outside Fort Sill. The agent states in his government reports that Dangerous Eagle and Big Tree brought H in. Sanckyaptw was called as interpreter. Sanckyaptw asked them why they had come, and they told him that H was the one who had killed the woman and that they were going into Fort Sill. Sanckyaptw said they had done the right thing, and that he probably wouldn't get a long sentence.

When they came into Fort Sill the interpreter went first, and the officer asked them to come in and sit down. He asked them what they wanted, and they told him they had come to surrender. The officer said that H had done the right thing to come in, and that if he would tell him why he had killed the woman he would get off easy. H told how he had been married, and how he had come to kill his wife when she refused him. The army officer told him that he had done the right thing, since it was his wife and that the law would back him up, but that he'd have to sentence him. He said that he would have to go into the guard house that night, but the next day he would have to mow the lawn and clean up the whole post and then he could go free. H agreed to this, and his brother went home. In the morning they let him out and he cut the lawn and burned the weeds, etc. till the whole post was cleaned up. H worked in the garden for a year and a half, and then was set free. "He was a different man when he came out." H was pursued by taido [shame], however, for the rest of his life. He went to live with the Kiowa Apache, where he married and was always very good to his wife. W's relatives made no attempt to get revenge.

CASE VI: DEATH BY SHAME: IN THE NAME OF JUSTICE

A man was known for attacking women when they were getting wood and water. He would lie in wait and rape them. Finally the women talked among themselves and banded together, planning to punish him. They chose a young and beautiful woman and sent her for water while they lay in ambush. Sure enough he came, and as he attacked the girl the women all jumped out and grabbed him. Some took his arms, some took his legs, and some even held him by the hair so he couldn't turn his head. Then they lifted up their skirts, and one by one squatted on his face. Some of them were menstruating and he got blood all over his face and in his mouth. He became very sick and vomited and vomited. When they finally let him go he was very weak. He was sick and very ashamed. A few days after this he died of shame (not suicide). It was felt "he got his due".

NDEMBU OF CENTRAL AFRICA

V. W. Turner
Schism and Continuity in an African Society
Fieldwork 1953, pp. 95–164, Selections

CASE I: SANDOMBU AND THE DEATH OF KAHALI CHANDENDA

The persons are:

Sandombu, about whom the sequence revolves.

Kahali Chandenda, his mother's brother, headman of the village.

Mukanza Kabinda, who succeeds as headman of the village.

Kanyombu, his younger brother.

Time:

1947—several years before Turner's study began.

One day in 1947 Sandombu trapped a duiker and divided its meat between his village kin. His own mother's brother Kahali Chandenda was headman of the village and should have received by custom a back leg or the breast of the animal as his share. Sandombu, however, gave him part of a front leg only. Kahali refused to receive it, saying that Sandombu had shown that he despised his uncle. A few days afterwards Kahali went to a village about eight mile from Mukanza Village and snared a bush-buck. He sen his daughter back to Mukanza with the meat. Sandomb took the meat and proceeded to divide it, retaining th breast, liver, a front leg and the head, for himself an his wives. Next day Kahali returned, and finding San dombu away, asked Sandombu's wife Malona, from Angola for some food, for he had no wife of his own at tha time. She was insolently slow in preparing the food, an in the end he went to his classificatory sister Nyam waha, who gave him beer as well as food. At nigh Sandombu's sister and Kahali's own niece came to hir in private and told him, in anger and shame, how the mea had been divided.

Next morning Sandombu set off early to go twenty-fiv miles away, where he had seasonal employment as capitão in charge of road maintenance. Meanwhile Kaha spoke bitterly in the village forum (*chota*) about Sandom bu's action, and the latter's wife Malona wept tears at thi public shaming of her husband.

After a week Sandombu returned to Mukanza Villag and Malona reported Kahali's remarks to him. A fierc dispute arose between uncle and nephew, in the cours of which each threatened the other with "medicine", euphemism for sorcery. Sandombu ended by saying, " am going to Sailunga Area. The people of this villag are worthless. Some people must look out." By this peopl took him to mean that he was going to seek out th services of a notorious sorcerer, thought to be Sakasump of Shika Village, to kill Kahali. It was believed b Mukanza people that Kahali kept his familiar, an *ilomb* or water-snake which possesses the face of its owner, in stream in Sailunga Area; and that Sandombu had gone t pay Sakasumpa a fee to shoot the *ilomba* with his "nigh gun", a piece of human tibia carved in the form of muzzle-loader and primed with graveyard earth and de composing pieces of human bodies. When an *ilomba* ha been killed its owner also dies.

After a few days Kahali fell ill, and died shortly afte wards. A rumour came to Mukanza Village that Sandomb had boasted in Shika that he would kill his uncle by sorcery. No divination was made into the death since the people feared prosecution by the Government for making accusations of witchcraft. Besides, some, including Mukanza Kabinda and Kanyombu, classificatory matrilineal "brothers" of Kahali, said that Sandombu had condemned himself out of his own mouth both in Mukanza and in Shika Village. Sandombu returned to his place of employment and Mukanza people said that Sandombu must not succeed Kahali, for he had shown himself to be a man with "a black liver", a selfish person and a sorcerer. The question of succession was left over for a time. Sandombu was not expelled from the village because there was no positive proof of his guilt, such as might be obtained from the diviner's basket. He had only spoken in heat as had Kahali himself, although good men did not speak this way.

Mukanza Kabinda was made headman with the approval of all, and confirmed in his office by the Government.

Case II: SANDOMBU ACTS IN PASSION AND REPENTS

The persons are:

As above—Mukanza Kabinda is headman of the village.

Zuliyana—daughter of Mukanza Kabinda, and second wife of Sandombu.

Kasonda—a young man, nephew of Mukanza Kabinda (and possible successor).

Nyamwaha, who dies—sister of Mukanza and mother of Kasonda.

Time:

Late 1948

Samdombu had married Mukanza Kabinda's daughter, Zuliyana. It may be supposed that he hoped by this means to attach himself securely to the two village matrilineages, since she was connected to both through her mother and father. He also hoped that she would give him children, for although he had married eight times, no wife, except his first, had borne him a child, and this was thought not to be his. He had divorced Malona before marrying Zuliyana, because she was not acceptable to Mukanza people, being reluctant to give them food and hospitality. One of the psychological drives behind Sandombu's persistent and openly expressed desire for headmanship probably consisted in the fact that the names of sterile persons are not given to children, or rather, to put it in Ndembu idiom, do not "come back to children to give them a name". Sterile people "die for ever", in that their names are not remembered and no shrines of quickset saplings are planted to honour them. Sandombu probably feared that his name, i.e. his social personality, would be forgotten, unless he became a headman, in which case he would be remembered as the occupant of a political position. After a year Zuliyana had borne no child although she came from a fertile family and Sandombu used to vent his spleen on her by frequently beating her.

Towards the end of 1948 an *Nkula* ritual was performed at Mukanza Village for Nyatioli. *Nkula* is most often performed for women with menstrual troubles, and it appears that Nyatioli was experiencing a difficult menopause, with much menstrual bleeding.

Sandombu, who was by this time working as a Road Capitão for the Public Works Department in a camp about a mile from Mukanza Village, was under the impression that an *Nkang'a* girl's puberty ritual was to be held that weekend, and not *Nkula*. He ordered Zuliyana to brew many calabashes of beer for the occasion, for at *Nkang'a* nearly all the people in a vicinage attend. At the concluding phase of *Nkula* many people also usually attend, but this was only a "small *Nkula*" confined to Mukanza Village and a few external kin and neighbors. Zuliyana brewed only two calabashes for this small ritual. When Samdombu came off duty—most Ndembu rituals today are held at weekends to accommodate those at work—he found only two calabashes of beer. Without waiting to hear the explanation he began to beat Zuliyana, who called out to her kinsfolk for help. Kasonda entered Sandombu's village hut and, according to his own account, remonstrated in a brotherly way with Sandombu. The latter's only response was to take a bamboo cane and thrash Zuliyana with it. Then a young man called Benson, just back from the Copperbelt, came in, snatched the cane from Sandombu and broke it across his knee. Sandombu lost his temper and his head completely, according to Benson and Kasonda, and accused Benson of being Zuliyana's lover. Others, by this time assembled in the doorway, heard him go on to say that he would make the members of Mukanza who were interfering with his married life pay for their intervention.

Next day, Sandombu was observed by Kanyombu, Mukanza Kabinda's youngest brother, and by their sister Nyamwaha, as he was stooping over the footpath between Mukanza and Benson's village. Then he circled the huts of Mukanza and Nyamwaha. He was heard, it was alleged, to have invoked the spirit of his deceased parallel cousin Lupinda, a hunter and powerful personality in his lifetime, to punish his enemies. He is then alleged to have said to those sitting in the *chota*, "I am not returning to Ikelenge Area. Tomorrow someone will die in this village. Mukanza people have no sense."

Early next morning while the aged Nyamwaha, sister of Mukanza and mother of Kasonda, was pounding cassava, she felt a spasm of pain and fell down in a helpless condition. Kasonda, who had been working as a garden boy, was informed of this and obtained permission to return to the village. Nyamwaha was gravely ill. Her last words before she died were "Sandombu has killed me."

Kasonda wrote an angry letter to Sandombu, retailing his mother's last words and demanding that he return to Mukanza and give a full explanation of his suspicious behavior. Sandombu came back and all the senior men of Mukanza assembled in the *chota* to hear what he had to say. It was put to him by Mukanza that he had cursed the village by invoking Lupinda's ghost. This form of curse is classed with sorcery. Sandombu denied that he had cursed the village in this way, but he admitted that he had been angry, and expostulated that he would never, under any circumstances, have killed his "mother", whom he loved. He took out a 10s note and said: "Here is my money. Go yourselves to a diviner in Angola, and find out the truth.' (The Portuguese, according to Ndembu, do not regard witchcraft accusations as a criminal offense, so that divination is legal in their territory.) Kanyombu, Mukanza's brother, took the money and demanded *£3.10s* in addition, saying that the compensation he should pay for causing Nyamwaha to die must be set at *£4*. It was no use, he went on, denying that he had threatened the village with sorcery. Many people had heard him, so that there was no need for a divination. But Sandombu insisted with tears in his eyes that under no circumstances would he kill his mother, or indeed, any of his kin. Kanyombu then said that after the mourning ritual Sandombu must leave the village, and stay away until he showed by his behaviour that he could live properly with his kin. The others agreed, and Sandombu left the village for about a year. In the end he humbly asked Mukanza for permission to return.

In the meanwhile, in view of Sandombu's evident sorrow at Nyamwaha's death, public opinion wavered as to the cause of death, and secret divination into it was made by means of a medicated pounding-pole, and blame was finally ascribed to the husband of Nyamwaha's daughter's daughter from Chibwakata Village in the same vicinage. It was alleged that Nyamwaha had tried to keep her granddaughter in Mukanza while her husband wanted to take her to his own village. In anger he had "shot medicine" at her and killed her.

Sandombu was absolved from the blame and allowed to return. But in order to show finally that "his liver was white" towards the people of Mukanza, dead and alive, he paid Mukanza a goat and took part in a village ritual performed to placate the restless spirit of Nyamwaha who had caused many people to dream of her and caused a minor epidemic of illness. It was thought that she was disturbed by the "troubles in the village". Sandombu planted a tree to his "mother" in front of Mukanza's hut. Both Sandombu and Mukanza prayed to Nyamwaha, and mentioned that they were now reconciled. Through the planting of the tree, they said, she would be remembered by her relatives. Finally, three lines of powdered white clay were sprinkled on the ground from the base of the tree by Mukanza, and all the members of Mukanza Village who were present, matrilineal, patrilineal and affinal, were anointed by Mukanza with white clay, symbolizing the basic values of Ndembu society—good health, fertility, respect for elders, observance of kinship dues, honesty, and the like.

The prodigal nephew had returned.

Case III: THE FURTHER ADVENTURES OF SANDOMBU

The persons are:

As above—Mukanza Kabinda is an aging headman.

Sakazao, brother-in-law to Mukanza Kabinda (and possible successor).

Nyamukola, sister of Sakazao, wife of Mukanza Kabinda, mother of Zuliyana.

Chibwakata and Anderson Mulumbi—chronic enemies of the village.

Time:

1953—the anthropologist is resident in the village.

At the beginning of 1951 I employed Kasonda as a cook and general henchman. After a time I made a permanent camp in Chief Ikelenge's area, returning to Mukanza Village on intermittent visits to watch the progress of events. In June of that year Kanyombu, Mukanza's younger brother and a leading doctor in several cults, died after a protracted illness. Kasonda told me that the cause of his death was probably Sandombu's sorcery. He had received a letter from Sakazao. Later in fact the myth became established that Nyatioli, sister of Nyamukola, and divorced wife of Kanyombu, had bewitched the old man. They had lived a married life of continual domestic bickering and Nyatioli had developed a grudge against her former husband. Women are believed to possess familiars of a kind different from, and more dangerous than, those owned by men. They are called *tuyebela,* and have the variable forms of little men with reversed feet, hyenas, jackals, owls or small rodents. *Tuyebela* are exceptionally active if their owner has a grudge against someone, when they are liable to take instant action against him without asking their owner. Nyatioli had been suspected for some time of having *tuyebela*. Sandombu continued to visit the *chota* every day, to take part in discussions on such important matters as bride-wealth, the holding of rituals, death-payments, cases of petty theft, slander, etc., and to state his opinions forcefully and authoritatively. It was clear that at some time or other he would make another bid for the headmanship.

By the middle of 1953 it became obvious that the headman Mukanza Kabinda was becoming very old and infirm. He spent much of his time dozing in his kitchen, and although he still went into the bush to hunt, he seldom killed anything. The question of succession to headmanship was once more beginning to disturb the village. By this time I had made my permanent camp just on the outskirts of the village, not far from Mukanza's own huts. I was, therefore, in a position to observe the trend of events far more closely than before. Kasonda, still my cook, was now making plans to found a farm of his own. He said that when Mukanza died the village would break up, some going with him, others going with Sandombu, and others staying with Sakazao. Shortly after I arrived Mukanza publicly announced in the *chota* that he had appointed Sakazao as his successor. Sandombu was away at the time on a visit to Ikelenge Area. When he returned and heard the news, his first action was formally to succeed to the name of Kahali, the ancient title of the Mukanza headmanship. Mukanza publicly approved Sandombu's step, and said smilingly in the *chota,* when both Sandombu and I were present, "Now there are *two* villages, Mukanza and Kahali. Sakazao will succeed in Mukanza Village, and perhaps someone or other will succeed in Kahali." Sandombu said nothing but shortly rose and returned to his village. Trouble was patently brewing.

A week later Sandombu invited me to drink with him in his house. He was broodingly drunk when I arrived. Soon he asked abruptly, "What is the name of this village in the Government tax-register?" I said that it was written down as "Kahali-Mukanza." "Yes," he said, "in 1947 Bwana Heath [the District Commissioner] came to the village to collect tax and Kahali Chandenda, my uncle, told him to change the name in his book from Mukanza to Kahali, for the old name from long ago is Kahali; but Mukanza Kabinda and Sakazao told him that the village had been founded by Mukanza Kandulu and was known by all as Mukanza. So Bwana Heath was very clever and wrote down Kahali-Mukanza. But he was wrong. You have written our history and you know that the true name of the village is Kahali. Please go and tell the D.C. to change it to Kahali." I replied that although it was true that the village used to be Kahali, the majority of people today thought that the village should be called Mukanza.

But Sandombu went on drinking heavily, and in the evening another social drama began which revealed that the jealousy over succession had not been eradicated but had been festering beneath the show of outward harmony. Sandombu was well aware that Mukanza, Kasonda and Sakazao were attempting to seal him off from any possibility of succeeding, by asserting that his farm now constituted a separate village, and that Mukanza Village was not continuous with Kahali Village, which had, in their reckoning, become extinct. Perhaps he felt that he had made a mistake in taking the name of Kahali, and that Mukanza and Kasonda were chuckling over their exploitation of that mistake. Whatever the cause the fact was that by nightfall he was in a prodigious temper, and threw over the restraints he had imposed upon himself for years.

While Sandombu was drinking great excitement was aroused in the village by the arrival of a masked dancer from a Boys' Circumcision Camp some miles away. At a certain point in the seclusion period of the boys, the dancers emerge from the camp and visit neighbouring villages, accompanied by ritual officials from the camp, to obtain gifts in cash or kind from the villagers or to extract various kinds of forfeits from them. The whole village was in a condition of social excitement, with drumming, dancing, singing, and drinking. This reached a high point when my kitchen accidentally caught fire.

Zuliyana, Sandombu's junior wife and daughter of Mukanza and Nyamukola, went to join the other women who had assembled to sing and clap around the dancer. She came back in a temper because she did not possess a new dress as some of the other women did, and began to harangue Sandombu on this theme. She was assisted by Katiki, the senior wife, and both accused Sandombu of giving away large quantities of millet beer to ingratiate himself with people instead of selling some to buy them new cloths to be made up into dresses by Kasonda, who had by this time bought a sewing-machine. They said that Sandombu had done little in the way of cultivating the millet, while they had weeded it, harvested it, thrashed and winnowed it, ground it and made it into beer. Certainly he was the owner of the seed, but they were entitled to some reward for their labours. Zuliyana then said that Sandombu just wanted to make himself a big man; that was why he had taken the name of Kahali. He wanted to become headman of the whole village. In view of the previous arguments of the day that was an unfortunate remark and Sandombu staggered towards Zuliyana to beat her. But he was extremely drunk and she easily evaded him and ran off to her mother and father for protection. Sandombu did not beat Katiki, who seemed to possess some sort of influence over him, and she persuaded him to sleep off his rage.

But when he awoke later that night, his wrath had not abated and he rushed to Mukanza's hut. Meanwhile Zuliyana had told her father that Sandombu had been boasting to many people that he was the elder of the village while Mukanza was his junior, and that the name "Kahali" was a "heavier" name than "Mukanza." Mukanza had also been drinking and a major dispute developed between them. Sandombu accused Zuliyana of trying to bewitch him with *tuyebela* which she had been given by her mother Nyamukola. Zuliyana began to deny this energetically from the kitchen where she was sitting with her mother, but both men told her to keep quiet. Mukanza said: "Sandombu, you have slandered my wife, and I will give you a big case. Also you have been heard by others to have threatened me. Why do you want to kill me? Have I not given you my daughter? You have a very bad liver to speak as you do to me. You must take your wife back again, treat her well, and buy her a new cloth. If you want to speak in this way you must stay away from the *chota* of Mukanza." Sandombu refused to take back Zuliyana, and repeated that she and her mother wanted to bewitch him. He went back to his house and for a long time his voice could be heard roaring out abuse against the people of Mukanza, while those in the *chota* who were not immediately involved shook with suppressed laughter, especially the little boys.

Next day Sandombu came to the *chota* and demanded the return of his wife. She came back with him but Sandombu was told to return the day after to explain his conduct at a meeting of the village people. He did so and persisted in accusing his wife and mother-in-law of witchcraft. In such intra-village meetings in Mukanza the summing up was usually left to blind Chayangoma. He had neither wife nor child, and used to stress that he felt free to say what he liked as he was a "dead person." Since he was "already dead" no one had any motive for bewitching him, and he could speak impartially. In his summary of this case he said that grave charges had been made both by Sandombu and Mukanza, involving witchcraft. Therefore he thought it wise if the affair were kept within the village and not discussed by the local "law men," or vicinage elders with a high reputation for advocating and judging cases, since news might leak out and their relatives would be arrested. Sakazao said that Sandombu was drunk at the time and could not be held responsible for his words. If he apologized and paid 10s. to Nyamukola and a new cloth to Zuliyana nothing more need be said.

But Sandombu refused to pay. He said that he had been wronged by his wife, who had first caused trouble in the house by starting an argument and had then borne tales to her parents against her husband to cause trouble in the village. He had accepted her back and yet they still wanted him to pay. As for the accusations of witchcraft, both parties had made them in anger. He would pay nothing to Nyamukola, for he had been greatly provoked by both women.

It so happened that Sandombu himself at this very time was bringing an action for slander against the headman of a neighbouring village, Chibwakata. At a beer-drink at which I was present the day following the Zuliyana affair, headman Chibwakata had accused Sandombu of having accepted 10s. from Kasamba, Chibwakata's classificatory "son" by a slave mother, to kill the headman by sorcery. Sandombu at first thought that Chibwakata, who was his own classificatory "grandfather," was joking with him, and laughed heartily. But Chibwakata, who was drunk, became very angry and said that Anderson Mulumbi, another classificatory "son," had been witness of the transaction. Sandombu promptly charged Chibwakata and Anderson Mulumbi with slander.

Thus Sandombu was in the odd position of being defendant in one slander case and plaintiff in another at the same time, both cases involving accusations of sorcery and witchcraft.

The Kasamba case was settled first. After much argument the court said that Chibwakata ought to pay Sandombu 30s., and Kasamba the same amount. Anderson had to pay each of the plaintiffs 10s. In this case Sandombu identified himself with Mukanza Village and with the exception of Mukanza and Nyamukola all the Mukanza people were pleased with the decision. They had old scores to pay off against both Anderson and Chibwakata.

Next day the Zuliyana case was settled, still at the intravillage level. Chayangoma was again asked to arbitrate. Sakazao was suggested, but turned down by all parties who claimed that he had no inherent faculty for settling disputes. Besides, he was the brother of the co-plaintiff. Chayangoma said that Sandombu should pay Nyamukola 10s. for defaming her character, since the previous day he had obtained damages from Chibwakata for slander against himself. In both cases there had been witnesses and the fact of slander had been clearly established. Sandombu paid up, and people joked with him afterwards, saying that after all he had made a profit from his two cases. Peace was restored for a time in the village.

In this social drama it may be noted that Mukanza Village was by no means the same as at the time of the death of Kahali Chandenda. Former members had gone, new members had come into it. The conflict between Sandombu and the rest was in abeyance. But the case was undoubtedly brought in order to emphasize the fact that Sakazao and not Sandombu had been nominated by Mukanza as his successor. It was brought to signalize Sandombu's exclusion from the succession and to show that Kahali Farm was subordinate to Mukanza Village, and not the reverse. It was perhaps unfortunate from Mukanza's point of view that Sandombu should have been involved at that precise moment in a case in which he stood as the representative of the Mukanza group against their inveterate enemy, Anderson Mulumbi, and Chibwakata. Anderson Mulumbi, a farm head, a man of wealth, trader and tailor, had long been engaged in disputes with Mukanza people. Recently, he had accused some boys from Mukanza Village of having wounded his hunting dog and killed one of his goats. He had taken this case to court and judgment had been given against him. Kasonda was his principal foe, and economic rivalry was involved in their relationship, since both were tailors. Kasonda was delighted to see him in trouble. In this situation, therefore, Sandombu had the tacit support of the majority of Mukanza people, and it would have been difficult to penalize him severely in one situation and applaud him in another on the following day.

But apart from these considerations, Sandombu had in other respects improved his position in the years that intervened. He was now a farm head with a following. He had obtained work for many Mukanza men. He had been liberal in offering beer to villagers and to many others in the vicinage. There were even some who would support his future claims to village headmanship. Even if he did not succeed in Mukanza Village, he might yet be headman of a large farm and resuscitate the title of Kahali.

It is this heightened importance of Sandombu that was

responsible for the way the case was played down and kept within the village, for the small amount of the fine imposed, and for the fact that Kasonda kept in the background instead of openly giving Mukanza his support. A conciliatory tone was adopted towards Sandombu throughout, no attempt was made to retain his wife, and after the case was over it was joked about. Although Sandombu paid damages to Nyamukola he did not lose face thereby. In the altered climate of opinion, as he had just scored a victory of Chibwakata and Anderson Mulumbi, it was in Sandombu's interest to make a gesture of goodwill towards the village. On balance he had considerably improved his position after these two cases, and Mukanza's refusal to have anything to do with a case involving Sandombu had not added to the old man's popularity when Sandombu had been disputing with a major enemy of Mukanza Village.

TANGU OF NEW GUINEA

Kenelm O. L. Burridge
"Disputing in Tangu"
Fieldwork 1952, Selected Passages

TANGU SCENES

Tangu live in hilly terrain some fifteen miles inland from Bogia Bay on the north coast of New Guinea. Composing in all some two thousand people distributed through about thirty settlements of varying sizes, and grouped into four named neighborhoods, they are hunters, gatherers, and gardeners whose known history has been characterized in the last fifty years by upheaval and instability. An epidemic plague or, as Tangu view the event, a particularly violent and uncontrolled increase in sorcery, helped to set in motion, at the turn of the century, a series of migrations combined with much internecine fighting which broke down the former large communities. The larger kin and local residential units—which were also jural groups and landholding units—fragmented into households and, extensive tracts of unsettled land then being available, segments of varying size and composition scattered and resettled themselves over a relatively wide area. Soon afterward the first Europeans came to the region. Over the next thirty years Tangu were gradually brought under control: peace was enforced, labor recruiting became ordered, a mission station was established, and native administrative representatives were appointed. However, the population remained dispersed—indeed, additional settlements were founded. When, after the Japanese war, Tangu were persuaded to concentrate into larger aggregations, it was not long before families began to return to their old homes in the bush. During daylight the settlements are deserted. Families are out in the surrounding countryside in their hunting lodges, tending their gardens, or visiting friends or kinfolk. Only at dusk, on festive occasions, or when some community task is afoot is any substantial proportion of a settlement present. Tangu say, "There is always trouble and quarreling in large villages or when we gather together."

Within Tangu there are cultural diversities. Among individuals there is disagreement on the significance and implications of many situations, and where a consensus is found it often happens that nothing is done by way of enforcement. Lacking a permanent corporate group recruited of genealogical kin, the strongest loyalties are to the household, the nuclear family, at the expense of the community as a whole. Yet, intermarriage between members of different settlements, communities, and neighborhoods is frequent, internal trading and exchange relationships are numerous and regularly maintained, and while participation in the political activity, *br'ngun'guni*, is theoretically open to outsiders, examination shows it to be virtually confined to those who call themselves Tangu.

Everywhere in Tangu the basic and definitive social and economic unit is the household; and households are in significant relationships with each other as they co-operate, exchange, or are *mngwotngwotiki*—an agreement by free and mutual consent neither to exchange nor to co-operate. The work done by the members of a household goes into subsistence, exchanges with other households, and feasting and dancing exchanges which take place regularly during the harvesting months between two principal but temporary co-operative groups to which the other households in the community attach themselves. The co-operative relationship implies that the husbands of the households concerned are brothers or that the wives are sisters, while the exchange or oppositional relationship connotes households, severally or grouped, where the wife of one is the sister of the husband of the other. That is, the households of married siblings of the same sex are in actual or potential co-operative relationships, and the households of married siblings of different sexes are in actual or potential exchange relationships. However, the kin categories are in large measure putative. Though the kin idiom is always used, and though the core of a feasting exchange may consist of men and women in the requisite categories of genealogical kinship, there always remain households which find themselves equivocally placed in the particular feasting series and which are persuaded into joining one or another groups of households by influential men—managers.

Managers create alliances—make for themselves brothers—by persuasive oratory, cunning, and making good their claims to productive ability. Normally, in each community, alliances are forged at the beginning of each horticultural cycle so that the participating households form two approximately equivalent groups in a mutual exchange relationship. During such feasting exchanges, in the intervals between different phases of the dance, as food is placed before the exhausted dancers, men from either group of households make speeches. This is formal br'ngun'guni. The oratory is accompanied by staccato beats on the hand-drum, thwacking the buttocks, and, if a man is really excited, wild leaps into the air. Men boast of their prowess in the gardens and bush, comment on the dancing, and throw out disparaging hints as to the productive abilities of others. Some take the opportunity to remind the assembly that it is time to harvest the yams, cut new garden sites, or that work in the rice field is lagging behind. Others bring up their grievances whether they relate to hunting, fishing, gardening, administrative, mission, or kin matters, exchange obligations, or suspicions of sorcery. Visitors from other communities come to these feasts not only because they enjoy a party but because formal br'ngun'guni is the explicit occasion for submitting a cause or attempting to establish a claim. As the result of anger or an announcement or a complaint, however, br'ngun'guni may occur ad hoc, and though in the unexpectedness and heat of the moment many of the formal niceties may be omitted, the procedure, ends, and means are much the same. Managers are concerned with oratory, in the interplay of comment and discussion—in order to recruit allies, challenge other managers, and put to the test the abilities they believe themselves to have; individuals mediate, soften the hard lines of parry and thrust; the community in general works to restore equilibrium.

The political maneuvering and the domestic and kinship activities which lead to a feasting exchange and br'ngun'guni, or which results from a br'ngun'guni undertaken ad hoc, are dominated by a few firmly held and interrelated axioms. Amity exists within its own moral right, explicitly governs all Tangu relationships, and characterizes the ideal equilibrium. Mutual relationships tend to shift toward some kind of overt conformity with amity. At the same time, amity is no vague and emotional goodwill: it is expressed in and depends on equivalence, a notion of moral equality between persons which must be continually reaffirmed and reiterated lest someone become dominant. The focal assertion of equivalence occurs in food exchanges at every level of organization, whether the exchange is completed within the space of a day, weeks, or months. All such exchanges must be equivalent. If they are not, expectations are disappointed and trouble results. Yet no food exchange can be precisely equivalent; and because resources are limited households are forced to establish a scale of priorities, necessarily disappointing some to satisfy others. Since, in these circumstances, there is always room to find fault, exchanges that are regarded as equivalent reflect a true moral equivalence—and when this happens they speak of the households as being mngwotngwotiki: they have achieved equivalence, and neither exchange nor co-operate. An exchange that is not regarded as precisely equivalent, or remains not fully honored for long, indicates a lack of moral equivalence. One or the other party is thought to be attempting to demonstrate a dominance. The one is suspected of trying to establish an overall dominance in virtue of what may be a simple physical competence, the other may be suspected of contempt, and either may be suspected of resorting to a technique to shroud the other in obloquy. The necessity for maintaining equivalence in this way, or for working toward a moral equivalence, results in a critical attitude which, together with disappointed expectations, may lead into expressions of anger and indignation.

Tangu have no noun to denote anger; it does not exist as an abstraction. Men are angry with one another, not merely angry; it is a transitive verb. Anger kept in the heart leads to sorcery and means sickness or death for someone. Anger made public, normally by a rapid onomatopoeic drumming on a slit-gong, may lead into a complaint and thence into br'ngun'guni. An angry man is a dangerous man, and the signal on the slit-gong is both a warning to keep clear and an invitation to a close friend or kinsman to inquire what the matter might be. Whatever may lie behind a particular show of anger, whether it is expressed as an unsettling device or whether it actually derives from some substantial antecedent cause, it is almost always explicitly related to a misdemeanor over food and its production. A theft is denying food or tools to another, a trespass implies the intent to seize flesh, fish, or fruits from another; either renders the wronged person less able to maintain equivalence with others through food exchanges. The breach of the norm finds concrete expression in relation to food, and restitution demands further activities in relation to food: anger indicates a breach of equivalence, and normally predicates a series of feasting exchanges in which br'ngun'guni will occur and through which public equivalence may be re-established.

Either formally, or by precipitating br'ngun'guni by an expression of anger when the opportunity allows, managers attempt to secure and define co-operative alliances. Since they may not dominate but have to maintain equivalence with all in the community, managers must control themselves and challenge men of roughly equivalent abilities and resources. To challenge a small man would be fruitless: if equivalence is adhered to, no evidence of productive ability emerges; if equivalence is breached, the offender becomes the target for mystical attack which—even if the manager himself is oblivious—results in the defection of allies. Ideally, the successful manager is one who, in spite of great productive ability, is able to maintain equivalence and can resist the temptation to dominate. One br'ngun'guni is the springboard for another; each subtly confirms or refutes existing alliances and mutual interrelationships, the latter tending to shift so that amity can find expression in its most conventional forms. Formally, br'ngun'guni is a deliberative device which provides implicit authority for a series of activities; it is a mechanism for initiating, continuing, containing, or resolving disputes, and it is a vehicle for political management. Br'ngun'guni does not, and cannot, make any defined and explicit reallocations of claims to exercise rights.

CASE I: KWALING AND REAMAI: IN WHICH KWALING BECOMES THE BULLY BUT FAILS TO GAIN THEREBY

The persons are:

Kwaling, a "manager" and a "brother" to Meakriz and Reamai.

—Juatak, his wife (a sister of Nuok).

—Nuongweram, his half-sister.

Meakriz, the Luluai, *government-named headman. A widower.*

—Mureg, his sister, who cooks for him.

—Igamas and Bunjerai, his sons.

—Bwatam, another sister, who may take Mureg's place.

Reamai, half-brother to Meakriz and hence classificatory "brother" to Kwaling; like Kwaling, a "manager."

Nuok, Mureg's husband and Juatak's brother; not a strong man.

Time:

1952

One afternoon two teams of brothers were building houses for their sisters, Juatak, wife of Kwaling, and Nuongweram, Turai's wife and Kwaling's half-sister. Kwaling and Juatak were distributing food to the latter's brothers, and Nuongweram's brothers were working. The atmosphere was one of quiet and cheerful industry as men and women went about their tasks, smoked, talked, or chewed betel nut. Presently, Meakriz, the Luluai, was approached by Igamas, his natural son, and Bunjerai, his adopted son. There was a short whispered conversation, and all three ran off into the bush.

The incident created a small stir. People thought a pig had been trapped, and expectations were aroused.

Sure enough, half an hour later the cries of a party returning with a pig were heard. There was a short pause and then, from a group of homesteads separated from the main settlement, the beaten rhythm of a slit-gong announced the trapping of a pig and to whom it was going to be given.

Mureg, who is a sister to Meakriz and his half-brother Reamai, and who, since Meakriz is a widower, normally cooks for him and his sons, was disappointed. She said in a loud voice to her husband, Nuok, "What is this? Why does he not bring the pig down here, carve it under my porch and give it to me to distribute? Why is he giving it to Bwatam? I cook for him every day."

Nuok, friend of Kwaling and brother to Juatak, stepped out onto the dancing space to support his wife. "Why was the pig going to Bwatam? Why not to Mureg who cooked for Meakriz daily? Nuongweram's brother had killed a pig the day before and had given it to Nuongweram to distribute to the brothers building her house. It was appropriate that Meakriz and Reamai should give their pig to their sister Mureg to divide between the brothers building Juatak's house. Were not Kwaling, Meakriz, and Reamai brothers?"

Reamai, who had actually trapped the pig and who was annoyed that his choice should be questioned, came down from the upper portion of the village and confronted Nuok. "We will do what we like with our pig," he said. "We are giving it to our sister, Bwatam."

"Who cooks for Meakriz?" asked Nuok. "Bwatam?"

Reamai did not answer. He strode away angrily, asserting that the pig would be given to Bwatam. Nuok walked off in disgust.

Suddenly—perhaps Mureg had fired a parting shot—Reamai lost his temper. Turning on his heel he ran back to Mureg's house, forced his way in, and started to thrash her.

Mureg screamed. She was still screaming when Nuok, hurrying to the rescue, confronted Reamai emerging from his hut. Nuok stooped, picked up a clod of dried earth and flung it at Reamai. He missed.

Reamai sprang to the attack. Being smaller and frailer, Nuok fled. Reamai gave chase and grappled. Meakriz pounced on them both, trying to separate them. Reamai whooped, Nuok cried for help, and others rushed yelling to the scene.

Kwaling was among them, a heavy digging stick in his hands. Bounding into the melee with a whoop, he cracked Reamai across the head. Reamai staggered back, blood spurting from his temples and pouring down his chest. Nuok broke free. Kwaling retreated. Women scuttled around to the backs of their huts. The village was in uproar.

Br'ngun'guni commenced.

Why has brother struck brother? Both Kwaling and Reamai are managers. They are classificatory brothers who ought to be in an amicable co-operative relationship, but they have been quarreling since boyhood and they dislike each other intensely. Reamai is the younger of the two, boastful, hot tempered, and very proud of being the son of a famous father: He is an excellent gardener, hunter, and dancer. Nevertheless, he is jealous of Kwaling who is quiet, withdrawn, cool, well-known and respected far beyond the boundaries of Tangu. As Luluai of the village, Meakriz is responsible for keeping order, apprehending wrongdoers, and reporting misdemeanors to the administration. Because he is a widower with children, his sister Mureg has given him shelter, and has cooked for him and generally looked after him. She can reasonably expect generosity in return. However, Meakriz cannot find a new wife and he had been thinking of having his sons adopted by either Mureg or Bwatam on a more or less permanent basis. This means putting his potential as a food producer at the disposal of either Bwatam or Mureg—a matter on which the two women had come to blows and which had resulted in Bwatam moving her house from the main part of the settlement to the outlying cluster of homesteads.

Even apart from the economic issue, the two women have little love for each other. Bwatam is an attractive creature well liked by the men of the community, and it is no secret that Meakriz expresses his affection for her by many small favors. Having eaten a meal cooked by Mureg, Meakriz is wont to stroll over to Bwatam's house and there enjoy his leisure with tobacco and betel nut. Mureg herself swings her hips to some effect and enjoys the reputation she has among men of being somebody else's mistress. Reamai, however, regards Mureg's reputation as a blot on his name; he has had words with her before, and he has beaten her. Quite recently he had embroiled himself over an alleged theft of areca nuts and, since the popular suspect stood to him as son, he had attempted to clinch matters by threatening to beat up anyone who continued to speak of his son as a thief.

Into this general uneasy situation has come a stroke of good fortune—the capture of a pig. Meakriz and Reamai are burdened with a choice, and their decision has angered and disappointed Mureg. Nuok, her husband, has made a complaint, and the impending dispute is across the brother-sister link. Reamai was presented with a second choice, for he might have returned with dignity to his pig and carved it notwithstanding. Instead, angered, he chose to beat Mureg. In consequence, Nuok was angry, the two men start fighting, and Meakriz, as Luluai, tries to separate them. Kwaling has the choice of helping Reamai who is his brother, or Nuok who is his friend, or, like Meakriz, he might have tried to make peace. He chose deliberately to strike Reamai.

Shouting, leaping, whooping, beating their buttocks with the palms of their hands, Kwaling, Reamai, and Meakriz ran up and down the dancing space, sweating, furious, livid with anger; boasting, threatening, calling witness. Nuok made himself scarce. Kwaling had taken the quarrel out of his hands and made it his own.

The blood streaming down Reamai's body was prima facie evidence of a breach of amity. Meakriz, running, leaping, and thwacking his buttocks, said it was a deliberate assault and that he would take Kwaling to court at Bogia on the morrow.

Reamai passionately endorsed the proposal. Dizzy, eyes glazed, rubbing his hands in the blood, he demanded the court.

Kwaling countered. Reamai had beaten his sister, he said, and was in the act of assaulting Nuok when the blow was delivered. Should a man not go to the aid of his friend? His father and Reamai's father had been very close to each other. They had lived together in amity and co-operation, and their sons should behave in the same way. Right. Go to court. Tell the white men how they behaved—how a man of the village had beaten his sister, beat the husband who came to the rescue, and had threatened to beat others.

Meakriz withdrew, sitting down in silence.

Reamai and he, continued Kwaling, had been brought up together. They were brothers. Was it necessary to fight?

Still dazed by the blow, Reamai stuck doggedly to court, rebutting the appeal to amity by stressing the deeper issues between them. Kwaling disliked him and had hit him on purpose from spite. Court was the only way to settle it.

Kwaling continued to conjure moral or "ought to be" relationships, and by so doing he was looking ahead and placing himself in the stream of public opinion. He had taken advantage of the opportunity to give Reamai a knock and had everything to gain by returning to amity as quickly as possible. Reamai, on the other hand, was handicapped. He had suffered and wanted redress, yet it was not a fruitful course to pursue. If he was in earnest in calling for the court, and succeeded, it could only further postpone the eventual return to amity. If he was bluffing, and threatening to go to court is a stock maneuvering weapon, he was also invoking nontraditional values and procedures—a tactic in strong contrast to Kwaling who was referring the quarrel only to what was traditional, and who had also pointed out that the court might be equally severe about Mureg's bruises. Meakriz's withdrawal was a tacit admission that going to court was not a practical solution. By revealing the real relationship between himself and Kwaling, Reamai was deepening the rift and flying in the face of public opinion by making it so much the harder to return to amity. Kwaling withdrew from br'ngun'guni from time to time to have a smoke, a maneuver which highlighted Reamai's temperament and made it quite plain who was upset. Then other things came up.

Each accused the other of cheating in food exchanges. Each boasted of his own ability in producing food and accused the other of trying to steal the limelight when they had co-operated. Reamai called Mangai, his wife's brother. Mangai, an old manager, pointed to the blood, remonstrated with Kwaling, pleaded with Reamai not to make too much of it, and was emphatic that the affair should not go to court. Womak, a close friend of Kwaling, tried to pacify Reamai; what other way was there? Kusai, mother's brother to Kwaling and father to Reamai, scolded Kwaling, saying he ought to go into the deep bush and stay there awhile. Then, turning on Reamai, he entreated him to be more reasonable. Dimunk, called by Kwaling, remarked only that this was an affair between brothers.

The matter of the adoption of Meakriz's sons was brought up, and the incident between Bwatam and Mureg was discussed. Previous assaults by Reamai on Mureg were remembered, and the recent theft of betel and its consequences were thrown in as a makeweight. The air was clearing.

As the examples show, those who interjected remarks—and many did so whether they were asked or not—did not take sides. Explicitly supporting neither party nor blaming both, the remarks were designed to mollify anger, soothe the hurt pride, and prepare the ground for re-establishing equivalence and amity. The specific issues which triggered the incident could not be considered as isolated acts, for each formed part of a complex of disappointments and Reamai, which has become a political rivalry. The principal disputants interacted with each other and also with the community, the former attempting to influence and to manage, the latter to mediate—a process which may be described as "mutual steering" to equivalence and amity. What is also evident is a "looking to consequences." From the moment he grasped his digging stick, Kwaling seems to have been looking several moves ahead, and Meakriz's behavior reveals the same concern for what the future might have in store. Juatak and Nuongweram had fled from the scene as soon as the fracas started. As far as the trapped pig was concerned, Nuok's complaint had ranged their brothers in opposition, and the presence of the sisters might have provided concrete mobilizing points. After it was all over Nuongweram said, "We went away because we might have had to say something which would have made more trouble." Only Reamai seems to have been hopelessly entangled in himself.

The pig was eventually shared between all those who turned up to work in the rice field the next day. That is, it came from Meakriz, the administrative representative, to all those who engaged in an administrative task, irrespective of kin affiliation or co-operative alliance. But the disposal of the pig that had triggered the events only marked the end of a phase. Reamai and Kwaling were committed to feasting each other and finding public equivalence through hard work and recruiting help. In the feasting exchanges more br'ngun'guni will occur. Meakriz shifted his residence to a site almost a mile distant from the larger settlement, and Bwatam and her husband went with him. Bwatam will look after Igamas and Bunjerai and Meakriz will work with Bwatam's husband in alliance with Reamai, who was left with the opportunity for making good his claims to respect and managerial ability: he has something to win. Kwaling, whose position before the incident had been fairly secure, was shaken. First, he is past his peak in physical energy and competence, and no amount of cunning or high reputation will offset his smaller production. Tangu prefer to be allied to plenty of yams in the present than to yesterday's reputation. Second, he made Remai look small. He was beginning to dominate, and "fence-sitters" went over to Reamai. Those who have been with Kwaling had their first apprehensions about the future, and in the days that followed Kwaling himself began to brood and think about sorcery. On the other hand, Reamai brightened and became cock-a-whoop.

CASE II: KWALING AND GEENGAI: IN WHICH KWALING MANAGES HIS OWN RECOVERY IN THE PUBLIC EYE

The persons are:

Kwaling and his wife, Juatak, and others as above.
—Twambar, the four-year-old son of Kwaling and Juatak.
—Luassi, Kwaling's aged mother, owner of the piglet.
Geengai, the local jokester.
—Manduz and Kandidi, Geengai's sons.

Time:

1952—*a fortnight later.*

Perhaps the most fascinating aspect of the first dispute is the personality of Kwaling and what he represents. He was too good for his nearest rival, too cunning and too shrewd. He lost out because by being too good he was unable to maintain equivalence, and a fortnight later he exploded again.

Twambar, Kwaling's four-year-old son, was playing with Geengai's young sons, Kandidi and Manduz. They saw a piglet defecating and, as children will, decided to stone the animal for being thus ungracious. Kandidi struck hard and true, crushing the delicate skull. Death was almost instantaneous.

Geengai, the local jokester, cackled with mirth. "Oh, well hit, well hit!" he cried.

The owner of the pig, Luassi, Kwaling's aged mother, started to grieve, complain, and scold. Kwaling himself tucked his pipe into his armlet, leaped to his feet, and grasping a large hunk of firewood gave chase. Whooping loudly he hurled his log, hit Twambar in the back of the neck, and brought him down. Juatak hurried to the rescue and dragged the screaming child to a safe place. Br'ngun'guni commenced.

Whooping, yelling, leaping into the air, and thwacking his buttocks, Kwaling had everyone's attention. Children fled from the dancing space, women sought out their huts, and a few men who were stitching sago fronds into roofing strips continued their work with studied concentration.

Geengai made a few half-hearted runs and then retired to his hut. Kwaling wanted to know what Geengai was about. Did he want a fight? What then? Did he think he had a garden of worth? Did he want a feasting exchange? Ha!

Luassi intervened. This, she said, was a fuss about little. The pig was dead. Kandidi was only a child.

Gently but firmly, Kwaling hustled her off and returned to the dancing space. Meakriz, who was sitting nearby, rose to his feet, but he had barely opened his mouth when Kwaling let fly at him. The Luluai sat down in silence. Luassi came forward again, imploring her son to desist. Kwaling only took her by the shoulders and led her, protesting, back to her hut.

Geengai, who is an easy-going man with no pretensions to managerial ability, had seemed transfixed. However, at last he gave voice. He pointed out that the piglet deserved stoning; it should not foul the village. Everyone stoned piglets that defecated in the village; who could tell it would be killed? Besides, Kwaling ought to take more care of his pigs. Kwaling's pig had been into his garden, rooting and eating his yams.

"Come out of your hut!" Kwaling cried, livid and bouncing with rage. "Come out into the open!"

Geengai refused. He has a big enough garden, but as the village jester he is wont to laugh at the things others take seriously. He is not interested in prestige and influence; his metier is gossip, turning the phrase, mimicry, making fun of the pompous. He likes his joke.

"Ha!" With a last flourish and thwack of the buttocks, Kwaling sat down to relight his pipe. The village fell silent.

Seconds later, Geengai emerged from his hut, axe in hand. Walking deliberately, he went around to the back of his hut—to his coconuts.

Immediately there was uproar. Geengai's wife's brothers rushed down and pushed Geengai away from his coconuts. They argued, they placed themselves between Geengai and his coconuts, hugging the trees; gently, they relieved him of his axe. No, he must not cut down his coconuts.

Geengai said little. With a gesture of resignation he turned and went into his hut. In a few moments he emerged, spear on his shoulder, and, with Manduz following, he walked disdainfully out of the village.

Though the incident arose from the irresponsible act of a small boy who had not reached years of discretion, the critical choices cleared the way for a speedy return to amity. Kwaling had an interest in the piglet and there is no doubt he was angry over its death, yet he is in no kind of competitive relationship with Geengai. He struck Twambar, his own son, not Kandidi who had done the deed, and by so doing avoided a major issue with Kandidi's mother's brothers. Nor was the act an accident; it was done, as Kwaling afterward explained, specifically to avoid further entanglements. He was looking to consequences. The br'ngun'guni had to happen. The pig was dead, killed in public, and Geengai had laughed. Something had to be done. Nothing could bring the pig back to life but, especially in view of what had happened with Reamai, there had to be a retort.

Geengai refused to accommodate Kwaling. In his way a philosopher, and a Christian, Geengai had spent the last two weeks bringing out the funny side of the Reamai affair, and he had even succeeded in making it look ridiculous—a joke hardly appreciated by Kwaling. Yet, though Geengai refused to meet Kwaling on a ground of his own choice, he is so far locked in traditional values, that the reply he made referred to the ravages of Kwaling's pig in his garden; and his final act, an apparent attempt to sever his connection with the village by cutting his coconuts, shows that he felt keenly his inability or reluctance to maintain equivalence in the traditional way. In the eyes of his friends and relations he was failing quite miserably.

Nobody will ever know whether Geengai was bluffing or whether he really meant to cut his coconuts. He had more to lose than to gain by so doing, but points in his hand if someone would stop him: his wife's brothers could hardly have been more timely. Kwaling had dominated in br'ngun'guni, but this was because Geengai had refused to accept. If Geengai had wholly submitted, sympathy would have gone to Kwaling because Geengai's behavior would have been thought contemptuous and therefore a deliberate breach of equivalence. Further, no one in the community would have failed to impute to Geengai a deliberate and malicious intent to get his own back by sorcery—a flagrant intent to do evil which would have made him very unpopular and an outlaw. If Geengai had succeeded in cutting his coconuts, the community would have fallen to pieces. Kwaling's reaction to the death of the pig was expectable and, in the circumstances, natural; Geengai ought to have engaged in br'ngun'guni. Yet no one would have had sympathy either for Geengai or for Kwaling had the coconuts fallen: Geengai should not have done it, nor should Kwaling have driven him to it. The whole village would have had to rearrange itself and most would have gone off into the bush to found new settlements. On the other hand, the evidence of intent served to equalize. Kwaling and Geengai went off into the bush an kept out of each other's way and three weeks later rel tions between them seemed to be quite normal. Geeng was as cheerful as ever, and Kwaling had recovered h confidence. They had finished equivalent.

CASE III: THE PERSISTENT WHISTLERS AND A TULTUL' TOE: DIPLOMACY IN INTERVILLAGE AFFAIRS

The persons are:

Ndori, Luluai of neighborhood M (administrative hea man).

Wapai, Luluai of neighborhood B.

Kavak, the Tultul of B, assistant to Wapai.

Time:

1952

It was thought in neighborhood M that a man of neigh borhood B, who was a renowned and skillful hunter an who had been giving a series of feasts, had been takin his game from bush habitually used by a man of M. Privat representations had been made to the people of B, but stil the game was elusive. The conclusion in M was that th trespasser was continuing his mischief.

One night, at the start of a regular community feastin and dancing exchange in M, Ndori, the Luluai, who wa leading the dance, became dissatisfied with some of hi team who were blowing whistles. He halted the dance an asked his brothers to stop blowing their whistles. They nod ded compliance and the dance continued.

A few minutes later, quite firmly, the whistlers piped u again.

Again, Ndori stopped the dance. It was his favorit dance, and he didn't want any whistling. Was that under stood? Yes, it was. The dancers resumed their places in the line and the dance recommenced.

But the whistlers wanted to whistle. Gradually the sof little "peeps" grew into a chorus of shrill, fully-blow screams. Ndori was obviously under some strain; glowering, stamping too hard, and cracking his hand-drum in temper, he said nothing. Nearly everyone was whistling.

Suddenly, Ndori straightened. Tearing off his headdress of cockatoo plumes, he flung it to the ground, stamped it to pieces, and strode off to his hut.

The dance stopped. Nobody spoke. Seconds later the rapid tattoo on a slit-gong and the clatter of the wand being flung into the body of the instrument informed all within earshot that Ndori was very angry indeed.

After a hasty consultation the dancers decided that the mission boss-boy should go to Ndori and try to persuade him to rejoin the dance. But when he returned a few minutes later, he could only report complete failure. Ndori had shut himself in his hut, was very angry, and would speak to no one. "Let us stop dancing," suggested the boss-boy. "If we go on it will make him angrier."

There was general opposition to this. Someone struck up on a hand-drum and the dancers resumed.

An hour later the boss-boy again repaired to the Luluai. He returned with the news that Ndori had gone to the stream to wash himself of paint. Speaking in formal br'ngun'guni, he exhorted all those present to abandon the dance. They refused. The boss-boy started to lobby individuals, pointing out that Ndori could use his office of Luluai to stop dancing for the year. He went again to see Ndori and spoke twice in formal br'ngun'guni, but to no effect. Someone always struck up on a drum and the dance continued.

A little after midnight Kavak, Tultul of B, who was attending the dance, rose to speak in formal br'ngun'guni. He was sorry, he said, very sorry indeed to see Ndori so angry. Why was Ndori so angry? There was nothing to be angry about. Perhaps it was the matter of—but no! Allegations of trespass could be settled in amity, by talking. True, there had been a little wild talk, but it could never be seriously meant. True, the men of B were tired of being accused of trespassing and there were some loose and irresponsible people who had spoken of stopping the trade in cooking pots if the accusations went on in this way. But now? Now it was different. Ndori was angry, angry in a dance! Angry because he had seen a man of B—himself! Right! (Kavak thwacked his buttocks and leapt into the air.) They of B would let no cooking pots into M; they would smash them to make sure! Anger such as this over an unproven trespass!

Kavak did not get through his speech without interruption. It was pointed out that Ndori's anger had nothing to do with the trespass, nor was it a reply to the threat of an embargo on cooking pots. It had to do with the whistling.

"Whistling?" cried Kavak. "Bah!"

Many muttered expletives under their breath. Others shouted, "You are a good fellow—come again next week!" Or, "Speak up—I cannot hear." Or, "We like you. Let us get on with the dance!" Or, "Oh true, oh true!"—a phrase always carrying explicit agreement but importing overtones of scepticism or frank or aggressive disagreement. One man sitting next to the writer gently exploded with wrath.

Kavak whipped around. "Never mind!" cried the man. "You're a good chap. You carry on!"

But the position was serious. No one in M could make a clay cooking pot; they had to get them from B. The threat of the embargo was a fair weapon to use in reply to the allegations of trespass, but failure to establish Ndori's anger as resulting from the threat—followed up by carrying out the threat—was answering a pinprick with a bombshell. M was to be without pots, and unless B could establish anger in M, Kavak, as representative of B, had overreached himself.

The following night there was a dance in B, and to it went several men of M including Ndori. The Luluai had recovered his poise, but nevertheless the men of B studiously avoided him during the feast. Toward dawn, however, Wapai, Luluai of B, approached Ndori, offering betel and tobacco, and cautiously felt his way into a conversation. He joked, mentioning casually that there was no need for anger in this matter. He laughed with spirited gaiety. As tactfully, and quite as obstinately, Ndori refused to be drawn. In a few minutes Kavak joined them and contributed his quip. It was soon evident that he had abandoned his position of the previous night, and that his kinsmen in M had persuaded him that Ndori had been angry over the whistling and not over the threat to place an embargo on pots. Without taking sides, he became a mediator. He tried to show both Wapai—who, sincerely convinced or otherwise, would have liked the anger pinned to the trespass—and Ndori that it was an understandable mistake that Ndori's anger should have been connected with the trespass. Ndori said little.

Nor were they the only men talking. It had become recognized that although B was committed to stopping the trade in pots, the individuals concerned would like to recant without climbing down. If Ndori, or someone in M, would admit Ndori's anger to have been over the trespass all would have been clear sailing, but no one in M was willing to do this. Nevertheless, reconciliation had entered the decisive stage when it was agreed that B should come to dance in M. Throughout the interval between the feast in B and that to be held in M, there were meetings between private individuals. Kin links between the two neighborhoods facilitated the talks, but one factor stood out: how, in the circumstances, could one neighborhood reach equivalence with the other?

During the feast in M the men of B danced very well, but when food was placed before them there was no meat and the tubers were not so well cooked as they might have been. The men of B were highly indignant. One after the other they spoke in formal br'ngun'guni. Why was there no meat? What had they done? Were the men of M really this impossible? First there were allegations of trespass, then Ndori had been angry, and now there was no meat!

No one from M spoke a word. They gathered the empty food bowls in silence, and the dance petered to an end.

As soon as the dance was abandoned there was jubilation in both camps. "Now all the trouble is over," said a man of M. "We gave them no meat." A man of B said, "We shall have another feast. It is finished already but another feast will finish it properly." One insult had cancelled the other.

With the parties roughly equivalent there only remained a few niceties of wit to show how close to one-up equivalence can be. Two days after the feast in M the slit-gongs of B announced the concluding feast together with dance *Surai.* When he heard the slit-gongs the Tultul of M, who was to lead the dancers, at once let it be known in B that he had a sore toe and would be unable to dance Surai. There was much indignation in B, since the Tultul's refusal was good for all of M. It was noted, however, that the refusal had not come by slit-gong but by messengers. Those with kinsfolk in M took up their spears, girded their betel bags, and set off for M.

Meanwhile, the Tultul sat on the platform of his hut, legs spread wide so that anyone who would might inspect his sore toe. "I do not like Surai," he confided in a whisper. "Besides, I do not have the proper regalia." It was also common knowledge in the neighborhood that the Tultul was an expert at *Dumari.*

As men from B began arriving in M to visit their kinsfolk, they passed by the Tultul. Some inspected the toe, clucking their sympathy, and went on their way. Others may have noted the Dumari plumes carelessly hung in the doorway. At any rate, a couple of hours later the slit-gongs rang out again from B. Surai was cancelled, and Dumari was on.

Dumari in B was a great occasion. The man of M who had first alleged a trespass went, and the alleged trespasser provided most of the food. All the speeches in br'ngun'guni were conciliatory; the quarrel, the "talk," was dead. Both neighborhoods appeared to have clean sheets before them. The atmosphere was gay, the food excellent and prodigious, the dancing superb.

Then Ndori made a speech in formal br'ngun'guni, the last to be made. He praised the food, soberly approving its quality and quantity, and he remarked on the skill, industry, and generosity that had gone into the preparation of such a feast. There had been some trouble, he said, the beat of his hand-drum beginning to quicken. There had been some talk, but now it was over. Ndori thwacked his buttocks for emphasis. He leaped into the air, bounding up and down the dancing space. Ha—what a feast! But let the men of B come to M! Let them come to show how they could dance! Let them come and see if they could eat all that M would provide!

A chorus of yells greeted this outburst. "Have you no shame? The talk is dead! There is no quarrel between us!"

Ndori sat down, gleeful and unchastened, and the hubbub died down.

With the dawn came the end of the dance. As men and women stole away to their huts or to their gardens to sleep, one or two remarked on the portent of Ndori's speech. Two months later men's ears were pricking as they reminded one another of what Ndori had said. For, though the two neighborhoods are separate entities, only fifteen minutes' walk lies between them, the kin links are many and strong, and both sides enjoy having reasons to entertain each other at feasts.

Ndori is a manager. He had failed to get his way with the whistling, but in his final speech in B he equalized personally and he also opened the door for another series to be settled by interneighborhood feasting. His last speech is the peg on which the future issues will be hung. Other managers, looking to consequences and susceptible to mediation, also tried to influence the course of events. The mission boss-boy, anxious because Ndori was angry and might stop dancing altogether, tried to have the first dance abandoned. Kavak used Ndori's anger to bring the bush dispute into the open, and to crystallize and justify what hitherto had only been rumored—an embargo on cooking pots. Later, knowing he had overreached himself, he was among the first to attempt to restore equivalence through mediation, particularly choosing Ndori who had become, as it were, the fulcrum of the dispute. Others, in other directions, were not slow to follow his example. Some managers in M felt that huge quantities of meat in the third dance, rather than no meat, was the proper response. Either would have neutralized the insult of placing an embargo on pots, but the scarcity of game forced them to select the cheaper way. Wapai, a manager, called for dance Surai. In B they were experts at Surai, well qualified to criticize others who attempted the dance. Knowing this, the Tultul of M, also a manager, maneuvered Wapai into cancelling Surai and substituting Dumari, thereby serving a political as well as a personal interest. Finally, although Ndori's anger was over the whistling, it started the train of events, was used to make other issues explicit, and was directly responsible for reopening further possibilities between the two neighborhoods.

FOOD AS A "POLITICAL" GOOD: SOME CONDITION FOR GOVERNMENT BY FORMAL DISPUTATION

Br'ngun'guni is an activity designed not to make explicit decisions. It allows personal relationships to work themselves out in relation to the community. Brothers, such as Kwaling and Reamai, should ideally be in a co-operative relationship. But it so happens that, first, they are the two best food producers in the community and, second, there is a personal antagonism between them. In a co-operative relationship the discord becomes vicious and cannot conform to amity. In an exchange relationship, on the other hand, personal animosity becomes larded with mutual respect which in turn lays the basis for equivalence. It may even be that Kwaling and Reamai will end up mngwotngwotiks —precisely equivalent. Finally, since Kwaling and Reamai are the two best producers, with whom can they exchange and at the same time maintain equivalence and a reputation for productive ability if they co-operate? What is personally apparently desirable also emerges as a structural necessity. Only by shifting from the co-operative to the exchange relationship can they work toward a personal equivalence. Other households will join with them, help them toward their personal equivalence, and also work out their own equivalences.

The techniques of br'ngun'guni appear to be consistent with the ends. Management is the dynamic element. Managers rise and fall, gain adherents and lose them. They are not what they are by virtue of their positions within a network of kinfolk, but because of their competences—productive ability, shrewdness, and convincing oratory. Each br'ngun'guni subtly redefines the expectations contained within personal and interhousehold relationships. Anger is evidence of unsatisfactory relationships, of inequivalence, and on anger's expression the community seems to be on the point of disrupting—but the contrary happens. Individuals collect as an aggregation, disputants and others interact, and expectations become redefined. In terms of the interrelationships of individuals and households, br'ngun'guni changes the community. Mediation, whether as an interruption in br'ngun'guni or in the form of private conversations, lobbying, or carefully prepared small-talk, shades black into white and lays the foundation for re-establishing equivalence. Looking to consequences might, but does not, proceed from the idea of a precedent; it is a technique related to situations of choice, the inevitability of disappointed expectations, mutual participation and interdependencies, and the necessity to establish equivalence in order to have amity. The most common, generalized, and conventional technique is retiring to the bush so that an angry relationship is not sparked by personal contact into a series of incidents which may lead the persons concerned to a point of no return.

There is little doubt that as individuals managers are restrained by the fear of sorcery—mystical consequences. At the same time, so long as equivalence remains a firm value expressed in equivalent exchanges of foodstuffs, it is evident that no manager can possibly attain an outright dominance; sorcery acts in concert with, but independently of, the other factors involved. In the first dispute Meakriz, as Luluai, had to try to make peace. As Reamai's half-brother he came to his aid; as Luluai he demanded the court; and as Meakriz, the Luluai, a member of the community with a personal interest, he abandoned the idea. His behavior in the second dispute, where he might have made an ass of himself by trying to be Luluai, as well as the behavior of Kwaling, Reamai, Ndori, Kavak, Wapai, and the Tultul of M, shows a close coincidence of personal interest, political ends, and structural forms.

When anger cannot be related to food and its production, br'ngun'guni cannot occur. In the old days an offense

such as incest would have been dealt with on the level c
the jural group through the club-house organization, whic
included secret societies of sorcerers. Today, lacking bot
there exists no machinery for dealing with such crim
apart from bringing in the administration, which Tangu d
not like to do. One heinous incest on record, involving f
ther and daughter, revealed that at the time when the a
first became public knowledge there was general ar
hearty disapproval, but it was only diffuse. The union ha
persisted for over a year and had come to be accepted
a fait accompli—a claim made good and maintained in th
face of an opinion which could not grow "teeth." Le
serious incests gain disapproval and, in effect, "Oh we
that is how it is these days," if the parties adhere to the
union. Complaints of adultery may be expressed throug
or worked into, a br'ngun'guni but again only on the lev
of the Tultul's toe. Adultery is a personal, nonpolitical i
sue; there are divorce, compensation in valuables, and so
cery. Equivalence can be found in more ways than one. I
Tangu political power depends primarily on the produ
tion, exchange, and distribution of foodstuffs under equiva
lence, and these community issues br'ngun'guni deals wit
It cannot cope with personal problems unless they are als
politically relevant.

SECTION THREE

SOCIAL STRUCTURE AND CHARACTER

DISTINGUISHING CHARACTER AND PERSONALITY

Hobbes wrote: "so far as I am a person I am an actor, ıether on the stage or at my everyday tasks." The atmpt to reduce all I do to a matter of personal appetites and ·linations is like an effort to explain Hamlet in terms of Sir ıwrence Olivier's personal psychology—or, for that matter, ıakespeare's. Whatever my own motives, and however inısely I may labor (in the role) to make Hamlet express em, he remains an other and a fictional person. In the lanage of the theater, Hamlet *is* "a part"—a role inseparable om the network of roles comprising the play. My performce doesn't alter either the whole or any part. That is, the ucture of the drama remains. Like the works of a watch, it s logic and intricate articulation; its parts are finely and ost accommodatingly shaped.

So also in "common Conversation": we take and play roles. ır reasons for taking them are not the same as the motives plicit in our "parts"—we play Santa Claus for profit, and ofiteer for love of our children. So far as a social institution comprised of social roles it is not to be explained as a sime product of the concatenation of individual human wills. ıe motives people have for marrying and continuing their ırriages are diverse; but the roles of husband, wife, and rent can be surprisingly uniform for a very large population. The reason is that they *are* roles—parts in a set drama.

We don't have to deal with millions of men and women dependently deciding, without any prior bias, that the m should be the breadwinner and mechanic, while the wor should cook and be attractive. There are elaborately p suasive forces at work throughout the vast international m dle-class world, supporting the conventional sexual division labor. The chronicle of obstacles encountered by any n conformist family is almost endless. The concept of soc role refers to something quite real and institutionally (str turally) shaped. "Role" is not simply a label we apply to c aspect of your spontaneous personal behavior, as a seman convenience; the word is a clue to the limits of your sp taneity.

If an institution is composed of parts in the same sense t a dramatic play is, men will be engaged in pursuing fa standard strategies. The explanation of that individual act which comprises the routine life of an institution will *norma* require attention not only to the motivation of the person— "psychology"—but also to the motivation of the role i which he has been cast. In structural terms, the "motivat of the role" is governed by the whole pattern of rights a obligations, immunities and privileges, and odds for loss a gain which in a particular social structure attend the pa The source of the motivation of the person is called the *p sonality*. The corresponding source in the actor of the mo vation of the role is what we have been calling his *charact* We considered that distinction before our examination cases. It will be my task now to show, in the light of th cases, that the analysis of action in structured situations ca proceed on the assumption that the motivation of persons enough to explain what happens.

One of the special puzzles with which every system of p sonality psychology must deal is the question, how far "I" can determine the attributes of a "myself." It is the bo strap puzzle in a particular form: where the medieval Ch tian may have seen it in relation to sainthood and found resolution in a theory of divine grace, today we tend to se in terms of therapy and its limitations. Ironically, some the pists approach their task in the conviction that personality always rigid in all essentials: the best "I" can expect is learn to live with the "myself" inherited from childhood years. But when we view social action in a structured context we see that our participation in an institutional life is one of practicing different selves—in the terms of Hobbes (p. 3), putting on different *personae*, or masks. Privately, that would be cultivating one's *character* along different lines. The question how far you can cultivate or change your *personality* remains a puzzle, only the deeper for the admission that the psychic surface of our adult lives is ordinarily colored over heavily with role-motivated, characterological concerns. But that admission does make clear that in one sense the "I" is continually engaged in cramping, stretching, trimming, and shaping a "myself."

I don't mean to say that anyone's personality is ever completely hidden away. If I use "personality" to refer to that locus within myself whence spring my most-personal intentions, I use "character" to mean the tangible results in me of those intentions, tested in action. My character is accumulated through the playing of parts, the assumption of roles, the acceptance of tasks open to public sanction, the playing for reputational stakes "in Tribunalls, as Theaters." The fact that men, as consistently as they do, will engage in playing at the games of character is the fact which, in principle, clears up the puzzle of motivation. Man seems to be in a social context always creatively conventional. I'm continually involved in the making and defending of my character, tasks to which all the resources of my personality may be turned. Together, my personality and character perhaps comprise what some would still care to call my *psyche*. In the spirit of the original Greek word, your psyche is your very contribution, fragile and elusive as a butterfly, to being. But in the face of the uncertainties of human existence, it can be comforting to think that there is in each of us a nonfragile core of personality—that we *are* something definite, even if our wonted roles be taken from us. The idea of personality only begins to make us squirm when it is pressed so hard that it would squeeze out our freedom to become in some good measure what we would become, to take on new identities or build old identities into a consistent and viable character.

SHAME AND MEN'S MOTIVES: KIOWA CASES

A general principle can be said to emerge from the Kiowa cases which have been presented. Taken together, they illustrate the procedures provided in Kiowa culture for dealing with individuals who weren't responsive to the ethical standards which their fellow men had set for themselves. Kiowa society is one in which public shaming could transform a man's character. The Kiowa idea of *taido*, or shame, is one which presupposes the importance of character—as against personality—in the social motivations of men. A man whose heart is *taido* is not the man he was; and to merit the public shaming he must have acted in a way most men would not: he must have broken through the ethical restraints which are normal attributes of Kiowa character.

The general principle with which we have to deal is this: In the normal social situation the vehicle of individual motivation is found in personal character, which commits men to acting in ethically expected ways. In any society these are the role-ways, ways considered reasonable. When we speak of the "character values" of the Kiowa we mean the ethical criteria by which Kiowa judge another man's behavior. Character values are seldom explicitly formulated, for they are subtle and apply in very different ways to different social roles and situations. Though we often feel them intensely, as in shame, our culture has always many voices, and we can easily fool ourselves about what they say. A man who is led to unreasonable acts need not loose his ethical self-awareness—he may know well how far he is risking, and twisting, his good character. Infamy, after all, is a kind of fame.

Consider the case of Twkoide, who killed his wife (p. 36). In holding that character, not personality, was the vehicle of motivation in that case we scarcely could mean to assert that the killing was a characteristic act for a Kiowa war chief. The individuality of the man is manifest, and his aggressive jealousy offers insight into his personality. In simple psychological terms we might guess that he had always been insecure in his relations with women, and so on. We could suppose that the personality set in childhood was the controlling factor in this as in other acts of violence, and essentially explained them. But then we should be faced with the report that, later, his "heart became poor like a pet dog," because he was reduced in men's eyes. For me, the idea of *personality* as a scientific concept would lose its usefulness if personalities were so easily changed; for we use the term to explain an individual's typical behavior and his reaction to crisis. In the case of the war chief Twkoide we need the concept of personality to explain not only the murder but also the aftermath —the reaction to disgrace when he lost his personal power among men but continued his cruelty to women. A more satisfactory understanding of the case emerges if we conceive of the murder itself as an act of character: that is, an act intended to meet the ethical standards of behavior for a Kiowa war chief. Then the tale is to be construed in this way: Twkoide saw that his wife was flauntingly contemptuous of him, seeking an affair with a younger lover. In such a case a war chief was nothing if he was not enraged and ready on the instant to destroy the person who sullied his honor. He did so with courage and boldness. At first the others seemed to see the act in that same way; but it was a doubtful issue—though revenge on the offending lover was bought off, the dead wife's relatives were also compensated; and in the end the act was seen as a cruel, unethical deed, unworthy of a ranking war chief. Twkoide lost, by the very act which should have saved it, the good character to which his performance in Kiowa life had been dedicated.

Such a construction of Case I is supported by the two cases which follow. In Case II (p. 38) a husband, finding himself deserted by his wife, is not overpowered by rage; he must have the fact and the adequacy of ethical motive established, and to that end he waits to tell the story in the smoking tipi. Now the execution ethically falls upon the woman's brother, who normally would have been her first defender. In Case III (p. 38) we meet again Twkoide, much older and much the same: only without much semblance of ethical integrity. The marriage to a girl his own son was courting shows him grasping for stature as a man whose unethical whim knows no restraint. Whipped by his son, Twkoide does not best him as an ethical man but as a dastard. Yet the just anger of the son, in good Kiowa fashion, is restrained by the word he has given. At first reading, the cases may seem to reveal a people devoid of ethical character—unpredictable, individualistic, undisciplined by any restraints but those dictated by deep-seated fear and aggression. Our analysis does not bear out that view.

Character among the Kiowa is the normal vehicle of personal motivation even in critical situations where emotions are at their peak. Personality lurks, as it were, behind character: a man must assess for himself the values of his culture and find his own way to self-respect. In one sense of the term or the other, Kiowa who were not shameless could not continue to live with men.

Twkoide could not be shamed; but his son Iapa, in Case V (p. 40), who also must kill his wife when convinced that she did not respect him, at last was shamed and reborn. Yet we would miss the point of his tale, and the relevance of social relationships to it, if we didn't note that the new life must have been made in another, structurally separate, tribal group in which he could nonetheless be culturally at home. How can I resume an old life, when all I had won there is lost?

THE NETWORK AS A MORAL UNIVERSE: SANDOMBU SEQUENCE

If the vehicle of motivation in social situations is character, then the vehicle of character in its turn is the network of social relationships in which a man is committed to pursuing his self-respect. Sandombu can't prove to himself his own worth unless he first proves it to Mukanza village. In characterizing the Ndembu generally, the anthropologist Turner refers to a "stubborn individualism, barely concealed by the veneer of politeness and sociability."[3] He describes Sandombu himself as audaciously ambitious, hardworking, and generously hospitable to strangers—a trait which contrasts strongly with his difficult and demanding ways with the men and women of the village itself, with whom he was most closely tied. The career of Sandombu was subjected by Turner to careful analysis.[4] From it this clear picture emerges: Sandombu was for a host of subtle reasons cut off from becoming headman of his village, but desperately wanted to be chosen. With strangers he was able through hard work in his gardens and wage work to establish a positive character: he was hospitable and helpful. As capitão or foreman for a road crew he made himself valuable by securing jobs for young men; in that way he became a person to reckon with also within the village—that is, he was not a man whom you would readily expel on a permanent basis, though he was the center of a nest of hostile relations. The hostility stemmed from his character and his peculiar position in the social structure of Mukanza village. That position and some of its implications will appear as we examine the successive scenes of the drama as Turner has presented them.

It may help to make a simple point: Sandombu is not a "deviant personality" in Ndembu culture. As a person he is in the mainstream. Yet he did become widely known as a witch: in a less thorough and intimate study than Turner's, he might well have been described for that reason as deviant. It is only by pursuing with care the idea of structural analysis—the effort to understand individual behavior within the context of unyielding social relationships—that the anthropologist has been able to discover some of the nice vicissitudes of the human career which, armed only with the idea of personality and culture, an earlier generation of observers was unable to see.

Scene one of the drama (p. 43) begins with Sandombu's arrogation to himself of a privilege rightly due to the headman, Kahali. The act can't be construed in Ndembu culture

[3] Turner, p. 101.
[4] *Ibid.*, pp. 95–168.

as one of oversight: in the honorific sharing of meat with the headman is seen an express avowal of ethical subjection to him; and refusal of the duty is equally express, with an opposite meaning. When Sandombu again provoked Kahali, persons close to them both played informer: it had become a matter for anger and shame, and Kahali must denounce and publicly shame in return his sister's son Sandombu. Such were the well-known rules of the game: a move was made first against the character of Kahali, and he must defend with a decisive move against the other. A weak man doesn't become headman nor a weakened man last long at the job, in Ndembu village life. We don't need to suppose that Kahali died of either sorcery or suggestion: Sandombu was a man to push his luck, and when death by chance followed upon an idle if impassioned threat, the affair fell back upon Sandombu. He was given the blackest of characters, and another "mother's brother" to him was installed as headman. That is, the question of succession to the coveted office by a member of the next–Sandombu's–generation was postponed.

The second scene (p. 45) takes place a year later. Sandombu's new marriage is difficult: as a political move, designed to tie him more closely to the structural center of the village, it would have value only if it lasted and if Zuliyana bore children. But Sandombu, without apparently admitting it to himself, was sterile[5] and could not but suspect it: the continued infertility of the new marriage to a young wife exposed him, and he defended by attacking her character without what was felt to be sufficient reason. The scene within the hut is a critical one, for it does represent in dramatic form the critical relation between Sandombu's private and his public ambitions. The man who restrains him is a stranger, for those close to him, like his "brother" Kasonda, would not use force but only moral powers of remonstrance. Yet it is the people of Mukanza who are cursed: it is those who stand close to him whom he conceives to be interfering, for it is precisely the one who holds moral power over him who blocks the way. When death follows the curse, the strength and the overriding importance to him of that moral

[5] Turner, p. 107.

power are at once illuminated: Sandombu is tearful and sincere; after exile he returns.

The final scene (p. 49) took place about five years later. Sandombu had openly moved in a way which he thought would enhance him, and saw himself bested by Mukanza. By extending a provocation by Zuliyana to include her mother, the wife of Mukanza, Sandombu moved to attack that man himself. There are then, by chance as well as by reason of Sandombu's character, three moots. In the first, Sandombu refuses to humble himself before the village by making redress for his attack; in the second, however, he wins stature; and at last the circumstance is such that he can make redress and still have "made a profit."

If we now ask how Sandombu's ambition was made, two kinds of reply suggest themselves. We could regard it only as the irrational obsession of a disturbed personality: the ambition becomes then a radical constant, not subject to our analysis. But that reply is disturbing in the face of Sandombu's apparent normality in Ndembu culture—he is not, after all, the only seeker. His "brother" Kasonda, in fact, was playing the game and apparently would succeed: he stood in a better position, when all the complex ties making up the village were counted, and in building and defending his character he had in fact been more astute. The better reply is therefore one which emphasizes the reasonable, ethically self-regarding aspects of action. Ambition in the Ndembu village is, for men who are able, the very essence of the game of character and position which by their involvement in the village life they are bound to play. For the best, to be headman is the object of the game, to which all the moves are instrumental. Not every success game is built around worldly ambition, nor could all persons in any community be notable "strivers"; but it is an obvious and familiar motif.

Sandombu's situation can be compared to that of a politician anywhere who is personally well qualified for the office he seeks but can't win election because of the social position he was destined to acquire at birth: in the modern context, the religion, race, nationality, or social class position inherited from his parents fail to align him with the majority of voters. In the context of an Ndembu village what matters most is parentage and generation; ties made by marriage may help, but must be firmly established; and, of course, a man wants many descendants. On the score of his position in the structure of the village, so reckoned, Sandombu had little chance of being chosen; yet he was an able and otherwise influential man: he was successful within the work-gang structure, made up of village strangers without a set and constraining kinship organization, where he was made capitão. But the village, with its fuller life and more heightened values, was a grander stage on which to perform; and the rewards of character—of winning for one's self that fuller life and heightened moral value—are not to be found by those who hang back from the drama which their social life affords. The idea of social structure is consistent only with a view that links man's social motivation most strongly to the characterological values of his society, rather than deriving that motivation directly from the natural appetites which the daily routine must satisfy, or from inborn temperament. And since the idea of social structure embraces the notion that moral, or character, values have no existence except as they dramatically emerge in the actions of men, it is an idea of man as a creature bound to his fellow man and subject to the terms on which he can maintain his ties. In Sandombu and ourselves we perceive that no man can be tied to man in general, each of us is localized: you are a point in a network of reciprocity—of intensely particular relationships to others who hold, for you, the relevant moral power. Do we need to be reminded that public fame doesn't diminish a man's emotional involvement in a private life, not with "publics" but with persons?

PEACE BY DISPUTE: LEADERSHIP IN TANGU

The drama of Tangu village life (p. 56) has a structure and mood which distinguish the New Guinean from the African context we have been considering. There is no place in Tangu for the slow-moving, indirect politics of the Ndembu. As to differences of structure: we have noted that the Ndembu African village formally vested authority in a single headman, while it is clear that Tangu village has more than one manager—indeed, the status of manager there is not unreservedly to be compared with the formal office of headman in the African context. The two positions are alike in one important respect: both are out of reach of men deficient in moral strength of the sort required for effective political leadership. In that sense, both manager and headman are self-made men. But it will be remembered that Sandombu was, effectively, a successful manager in the eyes of his fellow villagers; and, in fact, his rival Kasonda enjoyed a similar importance because of his knowledge of English and his ability to deal with government documents.[6] If there had been no formal centralization of the village under a headman (supported by a regional subchief and a developed hierarchy of governing authority), we can imagine that Sandombu and the other important men would have tended to become more openly rivalrous; it is even possible to imagine that the *chota*—which Turner (p. 43) described as a village forum, a place of sober discussion—might have tended to take on something more of the mood of the New Guinea institution, the *br'ngun'guni:* that is, a dramatic confrontation in which it is rhetoric and public acclamation which decide an issue, rather than adjudication of evidence and argument by constituted authorities. But now, having imagined such a shift, we are in a position to see that the change of structure we have envisioned is hardly thinkable without a concomitant change of cultural style or mood. The two—structure and culture—go together.

There is more: we have remarked the indirection which is typical of Ndembu politics in contrast to the forthright chest-thumping (or rather, in the Tangu idiom, buttock-thwacking) of the New Guinea politician; and we have seen that the character of Sandombu was throughout dominated by that quality of indirection. The ethical mood of the African village is painted in the colors of rumor, reputational

[6] *Ibid.*, p. 103.

slander, and witchcraft accusation. Indirection is to be found in Tangu, but has there another quality: it is epitomized in the palpably crooked bit (p. 72) of the Tultul and his toe. When blood doesn't flow too freely in Tangu—and sometimes, perhaps, even when it does—the mood of political drama is close to the mood of farce. But Kasonda and Sandombu are characters of another genre: structure, character, and culture are of a piece in each society; there can be no free substitution of the players from one theater to the other.

The Ndembu/Tangu contrast and the idea of structural analysis is nicely illustrated in comparing the conditions which in each case govern the holding together or the falling apart of the village community. Consider the mislucked stratagem of Sandombu (p. 49), who, in succeeding to the name of his village's founder, falls into a trap: portrayed by the headman as one who would found a separate village, Sandombu is once again edged out of the central position he would like to claim—yet from the experience of his exiles, he knows that he has not the following to lead the dramatic secession required to found a new village. Such a move can be successful only if the old headman would be left alone with none but his immediate kin: the division of an Ndembu village is long in the plotting, for it is the prospect of secession as much as the prospect of high office which will control each small maneuver in the unending political drama there. Without people there can be no office of headman; if the people be not held together, and their offspring allowed to prosper, who will covet or carry that office with characteristic ambition or pride? Such is the stuff of Ndembu culture, character, and social structure. By contrast, the holding together of a Tangu village is a thing of social gymnastics, depending always upon the quick recovery of a balance which a child with a pebble can upset. That is the function—the restoration of equivalence among the leaders of important factions—which the anthropologist Kenelm O. L. Burridge has shown to control the design and working of *br'ngun'guni,* the remarkable governing institution of Tangu.

We have seen that shame is to be understood as the experience of losing character: as a person of modest character will blush and falter when uncharacteristically exposed, the

Kiowa rapist (p. 42) lost even the strength to live when he was bested by women and sickened with what he had lain in wait for. Character, as we here conceive it, is the vehicle of confident social motivation; loss of character brings a sort of social paralysis, whether it be only the passing fever of *pudeur*, spoiled chastity's shame, or the sickness unto death. But shame is a phenomenon of sudden and irreparable loss; its precondition is perhaps a measure of innocent, or naïve, self-conceit which does not in all societies equally flourish. For Sandombu (p. 43) the pendulum-swing might best be described as moving from pride (the insolence of the opening scene, the grandiose threats of sorcery) to humility (the demonstrations of grief and conciliation of the second scene, the final payment of damage for defamation of character). The game of character and social position for Sandombu was a sort of reputational chess: one endeavored to save more pieces than one spent in an encounter, and the game was long and thoughtful but played to win. The difference in Tangu was the openness of each challenge—the transparency of strategy, suiting a reputational game with a different object and different rules.

What shall we make of Kwaling and his undisguised attack on Reamai (p. 63), whose reputation and following on first sight do not seem to threaten Kwaling's own? The anthropologist Burridge explains that Kwaling lost out by being too good, "too cunning and too shrewd." The Tangu village is a context of social structure and ethical expectation in which a triumph like Kwaling's can't endure. The roles of Luluai (headman) and Tultul (his assistant) rest lightly on the players: they are roles which the European administration of New Guinea area would, but can't, vest with effective authority. For Tangu, a village can't belong to one man but is composed of many households each momentarily aligned in various ways with others. Burridge points out that ties of cooperation, exchange, or a special sort of neutrality may be formed on the basis of kinship and the chances of marriage; but that the rules allow ample play for equivocation and persuasion by the successful managers. In that context, to align oneself wholly upon one side of a dispute is to cut oneself off from some other ties. For a man to show himself too good is to threaten the fabric of ties which hold the village together.

The competitive motivation which accounts for such a structure is not difficult to see. The Tangu, unlike the Ndembu (p. 43), are without substantial kinship groups based on descent and affording each member a permanent basis of alignment with others; we see that Kwaling (p. 61) can place his friend before his brother; the quarrel has begun because ties of marriage and kinship are ill-defined—to bestow a pig on one sister and her household was to offend another. In the African case, the order of distribution was given; in New Guinea, it could be impossible not to offend. Each woman or man stood in a network of ties each of which must be maintained and exploited; no single and coherent set of ties was recognized which would isolate one faction of the village from another—even the two villages of M and B (p. 72) were held together by countless individual bonds. When Kwaling seemed through his shrewdness and cunning to have bested Reamai, the balance in the village was disturbed: while the two influential men maintained equivalence the pattern of existing ties could be maintained, but if one were shown stronger than the other then the powers were not held in check—sorcery must begin, and the disruption of ties of exchange and cooperation. In exposing his strength, Kwaling draws attention to his weakness: he is not the gardener he was, and can't practically support the following his moral strength would attract. In Tangu, the game of character is firmly tied to largesse, the distribution of meat and yams. To make a village there must be ambitious men, willing to feast the rest; there must be many such, for each depends upon his own traps and gardens; and they must be kept in moral equivalence, so that the villagers can play one against the other. The game centers on division, not aggregation.

Consider the case of Geengai, who will not stand up to Kwaling but none the less evens the score (p. 68). We do not have to deal here with a simple rivalry: Geengai is no manager but a mimic and pricker of the pompous. Yet again, Kwaling by showing his strength exposes his weakness. Geengai, because of Kwaling, would have wrecked the unity of the village. Already Meakriz, an important man, has withdrawn his residence. If Geengai had cut down his coconuts he could hardly have stayed in the village: we may see in them a symbol and a real tie to the fixed and settled life. For driving out Geengai, Kwaling must in turn have lost respect and following; in the idiom of Tangu, for any who had doubts, there was sure to be revenge on Kwaling by sorcery. Can we say at the end that Geengai and Kwaling are matched? They are not equivalent figures. What has been shown is that each can put the other in check. Where the Ndembu game was played to win, this one is played to stalemate. The structure and the corresponding demands on character are a little more open.

What constrains the Tangu manager from the kind of character-inflation which would put an end to equivalence can be simply shown. For a man who has "overreached himself" (Kwaling in Cases I and II; Kavak, who would have stopped the trade in pots, in Case II) is simply a man who has committed himself to a line of action in which his people won't support him. Kwaling at first would have dominated Reamai; but before many days had passed it was Kwaling himself who must begin "to brood and think about sorcery" because Reamai had gathered support at his expense. The encounter with Geengai shows the result: by the rules of the reputational game, Kwaling deserves more respect (for besting Reamai) than he has received; it is only through Geengai's desperate maneuver that the two are sobered, and Kwaling's aspirations are brought down to a level at which he can operate with confidence. For to "operate with confidence" means, in that context, to act within a known and predictable structure of support: within a firm clientele, the manager has no effective role. So it is also with Kavak and the embargo on pots: since it will not work, he must conciliate; a way must be found to make it clear that the village of Ndori (M) is the one which has been wronged, and not the village of Kavak (B). That is accomplished when the men of B realize that, having been insulted by a shabby feast, they have only to accept the insult with good grace and the trouble will be over. The affair of the Tultul's toe, and Ndori's shameless extravagance, are tests which establish the conciliatory mood of Kavak's party—that becomes, in the essential if not in the literal sense, a matter of record.

To rehearse: on first sight, the system by which Tangu maintains the peace—the system of seeking equivalence between quarreling parties—has something of that intricate look we have referred to in the "clockwork" analogy. The case then poses the puzzle of motivation: the natives don't seem to share the fine, Olympian viewpoint of the anthropologist who has analyzed their institutions; and even if they did see the matter as he does, why should they then go on playing each scene out to its conclusion as they do? Unless they are caught up in the game they won't play it, and it is of the essence of the game that one can't foretell the outcome. Further, it is obvious that keeping the peace is far from uppermost in their minds most of the time. The puzzle is then why they so often succeed in holding their villages together and maintaining cooperative relations between them.

Burridge has shown in the sequel to the cases cited that when Tangu quarreled (in the old days) with outsiders they were most often unable to settle the quarrels but went to war and feuding. The institutions of *br'ngun'guni*, conciliation, and exchange must therefore be considered the mainstay of Tangu government, the machinery by which their league of villages has been kept together. With structural analysis the puzzle of motivation does find resolution. Each participant in the drama of anger, insult, and reparation of the balance is adequately motivated: we need only see the situation of each actor clearly. When Kwaling first clubs Reamai the act is colored by emotional excitement—what we might call irrational motivation. Yet we have not seen the act clearly if we think it a random blow: Kwaling is playing the reputational game, striking a rival, not an ally. We may say that he is taking advantage of the *mêlée* to maximize his own characterological and positional gains. That is to say he is self-interested: the motivation is rational rather than irrational; it springs from character and from the strategy of the situation as the actor himself conceives it; to blame Kwaling's hostility, conceived as an attribute of his deeply rooted personality, is too simple.

REASON AND CUSTOM

The principle which needs now to be proclaimed is this: a man's self-interest in the drama of social interaction is colored by the fact that every social group is a structured group, and the career of each actor in it can be described in structural terms. When I say that the vehicle of social motivation is to be found in personal character I hope I won't be misunderstood. Character isn't made in a sort of ethical vacuum, each man acquiring his characteristic strengths and weaknesses in private contemplation; insofar as character has social relevance it is socially made. I'll go further: insofar as character is socially made it is dramatically made; it emerges in, and commits a sane person to, a social drama of unceasing interaction whose structure is external to each actor and sets the conditions under which he must flourish or falter. Always, the actor is caught up in the drama; always the outcome is in doubt. But the capital with which an actor enters each scene is what I've called his character: the current store of reputational and positional gains which he has built up, or to which he has fallen heir. So far as a man is an effective social agent, we conceive that it will be an overriding concern in all his involvements to maintain his character: defending what he has gained and adding, where he thinks he can add, to its ostensible value.

The idea of social structure demands that view of man's radical sociality and of the relativity of ethics to the demands of reputation. Character, in this view, is dramatically made within a structured network of social relationships. Each man is cast in a special role: he is surrounded by others whose expectations are patterned by culture and focused by the nice definitions of social structure. It is not all societies whose women a single, willful man can quickly master. Why does the Kiowa male wield a knife and the woman freeze before it? And how is it that a man will die of shame for having been overpowered by a group of women? It is a matter of role and structure, of the character values open to men and women in Kiowa culture. It is not all societies which can afford a Twkoide—one whose strength as a person is derived of shameless deeds; whose capital investment is in infamy, and must be guarded by a mask of murderous bravado, begetting bitterness and death. But the power to defy draws its strength everywhere from the power defied, and the devilish character appears in tales and in art where he can't appear in life; the antihero is, as much as the hero, a creature of the drama into which he has been cast.

For those of us who don't set out on the path of open defiance, motives are doubly fastened to the institutions our culture affords us: what we have to gain, we'll gain only through participation in the set dramas thrown up by events; by our most private motives we are drawn into the scene and involved; yet when once we are involved the privacy of our motives is altered, because the stakes for which the game is played are beyond our choosing. Cultures predefine for us the character values we may seek: that was the burden of Benedict's *Patterns of Culture.* But man doesn't stand on Olympus to greet his culture face to face. The meeting is in the village, the home, the fields; in each place one plays a particular role—one is man or woman, big man or little, challenged or bewildered, commanding or overreached. What we'll become is colored but not decided by the broad framework of usage we call culture. The same applies to the finer framework we call the structure of our society: we don't have the option to be merely passive creatures of culture and social structure but must strain to fulfill the parts we're given. Our scope of choice and chance for gain are contained in episode after episode, scene after scene—the phenomenal reality of life itself. To the actor involved in the drama there falls but this task: the characteristic exercise of reason on behalf of himself. It should no longer be a mystery to us that such exercise of reason, universally shared within any human community, leads to the predominance there of a pattern of ethical concerns which can continually reaffirm the prevailing structure of social roles and the relations of interdependence by which the community is held together.

That is the general view to which the idea of social structure has led us. The anthropologist, asserting his Olympian privilege, finds Kwaling, Sandombu, and even Twkoide reasonable men. The puzzle of motivation baffles us most when we are unable to see the creative role of reason in the unceasing making, maintaining, and remaking of men's social structures. It's true that each man's reason is very much his own, but that doesn't mean it is private. When we say a man is being unreasonable we mean two things: that the rest of us who are involved in a situation with him are having trouble bringing him around, and that we're determined to do so. I think this general view can be extended to encompass the round of life.

SOCIAL STRUCTURE AND CHAOS

For a student of social structure, the point of examining the microcultures (the thousands of minor traditions comparable to the Kiowa, Ndembu, or Tangu) is to achieve what the chemist can do in the laboratory. Having isolated the object of my curiosity, I subject it to observation in the most varied environments. In good measure that is the standard procedure we intuitively use when confronted with anything whose qualities are puzzling. And in refinement of that method, we often seek to vary the intensity or quantity of the thing we are studying, while holding the environment steady. Sometimes the result can tell us a great deal. In the case of social structure, variations of intensity imply a continuum from chaos to rigidity. There is a normal curve in the distribution of the world's societies along that continuum: most societies are roughly of middle intensity, and only a few groups fall out close to the extremes. Yet a look at the extremes will shed light on the rest, for there is a sense in which the normally viable social structure is always composed by a nice combination of rigidity with chaos.

During the decade 1935–45 the Nazi regime achieved in Germany a notable example of structural rigidity on a large scale. Toward the opposite extreme there are such societies as Tangu (p. 61), Kaingang (p. 27), and the Kiowa Indians (p. 36), where routine, ritual, and authoritarian action seem to be reduced to a minimum, and closely coordinated action is difficult to achieve. Twkoide (p. 36) apparently was not able to control his wife's behavior through discipline; that he must spy on her and would kill her in a fit of rage suggests the very opposite of well-structured authority. And the same fact suggests that the quality of the tie between husband and wife was not well defined in Kiowa society. After the deed public opinion was not easily settled on the rights and wrongs of the case: when you help or compensate both sides in a dispute you are stopping the fight at the expense of making clear for the future where justice lay. In the rigidly structured society, ambiguities of that sort are not tolerable, whether on the level of domestic relations or that of affairs of state. The caste village in India suggests the possibility of structural rigidity without authoritarian organization, and the Kiowa illustrate the rank-conscious society with only an ill-defined structure. Evidently there are various means by which in human societies order may be won out of chaos, structure out of fluidity. But does structure then mean any more or less than order? And will an unstructured group simply fall apart—or will the members fall at each other's throats?

The answers follow from all that we have so far discussed: social structure is a less inclusive idea than social order, and an unstructured group needn't be disorderly. Common norms and values may be the basis of social order. If two persons were left on an island and neither placed the other in any socially relevant category other than his own, though they shared the same language and culture they would not constitute a structured group. When Crusoe and Friday encountered one another, they fell almost instantly into a British master-servant relationship. If Friday had been a lady or a Martian we can assume that a different structure would have evolved. Structure presupposes complementary differentiation of status and role: a hundred identical wheels will not nake a watchworks, though they may all spin in unison. The dea we must hold of a complex social structure is that of a ast network of role relationships, each characterized by unctional complementarity—as with the "fit" of two parts of watch, or the nice balance which must be maintained in an lectronic system or living organism. A society composed (as Marx would have had it) of Jacks-of-all-trades would have he durability of a house of cards, in which each piece is uniorm. Although structure is not the only basis of social order, n the long run structure is necessary to orderly association among men; and it should be clear that well-defined social elationships normally presuppose a common culture and characterological values.

Yet if structure meant only differentiation and never equivalence, how could structure produce order? Surely chaos alone can result if two persons substantially alike can have no predictable relationship to each other? Studies suggest that an intimate association by two persons always gains structure —functional complementarity develops. In like manner, all of the role relationships in a society must fall into set patterns, characteristic of the group; and even so, it may be hard for individuals to judge what is expected of them. The set patterns have been called the organizing principles of a society; and you can often see the same principles at work at rather different levels of organization. If a patriarchal principle seems to dominate family organization, we can expect to find it also in the economic, political, and religious institutions of a people. If egalitarian principles are emphasized at one level, but significantly contradicted at others, we can expect social ferment.

Beyond the fact of set patterns, there is another sense in which every social structure must be enormously repetitive within itself. The analogy of the watchworks or the organism may be misleading if it is applied to the whole of a human society; for in many respects any human society is more like the biologist's colony than like his organism. A colony is an association of similar organisms. It may be far from formless, always taking a predictable and functionally efficient shape; the colony can be distinguished from an organism only by the fact that association at one stage is followed by dissociated life at another. A human society isn't composed c immovable cells, incapable of being rearranged and recom bined. The cell analogy will serve to give a sense for an ex treme of structural rigidity, in which no one can change hi position in the total network of social relationships excep through death. But actual societies could scarcely operat under such rigid conditions. No more can we expect to fin individuals somewhere totally free. Commonly, there ar family ties which ought not to be ruptured; and for access t wealth and the ordinary comforts one must maintain a con stant position; yet movement—of individuals, families, politica and economic groups—is as necessary and ordinary as stabil ity.

A society must be comprised of mobile groups, starting a the level of the intimate group which has a stable interna structure; and with overwhelming regularity in human socie ties around the world, the group which best suits this descrip tion can be called a family. Above that level there may b extended families, bands, lineages, clans, tribes, or just th familiar groupings based on neighborhood and territory. Bu at each level the same structure is replicated throughou society, according to a common plan; and each unit of th same type has roughly equivalent status to each other unit though some may in fact be weaker or stronger. Grouping with a territorial base are in contemporary urban societie usually not thought to be mobile; but in fact even territoria encroachment is common on certain levels, and neighborin towns are often inveterate competitors for population, for in dustry, for fetish shrines, or for whatever honors will seem tc place one community above another. If you allow that com petition for dominance is not possible without mobility modern nations tend to be as mobile in the international arena as their military strength and economic prowess permit. I have said that proximity and formal equivalence don't con stitute a structured relationship; rather, they tend to produce a condition of competitive mobility, which can be stabilized as structural opposition.

We've seen the structural opposition of villages in Tangu (p. 61) and in Ndembu life (p. 43). In principle, what we need to perceive is easily stated. Functional complementarity is the internal, or cohesive, aspect of social structure; structural opposition is its external, or mobilizing, aspect. Within the Tangu village there was structural opposition among rival managers; and to achieve stability they must achieve balance, or equivalence. In like fashion, between neighboring Tangu villages there was structural opposition, which required that a similar balance be achieved. The reason that balance can be reached in such cases is not that the strength of each party is pitted fully against the other and by chance they turn out to be even. Rather, the strength of one party can never be pitted fully against another's, because a small measure of victory is enough to soften the zeal of the aggressor, while a small measure of defeat will correspondingly harden the determination of the defender. We won't understand the structures in terms just adequate to animal psychology: an instinct of aggression or a blind ethnocentrism wouldn't produce behavior of this order. In a general way, the interchange between the two parties is a dramatic encounter, in which the other party is audience as well as antagonist. To impress him I must best him; but when I've done so I'm no longer sure he is worth impressing. What sort of team will keep playing in a league where it can't be beaten? The sense of equivalence must be maintained.

Concerning internal aspects of Tangu social structure we can gather only a little, though we see a pattern of complementarity between men and women, and the operation of a kinship network. The pattern in Sandombu's village is clearer (p. 43); and it is easier to perceive the relativity of internal and external structural principles. Sandombu's ambition for political ascendance, more than any other motive, accounts for his drive for success as foreman of a work crew, and his capacity to help others. But this same ambition, since it pits him in structural opposition to rivals for the headmanship, is itself to be accounted for by Sandombu's position *within* the lineage and affinal kin structure of the village; by virtue of his birth, he is the logical man to lead a certain faction in the village; and though it is a somewhat disadvantaged faction, there is hope for it with strong leadership, many offspring, and the adroit use of witchcraft. Structural opposition is not possible without some effective, overarching ties which tend to place the two parties in putatively equivalent status. For the Ndembu, the basic idiom is kinship and the headship of kin groupings; for the Tangu there are demonstrations of complementarity in trade relations, feasting and dance hospitality, and clientship, while opposition is expressed not in court suits and witchcraft but in formal *br'ngun'guni,* and an occasional free-for-all.

The two correlative principles, functional differentiation and structural opposition, combine in a great variety of ways on all levels of social structure in all human societies. Pushed to its logical extreme, functional differentiation would produce an impossibly rigid society in which mobility didn't exist for individuals or groups. But monolithic structures are usually more apparent than real. Flexibility on lower levels is introduced by structural opposition. Brothers within the household are rivals, though they present a solidary front to outsiders; lineages within the clan are in continual dispute, but fight together when the clan is attacked. Office mates are rivals for promotion, but constitute a solidary unit within the structure of the bureau. Middle-class neighbors stretch themselves to outdo one another in the game of conspicuous consumption, but unite to keep Jones from selling his house to a gentleman with an exotic face or threatening demeanor. Our account of the puzzle of motivation was not complete until now; for it is just by reason of structural opposition on all levels of our experience that we are most inexorably drawn into the expressive conventions proper to the status we hold and the roles we are expected to play.

PART TWO

FAMILY SYSTEMS

SECTION ONE

THE PRIMARY INSTITUTION

DOMICILED GROUPS

NATURAL/CONVENTIONAL

The idea of social structure is proper to the human condition: we're not called to reduce human behavior to terms which would serve as well for rats or baboons. We've agreed with Hobbes that a person "is the same that an *Actor* is, both on the Stage and in common Conversation" (p. 3); and you wouldn't predicate that of a rat. Motives such as sex, hunger, self-defense, and aggression apply as well to men as to mice or monkeys; but the distinctive character of human motivation lies in those qualities of self-concern and reasoned intention which make man an *Actor* even in the most passionate of the scenes he plays. The next step is a study of institutions within which social roles and character values gain definition. Since man is the most domesticated of all beasts, we can't understand him without reference to the demands domestic groups have put on him.

Although man has become domestic in that societies everywhere emphasize values associated with home and hearth, he has not been content with a single pattern. Men have produced a thousand varied institutions fit to be called domestic. Though Home and Adventure are two poles of our existence everywhere, nineteenth-century Kiowa domesticity (p. 36) would fall off the adventure end of the scale for even those intrepid bourgeois contemporaries of the Kiowa, Messrs. Pickwick and Snodgrass, or even Mr. Sam Weller. For all the variety, there is an underlying logic in the way men's intimate relations are arranged around the world. Domestic groups are enough alike that we can make some general statements about them. One is that the family in man is an artificial contrivance, not rooted in human nature.

It would be absurd to deny that family organization the world around revolves about sex, reproduction, and the socialization of children; but there is an enormous variety of arrangements for meeting the tasks set by nature. Even biological parenthood has turned out to be less decisive than one might have expected. The family is best conceived as a solution to structural, not to natural, problems. Human domesticity takes its character from the political even more than the biological ends it serves.

Consider paternity. In many societies a man who fathered a child may not know it. There may be a child I doubt is mine, or one I don't doubt though the mother knows it isn't mine. In one or two human societies the question, whose child is whose, has been a matter of no serious import, a subject of sporting speculation; though in the great majority of cultures that isn't the case, and the law is much concerned with paternity. Using the verbal resources of the Latin tradition, anthropologists have come to distinguish *genitor* (=biological father) and *pater*. The latter refers to a fact of social structure and, often, jurally sanctioned responsibility. *Pater* and *genitor* need not be the same person in any case, though in most societies they are likely to be. The *pater* of little Hans need not live with him; in some societies the child's home is always with his mother, however often her husbands change. The *genitor* of little Hans may live with him and yet not be his *pater;* for in other societies a child may legally belong to the mother's lawfully wedded spouse (of the time the child should have been conceived), however fickle may have been the lady's unlawful affections. In short, the constitution of a household is first a jural construct, a matter of social definition. What we may call natural paternity (the social position of the *genitor*) is universally an *object* of definition, and therefore doesn't control it.

But now consider the biological relation of mother and child. Most women in most societies suffer during childbirth; and it is a suffering which most women attribute to nature. The fabled joys of nursing are often conceived as a compensating gift of nature. We could conclude that the mother-child relationship begins with a stronger dose of "nature" than does the father-child relationship. Does that mean that the maternal role in human life is natural?

I think not. Consider cookery: is a cake not artificial, however natural the ingredients? The biologically grounded experiences of mother and child, like the sexual relationship in which the child may have been begotten, are standard ingredients of family systems almost everywhere; but when the family is regarded as an institution the question is not, What are the ingredients? but rather, What has been made of them? To continue the cookery parallel: give me the raw materials of an angel food cake and let me mix them at random—I'm fairly sure I could get an inedible result. An institution, like a cake, is a nonrandom combination of its ingredients. The differences between one family system and another—say, between nineteenth-century small-town Chinese and nineteenth-century small-town Canadian—will not be understood by a student who wants to reduce each system to its biological ingredients. Is the difference between a concubine and a wife a natural one? Is the possessive love of a woman for an adopted child *un*natural? Do bottle feeding and Caesarean section effectively remove the natural basis of maternity and necessarily produce a less natural sort of family? The anthropologist today can't take such questions with complete seriousness, for they are insensitive to the subtlety of nature's part in any human institution. They would be asked in a quite different way by someone familiar with the idea of social structure.

How much do social structure and natural instinct explain of marital behavior in the social group you know best? Much of the behavior of husband and wife toward each other has a natural (instinctual) basis: you can't be aware of your husband's halitosis without the proper natural equipment, and much the same applies to sexual awareness of others. But is it by nature (by instinct) that I avoid a person whose breath

I find fetid? Or can I sometimes go ahead as though I found it sweet? Do I habitually exercise discretion in my response? The answer is that nature initiates a problem for me but doesn't solve it; and the same answer applies to questions about sexual attraction and repulsion. When you grant that it's playful to talk of marriage among birds and artificial to talk of mating among ourselves you have begun to recognize the essentially conventional character of family systems.

GRANULAR STRUCTURES

Not all civilly constituted domestic groups are families, and of course not every family lives as a householding unit. Older children may be expected to live with their peers in village dormitories or away at school; barracks life may be found in the most disparate societies. The typical domestic group may be a big establishment, an extended family with hangers-on unrelated or married in, or a monogamous pair with children. Sometimes the observer may find that men are normally closer to and more responsible for sister's children than wife's: which is then a man's family? In some reports the men's club, ritual group, or honorary association is pictured as having more importance to men than their families; and in societies composed of small bands the individual families comprising them may only rarely operate as independent units. But for all the variety and the trouble with labels there is in every society a civilly constituted family system. In general, a domestic group suitably called a family will be the most numerous institution in any society; almost everyone will openly belong to one home household with only secondary ties to others, and it is at home that he will experience the closest ties with persons of different age and sex.

To say that a family is an institution means that, however spontaneous and natural the life of its members seems to be, it must stay within bounds set by social conventions. One set of limits applies to character: in a dour and parsimonious culture, children will not be encouraged to emulate the happy-go-lucky spendthrift. Another set of limits applies to the forms a family unit may take. If your society is monogamous you aren't allowed a plural marriage. That doesn't make a *ménage à trois* impossible, though it probably makes it difficult. But suppose concubinage is allowed: that means household organization isn't limited to elementary families, and something close to plural marriage is allowed. What happens then to your *ménage à trois*? A wife and concubine can't be equals, and you would be trying to make them so: we can predict they won't cooperate. Structural limits operate by sabotage and diversion as often as not.

One limitation which all societies place on their domestic groups is that they should be *replicable*. Consider a society of bees, and how its viability depends on the perfection with which its workers can be replicated as old individuals die off. A human society, however regimented, will never be the social machine that a beehive is; the resourcefulness of individuals will always be needed to keep a human society operating. If in some future Brave New World that presumption were to be out of tune with the facts of life, the idea of social structure outlined here would be obsolete. But as the world is now, the necessary resourcefulness of individuals is matched by the uniformity of the structure of domestic groups, supplying on an institutional level something of the regimentation of the insect world. So people in any society are free to be less alike than the families of which they are members.

While an insect society does have a center in its queen, the idea that the word "queen" suggests—autocratic rule by a superior creature possessing great intelligence—belongs to storytelling rather than to science. In fact, the viability of an ant society is vested in the replicated mechanism of the individual ant. The mechanism is fundamentally *social:* the ant was not first evolved as a self-reliant creature and then bound together with his fellows in a functioning society; social system and physical creature evolved together, though all the social mechanisms are vested in the replicated individuals. We may say that, in contrast to the centralized structure of the child's imaginary ant society, the real one has a *granular* structure. It is as if one were to take a pyramid made of pebbles and spread them out to form an even, solid floor. Probably there is no such thing as a society without a center; what matters is how much independent responsibility is left at the grass roots. In human societies this level is most characteristically represented not in the individual but in the stable domestic group; for individual participation ranges over all levels of organization, while family interests are rooted. So the stability of human societies depends on the maintenance of domestic institutions, as the social life of an anthill depends on the physiology of the individual ant. What the domestic institution does is to create a cell of self-responsibility and self-reliance, a cell which is far more steady than human individuals by themselves could be. Responsibility is normally inseparable from a structure of reciprocity and is heightened by enduring face-to-face relations.

Doesn't poor Tam O'Shanter have his counterpart in every human society? Individuals are prey to temptations that a corporate group is immune from, and the inner structure of the family sets it cleanly apart from other groups. Are cliques and gangs more solidary? They aren't as durable. Are cult groups more purposeful? They have a special-purpose character. Are communes more self-sufficient? They are also more readily divisible. Domestic groups are concerned with the whole activity of daily, yearly, and generational survival. There are always patterns of interestedness and exclusiveness, competition as well as cooperation among households. Coping with the problems of communal existence in this manner, always representing one's own domestic interests, is carrying ground-level social responsibility.

What I'm arguing is a point about social architecture. Consider me a partisan of the microcosm. I'm for cells, not crowds, an "egg-crate" structure for coexistence, not a pile. I'm for domestic institutions intervening as a base level of structure between individual and society or state, to maintain a granular distribution of responsibility to persons, property, and resources. Architectonically the object is to decentralize the keeping of the keys to social survival, and I argue that this calls for partition of the society into small groups, not individuals, and into groups more like families than corner gangs. If you prefer corner gangs and would like to be rid of the family, so be it; I only claim to be taking the part of realism, and you would have to admit that so far the anthropological evidence for the efficiency of family systems over alternatives is overwhelming. There must be self-reliant responsibility at the grass roots, and there are reasons why human societies have generally vested such responsibility with the units, specifically, of a family system: it is in the great catalog of tasks necessary to the successful rearing of children that ethical responsibility for another person has its most characteristic manifestations; the tying of sexual rewards to those responsibilities is a rather direct way of reinforcing them; and so on. Most obvious of all is the consideration that any society which would survive must provide both for a predictable heterosexual regime and for the survival of offspring through adequate personal care; and to do that in a decentralized fashion practically entails a family system.

In most societies there are some domestic groups which should not be called families. Sometimes young persons of the same sex or of both sexes live together in common residence; in various parts of the world there have been convents and monasteries; and adult persons may live alone. There are the longhouse societies, in which whole villages live under one roof, so that the separate families are in unguarded and frequent contact each with its neighbors in adjoining cubicles. And there are societies in which the successful family is like a village in itself, households within households. The African polygynist's compound could be such, when he had succeeded in getting many wives and each had many surviving children still remaining there and cooperating with the family economic enterprise. But such variations of form ought not to obscure the functional gain from uniformity which accounts for the proliferation in each society of domestic groups made to a characteristic, institutional model, so that each one substantially replicates the next and will behave over time in the same, predictable fashion.

AUTONOMY AND INTERDEPENDENCE

The idea of social structure does finally force one to the point of discussing the behavior of an institution like the domestic group in terms which owe little to psychology and would not be apt for discussing behavior in individual persons. When you see a family starting out on a journey you can personify the group and discuss its behavior as an active agent, even its motives and goals. But the behavior of a family *considered as an institution* ought not to be discussed in such terms. When a gang of African boys from Village Alpha steals and roasts and eats a goat from the herds of Village Beta you can predict that the next step in the drama will be, not another raid from Alpha on Beta but a counterraid to redress the balance. The reason lies not in human nature, which would obviously permit the boys of Alpha to follow up the one success with another; the reason lies rather in a structural principle, that is, in an observable regularity in the behavior of social systems, as distinct from the regularities of people. Social systems produce balanced opposition among groups; a society which has produced a series of politically coequal villages must, in order to have kept them equal, have worked up a system of balanced opposition among them. Goat-raiding by boys, like marriage contracts among adults, will be part of the balance. The ideas and values associated by individuals with goat-raiding and with marriage will be such that in the long run a balance of forces is maintained among the interraiding and intermarrying villages in the series. Raiding will be more a matter of one-upmanship than subsistence, wife-getting will be approached with a view to exploiting a bargaining relationship, not as sexual predation. We should look to the effort of men not just to feed their bellies and egos but to attain and show good character, if we would comprehend the process which negotiates the puzzling gap between individual and institutional planes of behavior.

The boys in the goat raid were identified with a particular village, just as boys of a football team may be identified with a school; and the analogy is apt, since the point of the raid was not so much the barbecue as a kind of scoring. But if the village were the lowest level of structure of an African society —if the adults, like the boys, were simply lumped together in village-wide gangs—it is hard to imagine that the system could maintain itself for long. The unitary, comparatively informal structure of a boys' gang (and they do seem to be much the same the world around) is nicely adapted to brief-lived common enterprises of the adventurous sort. A successful raid is a joy to all, and the braving of perils in common has its effect on morale even where all does not go well. But life is not all adventure, and neither team spirit nor local patriotism has ever sustained more than some of the people most of the time.

In contrast to the gang, the domestic group is organized about humdrum tasks and is dominated by sober values. Whether by chalk, masks, feathers, or uniform jackets the tendency of a gang is to fuse the identities of its members, such that none have goods withheld from the others. The tendency of the domestic group is to emphasize a fixed division of responsibilities and rights. There is a distinct manner of dress and comportment for each role position within the group, and mutual rights and obligations are unambiguously ascribed. One of a set of twins in some societies is always put away at birth, as though even so much fusion of statuses were anathema to the domestic institution, which must secure to each person born an unambiguous jural identity. On this will hinge his future rights and obligations—in sexual relations, in property and work, and in taking sides in conflict—toward each other member of the society. Social differentiation within the domestic group (and within the broader kinship units) is not so important in a hunting and gathering society, unless in connection with marriage rights, as in a herding or farming society, where it is likely that important rights in property must eventually be allocated within the family group—must, in fact, be reallocated within each generation. For some Bushman peoples of the Kalahari Desert, or among some forest peoples, or peoples hunting and gathering in an arid land like the Great Basin of North America, the local group may be so small that all can sit around a common fire in the evening, as if the village itself were no bigger than a gang of boys. But the structure of such a hunting band is more complex than that of a group of peers responsible only to themselves: as an aged face is more complex than a child's, the hunting group of three generations and two sexes falls at the opposite end of a scale from the group of boys. In a more populous and settled society the structure of the local group will be more complex, and the threshold between one family unit and another within the group will be more definite: each will at least have a separate fire, eating and conversing to itself. But however large or small the village or the wandering band, it will never fail to be comprised of component units (often elementary or nuclear families), and the thresholds will be there.

Considered as an institution, the domestic group comprises the stage upon which half of the episodes of any human life will be played out—and almost all the *scènes d'intérieur,* the transactions among intimates. Beyond or beneath the fact of the determinate relationship of right and responsibility, tying each member to each other, is the fact of being emotionally bound within the group. The intractableness of the tie between a woman and her son is celebrated in current cosmopolitan mythology under the title of the Oedipus complex; and other ties—especially the father-son—are equally hard to sunder. It is characteristic of the domestic institution that it begets and fosters a boundedness of emotional experience, ethical thought, and character which persons only lightly touched by the institution can never know. It is within the group that the rewards of the good life are liberally shared; that the most private drama of personal conflict, strain, and failure is up to the last contained; and that the resources of a man's character are, as nowhere else, laid bare to another's view. But if the domestic situation closets us in with the one hand, with the other it propels our thoughts outward. Each domestic unit competes as a microcosm with endless others for the fruits of the good life. The higher the threshold between them, the more surely they compete; for the sphere of cooperation is close at hand, and beyond is the great world.

In the vanishing universe of independent, unurbanized peoples there is often no constituted political group as such; and the management of peace beyond the domestic and close-at-hand poses a special problem. Politics can sometimes be said to consist in interdomestic relations. In what we may call the classic case of local exogamy each village is comprised of families closely related and on that ground disallowed intermarriage, with the result that all must marry, despite the sense of distance, outside the village; and politics has then become a blend of marital and intervillage relations, in which the main protagonists are domestic units. Why do men not simply throw custom to the winds and marry their cousins at home? An ancient but obsolete answer is: superstition. But that answer will satisfy only those for whom custom (here in the guise of "superstitious" belief and practice) is king and can't itself be explained except as a freak of history. For us the answer lies in a conception of the two villages as structurally opposed and balanced. A condition of the cooperation among males *within* the village has been the marrying out, for it is precisely that rule and practice which alone can really demonstrate the great weight which must be put on being closely related. Am I and my fourth cousin on my father's side closely related? Must I run to his side whenever he quarrels? This is a matter for social definition and varies from one people to another. Suppose I can't marry my first cousin but am free with my fourth: that defines the matter pretty clearly for me. By enjoining out-marriage a subsistence village has surrendered a great measure of the autonomy it might have had; but it had gained a structured, political relationship to other villages; and that, on the evidence, is the sort of behavior we should by now have learned to expect of a social system.

DOMESTIC GROUP AND SOCIAL SYSTEM

Consider an African society which practices the payment of heavy bridewealth to the father of a girl, in exchange for her hand in marriage. It is a cattle-keeping society which also practices agriculture; and we shall say that the usual bridewealth is thirty animals. What is the good of the practice? Why do they keep it? Where did it come from? It is not much help to suggest that the payment makes the girl's family willing to dispense with her services, for it is likely that the same family will have to pay out the same price in order to take on the services of a bride to one of its sons. The advantages do not seem rationally to outweigh the disadvantages, where income and outgo in the long run have to balance. Yet the idea of social structure suggests an answer, which relates cattle payment to the quality of inter-domestic relations. If we ask, *without* payment who could aspire to your daughter's hand? We find ourselves looking about for some pre-existing ties which you would like to affirm. The bridewealth custom serves to create a sort of open marriage market which, otherwise, we could hardly expect to find. *With* the payment you will not find it hard to believe that a perfect stranger is ready to place high value on your daughter. *Without* the payment what consideration could induce you to hold the same belief? In short, the custom of the bridewealth permits a broader-ranging system of outmarriage than otherwise would be feasible; and that, in turn, allows for the building of larger clusters of cooperating, closely related kin, who do not isolate themselves by inmarriage. When readiness with cattle is placed before all other criteria of eligibility for marriage in a polygynous society—and a society where wives themselves by their work beget wealth—a few men will tend to come into possession of much of the wealth in both cattle *and* women.

There are bridewealth systems in Africa which have a different character: the groups into which my daughter would marry are well known to me, and are distinct from the groups whence my daughters-in-law must come. My group thus participates in a system of generalized exchange, in that we help to circulate daughters in one direction and cattle (always given in exchange) in the other; and eventually, of course, the circle must be completed and the distant offspring of our own women and our own cattle will come back to us. The great difference between this and the "open marriage market" system is in the narrowing and channeling of the direction of flow. But what is important for us in either system is to notice in how great a degree *the norms of the domestic institution give form to the broader social system.* We are dealing here with a phenomenon which with some justification can be called an *interdomestic political system;* for the rules and conditions of marriage, ostensibly touching only the private affairs of families, are in each case very clearly related to the maintenance of peaceful relations over wide areas. Looking only at the motivation of the male role system, you have only to assume that the families engaged in a bridewealth system approve of it and want to keep it in good order, and it follows that they will tend to oppose unlimited cattle-raiding (and retribution), on the ground that no system of exchange can work where payments peacefully made are freely taken back by force. That is, if there is a widespread "marriage-cattle market" men must keep its peace. As to raiding for women, it goes without saying that warfare could not be carried so far without bringing down the whole, elaborate political system. That is the *point* of the system: it is a network of contractual relations with strangers who otherwise would be related to you only by structural opposition.

Polygyny itself—with or without bridewealths—is in a narrow sense only a rule of marriage; but where the practice is emphasized and has become the key, for men, to success in the game of character and repute, there the whole social system is affected. After all, a man who devotes his life to the accumulation of wives and children is a capitalist; and a society whose big men have influence mainly *because* of success in the game of polygyny is a capitalistic society. Sometimes in an aerial view of the country one can see, from the pattern of the dwellings, the cattle byres, and the tilled fields, the broad structure of the local social order. There can be an even scattering of similar households over broad areas, indicating a roughly egalitarian structure. Or there may be clusters of smaller dwellings about the impressive compounds of the big men. In both cases the granular distribution of ground-level responsibility can be seen, though it is not in both cases governed by egalitarian norms and practices. If we could stop in our aerial journey over such country, letting the years and even generations pass by, we should be able to watch the behavior of the domestic groups, as evidenced in the changes in their dwellings. We should probably notice in the capitalistic society that the big compounds did not last. Because of the rules—that is, marriage and filial ties—by which they were composed as social groups; and because all the ties hinged ultimately upon relationship to the household head; it would happen that when he died (or when the last brother died who could have inherited the wives and filled the place) the basis of unity in the group would die also. The compound would, in accordance with the ties still remaining intact, resolve into a series of lesser components. The wives who were young would marry again; if not inheritable, after mourning they might scatter to the four winds; but grown and married sons would be likely to stay, albeit in separated households, and on inheriting cattle an elder son could be in position to start the cycle of wife-accumulation over again. We should see the breakup, in short, of the large compound, and the scattering of a part of its population; the regrouping of what remained; and perhaps eventually a repetition of the cycle of growth and nucleation.

The society we have been picturing was one shaped by the ideals of polygynous marriage and tending to produce a cyclic pattern of domestic nucleation and dispersion. But consider now a society whose rules emphasize not marriage (affinal ties) but kinship by birth (common descent, consanguinity). Descent or blood relationships, until the whole group dies out, don't cease with the death of individuals: though my brother-in-law is no kin when the woman who linked us has died and been replaced by a stranger, my own brother always is mine, and all of our offspring are kin by birth. If we should view from the air domestic groups in a descent society, our first impression might be only of the similarity to what we had already seen; instead of an even scattering of homesteads over the country we might find a tendency to nucleation, or at least to a grouping together of separate households in hamlet clusters. But if we were to persist again in watching over the years and generations it is likely we should observe a different pattern in the behavior of the groups, reflecting the different rules by which the clusters were composed. If brothers (and male cousins descended from brothers) always tended to comprise closely cooperating groups then we could expect them to build in clusters of a handful of houses each. With time, their offspring would grow and marry, and there should soon be not a cluster of houses but a town. But in a primary horticultural economy that can't be expected. As the population of a particular kin group increased, the group would have to divide; and while one part might remain *in situ* the other must find a fresh site. The society would stress the unity of a set of full brothers; and it would not be surprising to find that the group setting off for a new place was such a set, whose own father had died. At that point, the sibling tie (of the *father* to *his* brother or brothers) which had bound the group to its kin would have dissolved; and the difficulty of getting a living in that place might well have begun to produce a certain friction among the groups—the several sets of brothers—related only by cousinhood. The phenomenon of "hiving off" or "segmentation" (following friction between potentially separate segments of a clustered kinship group) is typical of what are called descent societies; it is a phenomenon which can be said, for practical purposes, to have been entailed in the structural emphasis on consanguinity. For if inter-domestic relations are predicated on ties which can with time be indefinitely extended there will be no "dispersal to the winds" as with the breakup of the imagined polygynous compound; but the return to a more granular structure of society will be achieved by the hiving-off process instead.

Among the world's societies there seem to be none that make nothing at all of consanguinity, but there are some that make very little of it and make nothing of *descent:* they fail to align my offspring with my brother's or a woman's children with her sister's. There seem to be no societies that have no use for marriage ties, though a few have almost no use for them. But most of the world's societies make use of both consanguinity and affinity, and the result is an immensely varied lot of family systems. The systems are not so varied that they don't fall into types, but neither are they so true to type that the idiosyncrasies of each can be ignored. The wealth-oriented polygynist can't build his big compound without according tangible value to offspring: this tie of *filiation* is implied in any rationale you might find for collecting fertile wives. Putting a value on filiation may fall short of putting a value on descent, but the germ is there. Our wife- and cow-hoarding capitalist society is likely to have all the structural ideas needed to make it a descent society; the differences will be in emphases and the finer definitions.

In new circumstances old ideas will not work out as they did. Sometimes, as in rural China until recent times, a culture may almost obsessively emphasize the *idea* of descent without making much of it structurally. In Chinese villages (as distinct from the towns) the structural reality associated with the importance of ancestors was usually a very strong *filial* bond but little extension of the sense of consanguinity beyond the immediate household. In the absence of a son an unrelated male could be adopted in preference, say, to an eligible nephew, to carry on the family line: the important criterion was filial respect, not physical descent. Economic realities were pitted against cultural ideals. If he could, every household head would have found himself in his old age reigning over a vast domestic empire, an abundance of sons and grandchildren living under a single roof and taking their food in a single great room from a single stove. In fact, the competition for a livelihood from land or cottage industry was so pressing that the large household (rich enough that internal competition would be minimal and leisure might permit the cultivation of gentle arts) was no part of the villager's real world. The viable household unit was a small and lean one, the minimal unit capable of assuming ground-level responsibility and achieving permanence: dreams of grandeur helped to motivate responsibility as the myth of permanence helped to reconcile men to the failure of their worldly dreams. Instead of growing with the marriage of sons, families became quarrelsome and split up even before the old father's death. So the actual domestic or interdomestic structure of any society must be a subtle balance of ideal organizing principles, massively compromised by the possible.

SOCIETIES AS NETWORKS OF DOMESTIC GROUPS

DESCENT AND THE RELATIONS OF DOMESTIC GROUPS

If it is primarily domestic groups that compete with one another for the fruits of the good life—that is, if individuals *within* the household do not compete but freely share—then the nature of the family is going to affect the economic system. The style of economic motivation, and in good measure its ethics, should be fashioned at the domestic hearth. An economic system is a thing in itself, with its own laws, and is not reducible to its separate parts; but if you change the parts you are almost certainly going to change the system. This is equally true for other institutional orders. Consider not the economic system of a community but its system of sexual relations. The sexual style and ethics of a human community are no less important or characteristic than the economic; and here the influence of the domestic institution is even more apparent. The family everywhere is vested with special responsibility in the control of sexual relations from the discouraging of adultery and the prohibition of incest to the sponsoring of legitimate and (usually) extra-legitimate children. In short, the domestic institution affects in several distinguishable ways the general character and constitution of a society.

But that is a vague conclusion, and one whose obverse is equally true; economic and sexual ethics affect the structure of the family, also. And no family can ordinarily expect to change the laws which govern it; man's most modest cultural groups are like his grandest in that fact. Isn't incest almost everywhere prohibited? And aren't the rights and duties of marriage everywhere prescribed? Doesn't each society sanction and maintain a law of property and inheritance? of the status of women and dependent children? And doesn't society (or law or custom or tradition) state and maintain in detail the structural frame within which every man must find his way to the good life? The idea of social structure imposes a subtler view of human life than common sense. What I have to argue is that law, custom, and tradition—in a word, society—are not imposed on us from without but from within: and yet I don't mean "within" as a theologian or psychologist would mean the term. I would point to the inner structure not of man but of his social life.

When we think of systems of descent, and distinguish matrilineal from patrilineal patterns, we may be first inclined to think only in terms of persons and personal identities. Supposing that all men had surnames, our first thought might be that systems of descent pertained to them and to the vague identities which names imply. If you want a system of surnames you can't simply follow nature; doing that would mean that every child should bear the surnames of each parent, hyphenated, and after a few generations of such doubling-up a name would have become an extraordinary thing. Systems of descent must be selective: on what ground should they select? They must be exclusive: on what ground should they exclude? These are deceptively simple questions. Most microcultures are organized around kinship, and even where other principles of order (political, ritual, economic) are important these are likely to be conceived in a kinship idiom. A descent rule is certain to be tied in some way to residence rules (does a man move to his bride or she to him?), to the clustering and alignment of households for mutual aid, to questions of precedence and access to power, to land ownership and succession in an agricultural society, and to a host of more subtle matters of organization. To use a mathematical analogy, there is a long series of simultaneous equations whose values will be affected by any substitution in the rule of descent. Making sense of kinship systems is therefore an important task and a test of the idea of social structure: there is more in descent than a name. There can be, as we have begun to see, a sort of genetic code which will affect the shape of the whole society.

Usually the pattern of structural bonds has partial expression in the ordering of social space: if societies are not often neatly composed of territorially organized descent groups, in the fashion of the provinces making up some modern nations, a noticeable clustering of households by descent can be expected. Often it is a critical condition for the psychological reinforcement of kinship ties, by which they gain value to men. Genealogical relatedness which was never expressed in frequency, intensity, or intimacy of social contact could become rather tenuous. If you neither meet your cousin in daily life nor specially seek him out, he is not close to you in the way we usually use the term. On the other hand, the strength and durability of a structural bond can't be reduced to frequency of contact or familiarity. The matter wants more delicate analysis.

Let us begin with a classical problem, the position of the father where important things descend to his children not from him but from their mother and her kin. At first it might seem that reckoning descent through women would yield a simple mirror image of a system of descent through men. But descent systems don't work that way because men are everywhere more political than women, women are more domestic than men. A village of households hinged through women tends to be one whose menfolk—supposing most of them have married into the village from different places—do not comprise a strong political unit. At least, we should expect that a similar village, different only in being hinged together through men, would be likely to comprise a stronger unit; there the men are all agnates, that is, born to the same line. Differences of that sort matter a great deal in societies where responsibility for keeping the peace is emphatically decentralized. The institution of a rule of descent in a community means a hardening and systematizing of interdomestic relations—an effective guarantee that the domestic institution will work consistently from one end of the society to another, and will successfully replicate itself from generation to generation. But above all a descent rule means giving a particular character to the inner structure of the family itself, and to the network through which one household is likely to be related to another. It is through the hinging of each to others that the institutional character of domestic groups is most often guaranteed—their consistency in social space and time, and their capacity to function responsibly in relation to politico-military as well as economic ends.

The special qualities of a social group built up through what we can call matrilateral hinging can be suggested by considering a society which has succeeded in achieving political strength and coherence in the local settlement, while yet retaining a matrilineal emphasis. The Nayar castes of southwest India were organized to allow the men of a matrilineal group to live together in a compact settlement together with the women of their own matrilineages. But in order to achieve that arrangement, the Nayar had done away with the conjugal household: the husband-wife relationship, based on exclusive or limited sexual rights and daily economic responsibility, did not exist. A woman bore the children of various men, none of whom had rights over her or over any of her children. The lasting relationships in that society were not affinal but consanguineal—a man contributed to the support of his sister and her children, and more generally of the women of his matrilineal group; and he brought only free gifts to the women with whom he had arranged to have sexual relations. We can say that men lived with the women of their own matrilineage, and slept with the women of similar but unrelated groups. In considering the significance of such an arrangement it is convenient to think of a woman with her own children as making up in each case an elementary family or household. A good number of such households, matrilaterally hinged, comprised a compact matrilineage, which for men's work and for defense relied upon no husbands or visiting lovers but upon men of its own line. Both men and women, under such arrangements, are born and will die under the same roofs; but under any less extreme arrangement that could hardly be the case. It is more usual, where the rule of descent is matriliny, to find that matrilateral hinging of households is also the rule, but that it coexists with marriage and the conjugal household; that is, fatherhood exists and has some importance, even though the "unclehood" of a mother's brother may have more. From the child's point of view, the relationship to Father may be intimate and positively toned, but the tie to Mother's Brother carries authority and demands allegiance.

Consider the following summary statement by a distinguished anthropologist, discussing facts common to many societies. It is a passage which focuses on the relations of fathers and children, explaining a difference of pattern within the family in relation to the law—the jural sanctions—by which it has been constituted.

Meyer Fortes
An Analytical Essay 1958

It is because the father is not vested with jural authority over his son and the son has no ties to the inheritance of his father's properties or to succession to his offices and rank, that matrilineal fathers and sons have an affectionate, noncompetitive relationship. Conversely, it is because maternal uncles have jurally sanctioned rights over their nephews and the latter have jurally sanctioned claims on their uncles that there is tension in their relationship. And the pattern is reversed in patrilineal systems because the locus of rights and claims is jurally reversed. Matrilineal fatherhood is defined as primarily a domestic relationship with only a minimal function in the politico-jural domain. Hence its focus is the task of bringing up and educating a child and fathers must rely on moral and affectional sanctions to fulfill it. In the last resort society will stand behind them to prevent trespass on their prerogative but gives them no support in the enforcement of their will on their children. We can contrast this with the juridical support society gives to the matrilineal husband in enforcing his rights to the sexual services of his wife. A patrilineal father, on the other hand, has not only the domestic and parental roles of provider and educator. He has rights enforceable by juridical sanctions over and towards them and they have corresponding claims on him. He represents the power of society as a force within the domestic group in a way that the matrilineal father does not.

We have been given a picture of two sorts of domestic groups—two ideal types abstracted from the ethnographic descriptions of many societies. The domestic group in patriliny binds father and children in a tighter structural web than is the case in matriliny; and the reason has to do with the nature of the father's role in social control. Professor Fortes states the difference by distinguishing two sorts of sanction—on the one hand a set of "moral and affectional sanctions" and on the other "jural authority" or "rights enforceable by juridical sanctions." The difference is not simply one of mood: the two kinds of domestic group are different in structure. In the one, the father has both sets of sanction at his disposal; in the other, the juridical sanctions support not the father but the maternal uncle—that is, the children *belong to* the mother's kin. Let us suppose that the mother died in our matrilineal household: we could expect that the children would be reared by a kinsman of the mother, whereas in the patrilineal household children would remain with the father or would pass to his kinsmen to rear. In the case of divorce, our expectations would be similar: in patrilineal societies even an unborn child will probably revert to the father's care as soon as that is reckoned to be feasible. The rule of descent gives us a clue to the way one domestic group will be hinged to another—who belongs to whom when a family falls apart or needs assistance. The resulting network of households may be visible—the society may have local descent groups—or it may be otherwise. But if there is a rule of descent there must be a network of structured ties joining each household to some others. The strongest ligaments of the body politic are not always near the surface.

THE HINGING OF DOMESTIC GROUPS

Because descent is a universal structural device and because marriage and relationship through marriage is recognized everywhere, the hinging of domestic groups is often identified with kinship organization. In fact, kinship relations are often created to strengthen existing ties: two men who wish to erect their friendship into a permanent bond become blood brothers, and a client who would strengthen his ties to a patron offers a child in fosterage or symbolically as godchild. Consanguinity itself is best understood as conferring a right to alliance, not alliance itself. In many patrilineal societies, where it is expected that a man's sons will live near him in order to stand by him in case of trouble, there is nonetheless a minor pattern of living near your *mother's* patrikin. There may be sound economic or even political reasons for such a move; the custom is not just a safety valve where father and son can't agree. But that a man may choose between one descent group and another means that the tie of kinship between two household heads is not automatic. For example, a man may be entitled to marry his mother's brother's daughter or a more distant cousin who stands in the same relationship to him. There are many potential spouses for each girl, and not all the claims can be honored. The link that is made, however, will set the terms for future marriages of the same sort. Again, a choice has been taken within the framework of rights provided by a kinship system, and positive ties have been affirmed between two households.

I talk of hinging rather than bonding or forging links between two households because I want to suggest that the result is not a rigid tie putting an end to the autonomy of both parties. In some societies the strongest bond between two households is not consanguinity but friendship. This may be reinforced by work-sharing, wife-sharing, bed-sharing, or danger-sharing. But such ties are impermanent and reveal a preference for fluid social relations. As long as one's alliances are known and reliable the situation is adequately structured; and even the most rigidly genealogical systems of social organization offer a good deal of flexibility. It is not enough that the ethnographer learn the rules of residence; he must discover how far men live by the rules before he can say how households are actually hinged together.

In most societies even defense is not a function of any central government or territorial polity but of leagues of households constituted by the system of hinging. But more fundamental than defense are those welfare functions connected with the chronic uncertainties of domestic life. The most numerous household type in any society is the minimal one able to assume ground-level responsibility. There must be a regular process by which such households are formed and by which surviving members are redistributed among other units when a group dissolves. Often the system provides for keeping a young household intact, when the husband or wife dies, through obligatory replacement. It is logically possible that a society might have no rules to govern the disposition of responsibility toward orphans, widows with children, or aged survivors: the one rule could be voluntarism, each case to be handled as it came up, without attention to precedent, and an amicable solution to be found. Marriages in that society would be made on about the same basis, and dissolved as well in the name of amity, the children following where they pleased. What we are picturing by such reasoning might be called an unhinged society. It is a type some actual societies in some respects do approximate; but conversely it is a type from which most societies notably depart. If we can understand *why* men's social systems have departed from the apparent simplicity of granular structure, we can appreciate the reason for the great variety of family systems anthropologists have studied. The main consideration is obvious enough: history has judged that no one system is intrinsically superior to the others. Whatever rule of descent or of the hinging of households will not work must have long since gone into disuse, so that the patterns that survive and flourish must all be about equally adaptive, though different patterns may suit different human circumstances.

The domestic arrangements preferred by the Nayar—matrilineages emphasized to the point of doing away with the conjugal household—are extreme. They are seldom found, and that suggests that they don't suit many human situations. Another rare arrangement is customary among a people of western Borneo, the Iban, who have elaborated a system of filiation rather than descent. Filiation refers to the formation of a single filial link, while descent refers to a continuing chain of such links over many generations. The Iban custom is that a young couple when they marry should choose to move in either with his parents or with hers. This means that the type of filiation might shift with each generation, now being matrilineal, now patrilineal. Not many societies can succeed with such a rule. Considered as a device for hinging together households in a village, it poses problems. If half the men of a village had been born there while the other half were village strangers, there would be a potential for factional conflict or castelike domination. Stranger status would presumably deter men from choosing filiation to their wives' natal groups, and the system would break down. In Iban society this does not happen, partly because identification with a domestic unit is much more intense than with the local community, and partly because there is an unusual emphasis on equality of the sexes. As neither men nor women dominate, it is not clear that a faction of closely allied males would be more important than a complementary faction of females. But further, since the Iban do not think in terms of descent we have no reason to expect the descent-group pattern of alliance among men. In Iban thinking the crucial choice that must be made at marriage is between affiliation to the man's household and affiliation to the woman's. These households are apt to be located in different communities, but the choice is not between communities, it is between families. Families can easily shift from one community to another, but individuals do not move about, after a choice has been made, among families. That an intense kind of family loyalty can be maintained without extending to alliances among related households is an achievement of Iban social structure.

One condition is strict monogamy. A tendency toward polygyny or polyandry would be hard to combine with sexual equality and would certainly prejudice the choice of filiation to the family of bride or groom. Another condition seems to be a peculiar sort of political stability in the local community, allowing men to associate amicably *without* strong loyalties. It is hard to credit the Iban system working in Sandombu's political world (p. 43), where men sought power through their relations with women and their dealings with other men. In fact, the local settlement of the Iban is, by contrast to Sandombu's matrilineal/matrilocal village, an orderly one. There is no random clustering of huts. Physically the Iban settlement is a single longhouse in which each domestic unit is allotted only a one-room apartment. No family can be built to great size, since the apartments are standard and can't be enlarged. A family which grows must either divide, becoming two independent units, or export some of its members in marriage.

We know enough of human societies to recognize that Iban architecture and its consequences are not accidental—the apartments are not by pure chance built so as to be impossible to expand, but the physical scheme reflects and conditions the social scheme and its values. Domestic units are kept small and equivalent to one another through being housed in uniform, parallel apartments. A newly wed couple never regards itself as a self-sufficient unit but as part of one or the other natal family; and yet each couple aspires eventually to having its own household in which will be included a number of its dependents. Families everywhere are held together by a combination of consanguineal and conjugal ties, and in descent societies the tie of blood is the stronger. But among the Iban, though divorce is possible (and usually occurs as a consequence of discovered adultery), in the more usual crisis it is the tie of consanguinity–between siblings–which must be broken in favor of conjugality. When the members of a household can't get along in the village of Sandombu (p. 43) the question which arises is one of divorce; and so it must be in any society where the hinging of households together is by a rule of descent. But among the Iban the question concerns the separation of siblings. Two brothers or a brother and sister or two sisters, each with spouse and children, find they can't get along in a single apartment; and they decide usually that the junior couple should secede, perhaps building its own apartment onto the end of the long-house. The old unit remains: the Iban family, like the lineage of a descent society, is meant to last forever, always by taking in strangers through marriage to its young men or women.

The worst error for a student of the Iban would be to overlook the individualism associated with what J. D. Freeman calls the "sovereign family":

J. D. Freeman
"The Family System of the Iban of Borneo"
Fieldwork 1949–51, pp. 16–18

Casually regarded, all Iban long-houses do have the appearance of being compact architectural units, and this appearance has led some writers . . . to the supposition that the long-house is therefore the outcome of some kind of communal or group organization and ownership. For the Iban, however, this supposition is very far from the truth.

Although the platform and the gallery of the long-house do extend without interruption throughout its entire length, an Iban long-house is, in fact, made up of a series of independently owned apartments, and further, these apartments, although joined one to the other architecturally, are always the separate abodes of distinct and autonomous family groups. Indeed, the only parts of the whole long-house which are held in any sort of common ownership are the entry ladders; for the rest, every pile and every plank is privately owned by one of the community's component families. In a sense, then, the singular architecture of an Iban long-house is deceptive, for its gallery and its unbroken expanse of roof tend to cloak the fact that it is made up of a series of separate apartments, each of which is the property of a sovereign family group.

Among the various families which make up a long-house community there does always exist a network of relationships based on bilateral kinship. Thus, every family is always related cognatically to at least one of the other families of the community, usually to several, and quite often to many of them. However, it rarely, if ever, occurs that there is within a long-house community a degree of complete, or even nearly complete, interrelatedness among its various family groups. Furthermore, an Iban long-house community is an open and not a closed group, for its component family groups are joined in free association from which withdrawal is always possible, and there is, indeed, a good deal of movement, year by year, from one long-house to another.

Thus the rule that filiation and residence will be freely chosen at marriage implies that each family is regarded as freely joining its longhouse community; and the freedom to withdraw follows from the flexible manner in which they are hinged together. The kin to whom one might turn are scattered about, and there is no guarantee they will feel closely related to one another, since the household is the largest unit of allegiance based on kinship.

THE POLITICS OF PATRILINY

Any society at all may be conceived as a network of domestic groups: an army camp of barrack units or a large urban apartment complex is not a society until the units have some structural relations to each other. But sometimes direct network relations at the interdomestic level don't tell us much about the society. You could study the class system of London by prowling the interdomestic networks, but to understand how the system came about or where it is likely to go you would want to study it at a macrostructural level. Even in the microcultures where all the work of ordering social relations is vested in family and kinship groups, the network may seem to have little political significance. From the point of view of any householder, a few kin-related households are close allies, some others are more vaguely allied, and the great majority are unallied to him. The effect is like a tough wad of oakum which may be pulled this way or that and could be wrenched apart almost anywhere. A society beset by no political problems can perhaps put up with such a fibrous existence and no more. Politics always means more.

What politics adds is the superimposition of more inclusive groups upon the interdomestic network: the solidary matrilineage of the Nayar, the cooperative longhouse of the Iban, or some other form of political community. However it may have been recruited, a political community is one which customarily acts as an internally coordinated unit toward the attainment of common ends or maintaining the status quo. The most frequent political kin group is the patrilineage, expressing the solidarity of males claiming common agnatic descent. The varieties of patrilineage are legion, from the mainly patrilineal hunting band to the exclusive patriclan of the nomadic herdsman, and among agriculturists from the informal clustering of agnates in a hamlet to the territorially compact patriclan, comprising a major segment of a tribal society. Clan solidarity and tribal unity are important ideal values in many societies even where in fact they are little in evidence. As a result, the significance of the superimposed unit to the everyday ordering of life is easily overrepresented by an ethnographer, especially when he has to reconstruct his picture of a bygone life from older informants: politics is a self-dramatizing enterprise in any culture. The household is the repository of ground-level responsibility even in the most agnatic pastoral society, and for every occasion on which a household's autonomy is given up in favor of concerted action with others there is an occasion on which it is reasserted in divisiveness.

Patrilineal emphasis in some regions is associated with a religion of ancestors. Since politics and religion both lend themselves to the formation of community on the patriarchal model, they are often woven into the structure of patrilineal descent groups. Yet the seemingly logical extreme of the patrilineal emphasis is comparatively rare, like the extreme of matriliny exhibited by the Nayar. Kinship castles are no easier than any other kind to erect. The frequency of patrilineal emphasis in microcultural organization is probably due to its versatility rather than to its advantage for increasing solidarity. Often in shifting and nomadic cultures there is a premium on brief alliance among men, and that is more readily served by a patrilineal than a matrilineal emphasis, since patriliny gives a man a claim upon both his brothers and his (and their) sons, men he is apt to find together. As the genuinely matriarchal society is more legendary than real, while patriarchy is not so hard to find, the frequency of patriliny can be said to accord with the realities of male dominance, which is at least as frequent as sexual equality and much more frequent than any sort of female dominance. Finally, it is men who are the great braggarts, the mythmakers of the world, and descent groups are always founded in myth. This is not to say men can't help beating their drums harder than women, for there are cultures where they don't; but men are surely more prone to castle-building than women. Where polyandry occurs it is an unobtrusive institution, but that could hardly be said of polygyny. The men with the most power in a polygynous society are usually the men with the most wives.

To make sense of the variety of family systems which are found in the microcultures, to judge them as structural phenomena, we need to chart them. The figure on page 136 represents one way of setting family and kinship systems in logical connection to one another.

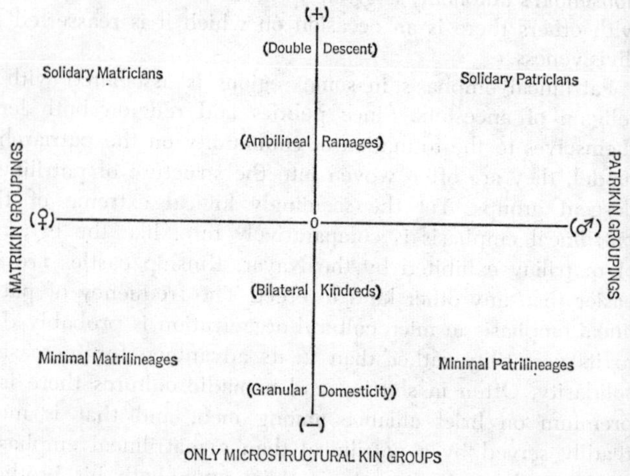

Kinship Coordinates

I use "macrostructure" to signify ordering of the public life and "microstructure" for the private. At the top of the chart belong all the strongest "descent" societies and at the bottom the many peoples who make no special political use of kinship.

The horizontal axis measures departure from symmetry in the way households are hinged together through kinship—principally through the maintenance of close familial ties between siblings, and between parent and offspring, after the young have formed households of their own. Bilaterality means that no preferential weight is put on relatedness through males *or* through females, but a unilateral emphasis is just as frequent, favoring links through one sex to the exclusion of the other for the most important kinds of interdomestic cooperation. There is a rough correspondence to descent, inheritance, and residence rules in a typical case, but the test remains practical, not ideal, norms. If politics is the coordination of individual wills in the form of group activity, then a rule of descent or residence that doesn't yield cooperation is a trivial one. In the urban-industrial West, inheritance and descent retain a patrilateral bias, but there is symmetry in the way domestic groups are tied to one another by sibling links. Many societies possess empty ideologies of descent: men may talk about their clans and clan totems while ignoring them in ordinary life. Inheritance can also be an empty exercise when there is little of value to inherit. What matters is what people recognize in practical situations, and this is what the horizontal axis is intended to represent.

The vertical axis represents the degree to which a society uses its kinship idiom in its political institutions. We can represent the two poles with the Eskimo, for whom politics was generally an interdomestic matter, and the Ashanti of Ghana, who used matriclans and patrilineal descent groups in the organization of an elaborate kingdom. The degree of political complexity *isn't* measured by the vertical axis, only the use of a clear kinship idiom; the urban-industrial states of the West fall at the bottom of the scale along with the Eskimo.

Nomadic societies with patrilineal bands fall to the right of the central axis; but if the band is only a loose league of related males with their dependents, hardly more than an extended family, the system would correspond to minimal patrilineages in the lower right quadrant. On the other hand, if recruitment of men to the band is based on other considerations than just genealogical position—for example, hunting skill, friendship, or affinal connections—these are aspects of band organization that can't be accounted for here.

One inadequacy of the schema is that even if you could place a society accurately on the grid you would not be able to indicate the effect of the interplay of rules, for example in matriliny. In a system which fails to provide for the continuous coresidence of male peer groups there is apt to be as much tension within as between local settlements. A matrilineal society is one that rears children to the kin group of their mother, not their father. But not every such society is matri*local,* ensuring that children will be reared *in* the matrikin group, along with their future peers. Sometimes the bride removes to the man's place of residence to rear her children, but when they are grown they return to live by her brothers. From the point of view of *descent*—the allocation of offspring to a unilineal group—the hinging of households is through women. Affiliation is to a matrikin group, whether the group is dominated by its male or female members, and control of agricultural land is likely to be vested in the matrikin. But from the point of view of *neighborhood* it may be that the core of every village is a group of lineage males with their wives and ungrown offspring—for purposes of local politics the hinging of households is through men. The fact that their myth of solidarity is rooted in a matrilineal ideology (and that therefore they grew up separately) may be secondary. For a male the rule of residence at marriage is avunculocal: he goes to an uncle on his mother's side. But for a female the rule is virilocal: she goes from her father's to her husband's place of residence, which is the one he moved to when he came of age. Hinging here is a nice combination of opposite asymmetrical principles which, being rigidly prescribed, don't just average out to a pattern of symmetry. We'd need more than two dimensions to take such variations into account.

Where in all this do the Iban belong? They are evenly balanced with respect to lineality and so should be placed across the vertical axis—but where? If the origin of the two axes can be taken as the mean, the Iban fall below it. Kin ties between households are unimportant in the political organization of the longhouse or in the men's ceremonial traditions. This means the Iban could be placed between a people like the early Irish, who expected a good deal of cooperation within the kindred, and the suburban bilateral nuclear family system, neither of them resembling the Iban. Here is another anomaly, but two dimensions have the undoubted virtue of fitting nicely on a piece of paper.

On the chart I have plotted *bilateral kindreds, ambilineal ramages,* and *double descent,* ranging up the axis of symmetry. Each of these terms refers to a scheme for elaborating kinship ties on the political plane, without skewing the system toward one-sided linkages through males or females. This does not necessarily entail equality of the sexes, however. The Irish kindred—not home to any women's liberation movement—can be reckoned as the group of relatives obliged to assemble at a wake. Since there is a distinct bilateral network concerned with almost every death, we are not dealing with a descent group, though on the level of interdomestic structure a kindred or a clan might function in about the same way to support a given family in need. Kindreds are normally balanced nicely: you are likely to have just as many relatives on your mother's as on your father's side, and to be just as close to them. Sometimes the limits of kinship are defined in such a way as to stop with third cousins, and in that case your kindred would include all your third cousins (with some of their parents but none of their children), whether the link be through your mother's father's parents, her mother's parents, your father's mother's parents, or his father's parents. Is it likely that such a collection would consider itself in any degree a political unit? Only, perhaps, if you were a king and so more important to anyone in the kindred than his hundred other relatives. Otherwise from the point of view of one of those other relatives *your* kindred will surely be invisible: how would he know even which of his own kin are somehow related to you? Kindred systems may, in fact, favor the rise of kingship because they inhibit the formation of large, potentially rivalrous descent groups which would reject an outsider's leadership. The balanced, bilateral method of reckoning kin generates meaningful links between families, allowing for the mobilization of kin at need, but generates no boundaries.

Could a kindred *become* a descent group? The nearest equivalent is the *ramage*, a politically active local group whose member households are recruited bilaterally. A household chooses to affiliate with one of several kin communities within which it will have family claims, reckoning these claims ambilineally—either through males or through females or through both. Political identity is more fluid than in the case of unilineal descent groups. But if a society can make use of both matriliny and patriliny there is the logical possibility that everyone at birth would be assigned to both matrikin and patrikin groups, with each of which he would be encouraged to maintain descent group membership. This logical possibility is realized in a few societies with elaborate systems of balanced *double descent:* separate identities, inheritances, and obligations descend to you from each of your parents, the male kind of descent being distinct from the female kind. The Ashanti of Ghana almost illustrate this, but they have the avunculocal complication (double asymmetry) involving an unsettling pattern of shifting residence and allegiance. Symmetry can best be achieved in much smaller societies with tightly knit city-state arrangements: compact and inmarrying societies where everyone lives close by both sets of kin, walking out to work each day and returning to organized activity in the evening. You might get fields from your mother and orchards through your father: if you are a man you pass on your trees to your son but your fields to your sister's son. Perhaps you live with your patrikin but sacrifice with your matrikin. In practice it would be more complicated than that: it is as though such a scheme could only be worked up by a community turned in upon itself and organizationally inclined to the point of preoccupation. A system of double descent can elaborate the web of kinship into a political, economic, and religious tapestry more subtle than any a unilineal system could weave.

How far is social structure a matter of legal fictions? Descent groups, like industrial corporations, are derived from everyday social forms. Patriclans, for instance, do represent an extension of the familiar into the political realm; but kinship there is backed up and transformed to its new tasks by jural-ritual sanctions. The most enormous political entity ever created, the British Empire, was officially conceived in the idiom of paternalism, even to the extent that the colonial "children" were expected in due time to attain their majority while continuing a filial and economic dependency on the motherland. In our studies of exotic cultures we may tend to treat legal fictions as if they must be sprung of intellectual error, while in relation to our own institutions we lend ourselves to the very sort of error which in others makes us smile. Are not our beliefs about human equality quite as vital to our kind of social order, and quite as baldly based on faith, as the belief in identity of blood has been for other cultures? In descent societies the elders can sometimes offer learned discussion of ancestral ties five generations dead and name lineal ancestors a dozen generations back: their legal fictions—the solidary descent groups, the land-holding corporations—are sanctioned by what they consider to be the important historical realities. But aren't the ancestors, in a strict sense, only imaginary? And what can be said for the divine right of kings and queens?

I persist in focusing on the role of myth, legal fictions, and what Freud called illusions in the constitution of political institutions because I want to emphasize the organization of life "on the ground" and to view the superstructures from below. In part, this strategy is aimed to redress the usual imbalance in the other direction. The main aim is to show the way in which a social system can be built on the radical decentralization of social responsibility—the sort of decentralization which is not found in a mental hospital or prison or some other total institution, and which is the enemy of totalitarian government.

My conclusion from the cases we have considered is this: The larger, political structure of any society—that is, its organization into local settlements and territorial segments, with or without formal governmental machinery—has always a molecular aspect in the structure of domestic groups and the manner in which one such group is hinged, by a network of recognized ties, to others. In the small, rural societies which comprise the vast majority of the societies anthropologists can study and compare, much use is made of kinship in the interdomestic network; and although in large, urban societies emphasis is more often on social class position, clubs, neighborhood, and similar qualifications, the conclusion holds true for both types of society. It is difficult even to conceive of stable political association among men without, first, the granular structure of social responsibility which is achieved by a family system, and, second, the hinging together of domestic units in coherent networks, whether through familistic or quite different institutional means.

What is the motivation of domesticity? What draws us back to it after we are grown and able to leave our natal families behind? There are enough who aren't drawn back to suggest that the answer isn't simple. What are the universal facts of the human condition that account for the vigor of descent and equivalent interdomestic systems wherever stable community life is found? Again there are enough exceptions. It is time to get down to more definite cases.

MINIMAL FAMILIES

A. R. Radcliffe-Brown
The Andaman Islanders
Fieldwork 1906–8

Nomadic hunting peoples are often classed as marginal because they have generally been pushed into poor areas by agricultural or pastoral populations with much greater political power. But when hunters are not refugees their social life may be nicely structured. The Andaman Islanders lived in small bands, accustomed to moving about, each within a recognized hunting territory, from one camping site to another in a seasonal pattern. Imagine ten or a dozen households, amounting to thirty or fifty persons, as a typical band. The Great Andamanese population was divided among some ten tribes, each composed of as many bands, each band in turn plying its local territory and making some effort to remain at peace with its neighbors. It is the relation of households to one another, especially within the local band and its common camp or village, which concerns us.

A whole band was housed under a single roof—a roughly circular, composite hut of, say, ten distinct sections, all facing a communal dancing ground. Otherwise, the same sort of elongated circle was formed around a larger dancing ground by constructing the distant sections as separated huts; but brothers could also make a sort of common household by placing their huts adjoining one another.[7] Each separate hut or residential section was occupied, with an exception, by a family. Radcliffe-Brown's definition is this: "A family consists of a man and his wife and such of their children own or adopted as are not of an age to be independent." He adds that each band contained a few unmarried males and females (of independent age), and that the bachelors, at least, lived

[7] Radcliffe-Brown, pp. 31–36.

n a hut to themselves—the occasional adolescent spinster would be housed with "some married relative, generally the parent or foster-parent."[8] Each hut had its own hearth, except that bachelors and widowers used a public cooking place near their hut.

Complex systems for reckoning and recognizing kinship ties are so frequent in the experience of anthropologists that the absence of such a system among Andaman Islanders has posed a special problem of explanation. The four northernmost tribes will serve as our example. The anthropologist states: "I did not discover any terms whatever by which a man can distinguish his own brother or sister from any other man or woman of the same age."[9] Again: "There are no terms of address that imply any relationship of consanguinity between the person speaking and the person whom he addresses."[10] To distinguish my own father from some other man of the same age I would say the equivalent of "my male elder"; for my mother I would say "my female elder." In mentioning my son or daughter, I would simply say "my child"; for my elder brother I would say, "my person-who-was-born-before-me"; and so also with a sister. One may infer from the anthropologist's report that the only kinship terms employed are those for "parent-in-law" and its reciprocal—that is, the term your parent-in-law would use to refer to you. Only those two terms, it appears, do not reduce to the formula which the others take: the others reduce to a noun *not* indicative of kinship, preceded by a possessive prefix. To indicate my husband or wife, I simply say "the person to whom I am married." The anthropologist concludes by noting that he could discover no terms "for grandfather, grandmother, uncle, aunt, cousin, etc.," although there were locutions by which a genealogical relationship of such kind could be described.[11]

That exercise in Andamanese terminology was wanted in order that we could state a general proposition concerning their domestic constitution: it does not create and emphasize social ties on the basis of what we usually call blood or con-

[8] *Ibid.*, pp. 35–36.
[9] *Ibid.*, p. 56.
[10] *Ibid.*, p. 53.
[11] *Ibid.*, pp. 53–56.

sanguinity. If there is a hint in Andaman terminology of a kinship tie beyond the nuclear family, it is only in the tie by marriage to elders in the nuclear family of one's spouse, and the reciprocal of that tie. The Andaman domestic constitution, in its failure to emphasize kindship, may be unique; but if one society can be made to work without a system of descent and collateral consanguinity, why can't others?

The answer should begin with comprehension of the Andaman system—how it worked, how its domestic constitution met the dual problem of responsibility and order. In human societies the domestic group must first be vested with self-reliance in the pursuit of the good life, and further maintained in its institutional character as a "chartered" or constituted agency of the larger society. We've seen that each Andaman domestic group, except that of the bachelors' hut was constituted by a marriage. There were no exceptions to the rule of monogamy, and the only adults in the standard household were therefore a man and his wife. Childhood endured only until the onset of maturity—menarche for the girl, a less definite event for the boy: initiation rites, particularly for the girl, were solemn and effective in banishing the manners and the dependent status of childhood. Although a girl might, for a time, have no household of her own, she could also join with another unmarried girl in a separate hut; and a young man was always removed to the bachelor hut. Both would soon be married, for marriages were engineered by the responsible elders at the first opportunity. There was a comprehensive set of rules, well understood and well looked after, assuring that the population of any local band would be sorted efficiently into the proper, minimal domestic units. Divorce didn't occur; and obligatory arrangements for remarriage applied at the premature death of a spouse.

The conclusion so far must be that the principle of decentralized structure in Andaman society was carried to a logical extreme; for it would be hard to design a workable system that carried the principle further. Yet in a special sense, the Andaman peoples did take it further, diminishing the nuclear family to a yet tinier granule. They had developed a system of fosterage to the point where the child attaining puberty and preparing to assume adult status in his local group was usually far removed from the places and the parents he had known in early childhood. Children of seven or eight years, or a little older, were of an age for fosterage—or what we might call the Andaman institution of free adoption. A man who had come to visit from a neighboring band would compliment his host by asking for a child to adopt: it was a society in which requests were freely made, and valuables as freely passed from hand to hand. Presented then, as a gift to the visitor, the child would pass over to another locality and become the child of another married couple; in time he might pass on to still another place and another family, until he ceased to be a child and was initiated into manhood. For a girl the case was not different, and marriage could often result of an attachment between a boy and his foster sister. The point is not, certainly, that little value was attached to children—the evidence is rather the opposite, for they were always well treated, and frequently visited by their own parents, who were promptly notified of their children's moves from place to place.[12]

Yet to the student of social structure the Andaman institution of fosterage does have a special point. It is suggested in the motives which governed such free-handed giving: for giving in Andaman society, even in the everyday life of the camp, was an unceasing obligation which men freely put upon themselves—it was at once an accommodation to another and a matter of self-pride. The system of responsibility and order which we can begin to perceive as the genius of the Andaman constitution is one which makes the least it can of domestic privacy and autonomy, and the most of what we might call the antidomestic values of openness to others. A well-constituted and self-involved domestic group was wanted to begin with; yet from the open-sided houses in which they dwelt, gathered always around a common camping ground, to their unexceptioned sharing of food and possessions, and the exchanging of gifts and children in every meeting with the folk of another band, the customs of the Andaman people seem to have been guided by a single ethical ideal. It is not easy to name, for though it might be taken for a sort of

[12] *Ibid.*, pp. 72–77.

communism it is not simply that but begins, as a gift always must, with individual right and private ownership. The hunter whose arrow first struck the wild pig was the owner of it: it was his pleasure to see it publicly cooked and distributed, not to see the best of it go to his own wife and children. The maker of a bow is its owner; it would be a breach of good manners to refuse a man who asked for it. A person has first a responsibility to himself and to his family: husband and wife are obliged to keep their huts and belongings in repair; a wife must cook for her family with water and firewood and utensils and gathered foods of her own making or getting; as parents or foster parents both are much taken up with the care and instruction of their children; children themselves in their later years and in the time of adulthood before marriage are much employed in assisting their parents or foster parents. But as the hunter must substitute moral pride for material possession in the case of his pig or sea turtle, so is it with the parent of a child: pride begins with possession but can't end in possessiveness. I've said that character is the vehicle of conventional motives. I've carried the argument further, to the proposition that a social structure will function as the matrix in which character is formed. The constitution of Andaman society put difficult demands on character: we should perhaps admit that the ethnographic uniqueness of that constitution may be partly due to the difficulty of creating a social life in which men set and meet such demands on themselves. After all, it is from the limits of cultural variability that we must infer the inflexible qualities of man's nature, of which we otherwise know nothing.

One further feature of Andaman life especially wants considering. The local band of ten or a dozen households had no formal system of government or organized sanctions; it was in that respect more nearly a free association of coequal households, among which the peace must be maintained by the universal system of muddling through—a murder might or might not be avenged, an unmanageable man might or might not be shamed into manageability. But in another and important manner the local group, as a whole, was highly organized; for each of its members knew and must recognize in all of his dealings with others the place of each in a ructure of rank based on age. Where in another society enealogical relationship might decide the connection of each ɔ each in such a band, for the Andaman people social posi-ion was first of all a function of relative age. Among adults, lders were most privileged in the way food must be distrib-ted, and they were advantaged over younger persons in he giving and receiving of gifts as well—they need not return ɔ much as they had received, if the giver was much younger han they. After the indulgences of childhood, the initiation ɔ adulthood was a stern rite of deprivation, and it was fol-ɔwed by a long series of food restrictions through which very elder in his turn had earlier passed: aging and the at-aining of privilege were subject to an effective system of pro-edures, informed by ethical values and religious beliefs to vhich each individual would learn to subscribe. On the vhole, life within the band followed an orderly pattern; and here were provisions—in the exchange of gifts and the adop-ion of children who were approaching the age of marriage—or maintaining the expectation of peace with neighboring ands. Yet those arrangements did often fail of what we can all their implicit purpose; and the Andamanese knew as nuch of danger as of safety, of feud as of amity, of attack nd panic by night as of ceremonial exchange by day. If, vhen all has been said, the phenomenon of social structure is othing less than a massive body of testimony to man's un-easing effort to cope with the problem of order in human af-airs, then we should judge that the Andaman constitution vorked as well as many others, though probably no better han most.

The studies which follow explore other family systems, vhose tendency is more firmly toward domesticity. There ve'll find that the pursuit of the good life is somewhat more venly balanced between the public and the private places of nen. But we'll also find that much of what for the Andaman-se lay outside in the public domain is elsewhere brought vithin the domain of private life; and that in the exchange he quality and structure of domesticity are altered.

SECTION TWO

CASE STUDIES IN INTERDOMESTIC RELATIONS

TROBRIAND ISLANDERS

Bronislaw Malinowski—from three works on the Trobriand Islanders: Fieldwork 1915–18.

The Sexual Life of Savages in Northwestern Melanesia, pp. 122–24, 130–31

Coral Gardens and Their Magic, pp. 198–211

Argonauts of the Western Pacific, pp. 62–65

WHOSE IS THE HARVEST?

The harvest of the main gardens inaugurates a long and elaborate series of activities, associated with the offering of annual gifts. The members of each household—for digging is always done *en famille*—repair to their own garden-plot within the large, communal enclosure. The yams of the small variety, called *taytu,* which are by far the most important of all native vegetables, are then dug up by means of pointed sticks and carried to a shady arbour made of poles and yam vine, where the family group sit down and carefully clean the dug-up tubers, shaking the earth from them and shaving off the hairs with sharpened shells. Then a selection is made. All that the man produces for his own use is called by the generic term *taytumwala;* what he grows for his women-folk and their husbands is called *urigubu.*

The best yams are placed in a large conical heap in the middle, and this is the *urigubu* yield. The rest are stowed away in the corners in less regular and much smaller heaps. The main heap is constructed with almost geometrical precision, with the best yams carefully distributed all over its surface, for it will remain in the little shed for some time, to be admired by people from the village and neighbouring communities. All this part of the work, which, as can easily be seen, has no utilitarian value, is done eagerly, with interest and *con amore,* under the stimulus of vanity and ambition. The chief pride of a Trobriander is to gain renown as a "master-gardener." And to achieve this, he will make great efforts and till many plots in order to produce a considerable number of heaps with a large quantity of yams in each. It must also be remembered that the marriage gift is the chief and most ostentatious product of the garden work.

To the European reader the whole arrangement of harvesting must appear absurd. Economically it is cumbersome. A great deal of time and labour has to be wasted on transport and also on display, on cleaning and on other aesthetic trappings which are obviously connected with the fact that the *dodige bwayma* is a ceremonial act. The transport is necessary because marriage is patrilocal, that is, the wife lives in the husband's community; while household economics are matrilocal, in that the brother has to produce the harvest in his own village and carry it thence to his sister's husband. This of course could be simplified if it were possible to regard the *urigubu* as a commercial transaction; that is, if the wife's brother could arrange for someone in his sister's community to provide for her while he in turn provided for someone in his own community. But this is not allowed by the customary law of the Trobriands. Each man must offer to his sister taytu grown by himself on his own land and carried to her by his own kinsfolk and relatives-in-law.

It is only if we understand how much personal pride as well as moral duty is involved in a man's producing a generous share for his sister's household; how much a gardener identifies himself with his crops, and especially that part of the crops offered as the *urigubu* gift, that we can realise why a simple commercial exchange is not possible here, though it obtains in so many other transactions.

The scheme is not only economically clumsy to the European, it is also morally unfair. If I am industrious, if I am a good gardener, if I strain all my forces, somebody else derives the benefit from it. If my wife's brother is lazy, incompetent, or in bad health, I suffer for it. This is in a way true but with the Trobriander the argument does not hold, because, as we shall see, a Trobriander has, sociologically speaking, a split identity; on the one hand his interests and his heart are in his own household, in the household, that is, of his wife and children; on the other hand his pride and his moral duties are in the household of his sister.

What puzzles the European most, what puzzled me for a long time very badly, is the question of motive. Why does the Trobriander spend an enormous amount of time and energy in work for someone else? What spurs him to such endeavour? Here again the split or double set of interests, ambitions and emotional incentives will supply the answer.

MARRIAGE AGAINST KINSHIP

The *urigubu* principle is the very core of both social and economic life. To understand it on the economic side it is necessary to grasp the law of marriage, native ideas about procreation and the native system of kinship. To begin with the law of marriage. In the Trobriands marriage puts the wife's matrilineal kinsmen under a permanent tributary obligation to the husband, to whom they have to pay yearly gifts of *urigubu* for as long as marriage lasts. The marriage contract is effected by the exchange of reciprocated gifts, the balance of which is on the whole favourable to the husband, or rather to the new household, mainly owing to the large gift of *taytu* presented at the harvest immediately following the union. This is packed into decorative, oblong prism-shaped receptacles which are erected by the brother in front of the freshly constructed yam-house of the new household. This gift is the first installment of the *urigubu* contributions, which year after year will be placed on the same spot as that where the prism-shaped receptacle now stands, though later contributions will on the whole be less substantial and will be arranged simply in heaps. These gifts are every few years repaid by the husband, with a gift of valuables to his wife's brother. But such gifts never total to the economic equivalent of the *urigubu*.

Kinship is counted only in the maternal line. The children of a union are not in any way regarded as kin ("kindred his") to their father or to his lineage. They are of the same body as their mother: she has made them with her own blood; they belong to her clan and sub-clan; they are members of her village community. They are successors to her brother. That is, her male children have the right to the offices, positions, and social status which is now occupied by her brothers. Her daughters will continue the lineage and bear children who will belong to the same kindred group. The unit of filiation, the group, that is, which embraces successive generations bound together by identity of flesh, is then not husband, wife and children, but brother, sister and her offspring. I say advisedly the brother and his sister, for wherever there are several brothers and sisters, one brother is specially paired off with one sister.

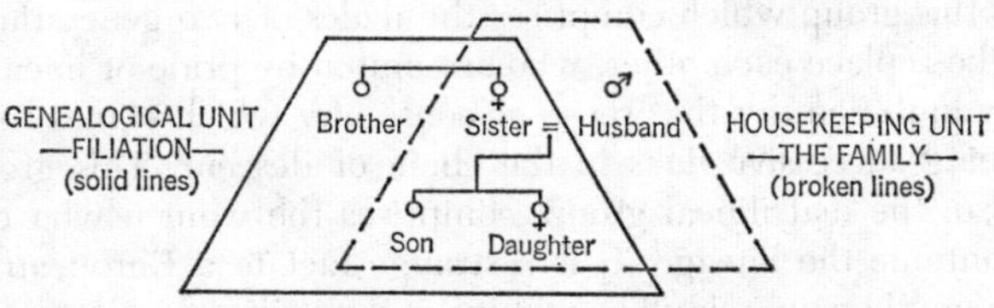

The above diagram, superfluous for the sociologically trained reader, will yet bring these conditions clearly to the eyes of one not so familiar with primitive kinship. The husband, though head of his own household, is outside the group of kindred, in the legal sense of the Trobriand word. Brother, sister and her children are the real genealogical unit of descent. In the Trobriands, as the diagram shows, there are therefore two units which correspond to our term "family". One of the units is the physiological procreati group, the husband, wife and her offspring. This group, among ourselves, is united by the intimacy of daily life, b the economic interests of direct housekeeping, by the sent mental ties which spring out of daily contacts on the bas of innate emotional tendencies. This group is very clear defined by the Trobriand law of marriage. But it must b carefully noted that in speaking about the physiologic foundation of the group, about the procreative unit an about the bonds of blood which unite this group, I hav been speaking as a sociologist and not reproducing th native point of view. For the natives have a procreati theory which, by ignoring the father's share in pregnanc and ascribing it to the influence of the wife's dead ance tors, supplies the dogmatic foundation for the matriline doctrine of bodily identity only and exclusively in the fe male line. The husband presides over the household as member extraneous in all matters of legal kinship. He styled *tomakava* (stranger, outsider). He is united only t his wife by the contract of marriage and only through he and indirectly is he related to her children and to he brother.

The other unit which, in one way and in one way only corresponds to our term "family" is the filiational or genea logical group formed by brother, sister and her children. I is this group which comprises the males of two generation who replace each other, who are united by pride of lineage by ambition, by that sense of continuity which comes fro being successive links in the chain of descent. This grou also, the matrilineal group, comprises the women who ca continue the lineage. It is a strange fact to a European o to any human being brought up in a patrilineal culture, bu it must be clearly realised: in the Trobriands, as in an other matrilineal society, a man is a barren shoot on the ge nealogical tree. In the Trobriands, moreover, and in thos communities which like the Trobrianders or the Centra Australians do not admit physiological paternity—a man ca have no bodily issue in his own right by virtue of his ow physiological contributions. The only children to whom h is related by blood are his sister's children. They are hi legal issue, as they are in any matrilineal society, even though, in such a society, it were known that he had physiologically procreated the children of his wife.

It is best, therefore, in the Trobriands to apply the term "family" to the paternal household, to the group of husband, wife and children. The other group I have termed here "genealogical unit," because all relevant genealogies are to the natives in the mother line, but perhaps "unit of filiation" would be the most suitable expression. The two groups, the family and the unit of filiation, are held together by the law of marriage and by the marriage contract.

FATHERHOOD AND HUSBANDHOOD: MOTIVATIONAL PUZZLES

One question arises out of this duality of grouping. If the Trobrianders do not admit physiological paternity, if a woman conceives and produces children by the agency of her own dead kinswomen and bears a child for her own kinsfolk, particularly for one of her brothers, why is the husband necessary at all? What is his place in the household? Is he merely a drone who lives on his wife and benefits from her brothers? The answer to this is two-fold. In biological and psychological reality, the husband lives with his wife because he is attached to her and is fond of her, because he was at one time in love with her and married her very largely for that reason. He also has received by the fact of marriage a much higher social status, and a comfortable home to live in. He looks after the children because he is fond of them, because he has desired to have them, even as his wife has. This is the reality of living men and women in the Trobriands, as elsewhere—a reality which, however, can only be ascertained and formulated by an outside observer and of which the natives themselves are unaware and could not put into words.

If you were to enquire into native theory and collect native opinions, you would receive an answer in a way less true but more interesting and sociologically more relevant. The husband, you would be told, has married the woman because a man without a household is not a real adult man. He has married her also because a grown-up man must have a woman who lives sexually with him and with him only. It is good for young people to have all kinds of intrigues, but a mature man must have a wife. In the Trobriands, however, a wife marries her husband as much as she is married by him. And if you enquired into her motives the answers would be even more illuminating. A woman does not need a husband as a legal guardian: her legal guardian is her brother, who remains in that relation to her after she marries, quite as much as before. But her brother is absolutely debarred from one whole side of her life. There is an extremely rigid and all-embracing taboo forbidding any friendly intimacies between brother and sister, and forbidding a man to take any interest whatever in his sister's sexual affairs or reproductive processes. For that purpose another man is necessary. Not only that, but this other man, the husband, is indispensable in order to render her reproductive functions honourable, in order to give her offspring full tribal status within the community. Although the sexual life of the natives is very lax and unmarried girls can have as many lovers as they like, a girl is not supposed to become pregnant before she is married.

Marriage is thus an absolute prerequisite of maternity, of the legal status of the offspring, and hence of the honourable continuity of lineage. A brother who is directly interested in having his lineage honourably continued, of having his nephews "real young men" and not "bastards" is, therefore, directly interested in the sister becoming married. A husband is indispensable.

The brother has therefore at a certain time of his sister's life to waive his rights of guardianship over her and allow her to go under the direct and intimate control of another man. The brother never does exercise any intimate control over the sister's affairs. Up to her marriage such little control of a girl's private life as is exercised, together with all arrangements connected with her marriage, have been in the hands of her father, who here again acts as the delegate of the girl's matrilineal kindred; and after marriage the real supervision of his wife's sexual and reproductive processes is vested in the husband.

This is connected with the principle of patrilocal marriage. The girl joins her husband in his village and in his house, and henceforth, having a joint household to run, the two must have a number of interests in common. They have joint economic duties and obligations; the husband watches over his wife's interests in many matters, and, when the children come, he undertakes a number of educational duties, especially with the sons, and advises and protects his daughters in their prematrimonial affairs. When the daughter becomes pregnant, it is his sisters who will take her pregnancy concerns and ceremonies in hand.

We see, therefore, how out of the native concept of marriage the idea of fatherhood gradually emerges, and that the role of the father and his relation to the children are derived from and based upon his personal relation to his wife. Let us gain a clearer insight into this relation.

MARRIAGE AS CONTRACT AND AS "COMPLICATED RELATIONSHIP"

Marriage is, in the Trobriands, the outcome of a series of intrigues. It is the intrigue which has endured, the intrigue which has been accepted by the girl's family as a permanent arrangement, and been legalised by them in a series of gifts, that finally, by public eating in common and the open cohabitation of the two, becomes legal marriage. Now since we are studying here the economic side of legal relations, what is the economic aspect of a sexual liaison? All sexual services in the Trobriands are repayable by gifts which have a special name, *buwana* or *sebuwana.* Not that the natives regard the pleasure derived from intercourse as one-sided, or that women in the Trobriands take a passive or retiring part in it; on the contrary, both in behaviour and in theory, female initiative and the female share in a liaison is equivalent to that of the man. But with the characteristic inconsistency of traditional decree, custom has it that for almost every sexual act, and certainly for continued sexual relationship, the man should pay and the woman should receive gifts. It is the payment "for her scarlet," by which generic name natives describe the female genitals.

Marriage differs from a sexual liaison in two respects. In the first place marriage is a contract which leads inevitably to the establishment of a new household, it is the foundation of a new type of social grouping, the family. This means that, in its personal aspect, marriage is a much fuller and more complicated relationship between man and woman than that which obtains between two lovers. In the second place, it is a publicly acknowledged relation, approved and accepted by the girl's family, and binding them to definite economic prestation.* Consequently the economic side of the relationship is complicated and two-fold. No longer free to give her body to anyone she wants to, the woman is now under severe sanctions bound to be for her husband's exclusive sexual pleasure. He, on the other hand, is expected still to go on repaying the sexual gifts which he receives from his wife. This he does, not by occasional gifts, but by continuous services rendered to her, and above all by services rendered to her children. The children are regarded legally as hers and not his, the love and care and the material benefits which he bestows on them are, by the traditional convention, regarded as a repayment: "the payment for the mother's scarlet," such and similar phrases are the stock answer to the question, Why does the father care for his children?

The wife, besides the erotic services which she renders to her husband, has also to cook for him, prepare his food, bring his water in the water-bottles, look after him when he is sick, and mourn for him when he is dead. Her brothers have to assist her by supplying the *urigubu* gift, in watching over him in illness, in defending his interests, and by being ready to do work for him whenever communal labour is necessary.

The *urigubu*, as we know already, designates not merely

* Since the English language has a really unaccountable and intolerable gap, I am deliberately introducing here the word "prestation" in the French sense, that is, of legally defined services to be rendered by one individual or group to another.

the annual gift at harvest, but comprises also the other services due from the wife's family to the husband.† Naturally, therefore, it is one of the central features of the marriage contract, which again is the result of native ideas about procreation, their doctrines of kinship and relationship, and of the moral duty of the brother to look after his sister and her offspring; and the equally important and more arresting moral duty of brother and sister to avoid each other.

FATHERS AND SONS: RECIPROCAL CLAIMS

With all this it must be repeated once more that the father loves his children, that he needs them emotionally, that sociologically his status is enhanced by them. He is their assistant nurse when they are young, he is their companion when they are growing up, he educates his sons and looks after his daughters. Paternity devoid of the rigid legal guardianship which devolves on the mother's brother becomes a lively companionship and real friendship. The father, in actual fact, always tries to give as much as he can to his own sons at the expense of those of his sister, who are his legal heirs. His natural inclinations are seconded by customary usage which almost defies and certainly circumvents the rigid matrilineal law, by giving the father a number of opportunities to favour his sons and to curtail the rights of his matrilineal nephews.

Thus the sons receive a great many benefits, especially in the form of certain kinds of magic, as a free gift from their father, while the nephew has to buy such benefits from his maternal uncle. The father usually tries to arrange for a cross-cousin marriage between his son and his sister's daughter, whereby he places his son in the position of an intermediate heir. Cross-cousin marriages, moreover, in opposition to ordinary ones, are matrilocal; that is, the son

† Communal labour is used in a far wider range of pursuits than gardening. The communal labour supplied by wife's brothers and kinsmen refers more to such matters as carrying heavy weights, fishing, constuction of canoe, storehouse, or dwelling, etc.

remains in his father's community, which is also the community of the father's matrilineal niece.‡

Thus the attitude of the father towards his children is built up very much on the same pattern as the patriarchal attitude, with a few important differences. The father has no legal power over the children; he is therefore much nearer to them emotionally, he tries to win their affection and usually succeeds in doing so. The father has no right officially to control the destinies of his sons, nor of his daughters after marriage. Both of them have to leave his house and his community when they reach the age of full citizenship, that is some time between eighteen and twenty-two. The sons, according to the strict law, should go to the village community of their maternal uncle.

The father, however, has definite claims, reciprocal claims, that is, on the services of his children, and above all of his sons. When they are young they both work on their father's plots and in his village, and with their maternal uncle for their mother's *urigubu.* In the latter case they would have to repair to their maternal uncle's community. Either way they contribute yams for use in their own household. Also the sons as successors and helpmates of their mother's brother are at their father's service. Thus, though in theory the fact that they are legally beholden to their maternal uncle fundamentally alters the normal son-to-father relationship as familiar to us in patrilineal societies, in practice it seldom makes much apparent difference. It does, however, mean that before acceding to the wishes of their father in any important matter they would have first to consult their uncle.

Later on they either remain with their father—through cross-cousin marriage, or, when he is a chief or a man of power, through his arbitrary decision—and then help him in his own community; or else they return to the maternal uncle and from there work for their father's and mother's *urigubu* each year in the gardens of their own village.

‡ Matrilocal marriage in the Trobriands often presents the paradox of the husband remaining in the village of his birth and adolescence, and the girl joining him there. Citizenship in a community and early residence there hardly ever coincide.

At the father's death it is the sons who carry out most of the services. They have to wash and adorn the corpse, bury it, and carry out some revolting mortuary duties, such as tasting the dead man's flesh, using certain pieces of his bone as lime spatulae and his skull as a lime-pot—revolting, that is, not only to the missionary or ethnographer but to the natives themselves and regarded as such, or rather as onerous and exacting duties. Here once more we see the play of give and take, of repayment for services rendered. If you ask why a son should render these mortuary services to the father, reference is again made to the father's relation to the mother or else to his nursing and educating of the children. "It is the repayment for the father's hand that was soiled with the child's excrement, for the skin which was wetted with the child's urine." "The father has received the child in his arms and nursed it, now the child nurses the father's body."

Thus the relationship between father and children is founded on natural affection, the sentiment grown out of intimacy and love. It has as its legal framework an artificial but neatly balanced system of reciprocal duties, the centre of these remaining always the annual harvest gift, the *urigubu.*

MOTHER'S BROTHER AND SISTER'S CHILD

Let us in turn focus our attention on the group consisting of mother and children and the mother's brother. This group, as we know, forms the real unit of kinship in native theory. The females continue the line, the males represent it in each generation. The males inherit the property, the females through the *urigubu* gift are made to benefit from a large part of the males' stewardship. The males of several generations work for the females; the females, under the guardianship of their husbands or fathers, lead their sexual and reproductive lives, continuing the lineage of the kindred.

It must be emphatically stated here that it is not the "clan" which acts as a unit in this complementary division of functions, but definitely the group consisting of brother, sister, and her offspring.

The woman's brother then is her natural legal guardian. But he is not enough. He cannot enter in any way into his sister's sexual life, not even indirectly, not even from a great distance. He leases his sister's procreative life as well as her offspring to her husband, as his maternal uncle has leased his mother's reproductive life to his father. Since he has to keep at a distance, physically as well as morally, the marriage must be patrilocal. But with all this the fundamental principles of matrilineal kinship oppose the development of any strong patrilocal or patrilineal family life. In the first place, the matrilineal, that is to the Trobriander the real, kindred of the husband, do not want him to bestow too much attention, privileges and gifts on his children; for a man's possessions and advantages should be kept within his own matrilineal kindred. On the other hand the real, that is matrilineal, kindred of the children, want them back in their community, want them as helpmates and legal successors. The patrilocal household thus is usually broken up, the girls leave the paternal house to marry, the boys return to their maternal uncle. Husband and wife, both old, decrepit and dependent now, remain alone and are still maintained by the wife's family, including her sons.

THE REAL CONSTITUTION OF TROBRIAND KINSHIP GROUPS

We are now, after this long but necessary digression on kinship, in a position to understand the nature of the *urigubu* gift. We can also answer our previous questions, first as to the motives which make this gift be given and given generously; second, as to the reason for the elaborate and competitive display incidental to the giving; and third, as to the function of the obliqueness in the fulfilment of economic obligations.

The *urigubu* is the endowment by its real head of the matrilineal unit of filiation, and this real head is neither within the household, nor even, as a rule, in the same village. The patrilocal household, on the other hand, which benefits by this endowment has its real head within it. This head also contributes economically to it, but is regarded as a stranger in matters of kinship and his position is legal only in virtue of a series of reciprocities which bind him to his wife, to his wife's brother, and to her offspring.

The *urigubu* is, therefore, the expression of the real constitution of Trobriand kinship grouping. This grouping is not simple as with us, where it consists of one household, one family, and one unit of filiation. The kinship grouping in the Trobriands embraces on the one hand the unit of filiation—brother, sister and offspring; and on the other hand, the household—husband, wife and children, including sometimes old parents and more distant relatives. The core of the household is always the family; that is, to the sociologist, the reproductive unit, husband, wife and offspring; to the Trobriander, the matrimonial grouping, founded on the contract of marriage, which makes the husband the deputy guardian of his wife and her immature children. The *urigubu,* therefore, is the outcome and economic expression of a compromise of adjustment between the principles of the patrilocal household and matrilineal filiation. Into the composition of the *urigubu,* however, there also enters the brother-sister taboo, the principle of legitimacy which decrees that all children must have a father, and the customary rule that adult man and adult woman must enter into permanent and full sexual partnership.

We can now understand not merely the legal sanctions, but also the personal motives for the *urigubu.* If the *urigubu* is regarded as a gift from an outsider to a household which he is scarcely even permitted to visit, it appears absurd, unfair and cumbersome. But when the *urigubu* is understood as the endowment of his own kindred group by its head, it becomes natural, almost obvious. Exactly as in a patriarchal society the *pater familias* feeds his household and works for its firm economic foundation to endure after his death, so in the Trobriand matrilineal community the maternal uncle provides for his descendants freely, generously and with a will. In the process he also feeds his sister's husband, but the latter repays by reciprocal gifts that share of the *urigubu* which falls to him and furthermore himself contributes to the feeding of his wife and her children, that is of the filiational group, a group which is not his kindred. All in all the economic arrangements of a household reflect very neatly the various sociological, legal, moral and personal inclinations, interests and reciprocal duties of the native.

We can also perceive now why it is that a man will not procure *taytu* locally at so much a basket for his sister's household and pay for it by some service rendered in his own community. According to native law, custom and morals, his real duty lies with his sister's household. It is consequently for this household that he has to raise and harvest the "real" *taytu,* the "full" *taytu.* It is on the size and quality of this part of the result of his labours that his reputation as a gardener depends. Moreover, in the giving of it he satisfies both his vanity and his sentiment. For on the one hand he is giving to a stranger—a man who by definition belongs to another clan—his sister's husband, and of such a gift he is allowed to brag. But on the other hand he is providing for his sister, for his own descendants, for those who will in future work for him and for the glory of his lineage, and therefore his heart is in the work.

The *urigubu* gift therefore lends itself to that boasting, display, comparison—to the running mythological elaboration, which is so dear to the Melanesian's heart.*

The whole ceremonial side of the transaction is not merely an expression of a strong individual inclination; it contains also an effective sanction. The display, the measurement in public, the taking and recording of tally, provide both a psychological spur to the giver and a handle to the community, whether it be for praise or blame. When his work has been successful as well as efficient, the generous gift is appreciated, the glory of the giver and his lineage extolled, and the moral approbation of the community

* By "running mythological elaboration" I mean the stories which gather round the current events of tribal life, in time grow into legends and become the established verdict of tribal opinion.

bestowed, and this to a Trobriander is a great satisfaction and a real reward.

We see, therefore, that the idea of satisfying *urigubu* obligations by a simple commercial transaction would be grotesque as well as repellent to the natives. Whenever I propounded such an idea to my informants, or enquired why they did not simply *gimwali* (barter) the harvest gift, they took it as a joke in bad taste, and expressed their scorn clearly. We also see how a better understanding of native psychology and of the native social framework enables a European to appreciate the function of certain customs and their effective value for a community. Such white residents in the Trobriands as had even an inkling of what the *urigubu* was were extremely contemptuous of its useless waste of energy, and were keen on having it stopped by Government order. To us, however, it will be obvious that half the incentive of the Trobriander to work would be destroyed and more than half of his moral sense and sense of responsibility blighted if the *urigubu* were in any way interfered with.

We can also understand why a man may be a good gardener as long as his object is to satisfy the fundamental obligations of the *urigubu,* but that it is dangerous to be a good gardener on his own behalf. To have large gardens and to use them for his own food runs obviously counter to one of the fundamental principles of Trobriand sociology, and the community, there as elsewhere, reacts with a sound conservatism and deep hostility to anything which offends its established conceptions.

URIGUBU AND POLITICAL CONSTITUTION

We can now quite briefly assess the functions of the *urigubu,* the influence, that is to say, which it exerts on Trobriand social life. From all that has been said above it can be seen that it is one of the main elements in the stability of marriage. It is closely connected with the position of the father and his relations to the offspring, as well as with the latter's relations to the maternal uncle. But one of the most important elements in the *urigubu* is that it is the channel through which every headman of a village com munity, every chief of subsidiary rank in his district, as wel as the paramount chief of Omarakana, levies his tribute.

It will be best to illustrate by concrete examples. Let u visit at harvest-time a component village of Yalumugwa, typical medium-rank community. Eleven storehouses hav to be filled ceremonially.

The people who fill these storehouses are all closely re lated, and they all reside either in the same village cluste or near at hand. In such a village, the fillers or donor can be easily reached and the date arranged on which the will start bringing in the crops. On such a day, crowds o carriers will arrive at short intervals in ceremonial manne and erect the heaps in their proper places. Some donor may be behind-hand, and then the bringing in will exten over two or three days perhaps. In 1915, as far as remember, all the heaps were erected within three days i the component hamlet of Yalumugwa. The heaps will b displayed in such a village for some three to five days, o at the outside, for a week.

In much smaller villages the proceedings would be th same only on a smaller scale. Here the number of heap would be about a third or even a fourth of what we hav seen in Yalumugwa.

As regards the commoners who reside in a high rank vil lage, they receive one, two or three heaps each. Man commoners who live in a small village will just get on heap.

In smaller villages also the donors would live near-b and the whole ceremony would be over in a shorter time The heaps would be brought in in one day, left for twenty four hours, and then stored away.

In villages of chiefs of high rank or of great wealth th arrangements would be on a much larger scale.

In every community in the Trobriands, there is one ma who wields the greatest authority, though often this doe not amount to very much. He is, in many cases, nothin more than the *primus inter pares* in a group of villag elders, who deliberate on all important matters together and arrive at a decision by common consent. This village headman is, as a rule, therefore, not much more than a master of tribal ceremonies, and the main speaker within and without the tribe, whenever one is needed.

But the position of headman becomes much more than this, when he is a person of high rank, which is by no means always the case. He is in the first place the headman of his own village, and in contrast to the headmen of low rank, he has quite a considerable amount of power. His high rank inspires everyone about him with the greatest and most genuine respect and awe. Chieftainship in the Trobriands is the combination of two institutions: first, that of headmanship, or village authority; secondly, the division of the community into classes or castes, each with a certain more or less definite rank.

Not only does the chief—by which word I shall designate a headman of rank—possess a high degree of authority within his own village, but his sphere of influence extends far beyond it. A number of villages are tributary to him, and in several respects subject to his authority. In case of war, they are his allies, and have to foregather in his village. When he needs men to perform some task, he can send to his subject villages, and they will supply him with workers. In all big festivities the villages of his district will join, and the chief will act as master of ceremonies. Nevertheless, for all these services rendered to him he has to pay. He even has to pay for any tributes received out of his stores of wealth. Wealth, in the Trobriands, is the outward sign and the substance of power, and the means also of exercising it. But how does he acquire his wealth? And here we come to the main duty of the vassal villages to the chief. From each subject village, he takes a wife, whose family, according to the Trobriand law, has to supply him with large amounts of crops. This wife is always the sister or some relation of the headman of the subject village, and thus practically the whole community has to work for him. In olden days, the chief of Omarakana had up to forty consorts, and received perhaps as much as thirty to fifty per cent of all the garden produce of Kiriwina. Even now, when his wives number only sixteen, he has enormous storehouses, and they are full to the roof with yams every harvest time.

Polygamy is allowed by custom to people of higher rank or to those of great importance, such as, for instance, the sorcerers of renown. In certain cases, indeed, a man is obliged to have a great number of wives by virtue of his position. This is so with every chief, that is to say, every headman of high rank who exercises an over-rule in a more or less extended district. In order to wield his power and to fulfil the obligations of his position, he must possess wealth, and this in Trobriand social conditions is possible only through plurality of wives.

It is a very remarkable fact in the constitution of the tribe of which we are speaking, that the source of power is principally economic, and that the chief is able to carry out many of his executive functions and to claim certain of his privileges only because he is the wealthiest man in the community. A chief is entitled to receive tokens of high respect, to command observance and require services; he can ensure the participation of his subjects in war, in any expedition and in any festival; but he needs to pay heavily for all these things. He has to give great feasts and finance all enterprises by feeding the participants and rewarding the chief actors. Power in the Trobriands is essentially plutocratic. And a no less remarkable and unexpected feature of this system of government is that, although the chief needs a large revenue, there is nothing of the sort directly attached to his office: no substantial tributes are paid him by the inhabitants as from subject to chief. The small annual offerings or tribute in special dainties—the first fish caught, vegetable primitiae, special nuts and fruits—are by no means a source of revenue; in fact the chief has to repay them at full value. For his real income he has to rely entirely on his annual marriage contribution. This, however, in his case, is very large, for he has many wives, and each of them is far more richly dowered than if she had married a commoner.

With this supply, he is able to pay for the many services he requires, to furnish with food the participants in big feasts, in tribal gatherings or distant expedition. Part of the food he uses to acquire objects of native wealth, or to pay for the making of them. In brief, through his privilege of practising polygamy, the chief is kept supplied with an abundance of wealth in food stuffs and in valuables, which he uses to maintain his high position; to organize tribal festivities and enterprises, and to pay, according to custom, for the many personal services to which he is entitled.

Thus the chief's position can be grasped only through the realisation of the high importance of wealth, of the necessity of paying for everything, even for services which are due to him, and which could not be withheld. Again, this wealth comes to the chief from his relations-in-law, and it is through his right to practise polygamy that he actually achieves his position, and exercises his power.

PASTORAL FULANI OF WEST AFRICA

Derrick J. Stenning
"Household Viability"
Fulani Studies in Northern Nigeria 1951–53, Selected Passages

THE WODAABE

The Pastoral Fulani inhabit the savannah zone of the western and part of the eastern Sudan. The savannah zone of the western Sudan constitutes a transition area between the Guinea zone to the south and the Sahara desert to the north. From south to north it is characterized by a diminution of the mean annual rainfall, and progressive deterioration of the vegetation from tall tropical forest to sparse thorn scrub. Perennial tsetse fly infestation in the Guinea zone, and continuous shortage of pasture and water in the desert, preclude cattle-keeping in those zones, while the dominant characteristics of the savannah render it, in general, favourable for this form of exploitation.

But the savannah zone is not immutable as a cattle-keeping zone, and with the seasonal interplay of the wet south-west monsoon from the Atlantic and the dry north-east monsoon from the Sahara, its characteristics change. In the wet season the southerly part of the savannah zone tends to take on the characteristics of the neighbouring Guinea zone and becomes fly-infested. In the dry season, the northern part of the zone becomes practically desert as standing water is evaporated and herbage dried by the sun.

These conditions enjoin upon the Pastoral Fulani of the savannah zone a movement north in the wet season and south in the dry season. This transhumance has much variation in impetus depending upon local conditions of pastoral and sedentary population density and yearly variations in the onset, intensity and duration of the rains. In west Bornu, where low sedentary population density means that movement of pastoralists is practically unimpeded by farmland, the Wodaabe move uniformly, every two or three days, in accordance with the phases of the moon.

But it is not merely movement which is imposed by the changing seasons upon Pastoral Fulani if their herds are to be maintained. The wet season is marked by a congregation of family households to form camps, while at the height of the dry season much smaller groups of family households, single households, and even matricentral components of compound families camp on their own. In the wet season greater concentrations of cattle are possible since there is adequate pasture and water; and greater concentrations of humans dependent upon them follow. In the dry season, the grazing area of a herd must be much larger, and households are consequently dispersed.

THE DOMESTIC UNIT AND THE CYCLE OF LIFE

In Pastoral Fulani society, the domestic unit is based upon the simple family (a man, his wife and their offspring) and its extension in the compound family (a man, his several wives and their offspring). Ownership of herds is vested in the male heads of such families, whose members carry out the essential tasks connected with cattle husbandry, forming the nucleus of a household living in a distinct homestead.

Changes occur in the size and composition of simple and compound families. A simple family commences as a legal union of husband and wife in marriage. This union is devoted to the procreation of legitimate children, their care during infancy, their socialization, and their material support until sexually mature. This unequivocal process of expansion comes to an end when the first child, particularly the first male child, marries and reproduces, setting up a similar simple family. From now on, the original family is in a state of dissolution. This may be concealed, however, by the birth of further children to it when the full reproductive span of spouses, particularly the male spouse, is utilized in polygynous unions. Complete dissolution—excluding the eventuality of death or divorce of spouses—occurs when all their offspring have married.

The formal development of the simple family begins by definition when children are born to the spouses. But in Pastoral Fulani society this must be regarded as only one stage—although a crucial one—in the formation of a domestic unit based upon the family. Anterior events must be considered, and it is convenient to describe the whole formal development of the family in terms of a male who is to be a family head, a householder, and a herdowner.

In these terms, the process begins when an infant boy is given a name, seven days after birth. He now becomes a person as this is understood for males by Pastoral Fulani; he has cattle. In the presence of his male agnates, his father sets aside for him a calf or two which are the nucleus of his future herd.

The next important occasion is at his circumcision, at between seven and ten years of age. He now becomes a herdboy, competent to take cattle to daily grazing. He is given some useful token of this service—a leather apron, a gourd water bottle, or a set of Koranic charms. He is taken to his father's cattle corral and "shown his beasts", and further calves are again allocated to him, again in the presence of witnesses who are his male agnates. He has the nucleus of a herd, and every herd must have its dairy-woman, the wife of its owner. He is therefore betrothed to an infant girl.

The next stage, still a preliminary to the formation of a family, household and homestead, is the induction of a betrothed girl into the homestead of her future husband's father. This takes place when she is known by the latter to have begun menstruation, and is therefore believed capable of childbirth. The couple sleep together in the open at the boy's post on the perimeter of the cattle corral. In other respects—participation in ceremonial and in work—the couple have the status of unmarried youth and maiden. The youth still carries out his duties of herdsman to his father's herd, including those cattle set aside for him. The girl becomes, as it were, a daughter of her husband's father's household, and works under the supervision of one of his wives, properly the mother of her husband. The youth and girl continue to participate in ceremonials proper to those who are not herdowners or wives, and act mainly as instructors of song and dance to younger participants.

This ambiguous period ends with the conception of the couple's first child. When the girl's pregnancy is evident to her husband's father's wife, she is removed to her own father's household. There she undergoes a period of seclusion during her pregnancy, and remains for three wet seasons—two to two-and-a-half years—after which she returns to her husband.

On this occasion it is not a pair of spouses taking up residence, but a family, and all the appurtenances of family life—a distinct homestead and a distinct herd—are to be provided.

Compared with the clusters of circular, thatched mud huts which constitute in some form or other the hamlets and villages of most of the sedentary populations of the western Sudan, the homesteads, and camps, of the Pastoral Fulani seem haphazard and rudimentary. In the wet season even a large camp blends with the bush, and in the dry season it is possible to pass within a few yards of a homestead without realizing it is there, unless its herd is present. Household equipment is limited to the amount which may be carried on the head or on pack animals, and shelter must be made of whatever tree foliage the district has to offer.

In spite of the rudimentary and impermanent nature of the homestead, it exhibits an important degree of formality and uniformity.

Pastoral Fulani homesteads always face west. In all but overnight camps a curved back fence of branches cut from nearby trees is put up to ensure a measure of privacy, keep out hyena, and deflect the course of stampeding cattle frightened by their nightly visits in the wet season.

Immediately in front of the back fence are set the beds of the homestead, the essential poles, slats, and coverlets of which are transported when camp is moved. Over the bed is erected a structure similar to it which forms a platform on which are placed the household utensils. In the wet season this platform is elaborated to form a shelter. Its components are, again, transportable. Alongside, behind, or in front of the bed-shelters there may be other ancillary shelters put up for specific purposes. These are low, beehive huts of springy boughs covered with bark matting, or tall shelters of heavier leafy boughs. These shelters do not contain beds made with poles, but a rough couch made of bundled grass and bark mats.

In front of the bed shelters there is a domestic hearth, consisting of three stones or parts of white-ant nests as a support for a cooking pot, supplemented perhaps by an iron tripod.

Near these shelters and in front of them is kept household stock other than the herd of cattle—a horse or donkey hobbled and tethered to a forked stake, and a small flock of sheep or goats sheltered in a fold made of stout branches.

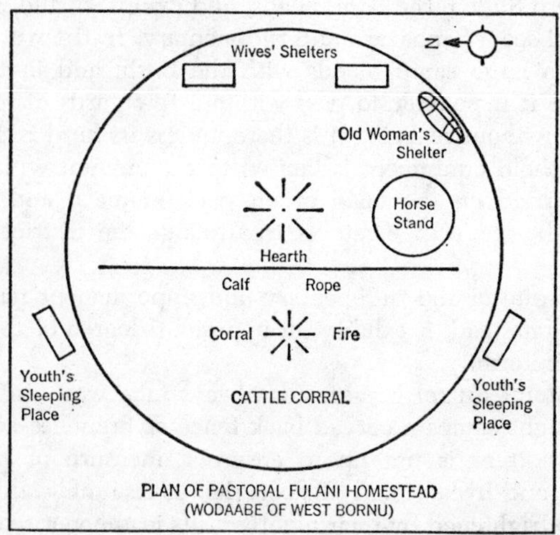

PLAN OF PASTORAL FULANI HOMESTEAD
(WODAABE OF WEST BORNU)

In front of this group of shelters is staked down a long two-stranded leather rope, to which the calves of the household herd are tethered whenever the herd is present, to prevent their suckling except when their dams are to be milked. In front again of the calf-rope is the cattle corral. This is usually just a circular patch of earth trampled by the beast's hooves, but where wood is plentiful a corral fence may be put up. Round the corral under convenient bushes or trees there may be rough beds of the type to be found in the ancillary shelters. In the centre of the cattle corral there is a smudge fire round which the cattle gather in the early morning and in the evening when they return from pasture. The fire is always lit, even in the rain, on the return of the cattle, and extinguished after they have gone out to pasture the next morning. The ritual importance of the corral fire is attested in the myths recounting the circumstances under which the first Fulani obtained cattle.

The whole homestead, consisting of one or more bed-shelters, ancillary shelters on occasion, calf-rope and cattle corral, is the basic residential unit of which all Pastoral Fulani local units, in the form of camps, are built up. The general shape of a camp is that of a rank of homesteads facing west, with their calf-ropes and bed-shelters in the same straight line from north to south. Larger camps are formed with the addition of other such ranks of homesteads pitched to the east and west, but never due east and west, for the first rank. There is no exact term for such camps in their residential aspect; the most general term for a camp is merely the plural of "homestead."

The essentials of the homestead—the bed, the domestic utensils, the calf-rope and the herd—are ceremonially brought together when the wife returns to her husband with their first-born child. There is a striking symmetry in the homestead plan, which canalizes the day-to-day life of family members, and the sources from which household property accrue to the new family.

The wife's natal family provide her with the objects of a wife and dairymaid. First among these is her bed. The bed poles are cut and trimmed by her brothers, and stained red by her sisters. The grass mats and bark coverlets are made or bought by her mother. The latter is also responsible for providing the ceremonial domestic equipment of a dairymaid—calabashes, dippers, churns, spoons and so on, lashed together with leather thonging in a traditional way. The site of the wife's domestic quarters lies alongside and to the north of her husband's father's homestead; it is cleared and fenced by the latter's sons. The husband's father also provides the pack-ox, with its harness, on which the new wife's bed and domestic equipment are transported when camp is moved. That part of the homestead which is predominantly the wife's, and which is essentially feminine in character, is thus complete.

The masculine component of the new homestead is the cattle corral, and this comes into being when the husband lights his corral fire in front of his wife's shelter.

One component of the new homestead remains—the calf rope. This is made by the husband's father and brothers, who peg it in position when the new homestead is being set up. The calf rope divides and yet unites the two halves of the homestead.

The wife's side of the homestead is to be given over exclusively to the day-to-day execution of women's tasks. A wife will maintain her own property. She will prepare milk and butter for sale, and milk and cereal foods for home consumption. Infants of both sexes and unmarried daughters will eat with her; they may be joined by the household head's son's childless wife, his daughter home for her first pregnancy, or his widowed mother. No female will eat outside this domestic area, and no male, other than infants, will eat inside it.

On the husband's side of the calf rope are the cattle, the main interest and preoccupation of the men, in their corral. Here, at dawn and dusk before milking time, the male household head will be joined, for an appraisal of the herd's condition, by his herdboy sons. The latter will sleep at the corral perimeter. The household head and his sons will eat in order of age seniority at a point on the western side of the corral. Here those males who are in camp during the day will work, mostly at making the many varieties of rope required in connection with livestock. Here they will also spend the evening round a fire, their circle often augmented by a ring of cattle who have "come to be admired."

As the family grows, the everyday activity of its members will be canalized by the division of the homestead into its male and female sections. In a general sense, entry into the corral is forbidden to females, entry into the wife's section is forbidden to males.

There are two important exceptions to this rule. A husband will cross the calf rope to enter his wife's shelter, to lie with her, to beget children. A wife will cross the calf rope to milk cattle whose calves have been released to them by her husband. The congress of husband and wife in the wife's shelter will concern children; the congress of husband and wife in the corral will concern calves.

Calves are identified with children, particularly male children, in many overt ways. A first-born son at his mother's back wears a ceremonial collar which is a replica of the halter which tethers calves to the calf rope. Boys below herding age are expected to take care of calves close to the homestead during the day while the herd is at pasture. A group of boys or youths in a dance who are age mates are called by the term for a calf rope.

But the calves at their calf rope play an important part in the ceremony at which the homestead is inaugurated. The homestead is prepared, the corral fire lit, but the new herd can be constituted in only one way. While the herd of the father of the new household head is away at pasture, the calves of his son are tethered to the calf rope of the new homestead. When the herd returns, cows allocated to the son find their calves elsewhere, and it is to the new homestead they go. The attachment, to the new herd, of cows which have no calves at the time of its constitution, must await calving, for which they are tethered in the corral of the new homestead. Bulls are separated by being tethered there for a few days and are then loosed in the evening when the herd returns from pasture, until finally they run exclusively with the new herd. But it is the transfer of calves which makes possible the orderly formation of the new herd. If the firstborn is a son, there is a calf or two in the newly constituted herd whose progeny will form the nucleus of a new herd at the third human generation.

The subsequent development of the simple family is in effect the marital history of the male household head, which takes place against the background of the expansion of the herd which he owns. Normally, sons and daughters are added to the simple family. It may be expanded into a compound family by the addition of wives up to the legal Muslim maximum of four, and, again, children may be added to these matricentral components. Divorce may take place, but normally the children born to a man stay with him, or are claimed by him when they are no longer infants, at the age of seven to ten. All these developments are crucial in considerations of the viability of the simple or compound family household.

But for the moment it is convenient to turn to the usages surrounding the dissolution of a family in the period of decline in the marital history of its head. Sons have been born to him and allocated cattle, which, in the normal course of events, have had their increase. His sons have shared the duties of herding and watering the whole herd, and, as their power and skill as herdsmen have increased, the cattle allocated to them have also increased. At the point at which, in addition, they have demonstrated their own powers of procreation, their allocations of cattle have been turned over to them on the formation of their homesteads and households. The herdsmen's skill has now been devoted to their own cattle, which in turn provide their dependents with subsistence. They have ceased to be sons, but have themselves become husbands and fathers.

But while these developments have been taking place, the father's personal power and skill as a herdsman and as a begetter have been waning. Although polygynous marriages and the children resulting from them may temporarily conceal the fact, he is steadily losing dependents as they get married. Allocations of cattle have depleted his herd. A man's last unmarried son herds his father's cattle, but on his marriage they all become his own.

Although distorted by the incidence of divorce and paternal rights to children, the case of a mother is parallel in Pastoral Fulani eyes. When her homestead was set up she was given decorated calabashes, which were never used but proudly displayed on ceremonial occasions, symbolizing her milking rights in virtue of her status as a mother. On the birth of daughters, decorated calabashes were given her by her mother and sisters. But as her children married her responsibilities for feeding them ended, while her reproductive faculties declined. She gave her own decorated calabashes to her daughters until finally, on the marriage of her last daughter, her stock of decorated calabashes and her responsibilities as a mother, housewife and dairywoman came to an end.

Sons and daughters married, the couple no longer constitute a family. The wife has no calabashes, because she has no milking rights; her husband has no herd in which she might milk. They no longer live in a homestead of their own. The shelter and the calf rope are abandoned. The couple take up residence as dependents, each with his or her eldest son, even where this involves living in the same homestead. The old woman lives in one of the ancillary beehive shelters behind her sons' wives' shelters. The old man sleeps in the open in front of his eldest son's corral. The old woman may be of use in caring for her son's infants, who may sleep in her shelter. But an old man is regarded as of little use. He may help in making rope, but he has no voice in planning the movements of the cattle of the household. Old people in this situation spend their last days on the periphery of the homestead, on the male and female sides respectively. This is where men and women are buried. They sleep, as it were, over their own graves, for they are already socially dead.

HERDS AND THE HUMAN FAMILY

The Fulani described here as "Pastoral" are part of that section of the Fulani population who are not farmers, fishers or traders as well as cattle owners, but whose subsistence and wealth derive solely from the herds they possess.

A herd is a distinct group of cattle consisting of at least one stock bull, and a complement of cows, heifers and calves, together with pack oxen. It is distinct in that it normally reproduces itself by in-breeding and line-breeding, spends the daytime period of grazing apart from other similar herds, is watered separately, and spends the night in a corral reserved or constructed for it and marked by its special smudge fire. As already stated, the corral is part of the homestead of the male herdowner, who is responsible for its day-to-day management and who directs the necessary activities of the simple or compound family subsisting on it.

Given circumstances in which cattle are the sole basis of subsistence for such a household, meat does not form a regular or staple diet and animals are not sold frequently, since this represents a draw on the capital stock of the herd. Killings are confined to male beasts, or where possible, sick, maimed or barren animals. Such killings occur only on important ceremonial occasions. Sellings take place only when an overriding need for cash occurs; for example to buy corn in the dry season, or to raise tax. The family, then, lives on milk; unlike some of the pastoralists to be found in East Africa, Fulani do not drink cattle blood or make blood foods. Either milk or milk products must be drunk and eaten *ad nauseam*, or milk must be sold or exchanged in favour of other foods. Thus the limiting factor in the subsistence of a given family upon its herd lies in the milk output of the latter. There is a minimum size, composition and (since lactation is a condition of reproduction) fertility of a herd in relation to the subsistence requirements of the family associated with it.

The herd has here been considered as supporting the family dependent upon it. But there is a sense in which the family supports the herd. Fulani cattle are not natural groups of wild animals followed and exploited intermittently by human groups. Fulani herds are in a particular way domesticated, and this domestication entails a degree of special organization in the families dependent upon them. The diverse pastoral skills of herdowners and their sons are directed towards the achievement or maintenance of a state in which the family can subsist on the herd's milk and the cereal foods for which it is exchanged. Desirable pastures have to be sought and cattle led to them. Water supplies have to be arranged and cattle watered regularly. Diseases and accidents of many kinds have to be avoided, or their results treated. Cattle have to be protected from the attacks of wild beasts, and thefts must be prevented. Pack oxen must be trained, and the birth of calves assisted.

The preoccupation of the wives of herdowners, helped by their daughters, is the control, by careful milking, of the supply of milk available to calves and humans, and the sale of butter-milk, butter and sour milk on as favourable terms as possible in such markets in cereal producing areas as are made available to them. The Pastoral Fulani family is a herdowning and milk selling enterprise.

Given this strict division of labour and a herd of a given size, a family must attain a certain size commensurate with its responsibilities towards its herd, and a composition which ensures that these are efficiently carried out by appropriate members of the family.

When the size and increase of the herd is adequate for the subsistence of the family, and the size and composition of the family are suitable for the control and deployment of the herd, then family and herd may be said to be in equilibrium, and the unit as a whole is viable. But both the human social unit and the means of subsistence associated with it are breeding concurrently, each within well-defined though different limits of fertility; the fertility of each affecting, indirectly, the fertility of the other.

INTERDOMESTIC STRUCTURE: MUTUAL AID THROUGH THE AGNATIC DESCENT GROUP

The fertility of the herd depends, first, upon the skill and diligence of the herdowner in securing for it the optimum conditions of reproduction within the limits of the habitat. A number of maxims and ceremonies, and much of Fulani notions of prestige, support this interpretation of the direct responsibility borne by the herdowner for the fertility of his herd. To this extent the responsibility of a Pastoral Fulani woman for her own fertility, and that of a man for the fertility of his herd, are comparable. Where a woman's fertility is inadequate she moves on, in divorce, to another man, and perhaps right outside the Pastoral Fulani community. But much can be done to prevent a herd's numbers sinking below the effective minimum, or, when they have done, to regain it, and to adjust the amount of labour available to the herd. Herdowners are members of agnatic descent groups whose members combine for greater or longer periods or in different ways to initiate, maintain, or reinstate families and herds in a state of viability.

Normally, where through dry season conditions there are not enough herdboys, two family households merge for the purpose of herding cattle. The homesteads are pitched side by side, and each herd spends the night in its own corral in which a corral fire is lit. But the herdboys of the two households are put on a common rota for herding, and look after both herds at once in the bush, for the herds do not merge when such temporary co-operation is carried out. The herds are watered separately, girls or women perhaps being brought in to help. The herds are milked separately by their respective dairywomen, and it should be noted that there may be milch cows borrowed from agnatic kinsmen in either herd. The herds are merged only for surveillance while grazing, and one form of co-operation does not rule out another.

The loss of viability due to irregular natural hazards is met again by the co-operation of herdowners of the same agnatic descent group. Where non-contagious diseases affect only parts of the herds, deficiencies are met by loans of stock on the pattern described above. Where a whole herd is stricken, and the herdowner cannot recoup by loans, he may do so by outright gifts from agnatic kinsmen and clansmen. Nowadays when slaughtering is enforced in outbreaks of infectious and contagious diseases, cash compensation is paid by the Administration. Among the Wodaabe the head of a herdowner's agnatic lineage group acts as his agent for the receipt of compensation. But although compensated, herdowners in many groups of Wodaabe are still reluctant to build up their herds again by purchases of stock in the open market. Indeed such purchases of unknown cattle are rightly believed to further the spread of virulent and lethal diseases like bovine pleuropneumonia. The agnatic kinsmen of such herdowners supply them with cattle in the traditional way, in return for a share in the compensation money, agreed between the giver of the stock, its recipient and the head of the agnatic lineage group. Such a persistence of the reciprocal rights and duties of agnatic kinsmen in emergencies of this kind is advantageous to all parties. The herd of the unfortunate cattle owner is re-established with cattle of the most desirable breed, whose history is known. The givers of cattle acquire a cash return which can be set against future expenses such as cattle tax. Both parties are saved the inconvenience of buying or selling in the open market, and avoid cash losses involved in the services of middlemen. The sole intermediary is the head of the agnatic descent group, and the proportion of the compensation which he receives is spent on objects such as a gown or a turban, a sword or horse trappings, which confirm his status and ultimately redound to the prestige of his followers.

When the dispersal of households is not enough to alleviate the worst effects of an epidemic, this reciprocity perforce breaks down. It is now that a herdowner may recoup on the basis of extra-clan ties arising from cattle exchanges, or on extra-clan affinal relations. But these are weaker both in number and in the material relief they bring than the co-operation of agnatic kinsmen. Although widespread epidemics thus involve the dispersal of agnatic descent groups, and their incorporation, by families or individuals, into other such groups they may also mean the removal of families from the pastoral community either temporarily or permanently.

In the context of the seasonal variations and irregular natural hazards, the agnatic descent group and the clan are agencies for the re-establishment of the viability of their constituent families. This function emerges primarily when non-viability is caused by shortages of cattle. Indeed the ability of an agnatic descent group to act in this way is contingent upon the dispersal of its constituent families. Only by endowing household heads with full responsibility for the fertility of their herds and full authority for their deployment is it possible to succour any member of the agnatic lineage group whose family cannot maintain its viability.

AUTONOMY AND DEPENDENCE IN THE TURNING OF THE GENERATIONS

It is at the inception of a family that both its requirements in cattle and in humans are most likely to be unsatisfied. Thus on the formation of a man's domestic unit, his new establishment lies, typically, alongside that of his father. The relation of father and son at this period is one in which the son is independent of his father in some respects, dependent upon him in others. A newly married son has, in theory, a certain independence. His wife may prepare food for him, which he may eat, if he chooses, in his own homestead. He may now sell cattle and may provide beasts for slaughter at ceremonies, the first of which is likely to be the name-giving of his second child. He may be responsible for raising his own share of cattle tax. He has a voice in camp councils, as a herdowner, and may give not only evidence, like a herdboy, but express opinions concerning it. He may move away from his father, and other agnatic kinsmen if he so desires, in the dry season.

In practice it is found that newly married sons stay with their fathers, often all the year round, eating in their father's homestead, being assisted by him in raising tax or ceremonial obligations, and siding firmly with him in camp councils. This association is one of dependence of the son upon the father, due to the latter's control of loans and gifts, and of the greater possibility of co-operation between agnatic kinsmen of the father's own generation than between those of the generation of his son. The minimum period of this association is five or six years.

Although a newly married man might decrease his herd, by sale or slaughter, and is bound to ensure its increase by careful deployment, the right to maintain it in adversity by loan or gift does not lie with him while his father is alive and in control of a herd of his own. For a son in this situation to ask for loans of cattle among his agnatic kinsmen of the same or senior generations is to repudiate all the efforts of his father as herdsman and begetter. This may take place, but in repudiating his father a man repudiates his agnatic descent group; the sign of such disaffection is not to return to the common wet-season camp.

The management of the inevitable period of non-viability in a newly formed household has been discussed on the assumption that a father sees all his son's marriages. But the formation of all a man's sons' homesteads and herds, much less their attainment of viability, is rare among the Wodaabe. It is more likely that physical death of the latter precedes the point of his social death, so that he leaves behind him unmarried children, fertile wives, and unallocated cattle.

In the case where none of the sons has married, it is a principle that the dead man's brother or patrilateral parallel cousin, usually a junior, shall act as the guardian of the dead man's children and supervise their betrothals. Under the witness of the family heads of the agnatic descent group, and with the mediation of its leader, he becomes the custodian of the dead man's herd, and turns over their portions to the dead man's sons as they marry. He should inherit at least one of the dead man's widows, particularly when of childbearing age. In a case of this kind, the dead man's brother or close agnatic kinsman of the same generation is as nearly as possible his substitute.

But where a family head dies leaving some sons married with families, homesteads and herds, and others without, this substitution in the collateral lines is not practised. Although the dead man's brothers or patrilateral parallel cousins may now act as adjudicators or witnesses in the settlement of his affairs, the guardianship of minors and the custody of the herd falls to the dead man's eldest son. A brother or cousin may marry the dead man's widow, and it is thought proper that this should happen, but in this case she and her offspring must be provided for out of his own herd.

All these arrangements are designed so that the simple or compound family may develop and exploit its means of subsistence in conditions which permit its greatest possible independence. This independence of economic action is secured for both men and women, and hence for the families to which they belong, by the help they can receive from agnatic kinsfolk.

In Wodaabe society, family development, in the sense of cyclical changes in the size and composition of viable domestic groupings based upon the family, must be regarded primarily as simple or compound family development. To the field observer this is obvious since dwelling units of a uniform pattern are referable to a simple or compound family as a household. More striking still is the association of herds with such family homesteads. Homesteads are grouped together, but this grouping is by no means indicative that they form joint domestic units. Where joint domestic units are formed, they are joint only in the limited sense of combining for the surveillance of cattle. Combinations of this sort are of short duration, breaking up again into their constituent simple or compound families. Other aspects of the non-viability of the family are met by forms of co-operation which do not involve the formation of wider domestic units. Most of these, like the formation of joint family units, are based upon the agnatic relationship of household heads. The functions of the agnatic lineage, and to a lesser extent the clan, are thus mainly those concerned with promoting the viability of their constituent domesti units.

THE ORGANIZATION OF A NOMADIC WAY OF LIFE

This family system may be regarded as an adaptation t a set of particular natural conditions in which seasona variations and irregular natural hazards, as well as the sc cial environment, encourage a high degree of autonomy i the smallest social units. The relationship between transfer of cattle, first marriage, and the inauguration of distinc households and homesteads suggests that the simple o compound family is the optimum viable domestic unit i Pastoral Fulani society. Fragmentation into domestic unit based upon the simple or compound family is made possi ble by an inheritance system which, in the main, through out a man's life matches the means of subsistence to whic he has title, or which he actively controls, to his own ski and strength as a herdsman or begetter of herdsmen.

SECTION THREE

FREEDOM AND STRUCTURE IN EVERYDAY LIFE

THE PERSON AS ACTOR

The Andaman tribes (p. 142) were broken down to the smallest households, among which the distribution of children could be kept even through the system of open adoption. If one tribe was growing small and its neighbor large, a simple remedy was available. In this Andaman tribes had a structural relationship similar to that of Tangu villages (p. 56), where tension and fear of fighting was resolved only when equivalence had been reached. The hunting-gathering economy of the Andamanese determined the size and composition of the group which exploited a single territory; and their prevalent procedures and attitudes maintained the viability of the band as a closely cooperating group. For the Fulani pastoralists the smallest viable unit was the individual household. But for the Andamanese so small a group had no security since the hunt is not so predictable from day to day as a herd's milk is. For hunters and gatherers the band must always have a certain size; and on an island where land is fully utilized there can be no splitting and joining of groups to maintain viability. The Andamanese tribes had fixed territories, entailing special problems of military security and food supply. There had to be a good number of men of the hunter-fighter age, yet not so many as to overhunt the woods or shores. Finally the tribe could not be so large, or so constituted, that factions were likely; for that would have necessitated, as among the Ndembu (p. 43), a formal system of authority for ruling disputes.

Could Andaman social structure have gone another way? The telling question is, What would have had to vary if it had? Hunting-gathering peoples are scattered widely about the world, and some are ethically like the Andamanese (Bushman groups in southern Africa) while others are not (the Kaingang of Brazil). Those groups that are not have a different *structure*. The relation between ethical character and social structure is not simple, but it is direct. The best way to show this is to ask how an Andaman tribe would make out in competition with a strange tribe ethically "of opposite sign"—exclusive, not open; given to bravado, not self-effacement; and so on. *Could* the two peoples, so different, establish equivalence? No. Could the new group organize itself in Andaman fashion, either domestically or as a territorial community? Not unless the Andaman ethos were adopted. More likely, if the new group proved strong it would inaugurate a period of change and adjustment. Neighboring groups would reorganize to meet the threat: they would strengthen alliances; if war became chronic, the strong hunter who now is specially honored only in death might be honored in life, being granted command. Andaman social structure would have shifted to compensate for the pressure upon it; the old ethical emphasis, for the time, would shift as well.

A drastic shift in structure—of a special sort—is probably possible without a great change in ethical emphasis. If the Andamanese took up farming their social structure would have to change far more than their ethos, if the change was economically easy. But the parts of a social structure are social roles, which are taken up and interpreted by persons who, in the long run, can't act out of character. If the new roles call for new ethics, then they won't be taken up except by persons who can find it in character to do so. In some directions, the structure *can't* change without a shift of ethical motivation.

The Trobriand Islanders (p. 148) have agriculture and live in far more populous communities. Like the Andaman islanders, they emphasize the conjugal household formed by a monogamous marriage and devoted more to sex and the rearng of children than to viability as a unit of economic produc-ion. Households are hinged according to the matrilineal cheme, a man having no jural rights over his offspring; but he local settlement pattern joins in a single hamlet grown *nen* of the same matrilineage, while the women are dispersed vherever they have married. A young man, when he is sexu-lly and economically mature, goes back to the mother's kin not where the mother was reared, but where her brothers vith their wives live). There he does not abandon the loy-lties of childhood, but takes part in the ceremonial circula-ion of yams according to the custom of *urigubu*, the harvest ift. The predominant character trait involved in this per-ormance was identified by Malinowski as vanity.

Imagine that the case was different—that the men of any natrilineage were chronically at war with their neighbors. It s inconceivable that they would send their male offspring way, knowing the young men were to become their mortal nemies. The structure as it is inhibits chronic war, at least mong the intermarrying lineages comprising a single chief-lom; and helps to make a chiefly organization possible, with-out any elaborate structure of secular authority. What nakes Trobriand social structure work is men and women onditioned by Trobriand culture: other values won't fit. The uccessful introduction of Presbyterianism to these islands vould presuppose a full-blown ethical-structural revolution. Most likely, *any* alien value system would contradict impor-ant principles of the social structure.

The Fulani (p. 167) are a pastoral and transhumant, pat-ilineal society. Their households are hinged through men; the onjugal bond is brittle; connections through women mean ittle or nothing. Divorce means only that your wife, with her milking pots, will cease to follow you, and you must find an-other who will take her place. The man, the cattle, and the sons to herd them remain when a woman leaves; by Fulani eckoning, the essential family is undisturbed. The social sys-tem depends on a rigid segregation within the household it-self. The principle of the calf rope and the two hearths is the first axiom of Fulani social organization. Its major corollary is that men shall not become sentimentally bound to women. It follows that men can't become bound *through* women.

To comprehend the *raison d'être* of the Fulani system, w must ask why a first marriage takes the form it does; or wh marriage ends when son, daughter, cattle, and calabash ar gone. When the adolescent girl first comes to sleep with he betrothed husband their relationship is, publicly, more int mate than it will subsequently be; yet they remain in th status of unmarried youth and maiden. Sentimentally, the are perhaps closely bound; structurally, the tie is not ye recognized; and it ends, in any event, with the girl's preg nancy. The relationship is renewed in marriage—an institu tion which cannot exist simply between man and woman, bu requires the presence of children and cattle, ending whe they are exhausted. Why does a man not cling to the last c his cattle, even when his sons and daughters are gone, in or der to retain his autonomy and his pride? At the height of h powers, a Fulani herdsman is a redoubtable fellow—and wh will he then be a foolish old man, whose counsel is ignored, dependent already "socially dead"? The first answer is that household constituted by a lone old man and woman is one c marginal viability. The welfare of cattle is more important i Fulani reckoning than human sensibilities. Further, the con jugal family is an instrumental arrangement, not somethin valued in and for itself. The patrilineage has a more soli metaphysical status, whose endless descent through time i concretely expressed in the continuity of the agnatic herd, which may be trimmed by sale or slaughter but which ough never to be supplied from alien, nonlineage strains. The polit cal group is the locus of values and expectations which mor typically would find their focus within the constituent do mestic units.

We must conclude that the quality of the person (chara ter) typical of a society is an expression of the social stru ture. One can't logically or intuitively derive the qualitie of Andaman or Trobriand moral life from a model of th social structure emptied of ethical information. But startin with a knowledge of the ethical demands of the roles he mus play one can put together a fair picture of the character person in either of those island cultures would be bound t acquire.

For Aristotle in the Poetics, character *was there* and wa

revealed, little by little, through critical decisions. But we are obliged to ask how character *comes to be there,* how it is won and lost, and we find it is not just exhibited but created in a man's critical decisions. A man is what he has done; and if in gaining his humanity he has wanted the recognition of others, he has had to renounce certain freedoms to be as he would be. There are also freedoms he will possess to the end but never have the chance to use: the Fulani elder, if he were valued and given a function, could be a different person in his death. A few hundred miles away westward the Dogon elder is encouraged to drink and babble, and is honored for it, being close to the ancestors who have departed along the same way. Six thousand miles to the east, the Andaman elder *has the function* of wise man, and much respect. Granted that I make my own character through the critical turnings I take, where I am free to choose—the rules of the game, particular to each culture, are also decisive.

The problem of freedom in everyday life has a facet which the anthropologist is best qualified to study. A generation ago, it might have been enough to say that freedom like other values was relative. Freedom was culturally determined—some cultures were permissive and others strict or authoritarian. That solution is too simple. Culture has many voices, all of them human. Men don't blindly discharge appointed roles. If suffering is imposed it is imposed not by culture on man but by men—role-motivated—on men.

Was the old Chinese custom of binding feet a cruel constraint or a guarantee that women would always be spared some of the burdens of hard labor? Much has been made of the agonies of bound feet. Should we believe that little girls were so hated that their suffering gave unnatural joy to their mothers? Or could so many women so hate themselves so perversely that they must displace their self-hate on their hapless daughters? These are attempts to explain the motivation of the role by way of the psychology of persons. It is not realistic to suppose there would have been so much psychic uniformity among so many women over twenty-five generations. A Chinese village is an acutely human place, not a personality factory. The uniformity must have been achieved on the level of role motivation, not personal expression. The question, Why? must be answered in terms c public values, not private inadequacies. But the custom wa more than an immense sacrifice to the idols of vanity.

The Western equivalent is hobbling the female with a inordinately expensive and unstable footgear which prevent her from taking natural steps and usually discourages th activity wanted for maintaining natural agility. Why d Western women cooperate in such customs? In both West an East we seem to be dealing with systems of meaningful act by which the claims of women in massively male-centere cultures are afforded a sort of left-handed vindicatior We know that the Chinese custom of binding feet sprea rapidly from the imperial courts (where it is first encoun tered) to the common folk, who took it to themselves an kept it up even in the face of official bans. Ordinary villager were binding the feet of every little girl for at least thre hundred years after the practice ceased to have prestig meaning in the urban culture. We could say that artificiall tiny feet came to have cardinal value in the plebeian cultur of Chinese women. The point at issue is not whether thes customs entail a loss of freedom to women: imposed suf fering or awkwardness is the very antithesis of freedom The point is whether the gains to women—the special im munities and rights accorded to them as physically less robus than men—are enough to make sense of the practice. Chines women bound the feet of their daughters so that womer might be proud of themselves, and Western women ar self-hobbled in a similar mood, trading off one kind o freedom for another. The treatment of feet is comparable t the disciplining of hair, which we so readily understand i terms of fashion and style. There is good reason for bindin feet, filing teeth, and tattooing or scarifying flesh: these ar ways of imposing style and its peculiar value upon our bodies Only the outsider to a culture, for whom its values do no yet exist, will be puzzled.

The case of Chinese feet is one of those most frequentl cited by social critics to demonstrate the arbitrary characte of culture. Their argument is for greater cultural *freedom* This means, in effect, less style, less culture, less standardiza tion of usage; more variety, more spontaneity, more scop r individuality. These are the attributes of the permissive ılture: doesn't anthropology support the tales brought back an Enlightened world with Bougainville from Tahiti, here bodies are all browned in the sun, food drops from ees, the great aim of life is pleasure? I'm afraid anthropolgy doesn't. Whatever the special tyrannies we wrestle with t home, there is a culture in which to escape them. But we ould only be trading them for others, not for cultural freeom. The Trobriand islander is free in his sex life—the typical iography there seems to include a lot of sex with a lot of eople and only occasionally trouble from it. But an eclectic eterosexuality is not a guarantee of freedom from the tyranies of sex: jealousy, scorning, deception, and desire for the orbidden are not banished from that sunny isle—they are nly couched there in an idiom of more open play than mong the Andamanese or the Fulani. The frustrated Fool in *he Yeomen of the Guard* wasn't allowed to be serious howver dejected he felt: play can exercise its tyrannies as well s soberness. Casanova was a driven man.

In short, the qualities of freedom are many. They are not be found all together. You will not find them outside the rame of culture and social structure, and to understand reedom is to understand that frame. We are ready then to ırn back to the family systems we've studied and put them nder greater magnification. The social relations on which we ocus will be those in which human nature seems to collide vith social structure: the sexual triangle among the Andamanse, the Trobrianders, and the Fulani, the classic situation f threat to the conjugal tie.

THE BREAKING OF MARRIAGES

Consider first what we already know or can figure out bout Andaman patterns for sexuality and aggression (p. 33). Can't we get at the main facts, simply from knowng the structure of the Andaman band and asking what eneral patterns of social motivation or character will fit in? Vithin the band young men may not assert themselves over heir elders; all men know precisely who was "born before" vhom, who through age should have priority in the daily distribution of meat. In a community so tightly organize no two men have formally equivalent respect status. It predetermined what person must yield, if any pair shou chance to stand in each other's way. The opposition-an equivalence game is not played within the band. And do that mean all is everywhere sweetness and light? It doesn When they conceive aggression is called for, it is not far find. If life within the solidary hunting band (before t advent of a European administration) called for a gener mood of mildness, the pattern of warfare as between ban called for displays of overt and passionate hostility—we ha not to deal here with mild *men* so much as mild *role* not harmless *persons* but harmless *personae*—the Andamans old seagoing lore were known as the very archetypal "ca nibal islands."

The ethnography shows that aggression is institutional called for only or mainly in the case of men, not women the "political nature" of the male and the "domestic nature" the female are re-created in Andaman as in so many oth human communities. Women are not physically incapable handling spears and waging war with all the viciousne their men can muster; the political/domestic distinction can be attributed to nature, as the Andamanese probably believ But if one sex is to be more domestic than the other in society close to nature, women will take the role. Huma sexual dimorphism is more striking in some populations tha others, but men are everywhere able to run down or escap their women—no society can count on Amazons to protect from enemy males, though technology has the potential changing this balance. It is structural convenience which nally accounts for the fact that the political/domestic distin tion appears almost everywhere in one form or another: yo *can* organize a society without it, but it is an uphill fight.

We have by this time learned enough of social structu to see that what we are discussing is not simply a set *norms* defining what is to comprise the male role (as again the female role) in Andaman society. Males and femal find themselves in structured situations; either they do or the don't recognize the plot in time to do the right thin and in this case it may be a matter of life and death. In

:uation of armed aggression an Andaman woman would ually be foolish to do anything but run, while a man must ten stand and fight to protect his life and interests. Women n expect to gain by running, men more often can't; that ch knows this instantly is a function of the fact that each eds only to react in character to be doing right. Each ene, however frightful, is for most participants only a brief tension to an old and epic plot, in which they have long ayed parts. But is adultery so serious, after all?

A. R. Radcliffe-Brown
The Andaman Islanders, p. 50

Cases of theft seem to have been rare. It was left to the aggrieved person to take vengeance upon the thief, but if he killed him or seriously wounded him he would have to expect the possible vengeance of the relatives and friends. Adultery was regarded as a form of theft. I gathered that a man had the right to punish his wife for unfaithfulness, but if the punishment were too severe it would be an occasion for a quarrel with her relatives. It was difficult for the aggrieved husband to punish the man who had offended against him. If he killed him he would lay himself open to the revenge of the relatives. The most he could do was to vent his anger in violent words. . . .

The frequent occurrence of serious quarrels is prevented both by the influence of the older men and by the fear that everyone has of the possible vengeance of others should he in any way offend them.

There is a certain style for dealing with others in Andaian society, and it is quick to assert itself even in disorinting situations like the discovery of adultery. Each person iust reflect on the instant what the consequence will be of cting this way or that. How far can the husband give vent o anger, inflating himself and showing power in response to he deflating and damaging discovery he has made? He knows hat if he resorts to physical violence he will be liable to vengeance. For the observer this calculus of probabilities an assessment of the relevant structural facts; for the thre participants it is a search for socially credible courses c action. They have found themselves in a fix.

Bronislaw Malinowski
The Sexual Life of Savages in North-Western Melanesia
Fieldwork 1915–18, pp. 144–46

An interesting case of matrimonial misfortune which le to divorce is that of Bagido'u, the heir apparent of Omara kana. His first wife and her son died, and he then marrie Dakiya, an extremely attractive woman who bore trace of her good looks even at the somewhat mature age a which I first saw her. Dakiya's younger sister Kamwalil was married to Manimuwa, a renowned sorcerer of Wa kayse. Kamwalila sickened, and her sister Dakiya went t nurse her. Then between her and her sister's husband evi things began. He made love magic over her. Her min was influenced, and they committed adultery then an there. When, after her sister's death, Dakiya returned t her husband Bagido'u, matters were not as before. H found his food tough, his water brackish, the coconu drinks bitter, and the betel nut without a bite in it. H would also discover small stones and bits of wood in hi lime pot, twigs lying about in the road where he used t pass, pieces of foreign matter in his food. He sickene and grew worse and worse, for all these substances were of course, vehicles of evil magic, performed by his enemy the sorcerer Manimuwa, assisted in this by the faithles wife. In the meantime, his wife trysted with her leman.

Bagido'u scolded and threatened her until one day sh ran away and went to live with Manimuwa, an altogethe irregular procedure. The power of the chiefs being nov only a shadow [of what it had been in precolonial times] Bagido'u could not use special force to bring her back so he took another wife—a broad-faced, sluggish, and some what cantankerous person by the name of Dagiribu'a Dakiya remained with her wizard lover, and married him

The unfortunate Bagido'u who obviously suffers from consumption, a disease with which all his family are more or less tainted, attributes his ills to his successful rival's sorcery, even now, as he believes, active against him. This is very galling, for he has the injury of black magic added to the insult of his wife's seduction.

Trobriand marriages are rarely chaste and are easily dis-olved. The rules are permissive, but the relationships which esult, as the tale shows, can be strained. The two men ini-ally enjoyed equivalent rank, although Bagido'u had better xpectations. Manimuwa's reputation as a sorcerer was not his nly asset: in love he was the stronger of the two men, aving his way through personal dominance. Bagido'u, on ie other hand, emerges as a loser, fatalistically accepting his npotence where a stronger man would have fought back vith countermagic.

The brittleness of Trobriand marriages and the defeat of agido'u offer clues to the inner quality of Trobriand social elations. Malinowski was told that a man had the right to ill his wife for adultery; but, he found, "the usual punish-ient is a thrashing, or perhaps merely remonstrance or a fit f the sulks."[13] A woman who wanted to leave her husband or another might simply pick a quarrel with him and run ome to Mother. There is little direct domination of others n Trobriand society. Where force is used on another person t is moral (psychological), not physical.

What is structure then and what is character? Male chau-inism among the Trobrianders seems to be a blend of law nd bravado. If men claim powers they do not exercise, how eal are their claims? If adultery is forbidden but everyone oes it, what is the structural norm? The relativity of tructure and character can be seen in the way Trobriand ublic sensitivities effectively control adultery by subverting ather than stigmatizing it. Love relations are subject to atastrophe anywhere, but this must be particularly so in the Trobriands, where the light and dark sides of love are dram-tized equally, the most active sort of hedonism being

[13] Malinowski, *Sexual Life*, p. 143.

matched by fears of sorcery, shame, and vengeance. Divorce which could make little sense to an Andaman couple, is an ever-present risk in the more histrionic atmosphere of Trobriand marriage. By contrast a Fulani marriage, demanding no more than a minimal investment of ego and personal reputation, is more simply broken.

Derrick J. Stenning
Savannah Nomads
Fieldwork 1951–53, pp. 173, 181–84

. . . In Pastoral Fulani society in general, the dissolution of marriage by divorce is permitted, easy, and frequent. It is allowed to both partners in a marriage, but it is probably easier, and therefore more frequent, for a man to divorce his wife than for a wife to divorce her husband. Wodaabe are well aware of the force of inertia which may keep marriages in being so long as the partners do not find their union intolerable. Asked to account for long-standing unions, elders would commonly answer with a single word *booral* ("familiarity"). Their attitude is that marriage, like other social relationships, must be carried on with patience and fortitude. When, owing to one or a combination of causes, patience becomes exhausted, then a marriage must be broken. . . .

The description of the procedure and symbolism of the establishment of a homestead and household by betrothal-marriage concluded with the suggestion that the marital contract in Wodaabe society was one in which the husband required of his wife that she should bear him children, particularly boys, the future inheritors of the herd; the wife's expectations were that the husband should maintain sufficient cattle for the maintenance of herself and her children.

If this is indeed the essence of the marital contract, it follows that the rupture of this contract by divorce should occur primarily when these expectations are not realized. Men may therefore be expected to divorce their wives when they do not bear children, women to divorce their husbands when insufficient cattle are provided for them to milk. . . .

If the likelihood of a woman's being divorced by her husband is greatest at the beginning and end of her child-bearing period and during the intervals in which she does not bear children, the fate of a barren woman is one of continual insecurity unless she can marry where her domestic virtues are more important than her reproductive capacities. A barren wife's best hope is in the fertility of her co-wives, for a woman who is childless but of equable disposition and a hard worker may, in certain circumstances, be a good foil to a co-wife whose main role is that of mother.

In Fulani society a love triangle would be a most abnormal thing. Trobriand marriage was personal, sentimental, highly ego-involved. Fulani marriage seems the opposite—a purely contractual, businesslike arrangement. Age, fertility, health, wealth—a few objectively given variables seem to control the fortunes of a Fulani family, rather than emotional involvements.

Stenning found that one marriage in three would end in divorce. Of marriages already discontinued, four out of five had ended in divorce rather than the wife's death or separation by reason of age.[14] Since there is no indication that the Fulani think marriages *ought* to be unbusinesslike, we shouldn't read Western values into these statistics. Even a long-continued union will dissolve when its work is done. Fulani do not mix sentiment into family affairs. A mother's ties to her child, sanctified in some societies, here are readily broken. They do not represent a major deterrent to divorce, in which case the children born to a man stay with him or are claimed by him when still young. The closest tie is that of father-son; yet an old man who joins his son's household may sit by the cattlefire at night for the discussion of plans *but have no influence* over the son's affairs—the old man is "socially dead."

The premises of ethical thought are distinctive in each

14 Stenning, *Nomads*, p. 181.

culture, but comparison justifies some general conclusions. It is a truism that, since goods are rarely to be had except through cooperation with others, a man has got to be social to be successfully selfish. In general, we have to keep up our good character with some of our fellow men if only for safety's sake. This means rational self-interest will always compromise itself in the direction of other-regarding behavior, but as a basis for understanding altruism this conclusion is of modest import. Should the scientist be delving for ulterior motives behind every seemly act he observes, in all cultures alike? Such a conviction can tyrannize the observer who doesn't distinguish the motives of persons, which are presumably egoistic, from those inherent in social roles. Compare the Fulani herdsman with the Trobriand gardener. When they are considered as persons, it would be hard to say which of them is the more egoistic. But the *role* of the gardener, oriented to the production of traditional harvest gifts, is altruistic where that of the pastoralist is not. The egoistic person loses himself in the roles he plays.

The shortcomings of an explanation through self-interest or egocentric motivation appear clearly in accounts of play and creativity, actions by which we directly undertake to escape or transcend ourselves. Sheer, unimaginative willfulness is comparatively rare in human affairs. Reflection on the case materials we've reviewed suggests that man's most characteristic stance may rather be, as Hobbes remarked, the pose of the actor.

PART THREE

RELIGION AND POLITICS

SECTION ONE

SOCIAL STRUCTURE AND PERSONAL INVOLVEMENT

THE CONDITIONS OF INTIMACY

THE TIES THAT BIND

Human intimacy has many contexts and styles. Anger eliminates distance even more quickly than sexual arousal. We can sometimes be freer with a stranger than with a friend. In North America, if you are a *fan* you want intimate knowledge of a person with whom you could never be on close terms. A young friend who inadvertently became a student of behavior in public transport (in the sixties) told me that Frenchmen predictably explored her charms by tactile rather than visual means. A Frenchman she brought back to her American university still claimed surprise to find himself gazing on intimacies which at home would be jealously private. Intricate little diagrams are sometimes made to chart who likes whom in the neighborhood playground. Whether they are models of real or imaginary structures, they offer us a clue to the way individuals become personally involved. Intimacy and distance, claim and immunity, are the stuff of which social structures are made in the playground and in more elegant places.

The Latin phrase *patria potestas* refers to the power of life and death which once was vested by Roman law in the family patriarch. The son had no rights *in law* against his father, who might sell him into slavery in order to retrieve a debt, or kill him as Abraham would have killed Isaac, or banish and disinherit him. Put this way, the law seems primitive, in being only half formed, unevolved, not wholly civilized. To later Romans, in fact, the early law of patriarchal authority did seem uncivilized: in a time when the father still could refuse to "take up" an infant into his household—that is, could practice infanticide by exposure—his right even to disinherit a son once "taken up" had been seriously restricted. Cultural change was removing *political* functions from the family; historically, the change in the family system was concomitant with the rise of a governmental establishment (a "superstructure") independent of a family and *gens*, or agnatic lineage—a chance toward a more complex organization for keeping the civil peace. As the Roman domestic group ceased to be the basic social unit for law enforcement, a less militaristic kin organization became appropriate. Fathers, in fact, seem to have become indulgent toward their sons by the time of Pliny the Younger (d. 112 A.D.), to the point of scandal. Can we say then that the father-son relationship had become more intimate?

The question is not whether fathers and sons were getting better acquainted in Pliny's day than they had been before; there was probably no change. What we do have evidence for is a great shift in political circumstance. That is a change of underlying structure; and it does not tell us much about the whole range of behavior that would have been subject still to personal inclination. Do I guarantee mutual understanding by either indulging my son or holding him to a rigid discipline? There is no necessary connection. But in another sense of *intimacy* the direction of change in the Roman family was toward less intimate association—that is, toward a looser association in which a man's wife or son might come or go more freely than had been the case before. A relationship which allows great mutual independence is less intimate than one from which there is no relief. When a son is bound as an expectant heir to his father until the latter dies, their bond is close. It may not be comfortable. When the son has a settlement at twenty-one, to do with as he will, the bond is loosened. So also is a marriage tie, if it can't be dissolved, made by that fact the more intimate, though it be colored not by warmth but by cold detestation.

Since structural ties are manifested in rights and obligations, we may distinguish the type of tie by the quality of mutual claims associated with it; and we may define the factor of intimacy and distance in human relationships as a matter of the intensity of mutual claims. We do not need to assume that such claims are in even balance for the bond to be a close one; but insofar as the tie is a *human* one the idea of mutuality will apply—how much could the Roman father expect from a son whom he didn't clothe and feed? A structurally intimate relation is one which will tolerate deep-reaching claims: an infant (once it is "taken up" into a community's social life) has such claims upon its mother, a wife upon her husband, a boy upon his friend. The maximal claim you may put on another can be called ultimate loyalty—that he should to the end put your welfare ahead of his own. Perhaps I am deprived in some deeply human way if there never has been one for whom I'd risk my life. It isn't hard to call to mind societies and situations in which the mother-child, husband-wife, and friend relationships can each in its own way call for ultimate loyalty. Yet each of the three may become a less intense relationship—one even of recognized alienation, whereby loyalties end. What is not true is that such a process of alienation could occur with equal ease, and by the same steps, in each case. Some ties of intimacy are ironclad, some blow off with the wind.

The ties hardest to break or dissipate are those which in any society will be regarded as ties "of blood" or "of birth"—that is, relationships of right and obligation which are attributed to nature itself. Ties of maximal intensity are so regarded; they are ties reinforced by a long period of intimacy—a sharing of the life of the same household. The scope and patterning of incest prohibitions indicate what ties a society attributes to nature (or God) and will not have man put asunder. The taboo of incestuous involvement within the consanguine tie sets it aside from one source of inconstancy; as a call for renunciation, the taboo projects clearly the element of altruism which must inhere in acts of loyalty.

Where the theory of divine kingship prevails, it may happen

that the God-and-nature formula, applied to the royal family, serves to stabilize succession through the automatic selection of an heir; and the concept of hereditary right has sometimes kept unlikely persons in positions of power. Because the political use of divinely or naturally given ties is not universal, and is out of fashion just now, it may seem contrived. But we have seen that the idea of nature is everywhere applied in comparable fashion to the structuring of family life; and the hereditary succession to farms, houses, and chattels is still built solidly into most codes of law. No system of role relationships is any more natural to man than the Arabic, Urdu, Eskimo, or English languages—all are contrived. But some ties are made to sever at need and others are not.

At the opposite end of a scale from the primally given ties, which must continue to exist even when they are ignored, are those human relationships whose quality is always contingent on actual affirmation. The two types can be distinguished as *axiomatic* and *contingent*. If a mother and child are still committed to maximal loyalty though they have spent their lives apart, that is not regularly true of friends or even of persons who were once husband and wife. In short, there are two sorts of strength which may characterize a human tie: one is the strength of richness of content or of depth, the other is infrangibility. The one begins with individual volition, while the other is immune from it. Emotional depth in a human relationship is a psychological fact with elemental structural relevance; the infrangibility of a tie, derived from its attribution to nature, is a structural fact with profound psychological relevance.

OEDIPUS AND ORPHEUS

Two myths (probably the two best known of the whole Western European heritage) define separate principles by which human intimacy may be structured—Oedipus and Orpheus. The lesson of the first is: a son who never knew father or mother is yet their son by nature and in the moral law. Oedipus killed his father and married his mother. That he knew nothing of the natural tie is inconsequential in the face of its axiomatic quality. We feel the double horror of patricide and incest, and so agree with the judgment of Oedipus upon himself at the moment of discovery. Such tales maintain the traditional teachings on kinship ties. The modern, Freudian version of the myth substitutes Eros for Moira, instinct for fate, and achieves a dramatic reversal—the turn from ignorance and innocence to discovery and guilt—through the subtle device of an unconscious mind, yet the lesson is the same: filial ties and obligations are built into human nature, to be violated at supreme cost.

The myth of Orpheus and Eurydice might be taken for mere romance, since it hinges on a man's love for his wife. But the tale doesn't conform to the rules of romantic literature, in that hero and heroine are not lovers barred by circumstance from union, but are joined in one flesh. The lesson of the myth is contained in its California Indian version, for when he comes to the land of the dead the husband discovers that his wife has returned to her own kin—it is a man's sister who sits with him there, not his wife. The intruder from the land of the living brings with him an incongruous attachment; the dead find it hard to tolerate his smell.

Theodora Kroeber
California Indian Legends Retold, pp. 148–49

After all this had happened . . . the chief came to the man to tell him that he could stay no longer, that the dead did not feel it to be right to allow a living person to remain among them. But, since he had grieved so deeply and gone through so much to be with his wife, the chief said that she would be allowed to return with him to her life in the world of the living. He made only one condition: during the trip home, which would take six days and six nights, and until they were home again, the man must not touch his wife. . . .

Together they left the land of the dead, going back across the bridge, between the moving rocks, and over the long trail, on and on until six days and five nights had come and gone and they were once more in country familiar to them. By the next day they would reach their own home.

But as darkness replaced the last of the light from the setting sun at their backs and the man could again see his wife looking quite as she had in life, he could wait no longer. He must and he would have her. She pleaded with him to wait through this one night. He could not. . . .

The sun was high in the sky the next day when hunters from his own village found the man. He was dead, lying face down, arms outstretched, on the trail which leads to the west.

To be sure, we are dealing with masculine impatience, but the end was inherent in the situation. Orpheus was fated to look back, and the condition set by the Chief of the Dead, though it seemed to suspend the laws of nature, ultimately could not. However intense the intimacy achieved by husband and wife, the tie begins to fade when it is not actively affirmed—so says the tale, in its fateful ending. Affinal ties are contracted by men, not given in nature. In the observable world, a man's loyalty to his wife may conflict with and overshadow the relationship to sister or mother; but in the ethical model of that world projected in the lore of nations, it is the tie "of blood" which is the stronger.

These considerations bear the following implications: first, that the strength of infrangibility will often outlast the strength born of mutual emotional commitment; and second, that as a contingent tie, initiating in personal involvement and gradually deepened by the prolongation of intimacy, gains strength, it takes on some of the qualities of the socially predefined or axiomatic tie. Trobriand marriage provides a nice example, for it begins casually as a love attachment which will become only by gradual deepening a mutual commitment to the conjugal life. Malinowski assures us that lovers are at first in no way beholden; young persons enjoy a ready but ephemeral intimacy. What prevents their continuing so indefinitely? why do they voluntarily submit to a tie of binding obligation? and in what precise sense, after all, *is* marriage such a tie in Trobriand culture?

Bronislaw Malinowski
The Sexual Life of Savages
Fieldwork 1915–18, pp. 114–15

Jealousy, with or without adequate reason, and adultery are the two factors in tribal life which put most strain on the marriage tie. In law, custom and public opinion, sexual appropriation is exclusive. There is no lending of wives, no exchange, no waiving of marital rights in favour of another man. Any breach of marital fidelity is as severely condemned in the Trobriands as it is in Christian principle and European law. . . . Needless to say, however, the rules are as often and as easily broken, circumvented, and condoned as in our own society.

In the Trobriands the norms are strict, and though deviations from them are frequent, they are neither open nor, if discovered, unatoned; they are certainly never taken as a matter of course.

To understand marriage in this culture we must see why the ease with which either partner may dissolve a marriage doesn't make a mockery of marital fidelity. A Trobriander is at once devoted to the maintenance of certain public codes or ideal norms (marital chastity, shunning incestuous attachments) and to the practical evasion of them in his own private affairs. The demands he will meet are those of persons, not abstract voices; and the wants of others are not always ethically toned—there is an alternate principle, which I call the romantic.

Human relationships gain strength either by attribution or by actual affirmation—these are the theoretically pure, limiting cases. They are realized, in pure form, only in myth. The axiomatic or primally given tie, unsupported by actual affirmation yet eternally binding, is found in the Oedipal tale. In the Orphic myth the gods and the laws of nature are set aside, overwhelmed by the affirmation of a private will and a private devotion. If marriages could be built wholly on romantic voluntarism, there need be no vows and no ceremonial recognition of the tie. But in real societies, though a marriage fails when it is not affirmed in actual contact, no marriage can continue for long on the pure affirmation of the archetypal lovers. In life, human relationships will fall between the limits of the involuntary, infrangible tie and the romantic, and men learn to cope with the tension between the two ideals.

If the world conformed to the romantic view, all institutions—government, property, marriage—would at all times perfectly express the wills of individuals; all social units above the level of the willing or unwilling individual would have nominal significance. But if the world conformed to an opposite view (which we may call an extreme of structuralism), human will would have to be dismissed as illusory. The true world combines elements of both of these extreme versions. Whatever you do, almost to the limits of actual patricide and incest, does not exempt you from filial ties or from the patterns of right and obligation therein entailed. To enjoy the full claim upon the other's loyalty you need meet no test of actual and recent performance—when the prodigal son returns he will be taken in. The myths of consanguinity and familism are maintained, affirmed. And the tie of marriage, though it is not always attributed to God and nature ("what He hath joined . . . in one flesh"), and though it inevitably must allow for a greater element of voluntarism than the tie of blood, has a similar prescriptive weight wherever it is found. Consider the Trobriand wife, so concerned as she is to maintain an air of fidelity. It is precisely that air which, in her circumstance, she owes her husband. She should spare him demeaning scandal, not wounding his vanity. The good wife will hide her own indiscretions and, where the matter is not publicly forced, condone those of her husband—to fail in such white deceit is to fail in one's obligations. Ethical agreement is for most men a recognizable good, worth affirming where it is not outweighed by some other and more urgent end, and we recognize the stable society by the absence of such ends.

Prolonging an intimate relationship erodes its voluntaristic character because each participant, having invented a role, is obliged to play it; and because with intimacy each will become involved in the network of rights and obligations in which the other person is already enmeshed. Affirming closeness to another means affirming the values of the good family member or friend. The Trobriander who delivers *urigubu* payments to the household of a particular sister is affirming a tie of blood whose meaning without that affirmation would be shadowy; when the same man allows himself to grow fond of his wife's children, he commits himself to maintaining a marriage even in the face of substantial differences in actual relations with the woman herself or her kin. Character involvement and structural involvement are universal accompaniments of intimacy in human affairs and explain how, through our own affirmation of intimacy with another, we become responsive to prevailing ethical values. An intricate but unbroken network of personal ties joins us ethically to others far beyond our knowing horizon: no man is an island.

FORM AND SUBSTANCE IN SOCIAL RELATIONS

THE ACCUMULATION OF CLAIMS

The experience of social structure from the inside is often one of constraint, since the substance of life is always protean in relation to the limiting demands of an institution. The establishment confronts the person, a sexual code confronts a Wilde or a Byron, law confronts charisma. But in the constant play between form and substance in social life, though behavior in the short run usually conforms to the limits of structure as water will run in its channels, a landscape in the long run is shaped by the flow of events.

Consider two people connected by an axiomatic tie who

have never met or corresponded. If, like Oedipus and his mother, they should meet without recognition, they might behave so as to breach the tie forever; but if they know one another at the start that is unlikely to happen. Their actions would be fitted scrupulously into the mold prescribed for them, though *as persons* they should scarcely exist for one another. When an Andaman child (p. 142) is taken away by his foster parents there is a similar discrepancy between form and substance—both parties understand the form of their relationship, or what it ought to be; but there are at first a few stiff moments, or worse. Yet with actual proximity, continuing to act within a well-defined frame of rules, the tie soon comes to have substance. Obversely the old ties between the child and his true parents come to be less substantial, though the roots of a deep commitment remain. Where social structure or some institution supplies the form or frame, a social relationship gains or loses structural weight with the use or disuse of demand rights by one person upon another.

But when people meet, they are not usually related. More often they meet in a trivial role relationship (clerk and customer, fellow traveler, fellow guest) and the acquaintance is extended beyond it. Then does not the *raison d'être* of that extension define the very nature of the new relationship? It may be friendship, hostility, the discovery of a mutual interest, or loneliness combined with anxious curiosity: intimacy is a door to many things. Yet as people continue to engage each other, they begin to establish claims each upon the other. In a small town, you expect the mailman to smile, and he can expect you to restrain your dog. On the beach, in exchange for allowing a flirting glance, the girl will expect the lifeguard's indulgence in the smallest things. On the road, when you are being patient you resent the driver who pushes impatiently by you—you consider retaliation, or you may even revile the fellow behind your closed windows, questioning his birth credentials. Involvements with others begin on a subtle plane of symbolic exchanges which often enough come to nothing, but which with continuation will inevitably accumulate and grow more substantial. Does that mean the form of the social life is importantly and inevitably *free,* and responsive to the whims and urgings of such as you and me? Where the institutional frame is not given at the outset, do we freely build our own?

Courtship which leads to marriage with all the due formalities illustrates a personal involvement which gradually moves toward and into an institutionalized frame. Antagonisms often move along the same route: a casual quarrel sets up antagonistic expectations; the involvement deepens, producing a serious altercation; with the attendant publicity, the affair is almost certain to move into the frame of court-case procedure—if, indeed, that frame is already available. Here we are dealing with social substance—or call it simply *privately motivated action*—which at the start has no ascertainable structural weight, but which gradually assumes form. Consider what follows the minor collision of two cars: an initial moment of emotional excitement (substance) provokes counterallegations and claims; credentials are demanded; the police are summoned; the case is pressed by the law's representatives into approved channels (form). But in such processes there is something more than the mere imposition from above of form upon substance. Whenever, be it out of love or jealousy or appetite or antagonism, we want to place a compelling claim upon another person, we are seeking to impose form upon our relationship. The imposition here is not from above but within. Short of magic or mesmerism, the only way that I can lodge such a claim so as to make it compel the other is through publicity—that is, I am prepared to invoke the law, the institutional forms of my society, such as marriage, or witchcraft accusation, or court process.

ENGAGEMENT AND DISENGAGEMENT

Over time, personal involvements which are not ephemeral will either deepen toward a maximal limit or (having achieved some depth) recede. The process is one of engagement or disengagement, undertaken in mutual awareness by both parties. But the process of engagement is one of *structural* deepening—the accumulation of valid claims and obligations. It is only in that way that the relationship can be fixed; it will otherwise be so fluid or volatile as to be emotionally unmanageable. Except in myth, a romantic attachment gains structure or else it blows with the wind. In fiction we find an obsessive love attached to an unworthy (irresponsible) object—for example, in Maugham's *Of Human Bondage*. In the archetypal European romance (*Tristan and Iseult*), a love without publicity and without recognition of claim or debt is the pure and lasting one. But what we find when we examine such mythic material is that the romantic motif requires, not engagement and deepening intimacy, but disengagement, the interposition of obstacles and distance (physical or social distance) between the lovers. Maugham himself opined that there were only two fitting conclusions in fiction—marriage and death. Marriage succeeds to and supplants romantic illusion as the social framework for love; but marriage is, in fact, often regularly preceded by a phased series of courtship stages, each (on the one hand) more formal and public than the prior stage, and each (on the other hand) legitimating heavier mutual demands in the realm of the personal and the private. Where courtship exists, and the patterning of legitimate premarital intimacy, we can expect to find romantic elements in the mythology, because such myths give sanction to voluntarism in sexual love; but the process of engagement is everywhere a movement from voluntarism to binding structure. The degree of intimacy which is sanctioned varies immensely—as from traditional Spain with its serenades and duennas to the frank sexuality of Trobriand youth—without affecting the predictability with which prolonged engagement with the other will lead to personal commitment and acceptance of the bonds of marriage. The process is one of a relationship gaining structural weight; it is the gradual accumulation of mutual claims, normally through a very subtle symbolic interchange, and through the mounting tendency to set precise conditions for the continuation of an emotional transaction which becomes the more intense as with time it becomes more exclusive of other emotional attachments. In some Norwegian valleys a surprising number of women bear children to their accepted lovers but are never married. The reason is not that their men are unfeeling scoundrels but that engagement there is not buttressed by formal, communal sanction.

If engagement entails the acceptance of claims, disengagement requires their settlement or abrogation. For the Fulani, divorce calls for no elaborate procedure—custom has already ensured that the marriage bond will have little more substance than that of an economic contract between two individuals. For the Trobriander, divorce is also easy in the formal sense, since the father has no jural claim upon the children, and their status as heirs to land is not dependent on the marriage, and so on. But Trobriand divorces are evidently not without emotional trauma—as personal involvement, the Trobriand marriage has typically a good deal more substance than the Fulani. Disengagement from an antagonistic involvement, where there are many particular claims to be settled, commonly calls for a system of arbitration, whether through a go-between or a truce or pact holder or by authority. Often, where it is not so much a matter of settling particular claims as of the cooling off of emotionally intense involvement, disengagement calls for solemn ritual and ceremony capable of a new engagement on the basis of amity. Peacemaking procedures are wanted wherever disengagement can't be achieved through the cessation of contact. The character of any relationship which is in being must be actually affirmed at every turn—deceit and ambiguity can't be indefinitely continued. The publicity of peace making is an effort to establish on both parts the expectation that amity will be the rule of interchange henceforth.

A BIAS TOWARD VOLUNTARISM

A great deal of behavior which *seems* to be free of a predefined structural frame is not. Obversely, no frame is so strictly sanctioned as to exclude all creativity which might have structural relevance: down in the dungeon you may have precious little effect on the king, but you may affect the character and role of the jailer, if there is any pattern at all of mutual expectation between you. The *substance* which fills the structural frame is eminently human, if not always humane. Even in anger, as in Kwaling's attack of Reamai (p. 61), social action is never insensitive to structured situation, never *merely* an expression of an internal psychic state. Similarly, action is never the wholly mechanical implementation of sanctioned obligation: if the soldier is not compulsively fitting his movements to the forms, he can't help showing that they irk him; if the typist is letter-perfect, she had best have recognition for it, or perfection will give way to error.

The most impersonal structure does not exclude personal involvement, though it may seal in men's emotions, denying them the kind of expression which might alter the structure; and the most intense personal involvement will not wholly blind men to the cold structural facts of their situation. But within such limits, social relationships are normally experienced in their aspect as human involvements rather than in their aspect as structural ties. There is a bias toward voluntarism in our perception of ourselves. No writer has been more concerned with the experience of structured relationships than Henry James. Here is a passage from "The Beast in the Jungle":

Henry James
Short Story, 1903, pp. 277–78

. . . He had no vision of her after this that was anything but darkness and doom. They had parted forever in that strange talk; access to her chamber of pain, rigidly guarded, was almost wholly forbidden him; he was feeling now moreover, in the face of doctors, nurses, the two or three relatives attracted doubtless by the presumption of what she had to "leave," how few were the rights, as they were called in such cases, that he had to put forward, and how odd it might even seem that their intimacy shouldn't have given him more of them. The stupidest fourth cousin had more, even though she had been nothing in such a person's life. She had been a feature of features in *his*, for what else was it to have been so indispensable? Strange beyond saying were the ways of existence, baffling for him the anomaly of his lack, as he felt it to be, of producible claim. A man might have been, as it were, everything to him, and it might yet present him in no connexion that anyone seemed held to recognise.

PERSONAL INVOLVEMENT/ IMPERSONAL STRUCTURE

IMPLICATIONS OF "STRUCTURAL WEIGHT"

The strength, or "structural weight," of a particular relationship has appeared in the foregoing discussion as a function of form and substance in combination. The structural weight of a tie between two persons is the probability that the tie will be honored by them—that their contacts will fall within the scope of extant mutual expectations, defining reciprocal rights, privileges, and immunities. So far as we can describe a social system by setting forth its axiomatic structure (that is, so far as the system consists in ties whose qualities and incidence are predefined), we can comprehend the social life as a mechanical system. But so far as actual affirmation —individual initiative—is a source of structure, the mechanical model fails. When you are dealing with probabilities you must turn to statistical models.

It follows that the probability of survival of a personal involvement is measured directly by its structural weight. That is, emotional involvements with others are, considered as events or episodes, ephemeral; and recurrent involvements gain, by the fact of recurrence, actual weight—expressible as a bond of mutually acknowledged personal claims. I don't doubt there is a philosophic sense in which the *natural* life of man is episodic, and sociocultural forms are always in constraint of nature. That suggests we enjoy not only civilization but even individual self-identity—the possibility of a meaningful life—by virtue of our tendency to build social structures. There are two corollaries which are of particular interest to us as we attempt to understand the principles on which structures may be vertically built up or laterally built out. First, there is the fact that axiomatic, socially predefined qualities in a relationship will need shielding and support, to prevent their being overshadowed by incongruous involvements. Second, there is the fact that ties which will have to bear an extraordinary strain will require to be strengthened by an extraordinary intensity of involvement, with a peculiarly appropriate emotional quality.

The first corollary is illustrated by the incest taboos, which are connected (especially through rules of exogamy in territorially stable communities) with the lateral building out of social structures. An incestuous involvement must occur within an axiomatic and—outside of myth—actually established tie of maximal weight. If there were no taboo of incest, the sexual involvement would come to form part of the substance of the relationship. What are the chances that the sexual involvement could be discontinued without otherwise breaking or suspending the tie? "Involvements within the tie" are practically ineradicable, short of breaking the tie itself. That follows from conceiving personal involvement as the *substance* corresponding to structural forms, and from associating structural weight with the combination of form and substance. An incest taboo is therefore a mechanism which makes it possible to exclude certain consanguine kin from the social field wherein you will seek your sexual involvement; so that one set of ties (of one special sort) can be built upon consanguinity, and another upon sexuality. Without that arrangement, the replication and hinging together of domestic groups, typical of the basic, granular structure of self-reproducing human groups, would not be feasible.

Other examples of the shielding of established ties from incongruous emotional involvements *within* the tie are all about us, though they sometimes are too easily taken for granted. In many societies sex is possessively toned, and the taboo of homosexuality (outside the kin group) protects the lightweight quality of man-to-man relations generally, on which flexibility of structure depends. Sexuality is also often excluded from master-servant (employer-employee, teacher-student, professional-client) relations. In general, role relationships must always be explicitly limited as to certain types of intimacy; looking at the same fact from the other side, persons are always granted some immunities from others in any institutional setting: there is always a boundary dividing what is tolerable from what is jurally (or morally) defined as abuse. Often, the problem is one of setting controls on power—power, after all, is not self-equilibrating. But the function of emotional insulation is at least as important: the physician is able enough to treat his own children, but not to recover from the emotional effects of a catastrophic error. The personal secretary is able enough to protect her virtue, but not to keep both that and her job, if she has no immunity from her employer's whim.

The second corollary is concerned not with limiting the structural weight of a tie but with maximizing it. Consider the phenomenon of power, first in the context of slavery and then in the context we call free. In the extreme situation, the slave need have no personal involvement with his master—the formal guarantees of obedience are so rigid that conformity is achieved out of fear. In the short run, there have been situations which approached such an extreme of mechanization. But in the long run, where the master makes no effort to win the emotional allegiance of the slave, the slave himself will yet supply that allegiance by "identification with the aggressor." That is, the utterly impersonal, utterly formal frame gives the relationship no personal substance, no motivationally relevant meaning. Since the slave or prisoner has no choice but to act as though he wanted to obey the master's every order, if there is personal proximity he must constantly exhibit the motivation of the role as his own. Evidently, it sometimes comes to be inseparable from his own, when the emotional strain is otherwise very great. Submitting wholly to the other as a person transforms the bond of slavery, at least, into a human relationship. Uncle Tom may not be a figure we respect but he is a figure we understand.

Power relationships in the "free" sector of society are not much different. In a bureaucracy, the formal sanctions on conformity are of a subtler sort than in a concentration camp or penitentiary (more like the minimum security penal institution, except that the office worker who drops out *may* gain from it). For the mass of persons who stay on, the surrender of autonomy even in routine and trivial things would be difficult if submission to the superior *person* were difficult.

One does not increase the efficiency of an office by attempting to eliminate personal feelings. Power relationships bear a special sort of strain; and a special sort of emotional involvement—which we call loyalty or allegiance—has been devised to meet that strain. The higher one goes in even the most efficient superstructure, the less is the importance of formal guarantees in maintaining the bonds of power and submission, and the greater the reliance on personal emotional involvement: must not Hitler trust his chauffeur? his valet? his second in command? Loyalty systems begin in the truth of this proposition: that we have only to ask where a man can't afford to be hated to know where he won't rest without assurance of something like love.

The second corollary applies also to lateral ties. The voluntaristic form of bourgeois marriage has always relied on romance: that is, we don't enter upon the dangerous waters of matrimony without achieving first an emotional high which is intense and lasting—comparable to the religious fervor of a young saint. Whatever difficulties such romantic illusions may foster, the mood of cold impersonality is at any rate no basis for a voluntaristic marriage. The bond is one which takes extraordinary stress, and that stress is matched only by intense involvement—the marriage, otherwise, lacks substance.

Another lateral tie which often wants strengthening is enmity. What is remarkable about war is not the strength but the weakness of the typical soldier's feelings of hostility and patriotic fervor. These feelings must be inflated lest a man lose his nerve when things get thick.

Taking the Olympian view, social structure may seem to be no more than law a respecter of persons: each should take up his role as it is laid out for him, and even make the motives of the role his own. But when we look at a social system from within we perceive that its vitality is, like that of a stage drama, never mechanically predictable. The extreme of structuralism is not better than the extreme position of romantic voluntarism. Human institutions don't suppress human passions but give them form; and the key to that form—though surely not to the nature of passion itself—is the idea of social structure, quite beyond the idea of the biopsychic individual. None the less we have argued that in the experience of life it is the substance and not the form which predominates; structure seldom obtrudes, and where it tends to, it is most often translated into personal equations. The anarchist does not simply hate the state, but reviles by name its head and its minions. The prisoner and the guard become victim and persecutor. Marriage is perceived as no impersonal bond but a balance of mutual claims and powers, commitments, lusts, and immunities. The state, the prison, the family, become for us the persons with whom we are caught up in a network of reciprocal involvements, which often run emotionally deeper than we would care to think. Something of the way structural involvement works is probably revealed only in pathology—where involvements spill out of their appointed paths. We take instances from Melanesia and Highland New Guinea.

EVENTS IN DOBU

The Dobuans, like the neighboring Trobrianders, are matrilineally organized; but their residential rule produces even less stability. On both Dobu and Tewara islands the matrilineage is a loyalty group (called the *susu*) and comprises the core of the local settlement—the "owners" of the village. You marry outside your own village but keep your land in your home territory—a man doesn't join his wife permanently in her group, nor will she join him permanently in his. The problem of cohabitation is resolved by moving back and forth, alternate years, from one *susu* village to the other. But the two villages are never friendly—the sojourn away from home is not a pleasant one.

Reo F. Fortune
Sorcerers of Dobu
Fieldwork 1930, pp. 57, 61–62

Occasionally a widower refuses to submit to mourning in his dead wife's village. He refuses to don the blackened mourning neck cord of pandanus fibre, blacken his body, eat poor food, refrain from dancing, smiling and possible intrigues with other women, and toil the while in his dead wife's kin's gardens, under a cloud in his dead wife's village. It is a hard ordeal. Nearly all men undergo it. But now and then it happens that a man is engaged in an intrigue with another woman when his wife dies. Then the ordeal appears in its worst aspect—a year's misery and drudgery. So some non-conformists go home to their own village and their freedom immediately. The village kin of the dead say: "There goes the man who did not mourn his wife" whenever they chance to meet him. It is felt as a stinging insult, but there are thick-skinned individuals. Such a man may have difficulty in getting another wife, but probably not much difficulty. Unfortunately I did not see the development of a case of a *wadai*, as this class of non-conformists are called. There is an equivalent class of women who elope with another man before their mourning for their dead husband is over.

If his children are young the widower invariably goes home to his own place after mourning, leaving them in the care of their mother's sisters and brothers, not often seeing them again. But if a child is full grown he or she may elect to desert his or her village and own dead mother's kin and follow the living father to his place. When the father dies such a child becomes boundary man and must go home to the mother's kin. In the interval between mother's death and father's death the grown child may stay most of the time in the father's place, cultivating his or her own kin by frequent visits back. In fact, I know of no case where a youth did this. But I found two cases where a grown unmarried girl was living with her father in his place after the death of the mother or her desertion by the husband. Public opinion was quite lenient to these cases, not caring whether the attachment was in part incestuous or whether it was not. If a man was *wadai*, however, such a course could hardly occur. I never saw any relevant case.

I heard of one case of son-mother incest outside my range of true knowledge. It is regarded as contamination, as father-daughter incest, or child and father's sister incest is not so seriously regarded. But greatest of all crimes, outrage of all outrages against the social system, is adultery between a man and his mother's brother's wife or a man and his sister's son's wife. Son-mother incest, after the father's death, is not interfered with actively. It is a private sin, not a public attack on the social system. Blood brother interfering with blood brother's wife, or blood brother blood sister incest I did not hear of. But I heard of two cases of trouble between sister's son and mother's brother over their wives. Here the *susu,* bulwark of Dobuan life, is rent, with difference in generation to make the matter worse. The mother's brother is guardian of the sister's son, his heir and ward. I heard of one such trouble in each group I was in—one historical case in Tewara Island, one more recent case in my locality of Dobu Island.

In Tewara a man committed adultery with his own sister's son's wife. His sister's son heard of it. He sought out his own mother's brother and drove a spear through his body killing him on the spot. The killer's mother sought out her village brothers and committed her own son to their vengeance urging them to take his blood for their and her brother's blood. His mother's village brothers so encouraged by their sister, his mother, pursued him through the island and into the sea at the straits of Gadimotu. There they hurled spears at the young man as he fled seawards until a spear thrown underwater caught him near the ankle. He collapsed and was killed. His mother went into mourning for her brother and her son. Then months after when the canoes were beached on the small island of Gabuwana many miles from home, the young true brothers of the hounded and slain young man slew the slayer who had thrown the spear which found its mark in their brother's ankle. They roasted the corpse and ate it. Other members of the party which pursued the boy trying to kill him took no vengeance on the boy's brothers for killing their brother's killer.

So the *susu* itself may be rent turning mother against son, and the village may be rent turning the young of one *susu* against the old of the other village *susu* who did no more than perform a mother's will against her son, the mother being their village sister. So, at least, runs the history vividly remembered by eyewitnesses, vividly and unmistakably told.

In Dobu Island a similar affair occurred less tragically, and under the eye of white government. A man committed adultery with his mother's brother's wife while his mother's brother was away at indentured labour. The mother's brother came back and heard of it, but not before his sister's son had left for a long term of indentured labour immediately he knew of his mother's brother's impending return. The elder man threw his wife out with scorn and passion. Several years after when the young man came back the elder was long remarried to another woman, and no word passed between them. Only one boy will say to another quietly and with much significance "I know of a man who slept with his own mother's brother's wife", with some awe and even horror in the tone. It is still a matter unforgotten. White government and indentured labour sanctuary for native crimes has taken much of the sting out of native sanctions. The culture tends to bend and weaken in action, but it still holds fast to its own ideas of right and wrong.

In the Tewara case we see exposed the strength of the brother-sister bond. A Dobuan tends to think of his sister first of all his ties when the question of breaking ties arises. Dobu practices the avunculate, inheritance from mother's brother to sister's son, but this is from no great sentiment between a man and his sister's son. Rather the sister enlists the brother in the interests of her children. Strength of sentiment obtains between brother and sister; and if a man punishes his sister's children over-severely it is his sister that expresses a sense as of a personal outrage upon her. In a village where a man has beaten his wards, their attitude is comparatively stoical. They may cry a little, but long after their crying has ceased one hears their mother wailing the lament that is otherwise only wailed over the dead.

In Dobu society, kinship and marriage are mixed with politics and local rivalry. Private and public trust are scarcely distinguished, and trust itself is at a premium. A man soon learns where it can and can't be placed—what ties will bear stress. Trust is vested not in *persons* but in *roles:* every Dobu woman can be trusted—by her brothers. The incidence of incest suggests a turning away, probably through hurt and suspicion, from distant contacts and a resort instead to sexual involvement within the consanguineal tie. The man who killed his mother's brother was outraged because this was one of the few men he *should* have been able to trust; the woman who exacted revenge on her son for the killing was moved by the same sort of betrayal. The psychology of social structure is a subject anthropology has only begun to touch; but there is such a subject, and it will take us deeply into the dynamics of human character. The Tewara killings were not so much *prescribed* by the social structure as *predestined*—if it were appropriately told, the tale would easily achieve the mood of solemn myth. For the Dobuan, it is a tale of rending involvement within the network of intimate ties attributed to nature. For us the level on which the tale can be explained is that of social structure interplaying with human character. There is no betrayal unless there is prior trust; there is no depth of feeling where there is no prior involvement; there is no involvement except through contact, the placing of claims on the other's loyalty. The Tewara tale is conditioned by the structure of trust and distrust in the society; none of the actions would make sense in a different culture. And the tale reminds us that what we mean by social structure is not a sterile set of norms according to which men behave for want of imagination and the sense for freedom, but structure in the dramatic sense: what happened had to happen, being ordained by what had gone before.

IN HIGHLAND NEW GUINEA

An important facet of the social structure of the mountain people called Kapauku (in the Central Highlands of Netherlands New Guinea) is egalitarianism. It is implicitly, not formally, guaranteed. In each village there will normally be one man who is recognized as the most powerful and can be called the headman; but he has only the power of one who can *actually* dominate others—he has no *given* power: that is, no constituted authority. He must maintain his position by generosity and by success in settling disputes; he must also stay rich, but avoid unpopularity on the score of his riches. The cases of Juw and Dimi show how an egalitarian balance is kept through a pattern of recurrent political involvement.

Leopold Pospisil
Highland New Guinea
Fieldwork 1954–55
Kapauku Papuans and Their Law, pp. 80, 244–45, 109–10

JUW: THE EXECUTION OF A RICH MAN

A man who steals from others, borrows without repaying, acquires money under false pretenses rather than through honest business deals, or a selfish individual who hoards money and does not lend it, never sees the time when his word will be taken seriously and his advice and decisions followed, no matter how rich he may become. The people believe that the only justification for becoming rich is to be able to redistribute the accumulated property among one's less fortunate fellows, a procedure which also gains their support. Thus, the emphasis upon capital and the acquisition of money is balanced by the highest value of the culture, "*ba cpi*, generosity." In the Kamu Valley, the rich men who fail to comply with this requirement are ostracised, reprimanded and thereby induced to become generous. In the Paniai Lake region, the people go so far as to kill a selfish rich man because of his "immorality." His own sons or brothers are induced by the rest of the members of the community to dispatch the first deadly arrow: "*Aki to tonowi beu, inii idikima enadani kodo to niitou* (you should not be the only rich man, we all should be the same, therefore you only stay equal with us)" was the reason given by the Paniai people for killing Mote Juw of Madi, a *tonowi* who was not generous enough. The people also resented the fact that his son who executed his "immoral" father was put into prison by the white man's police. It did not matter that he was sentenced for only three months.

Due to the fact that the highest status in the culture is achievable through the much publicized lending of money and that the hoarding of wealth for its own sake is considered unethical and is punishable by reprimands, ostracism and gossip, the people, although very willing to discuss their loans, are rather secretive about their cash. They are secretive so that no one can ask them for a loan or charge them with selfishness. A rich man in Kapauku society wears the same clothes as others, eats only a little better, and when he kills a pig he distributes all the meat without tasting a single piece. His house is large, but not because he would like to display his wealth; it is his many wives, children, "helping boys" and friends living in the *tonowi's* house who require for their own welfare a larger structure.

Juw was a very wealthy man but he failed to lend out his property in proportion to his fortune. People of his village, dissatisfied with the state of affairs, spoke to the paternal parallel cousins of the man and persuaded them to kill the culprit. They, in turn, talked to the man's eldest son who agreed to join them in the execution of his own father. He was promised a pig and 20 Km for his participation.

When the rich man was working in his garden, five men approached him and started to discharge their bamboo-tipped arrows into his body. His son was the first who shot him. Then his two paternal parallel cousins shot and finally two other men followed with their arrows. The executioners built a scaffold for the dead man and smeared their faces with ashes and soot, thus expressing grief over the necessary action. To avoid the vengeance of the dead man's "*tene,* the departed shadow," they slept for two nights in the bush. On the third day they came back to the village where they killed a pig of the dead man and distributed the meat to all people who came. The killers divided the dead man's property among themselves.

DIMI: A CASE FOR MAGICAL EXECUTION

Although today Botukebo presents the picture of a solid political unit under the uncontested leadership of Awi its affairs were different only two years ago when two people competed for primacy in the village. The internal strife was manifested by two political factions whose leaders were the present headman and Dimi of Botukebo. The latter was an eloquent and brave man. He was also very rich and had five wives. Rich and brave as he was, he could not match Awi in eloquence and number of wives. Although he tried very hard to become a headman and was ready at any time to contest the right in a stick fight, he never succeeded in "unseating" his opponent. This was mainly because Dimi failed to comply with the basic moral requirement for the *maagodo tonowi's* position. He was not only more selfish than the present headman, but he delighted in embezzling money, in borrowing under false pretenses, and he very seldom returned in full what he had borrowed. Consequently, only twelve people offered him support in his disputes, while Awi succeeded in rallying behind himself exactly twice the number of his opponent's helpers. Only close relatives helped Dimi, and even they did so only because of the kinship ties. All of them admitted that their late leader was a dishonest man and a troublemaker. "We had to help him in a stick fight. We knew he was wrong, but we felt sorry for the poor fellow who was left alone."

In the event of a stick fight, an impartial household sent half of its males to one side and half to the other. Consequently, Timaajokaimopaj and Timaajokaipouga, although identical twins, found themselves on opposite sides. "We never fought each other, of course. We just picked personal enemies who happened to be fighting for the other side and gave them a thorough thrashing." Thus, most of the fighting force had "combat motives" completely unrelated to the official cause of trouble. We may call this splitting up of households, which gives a fair chance to both sides, a Kapauku sense of sportsmanship.

In the long run, of course, Dimi suffered by distrust, ostracism, and a lack of people who would trust him or conclude business agreement with him. He sustained several public reprimands from Awi, who was supported by headmen from the other sublineages and lineages of the confederacy. Practically all the headmen of the confederacy finally decided on Dimi's execution. To make the execution as simple as possible, all of the headmen tried black magic. Thus, throngs of helping evil spirits and *tene* were believed to be attacking the body of the bad man until finally they succeeded in expelling the soul. Dimi died of pneumonia during the summer of 1953. There were not many people who wept. On the contrary, the name of the dead man is recalled in a derogatory way in most of the public reprimands administered today by the headman of the confederacy: "You are almost like Dimi. You had better change your ways or you will perish as he did." Strong is the magical power of the moral Ijaaj headmen!

There are few societies more informally structured than the Kapauku; yet the anthropologist Leopold Pospisil, by deliberately questioning the people about the settling of disputes, getting their statements as to ideal rules and comparing those with actual cases, codified a body of Kapauku "laws." Execution might be justified on egalitarian grounds alone. Here is another example.

Rule 117: If a man causes war by crime, and if there is much . . . loss of life among the home people, the culprit should be killed.[15]

Such a loosely formulated law, particularly in the absence of professional or representative jurors, leaves freedom of interpretation to those who become involved; it is a poor specimen of a law, from a lawyer's point of view. As a clue

[15] Pospisil, p. 245.

to one of the recurrent patterns of involvement which help to keep Kapauku society what it is, Pospisil's Rule 117 has the value of a descriptive generalization, based on informant statements and supported by some case evidence. Yet it is the sort of law which clearly substitutes for a more effective formal arrangement—a structure which might provide the means for negotiating a settlement with the enemy by some less drastic means. Kapauku society relies heavily upon informal, *ad hoc* actions by small groups who can count on the support of public opinion; in short, recurrent involvements fall into a pattern which serves to maintain social control in the absence of clearly constituted authority. With more formal structure, order would presumably be better kept.

The superstructure of Kapauku politics does not tower very high; the confederacy is loosely knit, hardly stronger than its weakest ties. But it reminds us that the central function of politics is in managing competition and conflict on the higher levels of structure. If the anthropologist has shown a tendency, moreover, to write of structure as though it consisted wholly of firm bonds, stabilized by functional differentiation and complementarity, the Kapauku, Tangu (p. 56), Dobu (p. 219), and Ndembu (p. 43) may serve in some measure as antidote. We are drawn into society, and out of ourselves and our families, as much by threat as by promise, as much by rivalry and conflict as by aspiration. From time to time the larger drama is sure to sweep us out on the public stage. It is through personal involvement, whether in anger or in lust, whether in altruistic mood or in secret search of gain, that we become subject to the claims of others and put demands in turn upon them—that we become an agent of society's structure. In great measure, the freedom we have in any society is only to withdraw, hold back, or to become involved. We can do little in the short run to alter the structure of the drama into which we would be drawn. Yet it is, paradoxically, by being drawn in that we become a part of the process of the making and breaking of structure; for in the long run involvement is the creative process and structure the result.

SECTION TWO

CASE STUDIES IN AUTHORITY AND CREDENCE

ANUAK OF THE SUDAN

Godfrey Lienhardt
Anuak Studies in Southeastern Sudan
Fieldwork 1952–54
"Anuak Village Headmen," Selected Passages

HEADMEN AND VILLAGE CULTURE

The Anuak are a Nilotic people of the south-east of the Sudan and adjacent Ethiopia. They may number between 30,000 and 40,000 people, of whom at least two thirds live in Ethiopia, where a number of difficulties prevented me from visiting them. Two somewhat different political systems and forms of rule and leadership are found in the villages of Anuakland. In the south-east, several ecological and other circumstances have favoured the spread of the influence of a noble clan, members of which reign in villages which, according to tradition, were at one time politically isolated from each other and autonomous under local headmen. These villages of the noble clan are drawn, through the nobles associated with them, into competition for the acquisition of a single set of royal emblems, of which the most important are several ancient bead-necklaces. It seems that the influence of this noble clan has spread and is even now spreading farther among the villages of Anuakland, though in the land as a whole most villages are still under the sway of headmen chosen from lineages which traditionally provided them. It is with the organization of these villages, and the way in which their members change their headmen, that this paper deals.

I first describe some features of Anuak village life and culture which are relevant to a study of the *agem,* the village "rebellion" by which Anuak villagers frequently change their headmen. Later, I consider Anuak village structure, and examine in some detail one particular example of the removal of a headman in a village in which I lived for a considerable time.

The Anuak are certainly among the least-administered people of the Southern Sudan, and as far as I could gather they are equally free from the control of any central government in Ethiopia. Even the administrative centre of Akobo, on the Sudan side, cannot exercise such control as might be expected over nearby Anuak villages, since dissident individuals and factions can with ease withdraw across the river into Ethiopia. These circumstances have favoured the continuance, if sometimes in modified form, of the Anuak custom of expelling unpopular headmen, despite the inconvenience of such frequent changes for a system of modern administration. I emphasize from the beginning this relative freedom of the Anuak from administration because it deeply affects the position of headmen even now, when they are treated as the official representatives of their villages in relation to the Sudan Government. They still depend, to a far greater extent than "official chiefs" in other parts of the Southern Sudan, upon maintaining a polity in accordance with their traditional view of the headman's office.

The villages of the north and west of Sudan Anuakland are situated for the most part in open savannah, which is widely flooded in the wet season. The villages are very clearly defined spatially, with stretches of uninhabited country between them. For the most part, in this region of Anuakland, they are built near the banks of rivers, where they vary in compactness according to the area of higher ground which they have at their disposal. Probably few villages have more than 300 inhabitants, and those I have visited had little more than 200. Some villages are extremely compact, and present to the eye a single dense cluster of small compounds, with the gardens of their owners stretching out around this central settlement. Others consist of several separate and distinct little hamlets, of from two or three to twenty homesteads each, separated from each other by their gardens, the whole occupying two or three square miles of land. Some villages in Ethiopia are said still to be stockaded, and there are the remains of a stockade and earthwork, similar to that even now in use at the Ethiopian frontier-post of Tiergol, at the village of Debango in Sudan Anuakland.

The Anuak are now primarily an agricultural people with few cattle, though there are indications of ancient pastoral interests in their elaborate vocabulary of cattle-colour names. Sheep and goats are kept in relatively small numbers. Neither they, nor cattle, accumulate for an Anuak as they do for the Nuer or Dinka, since they are often slaughtered for feasting. The essential parts of bridewealth payments are certain old beads and spear-heads, and the range of kin over which these are collected and distributed is relatively narrow. The only economic activities which require the cooperation of groups of people larger than the members of an individual homestead are occasional hunting forays, the erection of fishing-dams at certain seasons of the year, and special services to the headman of the village which will be described later. Of these, none is absolutely essential on economic grounds alone; it is quite possible for an Anuak family in isolation to produce for itself the material requirements of life.

The Anuak never speak of the villages of different headmen combining for aggressive action. Moreover, among the headmen's villages, there is no common political value (such as the royal emblems in the villages under the influence of nobles) which might give rise to competition and hostility. The spatial separation of villages prevents any quarrel over boundaries, and inter-village raiding would offer little to those taking part in it, compared with the booty in children, women, and cattle which the Anuak have in the past seized from the neighbouring Murle.

As the remains of stockading and the compactness of settlements suggest, the village is regarded primarily as a defensive unit, offering protection against Nuer raids, Murle reprisals, and perhaps also, in the past, against raiding parties from Ethiopia. Individual Anuak and small parties of companions travel widely in search of beads and other goods which are necessary for marriage, and which may be obtained by elaborate series of judicious exchanges of a purely commercial kind, which take advantage intelligently of relative scarcities of particular commodities in different parts of the country. Almost every Anuak knows of someone who has disappeared completely on such a journey, and it is assumed that he has been murdered or has settled permanently elsewhere. It is not difficult for a man to attach himself, through a headman or a noble whose prestige he involves in his protection, to a community other than his own village. Village affiliation as such thus ceases to count for much politically outside the immediate vicinity of the village, and, as Professor Evans-Pritchard has pointed out, there are no ecological factors, such as the transhumance of the Nuer and Dinka, which would favour the development of political relations over a wider field. In an analysis of the institution of headmanship in northern and western Anuakland, it is thus the internal affairs of each Anuak village which are primarily significant, though headmen have some significance in such inter-village relations as exist, as we later describe.

A description of certain features of the arrangement of each homestead and village indicates aspects of Anuak social life and values which are of importance for an understanding of headmanship and rebellion. Each homestead consists of two or three sleeping- and living-huts grouped around a small central courtyard. Its principal occupants are likely to be a man, with his wife or wives and some of their children, with such other kin as may be temporarily or permanently living with them.

There is often a refinement in construction in the form of a fenced-in veranda (*agola*) running round the hut. This is used for storing pots and gourds, and also as a shelter for visitors in rainy weather. It can be quickly removed to open a field of fire for the occupants, if necessary. In the courtyard a small hut or shelter is erected for cooking. Huts and courtyard are screened by a grass fence (*kal*), some five feet high, which is erected against the public paths of the village. The side of the homestead facing the gardens is often unscreened, but only members of the family, or enemies, would approach the home from that direction. The entrance to the enclosure is further screened, so that it is impossible for a passer-by to see into the courtyard through its entrance, or in any other way than by conspicuously peering over the fence. This would be extremely ill-mannered and suspicious behaviour for anyone who was not an intimate of the family. This form of construction gives an Anuak family, though living at very close quarters with its neighbours, a measure of personal privacy which, in my experience, no Dinka or Nuer expects.

The Anuak clearly regard the homestead as offering a series of possibilities of withdrawal, for there is a well-known story which tells how the Ethiopians first ask permission to shelter from the rain outside the fence, then ask if they may move inside, then beg to be admitted to the veranda, and finally occupy the hut, so that its owner is forced to leave it to them. The story is referred to proverbially, and is an indication of the way in which, the Anuak suppose, strangers may grow to importance in an Anuak village at the expense of their hosts. The possibility of privacy, together with the secrecy and plotting which can accompany it, is of importance for an understanding of the conduct of internal politics in an Anuak village.

Outside the fence of the homestead are the well-made granaries raised on piles; and outside the entrance to the courtyard there is a hearth (*wic mac*–literally 'headfire') for its menfolk and male visitors. This hearth is often marked by two forked branches standing a few feet apart. They are used as spear-rests, and between them a fire is kindled each evening. Skins are brought out, and men sit there until bed-time chatting, smoking, and watching the life of the village. It is at their exterior hearths that men discuss openly those matters which they choose to make public. More delicate schemes and negotiations, such as those for the removal of headmen, demand the privacy of the hut.

Each homestead thus indicates, by its physical arrangement, that a clear line is drawn between the private life of each domestic group and its participation in the public life of the village. A number of homesteads of the sort we have described, often with a little group of trees planted for shade, and consisting of related families of a small lineage and their kin, makes a hamlet. A few hamlets, distinguished from each other either by place-names or by the lineage-names of their principal inhabitants, together form a settlement. They do not form a village, completely furnished with the social amenities of village life, unless they are grouped around a traditional lineage of headmen, from which successive headmen are chosen. There are little settlements without headmen in Anuakland, but they consist of people who have formed a colony from some original village with its headman's homestead and court. This forms the centre of village social life, and differs from the other homesteads in ways we now describe.

The homestead of a village headman has a distinctive arrangement of quarters on the same principle as that of the homesteads of nobles, though somewhat less elaborate. Its constituent huts are not usually more numerous than in the homestead of any prosperous villager, but they tend to be rather larger and more solidly constructed, though not approaching the more fortlike qualities of the residences of important nobles in south-eastern Anuakland. What clearly marks the headman's homestead from the others is a profusion of decorative posts which support its fence. These posts (*dikweri*, so called after the horns of the waterbuck) are erected and carved by the villagers. The carving, which appears on the part of the posts which rises above the grass of the fence which they support, consists only of deeply incised rings and notches, sometimes upon single supports and sometimes upon supports which branch like the horns from which they get their name; but in their profusion they are not unimposing. Upon them are placed the horns and skulls of beasts killed for feasts given by the headman to his people. Bits of elephant-tail and hair from other large game found or killed on the headman's land, are also attached to the posts, while the most up-to-date headman of the Anuak, whose village is near Akobo, had in my time decorated his posts with the discarded headlamps of a government vehicle.

Buildings in the headman's homestead are known by names other than those in normal use for buildings which serve the same purpose in the homes of ordinary villagers. The sleeping hut of the senior wife is called the *pan dwong*, literally "the big home", and there is a special dining-hut (*ajom*) in a separate small courtyard. In this courtyard, the meat of the headman is on certain occasions cooked by boys and young men, though normally the headman is cooked for by his wives.

The immediate vicinity of the homestead of a headman, which has a special name (*labo kwaro*), is an area in which specially respectful behaviour of a kind later described is required. The sleeping hut of a headman also has a special name (*owinyo*), and his cooking shelter is called *amoa* (from *moa* "flour") while such shelters in ordinary homesteads are *abila*. Most important is the exterior hearth of the headman's homestead, the *wic mac* of ordinary men, which in the case of the headmen becomes a place of reception, or court, for villagers and guests. It is called *burra,* which may be connected with the *bur* or *jobur*, meaning "the people who traditionally own the village". It is partly surrounded by a fence like those of the courtyards of ordinary homesteads, but better-constructed and decorated with carved posts. On one side, it leads directly into the headman's own courtyard, from which it is divided by a fence and screen, and it opens on to the main dancing-ground of the village. Although partly open to the public places of the village, it is not treated as a thoroughfare and, unless they are visiting the headman, villagers do not pass through it in the course of daily movement to and from the gardens. The partial screening of the headman's court is so arranged that people may pass the court behind a screen, and avoid the ceremonial stooping which is necessary when passing the line of vision of the headman. This type of court, which is characteristic of the villages under the rule of headmen, does not seem to be a feature of the homesteads of ruling nobles, who receive guests in a special reception hut. Further, the numerous carved posts or *dikweri* with which the screens of a headman's homestead are decorated are not characteristic of the homes of nobles.

Besides the special terms we have mentioned, there are several others which are used only in relation to headmen and things connected with them. This "court vocabulary" of the headmen resembles in most details the court vocabulary of the nobles, though there are several significant differences. Most of the words of nobles' court language are, however, known to the headmen and their followers, and it is sometimes hard to decide whether or not informants have provided a term from the court language of nobles and applied it to headmen, in order to further dignify the headman and his court. Certain differences between headmen's and nobles' court language make it clear that neither is a mere imitation of the other.

The use of a special, if small, vocabulary in reference to those things most frequently used and touched by the headman contributes to the setting apart of the headman from ordinary villagers. The Anuak, who are mercurial in temperament and frequently aggressive and truculent, appear to enjoy the formalities connected with the *kar* or *kal boge,* "the place of leaves", as the headman's court is called in court language. It is so called because the headman in his court sits on the finest skins in the village, and a skin in court language is *bogo,* literally "leaf". A headman will not sit on the bare ground, and even headmen who have been ostracized from their own villages, and are living without following elsewhere, maintain this state.

Headmen never appear barefoot, for the removal of sandals is a sign of inferiority in status, and they do not observe the customs of ceremonial respect (*wudo*) for various categories of affinal relatives which are followed by ordinary men. Most striking at the headman's court is the ceremonial low-bowing posture (*gungi*), almost a crouch, adopted when approaching the headman or crossing his line of vision. Where men bow low, women proceed on their knees; and men also approach the headman in his court on their knees. These courtesies are shown to all headmen in their courts, and to ostracized headmen at the courts of those with whom they are staying. Travelling Anuak show perhaps more respect at the courts of headmen in villages other than their own than they show at home. It is the institution of headmanship, and not the particular headman, which prompts the ceremonial behaviour we have described.

The Anuak pride themselves upon these formalities of village life, which they contrast with the comparative informality of Nuer behaviour, and it is clear that for the most part they enjoy acting their parts in village ceremonial. The appropriate courtesies are also sanctioned by the collective action which villagers may take against individuals who lose their tempers and choose to neglect them. While a headman is in favour with the village as a whole, his people may seize a fine from anyone who fails in politeness, and perhaps bind the culprit and beat him. This is not done either at the headman's order or at his direct request; he can only draw attention to the offence, and leave it to his people to take action. A beast seized as a fine in such circumstances is not the property of the headman, but of the village, and it is slaughtered to provide a feast for the villagers.

GATHERING AND HOLDING A FOLLOWING

I have not seen the ceremony of creating a following, which the Anuak call *kwany ki lwop* or *kwany ki luobo*, *kwany* meaning "to gather". As the Anuak describe it, it is relevant to the type of prestige which the headman enjoys, and I therefore briefly mention here what I was told about it.

The Anuak do not have highly formalized age-sets, and there is no initiation ceremony, like the head-scarification of the Nuer and Dinka, by which it is possible to draw a strict line between youths and (in the social sense) adult men. When a group of youths of about the same age and in the same village are recognized (informally as among ourselves) to have grown to manhood, they select from the older and richer men of the village one whom they wish to make their leader or, more correctly, sponsor. This man is called their *kwai lwak*. The term *kwai* may be translated as "owner", and may be related to *kwayo*, "ancestor", and *lwak* is related to *lwaga*, "cattle-byre". If the man they have chosen agrees (and it is expected that he will be honoured to do so) they settle at his homestead or spend much of the day there, feasting on beasts which he has slaughtered and beer which he provides. In return, they may help him to hoe his cultivations and decorate his homestead with one or two of the carved posts similar to those found in much larger numbers on the fences of the headman's homestead. The *kwai lwak*, thereafter called the "sponsor" of this group of young men, gives them a name which is usually taken from some incident in the history of the village closely associated with their coming to maturity. The last *lwak* or age-group of Omeeda village, for example, is called Bong Dhiang, "no cows", because at the time of its creation the Government took energetic measures to prevent the raiding of Murle cattle.

Each age-group chooses its own sponsor, who must be a man of substance, with the result that each village consists of the age-groups of several different men, some living and some dead. A *lwak* may span five or six years, though now the system is difficult to observe on the Sudan side of the border at least, where it is breaking down, possibly as an indirect result of the difficulties of raiding cattle, and the consequent difficulty of providing feasts.

It is said that from time to time, perhaps every ten or fifteen years, a rich headman will *kwany ki lwop:* that is, he will gather together an army of men consisting of the junior age-groups extant in the village. Not every age-group is so honoured, and it seems that this creation of a headman's own following can only occur when the village is very prosperous and when particularly large numbers of young men are to be found in the junior age-groups. The *lwop* is in effect a temporary army of retainers bound specially to the headman himself. They settle for a period around his court, cook for themselves the beasts which he slaughters for them, and dance before him. Anuak say that when a *lwop* is first created, it can take control of the village, seizing the goods of those individuals who fall foul of it, dominating the dance with the type of self-display which we later describe, and enhancing its own and the headman's prestige by repairing his court and homestead. In the dance, members of the new *lwop* of the headman may be followed by other members of the village bearing torches to light up their handsomeness and prowess. They hoe a cultivation for the headman, and provide a male cook to prepare food for him at their feasts, which, however, he eats in privacy.

When the headman is no longer able to maintain them at his homestead, they disperse, and eventually cease to have any corporate existence except in the dance, when members of the same *lwak* enter and dance together. Eventually, however, as the village population changes and strangers come in while villagers leave, the principle upon which people combine in the dance is the more general one of age-grades (*tieng*), which are informal groupings of people of about the same generation. A rich headman thus establishes a relationship with the rising generation of the village, combining and welding to the headmanship age-groups formed by various different sponsors; and we suggest that there is a correspondence between this principle and that by which the various lineage factions of the village are temporarily agreed on the choice and support of a headman.

It is not every headman, nor any headman for the whole tenure of his office, who will have the support of a little army of the kind here described. The Anuak are quite ruthless in their treatment of past benefactors, once the immediate gratification of their desire for feasting and display can no longer be provided. Further, in the provision of bounty, it is the recipients and not the benefactor who are thought to render the greater honour. This point is of great importance for an understanding of village-headmanship, and explains why Europeans are often bound to regard the Anuak as mercenary. The prestige which a great man receives on account of his generosity is of more value to him than the material goods which he is bound lavishly to dispense in order to obtain it.

In internal polity, the headman cannot rely for long upon the swaggering support of a private army which he has created. In Anuak political theory (and the small scale of village politics does not reduce their intensity or subtlety) a successful headman must therefore be cunning as well as generous and dignified, and his diplomacy consists in part in maintaining within the village an adequate information service. It is in this connection that the possibilities of privacy and secrecy, which we earlier mentioned in relation to the physical layout of an Anuak village, become really important.

Headmen must spend much time receiving guests and talking to their people at their courts, from which it is not wise for them to absent themselves too frequently. Consequently, in order to transact necessary business in outlying hamlets of their villages or in other villages, they rely upon messengers (*nyiatwel*) chosen from among those of their followers whom they can really trust. The messenger also collects information about the village and on his return informs the headman and those who attend upon him. Within the village itself, there are informants (*nyimong*, from *mong*, a secret) though these are not in my experience regarded as court officials. Anyone who has private conversations with the headman is regarded as his *nyimong*, and if a plot to remove a headman is suspected, any representative of the party favouring the headman in power naturally retails to him such information as he has collected. Anuak say that such spies may stand quietly at the wall of a hut in order to hear what is being spoken of within.

Similar indications are given by traditions of the behaviour and policy of headmen in the past when, many

Anuak assert, they were more cunning and more careful than they now need to be in the security of a small measure of official government support. I was told that in the past headmen would send out their messengers through the village to visit any man who was sick. A messenger would wait in the homesteads of the dying to hear their last words, and stick a fishing-spear of the headman's in the grave to indicate that the last words had been officially heard by the headman's messenger. A man's last testament is of very great importance among the Anuak, for his dying wishes and intentions are thought to be extremely potent. This tradition of the behaviour of headmen in the past (for so far as I could find out nothing of the kind happens today) was explained as referring to the headman's desire to be sure that no one should curse him in his dying wishes. A man who dies with a grudge and a curse is believed to haunt, perhaps to death, those whom he has cursed. Where such a curse was uttered by a dying man upon the headman, I was told, the other villagers would despoil the homestead of the man responsible, seizing his property from his family. Then, in order to meet debts, his family would have to break some of their marriages in order to receive back the bridewealth.

It is said that after a raid the headman receives all the spoils, no matter how great, and from them selects what he wants for himself before distributing the rest among the villagers. In fact, from my own observation of the division of a game-animal by a headman, I should say that the Anuak would never tolerate an inequitable distribution in the headman's favour; for when a game-animal is so divided, it is the headman who eventually is left the worst provided for. A native comment on this distribution of spoils by the headman is of interest. An Anuak told me that, in the distribution, you might if you were unlucky receive little or nothing, even if the spoils were great; while if you were lucky, even if you yourself had seized nothing at all in the raid, you might receive a large reward. This gamble involved in relations with greater men (and it enters even more into the relations of the nobles with their followers) seems to exhilarate the Anuak. Their appetite, in all things, is for magnificence of gesture (as will later appear in reference to the dance), and they will impoverish themselves in order to attain this. There is no calculation (at least while a headman is popular) of the balance between the gifts which he makes to them and the services which they render to him. They receive as of right, and give and serve as of grace.

It is said that in the past a headman would not sleep at night, but would wander round the village hearing what was said and on the lookout for plots to ostracize him. He would even go so far, according to this report, as to leave some token of his visit in the grass near a homestead in which he had overheard something he disliked. The next day he would then have the drum beaten to draw people to his court, and when they were assembled, would address them in some such words as these: "People of my home, I am talking with this man [whose hostile comment he had overheard] because there is one small matter which I have to mention to him. Children of my lineage, I was walking about the village yesterday evening, and I found this man speaking my name thus and thus. And now I have nothing more to say in this business, it is your affair. You will hear nothing more of it from me, it is left to you." Then perhaps the people would seize the culprit and bind him and take a fine from him. Sometimes also, it is said, the headman would go at night to the homestead of a man whose attitude towards him he disliked, and splash his hand in a gourd of water. The man, within his hut, thinking that a dog was lapping from a gourd in the homestead, would cry out abuse such as the Anuak use to chase away animals from their cooking-pots. The headman would then later allege that he himself had been thus insulted.

THE BASES OF RESPECT IN ANUAKLAND

Professor Evans-Pritchard, with his experience of the Anuak in Ethiopia as well as those of the Sudan, has recorded that the headman nowhere seems to wield an authority which would enable him to control his people against their will. My more limited observations amply confirm this, and indeed it is part of the view of headmanship which the Anuak themselves openly express. They never leave the headman in any doubt that it is for their benefit (that is, the benefit of the village) that he is invested with the dignity of office and that the court and its ceremonies and social entertainments are maintained. A headman who is beginning to lose popularity may in fact be subtly insulted in various ways. People will remove their sandals a little nearer to his home than they would when his influence was greater, and their crouching as they pass him becomes more perfunctory, not sufficiently discourteous to be outrageous, but sufficiently so to be slightly demeaning for him. He can do nothing about this in these circumstances, for the minimum necessary formality is preserved, and it is only when the villagers act for him, on behalf of the village and not on his personal account, that he can resent the slights of individuals.

Paradoxically, but typically of the Anuak, however, they profess admiration for a strong headman, and there is a certain ambivalence of attitude in the way in which the Anuak near Akobo sometimes speak of the severity with which the Ethiopian headmen of the Gila river are supposed to treat individuals who have displeased them. Almost certainly such stories are much exaggerated, but they are significant in that they indicate the almost impossible combination of qualities which an ideal headman is thought to possess. He must not be "soft" (*mol*), yielding to everybody, for that is to be contemptible himself and to make his village contemptible in the eyes of others. I think I am right too in suggesting that *mol* in this connection has something of the sense of "insipid", as we apply that word to character. The Anuak easily lose interest in leaders or figureheads who have not the personality to supply them with drama, and whose evenness of temper gives them nothing to talk about, and truculence (*wini*) is a quality that in some circumstances they admire. Certainly the ordinary man would resent being referred to as *mol,* even in the sense of "gentle", far more than being referred to as *wini;* for a person who is *wini* is also, as we should say, "spirited". A headman who is truculent, however, will soon offend some powerful faction within his village (as in the case of a headman referred to in the second part of this article). Thus, in the Anuak view, what is most necessary in a successful headman, after great generosity, is a quality they call *atiedi,* which might be translated a "composure". It means, however, more than this. A *dhano mo tiedi,* a person who is *tiedi,* is one who appears to have reserves of strength, who keeps his head, who has the manner and habit of authority. He is the sort of person to whom people will listen. Such is the character of the ideal headman; and, in fact, people judge him according to their pursuit of their own interests, and a man who is too truculent or too insipid in one situation and from the point of view of one faction, may not evoke this criticism from another faction. While a headman is successful in retaining his position within the village, he correctly judges how far to yield, and how far to assert himself, when to dominate and when to be dominated by the people with whom he is dealing. If he is always dominated, he is insipid; if he is always dominating, he is truculent. To watch a headman in his court is to see how, in effect, he woos the villagers when they seem capricious and difficult, while they in turn submit to him in observing the formalities of the court, in occasional services rendered in his gardens, and in songs and dances in his honour.

The relations between a reigning headman and his people in fact resemble, in some aspects, the relations between the sexes in Anuakland, in which a similar alternation of dominance and submission is observable. The headman (as we later exemplify from his part in the dance) stands in relation to his people as husbands stand to wives, and as lovers stand to the girls they wish to please. Women approach their men-folk on their knees, as men approach the headman. The husband is expected to provide food and clothing for his wives, and the headman is expected to do so for his villagers to the limit of his capacity. A headman will not eat with or before his people, as an Anuak husband does not eat with or before his wife. In these ways (and in others more explicit in the relations of nobles with their people) the formal submissiveness of the people to the headman they have themselves chosen is a heightened form of the behaviour of women to their husbands. I have heard a poor youth say that, in order to make his fortune, he "would go to the court of a headman or a noble, and become like a wife to him".

But the outward respect which women show to men, and particularly wives to husbands, in Anuak society, is only superficially docile. In ways I do not here describe, married women exercise a great deal of power over their husbands; and unmarried girls are extremely capricious and difficult with their lovers. To court a girl is a very exacting matter for an Anuak—far more exacting than in Dinka or Nuer custom. Every submissiveness is required from him by the intended bride and her family. Her mother sends the suitor on long and often unnecessary errands, while many are the Anuak stories of maltreatment at the hands of prospective fathers-in-law. When a new wife is brought into a village, the young men have to go and make her many presents before she will consent to drink its water, and I have seen the calculation, and even apparent rapacity, with which the spokeswoman of such a wife has continued her demands for gifts. If the villagers are as women in relation to the headman, it is as Anuak women, whose outwardly submissive formal demeanour belies the actual extent of their control over and demands upon their menfolk.

CEREMONY AS AFFIRMATION OF STRUCTURE

The nature of this relationship between headmen and people is represented in dramatic form in the dance. The headman, as we describe in the second part of this article, has in his keeping the village drums. He may have had them made and paid for them, but they are nevertheless characteristically regarded as the property of the whole village. In these circumstances, in 1949, a case was brought to the Akobo court, in which a deposed chief had sold one of the village drums. He was required to return it to his successor in office. Outside the headman's court is the dancing ground of the village, and this is, for an Anuak, associated with the major pleasures and purpose of village life. In these days, when the Anuak village in the Sudan has little protective or defensive function, and for one reason or another small hamlets have grown up as colonies of the older villages, it is towards the drums and dancing-ground of the parent village that the outlying people will look with regret.

The headman's permission is required for a dance, and he will not allow small groups of young men to take out the drums and play them unless he judges that the village as a whole is anxious for a dance. Then, the drums are taken out and beaten, the girls arrive and start singing, and finally the men, who dress themselves elaborately for the occasion with scraps of coloured cloth and bells, enter the dance, where they are chosen as partners by the girls before whom they have displayed themselves. This is the usual dance at night, and the headman may watch it but does not, in my experience, take part. It is nevertheless a headman's dance, which means, for the Anuak, that if a fight should break out, the headman will intervene, and if a homicide should occur, compensation may have to be paid.

In the past there was also another kind of dance, which is of importance for an understanding of the full social significance of the headman's dance. This was a dance called *agaanya,* which the Government has now proscribed.

The significant features of the *agaanya* dance were that it was held away from the homestead of the headman, and with a drum which one of its participants had had made privately. The dancers did not, as in the official dance, retain the partners they had chosen. Instead, men would cut in on each other during the dance, and latecomers would try to wrest their partners from those who were already dancing. This gave rise to much fighting and many people are said to have been killed. No compensation was payable for homicide at the *agaanya* dance, for it was not a headman's dance with the village drums. It seems in fact to have been a type of orgiastic behaviour, inverting the principles of order found in the headman's dance. An Anuak said that dancers for the *agaanya* crept stealthily to the dancing-place "like thieves and like witches"—an indication of the explicitly antisocial principle of this dance. The *agaanya* and the headman's dance seen in relation to each other correspond to individual self-assertion in relation to the communal interest, the balance between private rights and appetites and public order in an Anuak village, of which we shall later have occasion to write.

When a headman is installed, the most important part of his installation is a dance (which may also be held at other times) in which he is honoured by the villagers and, in return, feasts them. Such a dance, for the provision of a feast by anyone of importance, is called *agwaga.* Small groups of women who want presents will often perform a little *agwaga,* dancing and singing at the homestead of someone from whom they expect to receive gifts, and the *agwaga* really compels the person whom it honours to give lavishly in return, whether he secretly wishes to do so or not. It is undoubtedly one factor in preventing any great inequalities in wealth in Anuakland, and as such requires analysis of a kind which is not here relevant.

The large *agwaga,* which both men and women perform for their headman is, however, a dramatic representation of the relation between a headman and his villagers, as we have mentioned, and is here described from that point of view.

The drums are taken out and tuned and beaten before dawn on the day of a headman's *agwaga.* An hour or so after sunrise, such men of the village as are not otherwise employed on necessary tasks arrive at the headman's homestead carrying spears and rifles, and run about the dancing-ground shouting ox-names, and uttering war-cries, gesturing with their weapons in a mock defense of and mock attack on the headman's home. In the course of this activity, at one *agwaga,* I frequently heard the word *agem,* "rebellion", shouted by the warriors, and a stranger might be under the impression that a real *agem* was about to take place, since the drums are beaten and an occasional shot is fired. Later in the morning, the young men arrive dressed in their best clothes and with their legs laced round with bells, and start to dance round the drums. They then sit in a semi-circle facing the headman's homestead and sing choruses, while old women occasionally enter the semi-circle and dance little solo-dances. After this, the men rise and, still singing, move in close formation to the entrance to the headman's home, to call him forth.

He meanwhile has dressed himself in his best clothes and, when his people have retired and formed themselves again into a semi-circle on the ground, he emerges. The rhythm of the chorus becomes more intense, and the women give their "luluing" cries. Carrying spears or a rifle, the headman dances before his seated people, and is joined by married women of the village, who enter the semi-circle one or two at a time and replace each other there. To these married women, the headman makes approaches in the normal manner of an Anuak beau when trying to attract a partner, drawing over their faces and breasts a switch of horsetail which is attached to his elbow and making various other gestures of self-display. Eventually, the headman is left alone in a vigorous war-dance before the assembled people, in which he mimes the firing of rifles and the throwing of spears. He shouts his ox-name.

The men then rise, and dance together towards the homestead of the headman. He retires from the dance, and they once more deploy over the whole dancing-ground, miming a skirmish with spears and rifles. In the course of this, I have seen mimed attacks upon the drums—a clear indication that part of the military action here mimed is the village rebellion, and not a raid or battle with strangers, since the seizing of the drums is the major objective of those who wish to depose a headman. Thereafter, the people disperse and rest for a while, and later in the day continue with the normal headman's dance.

This brief description makes it clear that the analogy with the relations of husband and wife, which we earlier used in describing a headman's relations with his people, is not purely fortuitous. The villagers dance before the headman arrives, and sing to encourage him to approach them, as the girls begin by singing in the ordinary Anuak dance. When the headman dances before his villagers, he courts the married women as it were on their behalf. The villagers in return dance again before the headman's court. Later in the dance, the headman's wife (who has the title of *gwanya*) leads the people. It is she who introduces the sequence of the normal dance, by dancing first alone before the men, who then join her one or two at a time as the married women join the headman in the *agwaga* we have described. When a headman's wife is dancing is the time of greatest excitement and display, and the elaborate Anuak customs of honouring (*ajiem*) at dances are then very evident. Men fire rifles near the girls whom they wish to attract, and the girls in return load those who have honoured them with bangles and sometimes hand over very valuable strings of old beads. These are later redeemed with smaller payments, which are acknowledged by further lavish presents. When the headman's wife is dancing, men slash each other with whips in mock hostility which, according to the Anuak, often springs from real hostility. It is clear that the headman's wife is the symbol of the girls and women of the village in relation to all their husbands and lovers, as the headman is the symbol of all the men in relation to their wives and lovers with whom he dances. It is said indeed that in the past the headman's first wife often was really the wife of the whole village, since her bridewealth was provided by the villagers and not by the headman. Consequently, in the event of the headman's being driven out, he had to leave his wife behind with the other village properties in his keeping.

In this article, I do not discuss the evidence which makes it possible to say that the Anuak village headman has very little religious importance. Neither the headman nor the nobles are at the centre of elaborate cultic practices, and the headmanship is to be understood in terms of its ceremonial, not its ritual, importance. It is an institution based upon Anuak notions of prestige, and its functioning is made possible by the intensely competitive nature of Anuak social life, by their personal independence, and by the privacy and secrecy with which they are able to conduct some of their affairs.

KACHINS OF BURMA

E. R. Leach
Political Systems of Highland Burma
Fieldwork 1939–40, pp. 172–95, Selected Passages

Kachins make use of concepts concerning the supernatural for practical (technical) as well as ritual ends. The illnesses of men and the diseases of crops and animals are alike attributed to the malicious attack of supernatural beings. There are many different categories of such supernatural beings, each thought to be responsible for different classes of symptoms. Treatment consists of a preliminary diagnosis to discover the type responsible, followed by a sacrificial offering to the spirit concerned. This is an essentially practical procedure no different in principle from our routine of taking one kind of pill for a headache and another for a stomach ache. With us, if one course of treatment fails, we try another; Kachins do likewise.

Offerings to the spirits have another practical aspect in that Kachins do not kill their domestic livestock except for sacrifice. A "spirit making" (*nat galaw*) is therefore a feast for all who attend it. Since rich people make larger sacrifices than poor people, sacrifices have the effect of equalising consumer distribution. It therefore does not greatly matter who owns the livestock; when they are finally killed, meat will always be shared around the whole village. This emphasises what has been said already to the effect that the value of property (e.g. livestock) to the individual is a prestige symbol rather than as an economic good.

It is, however, the ritual rather than the practical aspects of "spirit making" that mainly concern us in this book. Conceptually Kachin spirits (*nat*) are, in Lang's famous phrase, "magnified non-natural men". They simply extend the human class hierarchy to a higher level and are continuous with it. In the *nat* world, as in the human world, there are chiefs, aristocrats, commoners and slaves. The commoners of the *nat* world are simply the deceased ancestors of the commoners of the human world; the aristocrats of the *nat* world are deceased human chiefs. In order to obtain concessions from a human superior, a man starts proceedings by making a gift which thereby puts the superior person in his debt. To obtain concessions from the spirits one does likewise—one "gives them honour" (*hkungga jaw*) which, in this case, means making a sacrifice. In accepting the gift, the spirit only takes the "breath" or "essence" (*nsa*) of the offering, so that, conveniently, human beings are able to consume the carcase.

The ordered hierarchy of the spirits also reflects other ideas already familiar in the real world. In the real world if a poor commoner wishes to approach his chief, he will first approach a superior commoner (e.g. a village headman) to intercede on his behalf as agent (*kasa*). So too with the spirits; one must approach great deities by way of lesser ones.

Let me illustrate this. In Hpalang, as in most Kachin communities, an important religious ceremonial is held about the beginning of September. Its avowed purpose is to bring supernatural protection upon the crops which are just then coming into ear. It is a time when food stocks are very low so that it is not such a gay performance as the festivities that take place at harvest and at the time of sowing, but from the ritual point of view it is perhaps the most sacred of all regular annual ceremonials: the time is one of anxiety, will the crop flourish or fail?

Every household has a part to play in this ceremonial which ordinarily lasts three days and is then followed by four days tabooed holiday. On the first day each household makes an offering to its own ancestral spirits at home. These are small offerings; probably only chickens. On the second day offerings are made in the *numshang;* in this case pigs are offered and the ritual is in two parts, first there is an offering to the ancestors of the various village headmen other than the chief, and then an offering to the chief's ancestors. The pig given to the chief's ancestors will be a larger and better pig than that offered to the headmen's ancestors. On the third day, at the *numshang*, offerings are made to various sky nats on behalf of the commoners—usually the sky nats Musheng and his daughter Bunghpoi. Here probably Bunghpoi gets a pig and her father a buffalo. Then in the evening of the third day, in a ceremony from which everyone except the chief and his priests is excluded, an offering is made to the earth spirit Shadip. The offering is probably only a small pig, but it is a genuine sacrifice, the whole animal is buried; in all the previous cases the gift to the gods is only symbolic, the meat is eaten by the human participants. The proceedings close with a small offering to the luck spirits (*maraw*) which serves to de-sanctify the chief, the priests and the *numshang*.

This is but the skeleton of very long and intricate proceedings, but it suffices to show how the pattern of ritual "represents" or describes the status relations within the community. Rank is here represented in two ways, firstly by sequence—the order of sacrifice is: commoner ancestors, headmen's ancestors, chief's ancestors, junior sky spirit, senior sky spirit, earth spirit; secondly by the scale of offering: chicken, small pig, big pig, buffalo. Finally the exclusion of everyone except the chief and the priests from the final part of the ceremony sets off the chief as a person apart, possessed of spiritual powers distinct from those of ordinary mortals.*

Kachins have no separate category of performances which can be regarded as magical rather than religious. The explanation of all types of ritual activity is that offerings are being made to nats. Some types of nats, however, represent what in other cultural contexts anthropologists have described as witchcraft substance.

The practice of direct magical sorcery as opposed to the invocation of evil spirits seems to be very rare.

Kachins believe that people can be possessed by witch

* Distinctions in the degree of sanctity attaching to different nats is indicated also in various other ways such as the kind of costume worn by the officiating priest, the length of the priest's incantation and so on.

spirits even though they themselves are unaware of this malady. The taint is hereditary and there is no effective cure. Witches may cause all manner of sickness and misfortune; not to the person harbouring the witch spirit but to others. It is sometimes possible to treat the victim by exorcism, but the harbourer of a witch spirit is incurable. The only treatment is to destroy the human host and his or her family. The witch concept is thus a "scape-goat mechanism". Illness and misfortune is usually first diagnosed as due to punishment or attack by one or other category of nat; appropriate sacrifices follow. If these prove of no avail, another diagnosis may be tried, followed by further sacrifices. One possible form of diagnosis is to say that the cause of misfortune is a witch and to take appropriate vengeance.

Under the British regime it was illegal to accuse specific individuals of being witches and details are consequently unsatisfactory. In 1940 the concept of witchcraft was very much alive but distorted. Certain practitioners declared that they had acquired (from the Shans) techniques for exorcising witches from the victim without being too specific as to who was the human host of the witch spirit. My own cook was an expert at this kind of exorcism; but though I witnessed several spectacular cures of "witchcraft disease", I failed to identify any individual witch. From an anthropological point of view this is a pity, for the main interest in a witchcraft situation turns on techniques of divination and the relationship between witch and bewitched.

In former times families accused of witchcraft could be expelled from the village or even killed off. There is inadequate evidence as to how an accusation of witchcraft could be established or what sanctions could be invoked to achieve vengeance. This much, however, seems clear—one looks for witches in one's own community, not far afield. This has a bearing upon the stability of structural relationships within the local community.

From all this it becomes clear that the various nats of Kachin religious ideology are, in the last analysis, nothing more than ways of describing the formal relationships that exist between real persons and real groups in ordinary human Kachin society.

The gods denote the good relationships which carry honour and respect, the spooks and the witches denote the bad relationships of jealousy, malice and suspicion. Witchcraft becomes manifest when the moral constraints of the ideally correct social order lose their force.

CONCEPTS OF AUTHORITY: POLITICAL AND RELIGIOUS OFFICE

But if we have reduced the gods and the witches to mere manifestations of the human emotions, what becomes of the chief and the priests who derive their authority from their supposed power to control the gods?

In the literature of the Kachins it is implied that the "officials" in a Kachin community are always the holders of either secular or religious office. On the secular side are ranged the chief (*duwa*), and the elders (*salang*); on the religious side we have the priests of various grades (*jaiwa, dumsa, hkinjawng, hpunglum*) the diviners (*nwawt*) and the spirit mediums (*myihtoi*). But in fact the matter is not as simple as that. The chief, it is true, holds no priestly office; yet his power derives from a religious role; the diviner has no formal political power, yet he is in a position of considerable political influence.

Throughout this chapter I have stressed that the status of the individuals whom I describe as chief (*duwa*) is primarily defined in terms of prestige symbols. One can say then that the office of chief is a ritual though not a priestly office in the sense, for example, that the Lord Mayor of London has a ritual though not a priestly office. But how far is the Kachin chief's office also a political office of real power? Here the empirical situation (in 1940) was greatly confused by the fact that the British Administration had always taken it for granted that a Kachin chief *ought* to be an autocrat. He was expected to execute without question all instructions received from the British District Officer ("Assistant Superintendent") by way of the Government Native Officer (*taungok*); furthermore he was made responsible for the collection of house tax and he was entitled to a commission on his collection; he was also responsible for the law and order of his community and for adjudicating upon matters of native law and custom. Nearly all these functions are quite alien to the traditional role of a *duwa,* and most chiefs under the British found themselves in an awkwardly ambiguous position. In Hpalang, as it happened, the individual whom the Government treated as chief was not recognised as such by any sector of the community itself, and it was thus relatively easy for me to sort out the "proper traditional" attributes of a chief from those which were purely Government-inspired.

The role of the chief *vis-à-vis* other office holders can be best appreciated if we break down the concept of authority into a number of separate functional categories. What then is the chief's role in (a) judicial affairs, (b) military affairs, (c) economic affairs, (d) day-to-day executive decisions, (e) religious affairs? In each of these fields the chief has a role to play, but usually it is a minor one.

a. Judicial Leadership. Kachins have no native concept of a judge. The native Kachin idea is that disputes are settled by arbitration rather than arbitrary judgement. A lawsuit involving a debt (*hka*) and the settlement of the debt is a matter for the agents (*kasa*) of the disputing parties. The judicial body of a village cluster or domain is thus a body of arbitrators rather than a bench of magistrates; its function is to give a ruling as to what would be a fit and proper settlement of the issue in dispute. Before the coming of the British, such a body had little power to enforce its decisions. Once a judgement had been made it was up to the winner to extract the settlement *hpaga* from his opponent as best he could.

This judicial body—if it can be called such—was known as the *salang hpawng* (council of *salang*). The chief is a member of the *salang hpawng* simply in his capacity as head of his own lineage; he has no special judicial powers. Indeed because of his central position in the kinship network, the chief himself or some member of his lineage is likely to be a party to most disputes that crop up within the domain; the chief's role in the *salang hpawng* is thus more frequently that of litigant than that of arbitrator.

In theory a dispute between commoners should be arbitrated by *salang* (i.e. lineage heads); a dispute between *salang* should be arbitrated by other *salang* and by chiefs from outside communities; a dispute between chiefs will probably not be resolved at all for many years but when finally settled will be arbitrated by other chiefs, especially those of higher lineage status than the disputants.

But though the chief is not a judge, he has a personal interest in seeing that disputes within his territory are settled. If it is a case of violence, then the chief himself is necessarily a party to the dispute; if it is a civil offence such as bastardy or adultery, the chief is not necessarily immediately involved, but if the debt is not arbitrated quickly violence may result and then the chief will be directly involved.

A chief therefore may be expected to interest himself in the settlement of lawsuits even though he himself may play only a very minor role in any actual judicial procedure.

b. Military leadership. There are many societies where it is possible to define the political unit as the "largest community which considers that disputes between its members should be settled by arbitration and that it ought to combine against other communities of the same kind and against foreigners". But while a Kachin chief certainly likes to represent himself as the autocratic ruler of a domain (*mung*), it is quite clear that in practice Kachin warfare was seldom organised on a territorial basis. When Kachins talk of war (*majan*), they mean nothing more than a blood feud (*bunglat hka*) in which the lineages of two chiefs are involved and which on that account is difficult to bring to any immediate settlement. Only the lineages of the two chiefs are immediately concerned, and if other groups get involved, they do so as lineage groups, on the basis of kinship, and not as members of a territorial community. Thus if the chief of domain A is at feud with the chief of domain B, the chief of domain A cannot necessarily raise all the people of his domain to fight on his side. No doubt some will do so on the grounds of kinship, but others, being related to both sides, will prefer to take no part.

Moreover such enmities are not habitual. Nearly all feuds

start over a woman. Generally speaking, when the feud is finally settled "there is no question of the feud remaining outstanding as the parties have usually exchanged women between them and have (once more) become related groups." The actual fighting in such feud wars was always on a very minor scale. As in other types of debt settlement, the principals usually took no part directly. As already explained, the usual procedure was to hire agents, called *share,* to carry out the actual raids and assassinations.

Open warfare (*hpyen gasat*), when it occurred at all, consisted of marauding raids and ambuscades in which the short term objective was loot and the long term objective mainly to make life so generally unpleasant for the enemy that they would be willing to settle up outstanding "debts" or else pay handsomely for "protection".

But in all these military and para-military activities, the chiefs, even when they initiated a quarrel, did not themselves take a leading part as soldiers. Even today this is true. While persons rated as *salang* (lineage head) or *myit su* (wise man) have often had a distinguished career in the Burma Army or Military Police, the actual chief and his immediate heir has probably spent all his life at home. The Kachin Chief like the United States President is Commander-in-Chief. Neither of these social persons is expected to fight in battle.

c. The Chief's Role in Economic Affairs. We have already seen that the chief, by virtue of the fact that he is expected to give bigger and more frequent feasts than anyone else, plays an important part in the distribution of consumption goods. The right to receive meat tribute and to receive an enhanced scale of *hpaga* payments for the settlement of debts does not substantially increase the economic power of the individual chief, for his obligations increase proportionately to the increase of his receipts. Tribute in the form of paddy (rice) is not on quite the same footing. In pre-British days a very important function of leading Kachin chiefs was to offer "protection" to valley-dwelling wet-rice cultivators in return for tribute in rice. The procedure was to include the valley villages within the domain of the hill chief. Thereafter anyone who attacked the valley villages would find himself at feud with the Kachin chief.

Caravans of Chinese traders and the like passing through a chief's domain were "protected" in a similar way in return for tribute. The evidence makes it appear that all such tribute was always a perquisite of the chief and not of village headmen, and this would fit in with the general pattern of Kachin ideas about land rights. How the tribute was further distributed among the chief's own Kachin followers (*zaw*) is not apparent. It is clear, however, that in favourable cases the role of tribute holder gave the Kachin chief a position of real economic strength, provided, that is, that the tribute consisted of cash or rice or other economically valuable goods and not merely the orthodox ritual gift of meat.

d. Executive Leadership. Paradoxically, the executive initiative in such matters as the foregoing was not, in the pre-British period, necessarily a function of the chief. It was always open for a village headman (*salang*) of outstanding ability and personality to elevate himself into the position of being the "leader" (*bawmung*) of a domain for all everyday practical affairs the recognition of such commoner leadership by the Kachins themselves serves to stress the essentially ritual nature of the chiefly office. Kachin *theory* is that the chief rules (*up*) with autocratic power; in my actual fieldwork I seldom identified any instruction which had issued from a chief acting on his own initiative. Where he gave an order it was as mouthpiece of the Government or of the *salang hpawng* or of some oracle which he had first consulted.

It is entirely consistent with the ideas about kingship current in both Shan and Burmese society that the successful, economically powerful, leader should himself disdain to take an active part in day-to-day administrative affairs. Such practical matters are for underlings; the King himself should live apart in his palace surrounded by his numerous wives and concubines.

e. Leadership in Religious Affairs: the functions of priests. The chief's office, I suggested earlier, is a ritual but not a priestly office. It is a ritual office not merely because it is defined in terms of prestige symbols which do not necessarily carry with them any real political or economic power, but also because the chief is responsible for carrying out certain annual sacrifices on behalf of the community. His role is a passive one. The chief "gives" the sacrifice in the sense that he provides the animals for slaughter, but he is not a priest.

The same is true even when the chief holds *manau* and makes sacrifices to his personal deities for the enhancement of his own prestige. Although the right to "give" (*jaw*) the sacrifice is exclusive to the chief and is a valued possession, it consists merely in the right to provide the materials for the feast and to employ a priest to recite the appropriate ritual chants. A chief could never be priest (*dumsa*) at his own sacrificial feast and it is rare to find a chief who is qualified to act as priest even at other people's sacrifices. We need then to analyse the nature of the priestly office.

jaiwa–saga teller
dumsa–priest
hkinjawng–ritual butcher
hpunglum–assistant ritual butcher

The Kachin system provides a large number of priestly offices of one kind or another and entry into all of these is by apprenticeship and acquired skill. Hence they are non-hereditary. But practice of the priestly art, especially in its more elaborate forms, brings to the performer considerable perquisites and great prestige. Indeed in many ways the prestige of a great priest outshines that of a great chief.

The techniques necessary for the lower grades of the priesthood are not difficult to acquire and in most villages there are several people available who are competent to perform, let us say, the rituals of a *masha nat* sacrifice and to do the job for a quite nominal fee. But learning the rituals for a major sacrifice is quite another matter; it involves literally years of arduous apprenticeship. Thus in Hpalang in 1940 there must have been dozens of people qualified to recite the chants accompanying the sacrifice of a chicken in the ritual treatment of stomach ache, but there were only two men who knew the rituals for a *ga nat* sacrifice which, among other things, called for the intoning of a traditional saga for 8 to 10 hours at a stretch. At a *manau* the recitation of sagas can go on for days on end and the priests who can accomplish this feat have a special title *jaiwa.*

There is no particular rule as to who may or may not become a priest but the career tends to attract the able or ambitious man who does not hold office by hereditary right. Thus lineage heads who sit on the *salang hpawng* by right of birth are not likely to go to the bother of becoming celebrated as priests. But the elder brother of such a man or the illegitimate son of a chief who has, as it were, been defrauded of his natural status might have every incentive to seek the vicarious prestige attainable through priestly office. The priestly leaders of Laga village in Hpalang illustrated this point very well. Myihtoi Gam, as his name implied, was a medium as well as a priest; he was easily the most accomplished priest (*dumsa*) in Hpalang and his services were in constant demand. By birth he had been a distinctly frustrated character. His birth name was NhKum Gam and he was the eldest brother of NhKum Naw (Laga Naw), the headman of Laga village. He had a wall eye and a harelip and looked as if he must have suffered from rickets in his childhood. Second only to Myihtoi Gam in priestly influence was my neighbour Lahtaw Naw. As a priest (*dumsa*) he was of only medium competence—he was a *tsu dumsa,* he knew how to sacrifice pigs but not cattle—but he was immensely skilled as a ritual butcher (*hkinjawng*) and was present at almost every sacrifice to cut up the meat and see that the traditionally correct portions were allocated to the multifarious claimants both human and supernatural. Lahtaw Naw was also outstanding as a ritual dancer; he was always dance leader at the funerals which he attended and also (so I was told) at *manau.* Lahtaw Naw was married to the sister of Laga Naw the village headman, but he was of no status by birth. In discussions with me he was unusually reticent about his origin; local gossip alleged that he was an illegitimate son of an important Lahtaw chief 30 miles away to the south. Both Myithtoi Gam and Lahtaw Naw sat on the

Maran chief's *salang hpawng* in their capacity as "wise men". It is unlikely that either would have done so had they not become ritual experts.

nwawt—"diviner"; *myihtoi*—"medium"

Diviners (*nwawt*) and mediums (*myihtoi*) are not necessarily priests (*dumsa*), though the roles are often combined. Divining is resorted to very frequently for all kinds of purposes:—Where shall I site my house? Is X a suitable bride for my son Y? What has happened to the buffalo I lost last week? Is tomorrow a propitious day to go to market? All these and a host of similar and dissimilar questions may be answered by divination. Various techniques are practised. In theory the procedure is magical and automatic and requires no special skill. Large numbers of people claim to know how to divine. In practice all divination procedures call for interpretation by the diviner and certain people—usually priests—are recognized as specially expert. The office of diviner has very little prestige attached to it; in theory anyone can learn how to divine in half an hour or so. In reality it is quite clear that the diviner wields very considerable power, for his interpretations affect economic action and within wide limits his interpretations are free from all restraint.

Two very ordinary examples will serve to illustrate this. Firstly, when a feud is to be settled, each side chooses a body of elders and chiefs to act as its agents in the arbitration. Clearly much will depend upon who is chosen, but the decision does not rest with either of the interested parties, it is a matter for divination. Secondly, when a man is ill, it is the diviner who decides what nat is responsible and what sacrifice is called for. Now it must be remembered that the public at large will eat the meat of the sacrifice. It is not surprising therefore that the nats demand much bigger sacrifices from the wealthy than they do from the poor. But it is through the diviner that this discrimination is effected.

Mediums—*myihtoi*—have a considerably higher status than diviners, though their activities are somewhat similar.

In theory mediums are born not made; mediumship is a natural faculty, not something learnt from a master. The behaviour of mediums is, however, very stereotyped and is clearly learnt by imitation even if not by actual apprenticeship. I never heard any suggestion that the faculty was hereditary, it is supposed to crop up quite spasmodically. The incidence of mediums seems to be about the same as that of superior priests (*dumsa*). In Hpalang there were two mediums, one was also a senior priest. The ideology of mediumship is that the medium in a trance state is able to transport himself to the world of the nats and consult the nats in person, or alternatively that he can establish direct communication with the nats and persuade a junior nat, such as a recently deceased ancestor, to come and speak through his own human mouth.

Mediums are more expensive practitioners than ordinary diviners and they tend to be consulted when the procedures recommended by the diviner have led to no result. One very important function of the medium serves to limit the destructive implications of the religious theory. In theory, all illness is due to the persecution or displeasure of the nats. Consequently all illness is curable provided only that one can find the right sacrifice to make to the right nat. Kachins are of course perfectly well aware that death is the lot of all and that fatal illnesses may be very prolonged, but strict adherence to religious ideology would imply that the relatives of any dying man ought to be ruined in their attempts to buy off the nats by repeated sacrifices. Illnesses of important people do indeed provide the excuse for large scale sacrifices, but where an old man is obviously dying, his heirs are not usually prepared to see their whole patrimony squandered as a token of filial piety. Instead they employ a medium. In the course of a ceremony accompanied by a small sacrifice, the medium is supposed to transport himself to the nat world and make promises to the effect that, provided only the sick man is allowed to recover, much larger offerings will be made in the future. If then the sick man dies as expected, his heirs are absolved from further obligation to the nats who have not kept to their part of the bargain. The medium performs this ceremony on a bamboo platform (*hkinrawng*) some 20–30 feet high, erected for the occasion in front of the house of the sick man. After the ceremony this platform remains standing as a reminder that if the sick man recovers another sacrifice is still due.

Mediums are often credited with supernormal physical powers—they are supposed to be able to climb unscathed a ladder of upturned sword blades or walk along a suspended cotton thread. This, to some extent, is an index of the high esteem which attaches to the mediumistic faculty. Saga tellers (*jaiwa*) are similarly credited with the ability to ride around on tigers. I would suspect that mediums, like priests and diviners, are usually individuals who do not hold any political office by hereditary right, but I have no clear evidence that this is always the case.

Kachins appear to think of themselves as having a very clear-cut authority system. The chief is regarded as an autocrat placed at the peak of a hierarchy of ranked classes, differentiated from one another by rules of caste-like rigidity. In this ideal structural pattern everything fits together very perfectly, each person and each group of persons has an appointed place in a clearly defined system. But the reality does not correspond to the ideal. In the reality the chiefly office is only one of many offices which contain elements of authority; prestige and status do not really depend solely on birth status; the nicely ordered ranking of lineage seniority conceals a vicious element of competition. But it is competition for prestige and reputation rather than wealth.

It is, I think, relevant to note that Kachins share Chinese ideas about the paramount importance of reputation or "face". *Myi man sum*—"to lose face" corresponds precisely to the Chinese concept and has equal importance.

I assume that Kachins achieve personal satisfaction from being able to influence other people. Analysis shows that such influence is wielded in different ways through different channels. On the one hand recognised prestige attaches to certain formal offices—chief, lineage head, saga teller, medium—and those who can get themselves recognised as deserving these titles will have power and influence accordingly. But on the other hand there are offices such as that of diviner or junior priest or ritual butcher which carry very little prestige in themselves but which nevertheless provide channels through which influence can be exerted. The real Kachin society is not, I suggest, a rigidly structured hierarchy of fixed classes and well-defined offices, but a system in which there is constant and at times very rapid social mobility. The mobility is brought about in one of two ways. Either the holders of the minor unesteemed offices use their influence to manipulate their way into positions of higher recognised authority, or alternatively they become revolutionaries and repudiate the authority of the higher offices altogether.

GARDENERS OF SOUTH INDIA

Edward B. Harper
Studies of a Mysore Village, South India
Fieldwork 1954–56
"Hoylu: A Belief Relating Justice and the Supernatural,"
Selected Passages

INTRODUCTION

The purpose of this paper is to show how a particular religious concept, called a *hoylu,* is related to the social structure of a caste-stratified village in South India, and how the expression of this belief changes as other aspects of the culture change. The first part of the paper is a simplified explanation of how a hoylu operates and how it is distinguished from other types of appeal for aid from the spirit world. Next, a few case histories are followed by a discussion of how the theory and practice of giving a hoylu vary according to the motivation of the giver and the caste of the individuals involved. The questions of when a hoylu is given and how it is enforced are then examined. Finally, the relationship of a changing culture to varying hoylu patterns is discussed, with an analysis of the factors that may affect the future frequency and use of hoylus.

Materials for this discussion are drawn mainly from two castes in Totagadde, a village in the Western Ghats of Northwestern Mysore—Havik Brahmins who own and tend arecanut gardens, and a paddy-raising agricultural Sudra caste called Divarus (or Halepaika). A few examples involve two other paddy-raising Sudra castes. The fundamentals of the hoylu complex are the same for both the Brahmins and the Sudras, but the use and details differ considerably.

A hoylu is only one of several types of requests to the supernatural for aid. There are three commonly used terms for different types of appeals. One of these is *hurake,* usually translated as "vow," which is the most usual type. For example, if a person or animal is ill, either the spirit who is causing the illness will be offered a reward to induce it to leave, or another spirit will be promised payment if it can force the responsible spirit to desist. Another type is *māta,* best translated as "sorcery"; in this a spirit's help is enlisted to harm another person. The third type, hoylu, is a plea for help of a spirit to remedy an injustice.

In oversimplified form, the basis of a hoylu is that if a man feels cheated or feels that something has been taken from him by illegal or immoral means, he may ask for supernatural aid in recovering the lost property. A spirit does this by causing harm to the guilty party, and the punishment ceases only when the property is returned to the rightful owner. When this happens, the man who has given the hoylu renders payment to the spirit either in cash (a promised fixed sum for a percentage of the value of the restored property), or by giving a puja and a blood sacrifice. In village theory, any spirit or deity that is controlled by an individual can be directed to harm a wrongdoer. In practice, there are several spirits who have a reputation for doing hoylu work, and generally only these are asked. The spirit never undertakes to punish wrongdoers on its own, but only when requested by the person who influences it or through whom it speaks. This person is an intermediary, a shaman or priest, who enlists the aid of the spirit on his client's behalf.

Informants often state that hoylus have a built-in mechanism which prevents a person from unjustly enlisting the aid of a god to harm a personal enemy; this is the ability of the god to determine who is right. The god will punish only the wrongdoer, even if this involves punishing the giver of the hoylu if his claim is false.

There are several important distinctions between a hoylu, a vow, and sorcery. For instance, in a vow the goal set for the spirit is a socially desirable one, such as curing an ill man or animal or making a barren woman fertile. In sorcery, the goal is socially disapproved. The spirit is expected to cause harm (generally illness or death) to the individual, directly or through his family, and this harm is an end in itself. In a hoylu the spirit is requested to do good as well as evil. The spirit punishes, but only instrumentally.

Another distinction is that a hoylu is ordinarily public knowledge. Sorcery, to the extent that it really exists, is highly secretive. A vow is an individual or family matter, neither secret nor officially made public. In a hoylu, generally either a letter comes from the god's representative to the man against whom the complaint was lodged, or if the hoylu is given to a village god such as a *čaudi* (a minor local female spirit) it must be done in the presence of several people.

There is also a difference in the frequency with which the different types of supernatural aid are requested. A vow is a common everyday event, but hoylus are given infrequently. The most common reason for a Brahmin to give a hoylu is that he has lost all his land, a rare occurrence. Evidence for the frequency of the use of sorcery is not obtainable, but it appears to be rare.

The same gods are not necessarily appealed to in a vow, in a hoylu, or in sorcery. For a hoylu, only a few specialized gods are asked to help; for a vow, a person may appeal to a wide selection of deities. These include most of the local village gods as well as members of the Sanskritic pantheon, except Brahma. For sorcery, local non-

Sanskritic gods are generally used. Another difference between sorcery and hoylu is that the help of a shaman or priest is needed to counteract the former, while the effect of a hoylu can be removed only by returning the property and giving the spirit its promised reward.

In short, a vow is asking for a boon from a deity; sorcery is asking a spirit to injure a person; and a hoylu, ideally conceived, is asking for justice from the supernatural.

There are three main causes that may give rise to the use of hoylus: (1) land dispute cases; (2) theft of small movable objects, such as jewelry; and (3) unpaid debts. It will be shown that these three types of hoylu are functionally related, in this order, to three different economic patterns—those of the arecanut-raising Havik Brahmin, the paddy-farming Sudra, and the landless laborer. Although the type of hoylu and the economic system of the individuals involved tend to be associated, the correlation is not one to one.

CASE HISTORIES

The distinctive attributes, interrelations, and implications of the different systems can best be approached through a series of examples.

Hoylus between Havik Brahmins almost always take place over land disputes. A case of this type was related by a Havik after he had said that a land dispute case would sometimes be decided one way in court and the decision then reversed by the god Manjunatha in Dharmasthala, a large temple in South Canara about a hundred miles south of Totagadde. When asked for an example, he said:

In Halli there was a poor Havik named Narayanappa who had a court case with an important [Havik] man (*heggade*). The latter had loaned Narayanappa money. Narayanappa gave his land as security. When the loan came due Narayanappa, although he had repaid part, could not pay the remainder. The heggade obtained a judgment in court giving him Narayanappa's lands. A hoylu was given by Narayanappa against the heggade. The latter gave back the land to Narayanappa because the Dharmasthala priest said that Narayanappa was a very poor man.

Only two cases out of the dozen recounted by informants offer exceptions to the rule that hoylus between Haviks are given because of land disputes. One of these concerned a jewelry theft that had taken place about fifty years before, and in this case the hoylu was given to a village god. The other case occurred just before we left the field. Several brass articles had been stolen from a small Shiva temple in Totagadde, and the man whom many suspected of the theft made accusations that his worst enemy was guilty. An all-Brahmin village *panchayat* attempted to solve the problem by writing a letter to Dharmasthala, promising the items to that temple if they were returned.

Although the taking of a hoylu is ordinarily done by a man, a woman can also declare one. In one rare case, a Havik Brahmin woman took a hoylu against a Havik man. However, if she had not had a minor son to inherit the property she was trying to recover, it is doubtful that she would have taken this action. This hoylu case was related in connection with the story of an elderly Havik Brahmin man who suddenly became violently deranged:

Venkappa became mad (*hučča*) because of a hoylu. He was quite healthy and then suddenly this happened. His father, Ramappa, lived in Totagadde. Ramappa's wife's younger brother's wife was living in the house [in a neighboring village] where Venkappa now lives. When Ramappa's wife's younger brother died, Ramappa forged a document that the deceased owed him 800 rupees, then went to court and took the widow's land and house. Then he went to live in this house and began to farm her arecanut land. The widow gave a hoylu against Ramappa by writing a letter to Dharmasthala. Nothing ever happened to the father but now the sin has come to the son. . . . Anyone who knows that Venkappa's father had a hoylu taken against him will think that this is the reason Venkappa went mad.

A hoylu over a theft is nearly always taken to a local village god—usually a čaudi. The method of taking a hoylu to a čaudi was described by one Divaru informant in a hypothetical case:

A hoylu is given if someone steals a thing. Suppose some [brass] vessel is stolen in our hamlet. Then the owner of that vessel tells everyone that it has been stolen and that if he does not get it back he will give a hoylu to the Digadakoppa [name of a neighboring village] čaudi. After a week or ten days he brings a coconut and asks everyone in our hamlet to touch it saying he is not the thief (*kalla*). When this is done he goes to Digadakoppa and buries the coconut in the ground before the čaudi's stone. He should do this in the presence of ten people of that village, as it is necessary to inform them and have their consent for the čaudi to go out of their village and work for people from another village. The person taking the hoylu promises the čaudi a goat or chicken [in sacrifice] if the article is returned. Then the čaudi gives blows (*pettu*) to the thief.

When the thief begins to have trouble he will go to a shaman (*gadiga*) and thus learn the cause. Then he returns the article to the *pujari,* the man in Digadakoppa who worships the čaudi. The pujari then informs the owner that he must give the čaudi what has been promised as the article has come back. The thief should also give the čaudi a goat or a chicken for the wrong (*tappu*) he has done. This informant went on to give a case history:

Gaudru (a Lingayat) and Putta (a Divaru) once had a quarrel. Later Putta stole a plow that belonged to Gaudru that had been left in the field. Gaudru gave a hoylu to the Digadakoppa čaudi. The čaudi then gave blows to Putta—he lost his house by fire and his cattle died. Then he returned the plow to the Digadakoppa čaudi—he gave it to the pujari. The pujari forgot to inform Gaudru. Gaudru did not know that the plow had been returned so he did not give what was promised to the čaudi.

Then the čaudi turned against Gaudru and his whole family (*vamsha*) was ruined—the people and cattle died.

A third situation in which a hoylu is used involves a type of relationship that exists only between high and low caste individuals. Haviks cannot run their small areca-nut plantations without a certain amount of outside labor, and some of this labor may be supplied by a "master-servant" (*vadeya-okkalu*) system. A Havik Brahmin loans marriage money to a low caste person, who works for the Brahmin in return. This relationship does not always operate to the mutual benefit of both parties and sometimes the servant, the *okkalu,* will attempt to sever it. This may mean a financial loss to the Brahmin master, and he can theoretically resort to giving a hoylu against the low caste man. This has probably happened in the past, although informants who described it were unable to document it with case histories. But both low and high caste informants stated that Haviks frequently tried to prevent "servants" from breaking off the relationship or tried to recoup their money by threatening to give a hoylu.

DIFFERENCES IN HOYLU PATTERNS

One of the most striking subcultural differences between Brahmin and Sudra castes in Totagadde is the number of words used by or known to only one caste, or the use of the same term with different meanings. Hoylu falls into the latter category. Though both Haviks and Divarus use it to mean a way of influencing a wrongdoer to make amends, the circumstances under which a hoylu is given and the connotations of the act differ considerably. If we are to understand this more fully, we must note certain variables in taking a hoylu: whether a Havik Brahmin or a Divaru declares the hoylu; whether the hoylu is given to a Sanskritic god or to a local village spirit such as a čaudi; and whether the hoylu is given for a theft of jewelry or for a dispute over land. The majority of hoylus fall into one of the two types already described—a Havik giving a hoylu to a Sanskritic god over a land dispute, or a Divaru giving a hoylu to a village spirit over the theft of a small object.

The methods of giving a hoylu to the Sanskritic god (*dēvaru*) Manjunatha at Dharmasthala and of taking one to a čaudi in a village are quite different. Although occasionally someone may present his case to Dharmasthala in person, he usually writes a letter to the Dharmasthala priest explaining the case and stating what payment he will give when it is resolved. The priest may then write to the accused asking him to explain his side, or, speaking for the god, he may agree to undertake the case on the basis of the first letter. Sometimes a letter from Dharmasthala notifies the man who has committed the injustice to make it right, or letters may be sent to both parties asking them to come to the temple for arbitration of the case. If the accused is guilty and refuses to arbitrate or to return the property, the god will cause harm to him until he does. Informants of all castes emphasize the Dharmasthala god knows on whose side justice lies, and will not rest until the wrong is righted. Payment to the god is usually a certain percentage of the value of the land or object that is in dispute. Occasionally the object itself is promised to the god if it is returned.

The giving of a hoylu to a village čaudi is always done publicly, "in front of ten people from the village," and never by writing. It is done by presenting the claim to the shaman's familiar spirit. The hypothetical case given in the text above is a reasonably generalized and ideal description of the way in which a hoylu is given to a čaudi.

Punishment of the person who has committed the wrong, if he is known, begins at a set time. If the hoylu is given to Dharmasthala, the priest notifies the offender to rectify the injustice by a certain date; if he has not done so by this time, he can expect to suffer the consequences. Punishment by a čaudi begins immediately after she is asked to undertake the case. If the offender is named, he will soon come to know about the hoylu, but when he is not known, as in a case involving theft of jewelry, he is aware that action has been taken against him only after he or his family is harmed. Then he goes to a shaman (*gādiga* or *pātri*) or a priest (*bhattru, purōhita, mantra-*

vādi or *jōyisa*) and asks the cause of the misfortune. After the cause is determined, the harm ceases as soon as a vow is taken promising that the stolen goods will be returned.

Expectations differ as to how and when punishment will be administered by the Dharmasthala god and a village čaudi. A čaudi is believed to act in a more violent and bloody manner than does the Dharmasthala god, and within a relatively shorter time. The Sudra conception of the time lag between the request to a čaudi and the result seems to be not more than several years. However, it was stated by a Brahmin that if a čaudi acted at all, she would do so within one generation. Both castes consistently stated that although the Dharmasthala god invariably did harm, this might come at any time within three generations in patrilineal descent—that is, to a man's family, or to his son's or grandson's family.

There is a considerable difference in the length of time that the Dharmasthala god and the Digadakoppa čaudi have been used for hoylus. Dharmasthala is an elaborate and well established temple with an ancient tradition, and its god has been asked to give hoylus for as long as anyone can remember. This stability stands in striking contrast to the ephemeral nature of a hoylu čaudi. When the Digadakoppa čaudi was mentioned, informants frequently volunteered the information that people had, within the last several years, nearly stopped giving hoylus to this čaudi. The rationale for stopping was: "Why should a man endanger himself and his family, as well as other innocent people? Many people who have taken a hoylu to this čaudi have been injured by having the čaudi turn on them for one reason or another." But the specific story accounting for the cessation of requests, as related by a Divaru, is revealing:

There was a Divaru man in Uru village. He had paddy land leased from a Lingayat. One day for no reason at all the Lingayat asked the Divaru to give up the land. At first the tenant (*jaminu okkalu*) refused, but the Lingayat insisted. Thus hatred rose between the two. Then the Divaru who had been leasing the field went to the Digadakoppa čaudi and asked her to kill the Lingayat. The shaman for the Digadakoppa čaudi gave one of the čaudi's tridents to this man and told him to bury it in the contested field in Uru.

Two or three days later the čaudi came to the shaman in a dream and asked where her trident was. The shaman told the čaudi that she had to kill the enemy (*vairi*) before she would get her trident back. The čaudi left in a fury and killed the Lingayat. Then the čaudi came to the shaman and asked for the return of her trident, saying she had killed the enemy. The shaman told the Divaru what the čaudi had said. But this man replied: "Why should I give a puja? I have not gotten my land back."

Then the čaudi turned on the Divaru, the man who had given the hoylu, and killed him. Many people had trouble at this time. Even those who went to see this man when he died became frightened and when they were frightened the čaudi came on them and gave them trouble (*kasla*).

Full of anger the čaudi attacked the new tenant of the Lingayat's land and killed him. She again came to the shaman and said, "I have done harm in three directions [i.e., to the Lingayat, to the first tenant who gave the hoylu, and to the second tenant, who was farming the land in which the čaudi's trident was buried]. Still I have not been given my trident nor my puja. Now I want you to give them to me." But the shaman neither brought the trident back nor gave the puja. Within fifteen days both he and his son were dead.

But the čaudi went on giving trouble to all four of these families. Finally the shaman's family went to another shaman who told them why they were having so many bad things happen to them. Then they gave the čaudi her puja in front of five people from the village [who acted as witnesses], sacrificed a goat and brought back the trident. Now there are only two women left in the shaman's family and they have to do the work of landless laborers.

Within the last two generations there have been four čaudis in or near Totagadde that have been famous as hoylu-čaudis, but all are now in disrepute. The fact that even the latest, the Digadakoppa čaudi, is now seldom used, could lead to the conclusion that the practice of asking čaudis to do hoylu work is ceasing. However, I favor an interpretation that čaudis rise and fall in popularity, and that the Digadakoppa čaudi is now in disfavor because of a peculiar set of circumstances. Certainly the non-Brahmin belief in the effectiveness of hoylus to čaudis is strong, and thus another hoylu-spirit should replace the Digadakoppa čaudi.

The pattern seems to be that a čaudi who does hoylu work is popular for a limited time and then falls into disrepute and is replaced by another čaudi. The length of time varies according to the skill of the shaman controlling the čaudi and to the particular circumstances of the sickness and death of people involved with hoylus given to this čaudi. Also, the fact that a čaudi is expected to act within a relatively short time more easily leads to a loss of faith. But in order for the religious system to be maintained, the loss of faith must occur for a specific village spirit, not for these deities in general.

Now let us look at some of the distinctions between giving a hoylu because of a land dispute and giving one because of the theft of small movable objects. In hoylu cases involving land, the guilty party is always named by the person giving the hoylu; in cases of theft, this is not necessarily true. It is sometimes said that people are afraid to take a hoylu for small thefts when they do not know the thief, for fear that he may be a member of their own family.

Hoylus given over land are mainly the weapons of the weak and the poor against the wealthy and the powerful. The well-to-do land owners, who either loan money or lease out their land, are the recipients of the effect of such hoylus. However, this status relationship is usually reversed between individuals involved in a hoylu over stolen jewelry. Here the owner of the jewelry may be presumed to be better off than the person who has stolen it, and thus the wealthier person gives the hoylu against the poorer.

Hoylus over stolen jewelry are sometimes given more in a spirit of revenge than from a desire to recover lost property. For example, a spirit will occasionally be promised all that was stolen plus an extra inducement to effect the return of the missing goods. This motivation may be akin to that involved in sorcery. On the other hand, hoylus over land are primarily motivated by a desire for economic gain rather than for retaliation. Hoylus over the theft of small objects are more often given to a čaudi than to Manjunatha, and more often by a Divaru than by a Havik Brahmin.

Both Haviks and Divarus depend upon agriculture for their livelihood. An important question is thus raised: since land is the economic basis for both castes, why do Havik Brahmins generally use hoylus for recovering land, while Divarus give them most often for the theft of small items such as jewelry?

The answer to this may lie in the differential importance of land and jewelry to the two groups. Jewelry seems to be more important to a Divaru family than to a Havik family. Divarus use jewelry as a means of investing savings; Haviks do so only to a limited extent. A Divaru woman gains some economic independence by doing wage work for other castes, and she can most easily keep her own earnings by purchasing jewelry. Brahmin women have no money of their own; they obtain their jewelry as gifts from their natal or conjugal families, rather than by inheritance or purchase. The jewelry belonging to the Divaru family acts as a reserve for times of crisis, when it can be sold or pawned. The percentage of a Havik's wealth tied up in jewelry is relatively small, while the percentage of a Divaru's is relatively high.

The income of Haviks is derived mainly from arecanut land. Havik families usually own and farm arecanut gardens, and if a Havik loses his land, there are few alternate ways to make a living and still stay in the village. Because of the caste structure and his status position, a Havik cannot do the work of a coolie nor is he supposed to farm paddy land. On the other hand, Divarus more often lease than own paddy land, and land is therefore not a capital investment for them. If a Divaru loses a particular piece he can usually lease other land. Although he may be reduced from an owner to a tenant, or have to lease land from a different person, he has the possibility of remaining a farmer. Even if he cannot find new land he can work as a coolie, although he prefers not to do so. Loss of land is a serious blow to a Divaru but it is a death blow to a Havik Brahmin, and this seems to be an important factor in accounting for the different ways in which hoylu is used by the two castes.

HOYLU AND MORALITY

The moral nature of a hoylu has already been implied by the statement that a hoylu is effective only if the person taking it has justice on his side. However, the situation is more complex than this; the degree of morality varies according to whether it is a land-hoylu or an object-hoylu, and according to the spirit to which the appeal is made. In addition, these variables are associated with the caste of the person giving the hoylu.

The choice of the spirit whose help is enlisted by a Divaru or by a Havik reflects a difference in the religious orientation and values of the two castes: Manjunatha in Dharmasthala temple is most often utilized by Havik Brahmins; čaudi, a local non-Sanskritic spirit, is now used exclusively by non-Brahmins. The Divarus are firm believers in the efficacy of local village spirits and in their willingness to work for blood sacrifice as payment. Brahmins, however, have a great respect for the Sanskritic vegetarian gods worshipped by priests in an elaborate temple setting. Although informants' statements that deities will accept a hoylu only from a person with justice on his side were intended to apply to both the village gods and the Sanskritic gods, case histories make it clear that čaudis can be bribed to harm a person who is in the right. A čaudi who does hoylu work may also have a reputation for doing sorcery, while the Brahmanical god Manjunatha works only for ends that are socially approved or considered to be just. Divarus do not always make a clear distinction between hoylu and sorcery and, when speaking about cases of hoylu, easily disgress into cases of sorcery and occasionally use the terms interchangeably. Haviks do not confuse the two concepts in this way.

The difference of opinion on the propriety of a hoylu is related to the following facts: The Sanskritic temple has a wide reputation as a seat of learning and moral enlightenment, and the integrity of its priests is frequently eulogized by both Brahmins and Sudras. Shamans, who are usually Sudras, control čaudis who can use their power in a manner that is considered unpredictable, dangerous, and sometimes immoral. Also, čaudis may have an element of treachery in their personality; statements by informants reveal that, although most čaudis are honest and reliable, there are a few who do not always respect the contractual arrangements into which they have entered.

Within the framework of village concepts of right and wrong, the relative morality of hoylu depends more upon the god than upon the caste of the person giving it, and this is shown by the fact that the ethical connotations of a hoylu to Dharmasthala temple are the same for both Divarus and Havik Brahmins. However, there is some connection between caste and the morality of a hoylu, and this is related to the fact that Haviks generally give a hoylu for a land dispute only in cases of economic desperation, when their last bit of respectable livelihood is being taken from them. There are no examples of well-to-do Haviks resorting to hoylu against each other over land disputes, even where one man has obviously obtained a piece of land by chicanery. Such cases are resolved by courts and panchayats. Divarus, however, utilize hoylus in a wide range of circumstances—when land has been taken from one tenant and leased to another, or when agricultural implements or jewelry have been stolen. Several cases of hoylu by Sudras have involved men who were already enemies, while among Haviks enmity arises only after the hoylu has been given. In short, the Havik Brahmin's motivation for declaring a hoylu usually has a much stronger economic basis than does that of the Divaru.

ENFORCING MECHANISM

Why does the hoylu system work? What role is played by the elements of belief and fear? What other mechanisms support the enforcement of a hoylu? Before giving some possible answers to these questions, I should state that the effectiveness of the Sanskritic god appears to be greater than that of the village spirit. This does not seem unreasonable, considering the fact that in land-hoylu cases, which are usually given to the Sanskritic god, the offender is always known; in thefts, which are usually handled by čaudi, the guilty parties are unknown.

If a hoylu over theft is effective, one of the most convenient explanations is belief and fear—the offender's belief that the spirit will punish him, and his fear of this. The possibility remains that a feeling of guilt may be a factor in motivating the thief to return the property, but there is no evidence for this. The differing patterns of hoylus fit differing degrees of belief in the efficacy of supernatural sanctions: Divaru informants invariably maintained that they feared the powers possessed by the supernaturals; the more sophisticated and philosophically oriented Brahmins often boasted that they did not believe in these spirits or in their ability to cause harm. Belief in supernatural sanctions thus helps to explain the effectiveness of the Divaru system better than it explains the Brahmin system.

In answering these questions, an examination of the status pattern of people having a hoylu relationship is revealing. When a Havik Brahmin is involved in a land-hoylu case, it is always with another Havik Brahmin. The only examples of Haviks being involved in a hoylu with a non-Brahmin are in the vadeya-okkalu system, a formalized system of interdependence between Brahmins and Untouchables. Among paddy-farming Sudras, land-hoylus do cut across caste lines, but they usually involve castes which occupy fairly equal positions in the caste hierarchy and which are engaged in similar economic activities. The suspected offender in theft-hoylus among Sudras tends to be within the same village, and often within a hamlet and a caste. The common element is that the hoylu is between people who have a sense of unity, a common value system, and who are within the same orbit of social control—all of which should add to the effectiveness of a hoylu.

Haviks, who are coming to believe less in supernatural sanctions, still regard hoylus as an effective means of restoring lost property. The remainder of this section will be devoted to analyzing some of the factors that may account for this, but first I should like to point out two types of situations that could potentially inhibit the enforcement of a hoylu, and some of the reasons these situations do not occur.

Within the Brahmin community, feuds between two male heads of households are not uncommon, and such feuds may become so intense that a hoylu between these men would have little chance of resolution. However, this situation is almost impossible, because the status of individuals who have a hoylu relationship and those who have a feud relationship are diametrically opposed. Feuds take place between men somewhat equal in age, wealth, and interests, and who are therefore rivals. Hoylus between Haviks, however, involve individuals of unequal status—a man wealthy enough to be a moneylender and a man poor enough to borrow money on his last remaining plot of land.

Another type of situation that could impede the effectiveness of hoylus involves the ideal of family solidarity. Although there are many tensions within the Brahmin patrilineal family and quarrels over land are frequent between close agnates, hoylus do not occur between them. This situation cannot arise, according to informants, because the Dharmasthala god will not accept hoylus involving close agnatic kin.

The Brahmins' infrequent use of land-hoylus must help to account for their effectiveness. If hoylus were misused, that is, given by a man who had lost property to a moneylender when he was not on the verge of bankruptcy, then presumably their effectiveness would decrease. Why hoylus are not misused is a question I cannot answer, but attitudes toward aggression undoubtedly play a part in it. Acts of physical aggression between males are infrequent in all castes in the village, and are even more rare among Brahmins. The giving of a hoylu is considered an extreme form of aggression. It involves such a serious breach between two Brahmin families that the otherwise universal hospitality patterns are suspended; it is the only type of hostility relationship that precludes inviting a caste member from the same village to a major life-crisis ceremony. The failure of Brahmins to appeal to village spirits may also be related to sanctions against aggression, as the punishment inflicted by the village spirit is more harsh and bloody than that inflicted by the Sanskritic god.

The nature of the family structure is another factor which helps to maintain the effectiveness of hoylus. The harm that is destined to come to the guilty person may not fall on him as an individual; it may, and frequently does, come to other members of his family or may even be effected through the cattle belonging to the family. This collective responsibility and guilt may be an important factor in accounting for the success of hoylus, especially land-hoylus, as a man and his family know that the hoylu has been declared against him. The family is likely to attribute every misfortune to the hoylu and thus to exert pressure on the head of the household, who has it within his power to take the necessary steps to have the hoylu removed. The effectiveness of this family pressure can be inferred from the number of times the head of a Brahmin household performs a propitiatory act in which he has no personal faith. For example, a Brahmin man who professes not to believe in the local minor spirits, although the women in his house do, may nevertheless pay homage to these spirits in order to keep from being blamed by the women for any sickness the children or animals may contract.

A final hypothesis about the effectiveness of the Brahmin land-hoylu system is based on the fact that all married Havik males receive most of their income from arecanut gardens, and arecanut gardens in this area are generally owned by Havik Brahmins. Haviks seem to have an implicit belief in their own caste occupational unity, and this is probably the most important single element in enforcing Havik land hoylus. A common saying which illustrates this point is that Havik males without arecanut gardens do not marry, and this is true in actual practice. For example, although a Havik had trouble finding a husband for his unattractive daughter, he did not look with favor on a proposed alliance with a landless Havik who worked in a bank in town. Havik Brahmins feel that farming arecanut gardens is the only occupation they should follow, and that a wealthy man without arecanut land is not a substantial man.

The Brahmin land-hoylu system is used after land has been taken by legal means, that is, by foreclosure on a debt. If the ordinary legal system therefore works to the detriment of the Havik who owns only enough land for bare subsistence, the legal advantage of the moneylender over the borrower is subordinate to the more important value that a Havik remain within the caste economic structure.

CHANGING PATTERNS IN THE HOYLU SYSTEM

Two generations ago Haviks sometimes utilized the local village spirits for hoylus. Now few Brahmins have sufficient belief in the existence of these čaudis, or in their ability to inflict punishment, to withstand the criticism and ridicule from other members of their caste that would ensue if they patronized these spirits. Another reason for the Brahmins' reluctance to take advantage of local spirit aid is that these gods usually require blood payment, the sacrifice of an animal. Two decades ago Haviks occasionally gave animals in sacrifice to village deities, but this practice has given way to one that conforms more to the modern ethical system as contained in the ideology of Gandhianism. The combination of a diminishing belief in local spirits, and fear of a spirit's wrath if it did hoylu work but was not given blood, means that Haviks no longer make hoylu requests of local village deities.

What effect will withdrawal of the high status and often

imitated Brahmins from use of the local village deities for hoylus have upon the belief system of the Divarus? At the same time that Brahmins were occasionally appealing to local čaudis and offering blood sacrifices, they often ridiculed them. One suspects that the lack of Brahmin participation will not greatly affect the Divaru system, particularly since the Brahmin system continues to function with different gods. Also, Brahmins still do puja to many of the village gods, although they no longer offer them nonvegetarian food. A few Haviks believe that all of the local gods are imaginary, while others believe rather strongly in their existence and powers. There is a common tradition that the religious systems of the two castes differ —a tradition which is illustrated by the fact that Haviks tend disparagingly to call the village deities "Sudra gods," and by the Divaru statement that "we go to a shaman when ill, but Brahmins go to a doctor." Since there is a certain amount of mutual agreement that different systems exist, a change by one caste does not necessarily mean a change by the other.

While Havik Brahmins are drifting away from the use of village gods, Divarus tend increasingly to appeal to the god traditionally used by Brahmins in Dharmasthala temple. This may be an example of the process labeled "Sanskritization" by Srinivas (1956). The recency of this phenomenon is in part the result of modern governmental policies that stress education for all. Traditionally only Brahmins have been literate. As hoylus to Dharmasthala are usually taken by a written communication, this facility has been used principally by Brahmins. Within the past fifteen years a few Divaru men have learned to read and write, and thus are now better able to use Manjunatha for their hoylus.

Not only is the pattern of hoylu use among Divarus changing toward the employment of new gods, but it is also changing because of different economic motivations. Relatively more cases of hoylu are now given over land disputes and relatively fewer over jewelry. This might be expected from an examination of the changing patterns of availability of paddy land. Older Divaru informants remember when land went begging, and Brahmins actively sought tenants for their lands. It is only within the last few decades that population pressures have caused a scarcity of paddy lands. Now if a Divaru loses his paddy fields, he may encounter great difficulty in obtaining new ones. The more frequent requests for supernatural aid to recover land may reflect this insecurity and the increased importance of keeping the land one already has. Also, it helps explain why Divarus are turning to the more moral Dharmasthala god for solving land dispute cases.

Among Brahmins, the belief that Haviks have a fundamental right to own arecanut gardens is being put to a severe test. The area they reside in is becoming more densely populated, and the availability of new tillable land is decreasing. Because land is inherited equally by all sons, large landholders who can afford to return small plots of land acquired through the legal courts are lessening in numbers; thus there are fewer suitable persons against whom a hoylu may effectively be given. Conversely, as population increases and arecanut gardens are subdivided below the subsistence level, there should be more occasions for declaring hoylus. These opposing trends may undermine the structural basis of the Brahmin land-hoylu system and decrease its past high degree of effectiveness.

The changing pattern of moneylending tends to counterbalance the potentially greater use of hoylus by Brahmins. There are two main sources from which a Havik borrows —either from a wealthy Havik landowner or from a town-dwelling arecanut merchant, who usually loans by giving an advance on the next season's crop. Borrowing from a town-dwelling merchant of another caste is more common now than previously. If he forecloses on property, hoylus do not seem to be taken against him; even if they were, they would no doubt be less effective outside the orbit of village social pressure. If outside moneylenders continue to increase in importance, the frequency of Brahmin land hoylus may be expected to decrease.

SUMMARY AND CONCLUSIONS

The use of hoylu falls into three patterns which roughly correspond to three aspects of socioeconomic structure.

For garden-owning Brahmins, whose way of life depends upon arecanut land, the hoylu system is couched in terms of rigid morality and is used mainly over disputes involving land. Brahmins rarely abuse the system. The deity who decides the case and imposes punishment has an impeccable reputation for justice, strength, and righteousness, and a hoylu is effected by a respectable Sanskritic god surrounded by priests in a large temple.

As used by Brahmins, a hoylu acts to a very limited extent as an economic leveler; it takes from the wealthy and gives to the poor. But more importantly, it helps preserve the occupational homogeneity of Havik Brahmins. It is not a method for giving land to the poor or for making the poor wealthy, but is a device for allowing the near-bankrupt to retain a small piece of land. But because there is a certain fluctuation in family fortunes, this does not necessarily mean that the family is only postponing the economic decay that eventually results from natural population increase and land partition.

Hoylu, as used by Divarus, does not give so neat a picture. Only a minority of Divaru hoylus involve land disputes, but when they do occur, they may now be taken to Dharmasthala, the temple traditionally utilized by Brahmins. Most Divaru hoylus involve thefts of small items, often jewelry but sometimes objects of an inconsequential nature. In one case a whole family was wiped out by a hoylu against the head of the house for having stolen a plow, an easily replaceable item. Since the thief had returned the plow, it is difficult to see that the spirit acted upon the principle of causing harm only to the guilty person.

The differential morality of the Sanskritic god, used primarily by Brahmins, and of local village spirits, used mainly by non-Brahmins, is further shown by the fact that

Divarus do not always distinguish between hoylu and sorcery, while Haviks never confuse the two concepts.

The giving of a hoylu is involved with a third socio-economic pattern. It sometimes is used as a threat to reinforce the "master-servant" labor system in which a low-caste man, usually an Untouchable, borrows marriage money from a Brahmin and agrees to work in return.

There are several types of contractual relationships upon which the hoylu system impinges. First, it supports the sanctity of contract between a Brahmin "master" and his Untouchable "servant," a relationship which no longer has legal sanctions. Second, within the community of Havik Brahmins the hoylu system, under certain special circumstances, overrides the sanctity of contract between creditor and debtor. Third, the hoylu system supports an implicit but by no means absolute rule that the owner of paddy land should not dispossess his tenants.

It sometimes happens that through court action one man obtains an advantage over another which would push the defeated party out of the caste occupation, and the loser counters by attempting to force the application of a strong caste value through the hoylu system. Thus the system as utilized by Brahmins may supersede the State legal system as administered by courts of law. Thus it would appear that the morality of keeping a Havik Brahmin within the occupational fold is stronger than the morality of a contract between debtor and creditor, and this hierarchy of values has helped account for the effectiveness of land hoylus.

Enforcement of hoylu sanctions within the Brahmin community is a complex interplay of several factors: belief in supernatural punishments; belief in Havik Brahmin occupational unity; family pressure exerted on the wrongdoer in the house; and the excess of population over the availability of new cultivable land. With Divarus, the elements are less complex in that fear of supernatural retaliation seems to be more important. If this is true, the effectiveness of hoylus should decrease to the extent that secularization undermines the Divaru belief system.

Several trends can be noted. The use of the Dharmasthala god by Sudras has increased; although this development is an aspect of "Sanskritization," it also reflects modern educational policies and the increasing pressure on paddy lands. Brahmins have now almost completely stopped taking hoylus to local village spirits, an example in Totagadde of Brahmin withdrawal from village non-Sanskritic Hinduism.

The method of appealing to supernatural authority described in this paper points out basic features of the culture of a particular area of South India. It is one small aspect of Hinduism as a system of daily religious beliefs and actions, rather than as an elaborate philosophical system. As the hoylu pattern is probably restricted to a relatively small geographical unit, it shows how Hinduism is modified to fit special local circumstances. It also indicates some of the complex interrelations of one aspect of religion with the economic organization and social structure in a rural village area. But, perhaps most significantly, the hoylu system points out some of the important subcultural differences between castes or groups of castes within a restricted area. The term hoylu exists in both subcultures but its meanings are sharply divergent, in both subjective connotations and in actual practice.

SECTION THREE

REGULATION AND VITALITY

RECURRENT INVOLVEMENTS/SET PROCEDURES

Politics, like the elipse, has a double center. The ethnographic exhibits from Eastern Africa, India, and Burma represent a vast number and variety which show that the origin of politics lies as much in rebelliousness as in repression: without the tension between the two, politics would be like bought love, too easy to achieve the dignity of drama. You must seek beyond politics to the place of unopposed power—Belsen, Buchenwald, My Lai—to appreciate the sense in which countervailing opposition can be called the origin of politics. Where people have come to be not *others* but *things* they have no part in the social structure. Krupp's slave laborers didn't weigh on his conscience. The pattern of lynching in the Southern United States defined the condition a black must meet to be treated as human by the white: total ingratiation. But that condition reduces the political existence of the oppressed to a veiled nothingness.

The Kapauku are egalitarians—like the Anuak, they believe in obliging the rich to share. (pp. 224, 229) But the Anuak admire pomp and ceremony, the Kapauku admire wealth. Kachins "think of themselves as having a very clear-cut authority system," but an underlying principle of village structure is "competition for prestige and reputation." (p. 263) Recurrently, Kachins "become revolutionaries and repudiate the authority of the higher offices altogether." In each case there is a positive thrust toward the building up of superstructures, and a countervailing propensity for tearing them down. Implicit in the nature of the language we must use to discuss such processes is the notion of the greater legitimacy of the "constituted order" as contrasted to the assertion of rights expressed in "insurrection" or "revolution" or "rebellion." But the study of exotic societies, in which the anthropologist has specialized, helps to supply a comparative and longer-range perspective on rebellion. Seen as a recurrent phenomenon, with a characteristic pattern or style peculiar to each society where it is found, rebellion takes on a new appearance. The assertion of countervailing power, against established authority, has itself a regulative function —it acts as a control on personal power. The *hoylu,* in a village comprising no single hierarchy but a varied array of small power relationships, does much the same thing that an Anuak rebellion can do. Totagadde (p. 264) has not the kind of superstructure which can invite rebellion; the countervailing action there is appropriately undertaken within a religious frame. And in the case of the *hoylu,* a recurrent pattern of personal involvements has given rise to set procedures which are at once legitimate and counterstructural.

Juw and Dimi (p. 224) were bad examples among men of wealth and power; had no one feared the mischief which would result if other men followed their lead, public opinion would easily have been aligned against them. Evidently the balance in the Anuak case (p. 229) is a more sensitive one. There is more structure—the lines of authority are clearer, there is more formality. Awi and Dimi could compete for primacy in their village, but not contend for office. The Anuak commoner kowtows even to an ostracized headman, so unambiguous is the attribution to him of transcendent status. At the same time, the established leader walks by night, looking for signs of discontent; and he is sensitive to nuance in the signals he receives, where the Kapauku men seemed deaf. Paradoxically, rebellion seems to be a workable procedure for deposition of the village head in Anuakland—whereas it would break up a Kapauku community—precisely because of the well-structured nature of Anuak life. For the Kapauku, "most of the fighting force had 'combat motives' completely unrelated to the official cause of trouble." (p. 226) But Anuak rebellions are always carefully engineered and focused upon a clear political objective, which is to ostracize the current headman and replace him with a new favorite. It is said that virtually every Anuak village houses one or more deposed headmen, living in exile, and perhaps awaiting their chance to return with a change of fortune. Kapauku leadership is too much a thing of persons, not of offices, to allow for any procedure more refined than execution. Wherever a politician, once powerful, ceases to be so (that is, ceases to be dangerous) by the fact of being put out of office, we have there to deal with a firm political structure. Stability of structure doesn't call for immobility of persons.

Counterstructural procedures are then not *anti*structural in tendency but represent the principle of mobility within established frames. The Anuak do not speak disparagingly but with enthusiasm of their recurrent rebellions, which are certainly expressions of freedom from unpopular domination. In counterstructural movements we most clearly see the connection of personal involvement through conscious intention to institutional forms; but the same connections are to be seen in everyday life, though it may take a dramatic incident to exhibit them. Structure, unaffirmed, lacks vitality and substance; but mindless vitality doesn't make a social structure. For a case which dramatizes the conscious concern with structure, without which the intricate arrangements of our superstructures would surely never have been devised, we may turn back to the peripeties of Sandombu, the sometime witch of a small Ndembu village. (p. 43)

There is an anomaly in the way the two deaths, of which Sandombu was suspected, were handled. The headman Kahali Chandenda was a more important person than the woman Nyamwaha: but why, in that case, was divination used in the woman's inquest, while the guilt for a headman's death was never established? Presumably, the danger of (British) government intervention had not receded in the interval; it seems illogical, in a community given to blaming all sudden death on witchcraft, to make almost nothing of the question of guilt in a headman's passing, only a few days after a threat of sorcery. Sandombu was not even exiled from the village. He merely absented himself. Yet in the later case, though his denials seem to have convinced a good many, he was banished; and he was required to offer material and ritual tokens of remorse—of a change of will and character. (p. 45)

The anomaly can be explained if we grant that in each case the inquest served to intensify conscious concern with village structure. The meeting was in the *chota,* the court which is the locus of politics in an Ndembu community; and with Nyamwaha's death what we observe is a political trial. In response to accusation, a man speaks out. What grievances there are within the tightly knit community will appear. What reparations need to be made will be stated in circumstances of maximal collective authority—the high seriousness of the occasion makes possible a kind of transaction, with a depth of meaning, transcending the occurrences of everyday life. At the first death, the headmanship was empty and Sandombu by his own actions had removed himself from consideration for the office; if he had stayed and pressed his candidacy, the resistance would not have stopped short of the divining basket. At the second death, the headmanship was under attack. To leave Sandombu alone would be to let him claim not only the power to kill the sister of the headman, but immunity from legitimate controls still intact. The move to discipline Sandombu—to shame him and expel him—was a move to affirm the pattern of Ndembu village structure, just as the magical execution of Dimi affirmed the principles by which the Kapauku were willing to live, and to which they would hold their fellow man. Inquest and witchcraft accusation are elements of the political idiom of Ndembu, as retributive execution or disciplinary ostracism are elsewhere.

The Anuak (p. 229) allow no recriminations, and sanction no reparations, for deaths in a rebellion. When legitimate controls are not intact, there is no right and wrong. More precisely, morality is relative to structure; the structure of war sets its own rules, just as citizenship in a peaceful village implies acceptance of the rules of peaceful civility. Men generally act in fair knowledge of their structural circumstance. The drama of our lives is apt to sweep us away when the involvement is new, and we have no sense of an already trodden path. With recurrence we have begun to have standards for our performances; and standards, shared with the others involved, become procedures. The procedures for achieving a headmanship or for rebelling against an incumbent are more clear among the Ndembu than the Kapauku, more clear among the Anuak than the Ndembu. It would be harder to argue that events are more predictable among the Anuak than the Kapauku. However, the function of structure is not simply to produce monotony in human affairs. Arising in men's awareness of the social relevance of all that they do, structure turns involvement into intricate patterns of knowing relationship. What one knows (or soon learns) may be only how to proceed, once one has got involved—whether in marriage, adultery, or rebellion. But this is the kind of knowledge which, far from diminishing the need for personal judgment, calls for sophistication.

Structure *is* procedure: lineages, clans, classes, and castes can be described in terms of the procedures which maintain them; the life crises which give structure to the human career consist in procedural thresholds, sometimes ceremonially and otherwise contractually articulated; the settlement of disputes, the enforcement of authoritative orders, the seduction of the customer in the marketplace—all may be reduced to set procedures and well-rehearsed routines. In counterstructural action, which (though it be recurrent) is of an *ad hoc* sort, or in official action taken to curb the wayward, or in ritual acts and ceremonies, sanctioned procedures are explicitly recognized; in bureaucratic societies enrolling, licensing, favor-seeking, and tax-paying procedures punctuate the everyday existence of all respectable men with an inexorable rhythm. But the procedure of which we are conscious is the one which is new to us, which seems to be imposed on us; when it has been reduced to routine, we are beginning to see through it to the ends we would accomplish by it—it is the substance, not the form, of structure which preoccupies experience. Every procedure, after all, is imperiled by our consciousness of it; for the building, reforming, and tearing down of structures are consciously undertaken.

CEREMONY AND OFFICIALDOM

To see social structure in perspective we must learn how cultures grow and how regulative institutions achieve their vitality. The key question is not, How did it happen? but, How does it happen?

To see social structure in perspective we should ask how, in the context of culture growth, regulative institutions achieve their vitality. While this is a historical question, it is wholly general and can't be approached particularistically. The answer we require should apply to the Andamanese and the Papuans as well as to ourselves. I suggest that *it is the very recurrent involvements that most endanger the social structure, which provoke fresh forms and evoke renewed vitality.* Let us look at some indirect forms of social control.

Some societies possess yearly revitalization ceremonies, whose overt purpose is "world renewal." In some African societies a similar significance is attached to the great "bush schools" for young men and women, which alone can offer the credentials of adulthood. At such gatherings the central values of life are celebrated, and public feeling is heightened. The symbolism of an Australian fertility ceremony may be, on the one hand, bound up obscurely with the meaning of native myth; or, on the other hand, the symbolism may be crudely apparent; yet there is an intense presence of danger, felt as sacredness, in the proceedings. The ingredients of ceremony are those of the lives from which the ceremony has grown. How do you renew the world? take courage from the launching of a new generation? banish the darkness of spirit begotten of social isolation? As war games and dance may banish fear, sexual license may banish the sense of estrangement; and as we can expect to find the one in a warlike society, the other is proper to a society lacking permanent and well-bounded communities above the granular level of the household or band.

"Initiation rites" are dramatic statements of the condition of accession to adulthood. It isn't hard to see why, with their obviously tutelary function, they are widespread. Especially where an artificial, physical alteration of the body of the initiate is required as the overt ritual condition, the ceremony states that it is elders (of one's own sex category) who confer maturity on their successors; maturation isn't natural but social. But a statement to this effect would have no deep meaning if the atmosphere were not extraordinary and the path of learning tortuous: if the initiate weren't at once determined to endure, yet seized with dread, if the elders weren't obscure and overbearing. The conflict of generations is as much a part of the drama as is the act of will by which one generation gives over to the next (or inflicts on it?) the signs of power and vitality.

Why fear and cruel pain? Why circumcision, subincision, clitoridectomy? Why can't initiations be "civilized" everywhere, like confirmation ceremonies in the West or long-winded school graduations? Setting aside the possibility that some forms of oratory may be harder to endure than the flicker of a flint knife in a skilled hand, the effect of the latter is certainly more lasting and properly traumatic. The sharpness of meaning achieved with the knife could not be obtained by any less dramatic means. Circumcision is not word symbolism but the kind which plays with real stakes and undeniable meanings: it would take a man of the West, circumcised at infancy, to doubt that the prepuce is a powerful instrument of pleasure and miss the irony of equating its loss with manliness. In like fashion it would take a man of the West, never starved for meat, to miss the point of sacrifice, where men feast like the gods and so transcend the mundane.

Even if we conceived that the function of ceremony was only to entertain, we would have to concede that sure-fire entertainment can be hard to provide: a slight acquaintance with television could be enough to convince. Without vitality, ceremony is empty; and empty ceremonies are hard to repeat even once. In ceremony the relevant social world is assembled or represented; ceremony is distinguished from ritual by the degree of public participation. To achieve participation, ceremony must incorporate what matters. That is, in form and substance the ceremonial occasion must derive from and present a resolution to those recurrent involvements which most persistently beset the people.

If these ideas about ceremony are sound, it follows that you could infer the focal concerns of a society from the nature of its ceremonies. In some "circumcision societies," for instance, you could look for signs of strain, especially competition for women in polygynous societies, between adjacent generations of males: the ceremonial principle is much like hazing in the old bourgeois college fraternities of North America—an ambivalent welcome to the club of men, extended to those who will soon succeed you in power. You might look among societies with regular "world renewal" ceremonies to discover if it wasn't a lack of coherence above the level of the local settlement—a sort of social centrifugality—which was countered in the holiday gathering. Can one find a passionate localism reenacted, rearoused and resolved, in such massings of the people at a single dance-ground? or would one be led on to a more meticulous classification of ceremonial types and social structures? In politically-territorially segmented societies in Asia, Africa, and the New World a remarkably similar ceremony is found—the rekindling of all fires from a central one, kept at the place of the divine ruler. Does that not answer to the supreme political danger of such societies—that the prestige of the one acknowledged center of maximal power should fade? One would not expect such a ceremony where the kingship was securely backed by a secular, military hierarchy and an integral bureaucracy: in the modern state, it is a massive parade of centralized power and wealth, not a dramatization of the frail threads by which a people must cling to its unity, which we should expect. But where do we fit the massive monuments of Egypt's Early Kingdom, or the staggering rituals of bloody death toward which all of Aztec public life was bent?

Between those examples and the cases we have selected there is a great difference of scale; between the encyclopedic survey and the tiny sample at our disposal here there is the same difference of scale, and I confess to preferring the smaller scale and a few cases I can control; I'll be satisfied with something less than a theory of the pyramids. But those monuments are evidence enough of the power which can be acquired by a ceremonial tradition focused on the meaning of death and deity; and we are reminded how naturally such a ceremonial cult can become the property of a powerful officialdom. Our humbler ethnographic cases do only a little to illuminate the great theocracies of the past, but they do demonstrate the first principle—the wholeness of the political-ceremonial domain. I think this pvoides the key to what Ruth Benedict called a superstructure, and perhaps a clue to what Thomas Hobbes figured as Leviathan, a great multitude of men massed in the form of a monstrous organism.

The passage which follows describes a dance at an Australian "corroboree," in which the Aborigines respond to a parody of the typical official, representative of European rule, the native policeman. Humor, like intoxication, is a transformation of consciousness, not a distortion of perception—through the magnification of humor we often make more keen our perception of the social world, just as through the intensification of the dance we may present to our senses a social fact of which we otherwise are dimly aware.

R. M. & C. H. Berndt
The World of the First Australians, p. 324

In one scene a policeman, a "man with chains", was shown trying to bring in "witnesses" for a court case. The actors here were men, representing attractive young women all roped ("chained") together by the neck in a long line. The policeman led the way, dancing slowly around the clearing; but every now and then when he was looking the other way a small raggedy actor, a "bagman" or "swaggie", would come sneaking up from behind and try to take away one of the girls. The policeman, turning and seeing him, would drive him away, kicking at him and lashing out with a stick, with a great deal of noise and commotion:

he wanted the girls for himself. The side play, gestures and impromptu remarks of the actors, punctuating the singing, kept the audience in a state of hilarious laughter for over an hour.

This little Australian burlesque serves as a paradigm for the nature of ceremony and its relation to officialdom. The skit shows a miscarriage of authority. The laughter of the audience underwrites its discontent with injustice and gives a particular form to its concern for rectification: what is a laughing matter is not yet cause for revolution but is cause for reform. The people sanction officialdom. Officials are servants of the society taken collectively, though officials are masters in the reality of everyday life, when society's members are to be taken singly. It is through ceremony that the multitude can effectively be represented as one body, expressing a collective concern and exerting a collective power. It is when ceremony fails to unite the village that the Anuak turn to rebellion, and the attempt by force to reestablish the legitimacy of the official order. (p. 229)

In Anuakland, as in the Kachin Hills, officialdom is concentrated in a comparatively small fraction of the community; but in each case the controlling elite is in direct communication with the common citizen, through the channels held steady by ceremonial tradition. The South Indian caste village presents a different picture, particularly where the traditional village panchayat is found, expressing upper-caste paternalism. Stratic barriers reduce to a formality the direct communication between Brahmin official and lower caste or Untouchable citizen. And each caste possesses its own system of control, so that in certain matters—as the *hoylu* shows us—the sources of political, jural, or ritual intercession may be radically decentralized. The private creditor, regarded as a small-time banker, may even share in the style and functions of officialdom, for he may be subject through a *hoylu* to the same countersanctioning power which makes the official, in the end, the community's servant.

The difference between the caste village and the chiefly

village of the Kachins is instructive. Though the Kachins may have two styles of politics, the effect in any single village is a coherent set of procedures in which all citizens cooperate. In Totagadde, Havik and Divaru procedures are distinct, reflecting distinct schemes of value. It is rare that a religious complex is so eminently practical, and therefore so transparent as to its function, as the *hoylu* procedures Harper describes. (p. 264) The Sanskritic god is literate, irreproachably wise, dispassionate, and long of memory; the fickle village spirits are "more violent and bloody," inclined to self-serving and sorcery, and impatient. The two castes, with their two agricultural callings, have maintained two styles of life. Accordingly, they have devised procedures which presuppose two styles of supernatural service, suited each to the character of a distinct clientele.

In a footnote to the *Hoylu* paper, Harper wrote that a preliminary reader had asked. "Why do hoylus exist?"

> He suggested that certain types of authority are invested in the supernatural when the society lacks strong power positions; that is, when political equality precludes the existence of a type of political organization strong enough to enforce sanctions for the rules in question. This agrees quite well with the situation found in Totagadde. Certainly a degree of authority to punish thieves or to arbitrate land disputes is given to the supernatural that does not exist in any individual or group of individuals. This Brahmin community is well known for its lack of an effective political organization. There is a strong feeling of equality between Haviks that often overrides other values such as respect for age and status. Quarrels between individual Brahmins are relatively common and long lasting. Although these are often taken to panchayats for settlement, the panchayat members have few means of enforcing their decision. This is reflected by the frequency with which cases go to civil courts after being arbitrated by a panchayat. Divarus, who have a slightly more effective political organization than

do Brahmins, still have no individual or group of individuals who are given any strong political authority.[16]

It may seem anomalous to characterize a caste village by "political equality," but the phrase does apply to the relations among househoulds within a single caste, where considerable differences of wealth can't be reflected in congruent differences of official status. Politics and religion are not so alike in function as to be interchangeable; but they are complementary alternatives for handling of problems of order. The best-known statement of this principle is "Religion is the opiate of the people." When this Marxist battle cry is translated into dispassionate language the point is a worthy one. Religion is nothing if it isn't popular. Where religion is failing you can expect an urban proletariat to show the signs of social disorganization. Stratification alienates the common folk from officialdom, whose decisions become therefore unresponsive and exploitative. In many modern cities that tendency has been counteracted through the development of elaborate systems of patronage and corrupt dealing between the people and the petty officialdom. Where a democratic ballot or some other device has maintained credibility men may take comfort in a formal guarantee of responsive government; or it may be that the church is more responsive than the politician or labor-union official to some of the needs of some proletariats. Or, where caste cleavages only reinforce the isolation of police and government officials from an urban mass, and the established religion is not adequate to the times, there may be disorder and a reign of political and religious ferment. A social superstructure cannot be understood in isolation from the pattern of popular, recurrent involvements which are the insistent sources of structural vitality in any community.

There is a sense in which the "political" is identical with the "centralized" structure—for example, a highly centralized church is an authority-bearing church, whose central bureaucracy might be guilty of playing politics in the handling of certain issues. What changes are correlated with decentralization? or to put it otherwise, What replaces political

[16] Harper, p. 815.

authority in the superstructures of noncentralized societies? How widely could a politically powerful personage delegate his power, before it changed in quality or dissipated altogether? and how is the regulative function served if not through authoritative systems of control? A political superstructure is a pyramidal one; but as the pyramid is flattened the quality of the regulative function is changed, depending gradually less on the decisions of individuals and more on the maintenance of set, ceremonially sanctioned procedures. The Kachins, who from time to time become revolutionaries and repudiate their vertical structure of offices, provide us with a case in point.

The pattern of revolution of the Kachin village places it between the secular but heavily ceremonial constitution of the Anuak and that of the South Indian caste village. The Anuak do not revolt—that is, they do not level their village pyramid, but only replace its personnel. But, logically, the Anuak *could* become revolutionaries, however chaotic the consequence might be; for the political pyramid does exist, at least on the village level, and could be torn down. The practical difficulty is that Anuak culture does not supply an alternative basis of regulation, which would make village life feasible without concentrated political power—in the flattened condition of Totagadde Haviks or Divarus. That versatility is just what Kachin culture, with its peculiar blend of ritual-political emphases, makes possible. When a Kachin village faction revolts, its aim can't well be to unseat a chief and replace him: his office has strong ritual underpinnings, which can't be supplied at will in support of a usurper—if the office itself is legitimate, the authority of the incumbent can't be challenged. Countervailing action must be taken against the office itself, challenging its legitimacy. In practice, that means that the rebellious faction must move away and found a new village basing itself on a doctrine of political equality. Rank, with its scale of prestige and privilege, is done away with; and public ritual may be directed to a new set of (unaristocratic) spirits. But the revolutionaries don't have to invent their new structure—its rules are known everywhere, as part of standard Kachin lore. The Kachin village is dimorphic, knowing two polar sets of principles by which the regulative functions of a community may be organized, and able to achieve a fair degree of stability within either structural frame. Here, then, are villages which regularly build, tear down, and rebuild their superstructures over long cycles of time. Kachin culture offers a unique field of evidence for studying the viability of such structures.

TO AFFIRM OR DISAFFIRM

In Kachin society, open to fluctuation between flat and pyramidal distribution of political power and wealth, the *legitimation* of preeminent power and wealth is one of the central problems of the social structure. Where popular thought and behavior swing between an ethic of egalitarian cooperation and one of aristocratic *noblesse oblige*, the privilege of an aristocrat is in jeopardy if, first, the exaction of privilege is not matched in a rough way by assumption of equally tangible responsibilities; and, second, the reputation of the principle of aristocratic rule—its ethical value—is not maintained. We may call these the tangible (or practical) and intangible (or ideological) modes of legitimating power—of assuring its continued acceptance. For power in a human social system can't ultimately rest on physical strength or the *de facto* possession of physical weapons—that is easy for us to see, anyhow, in the context of Kachin culture; and it was clear to a man like Hitler in his own situation. If I can't go to sleep knowing that others will credit my authority tomorrow as they have today, then I possess no authority; no more is a hunted thief, who has a million dollars, a rich and powerful man. Authority and power rest on legitimacy. The legitimacy of an established order is normally affirmed through the idiom of ritual-ceremonial procedure.

The Kachins do not kill their domestic livestock casually for meat, but consume the meat only under the procedural rules of a sacrifice, sharing the meat around the whole village (p. 250). Rich men make larger sacrifices than poor men, and doing so compete "for prestige and reputation rather than wealth" (p. 263). The competition for prestige centers on sacrifice and the various roles and statuses which comprise ıe "priestly" side of Kachin officialdom. If we regard the iscrimination of rich and poor as a pervading aspect of the ·hole ritual-ceremonial complex among the Kachins, and re-ard it as a regular part of the procedure that "the nats de-ıand much bigger sacrifices from the wealthy than they do ·om the poor" (p. 261), we see that such procedures do not imply *reflect* the essential character of Kachin social struc-ıre, but in fact *contain and exhibit* that essential character. f "competition for prestige" is exhibited in the desire of the ich to display their wealth through sacrifice, and if the peo-·le *demand* such a display, then the institution which main-ains this reputational competition, and sets its style, *is* the in-titution of sacrifice.

This may lead us to conclude that the idea of social struc-ure is at odds with common sense. Is it not only a matter of ·ommon sense to regard a social structure as an *expression* ·f the character of a people? Was not the Nazi regime in Germany an expression of German national character (that s, "authoritarianism"—an endemic personality quirk among Germans)? And are not the institutions of democracy secure n all nations with a "democratic personality," while the same nstitutions can never take root in other countries, where a lifferent national culture prevails, with other character val-ıes? Again, in the "Free World" are not the totalitarians of he right and of the left, who would suspend civil freedoms n the name of some inscrutably higher good merely "psycho-logical cases"—in fact, deviants? Have we not argued in this book that character is the vehicle of structurally relevant mo-tivation? Evidently, if it is common sense to regard Kachin sacrificial practices as an expression of Kachin character; and if we are holding, on the contrary, that Kachin ritual-cere-monial practices represent the forge at which that character is made; then we are departing a little from the path of com-mon sense. Is it possible that religious practices, which so patently deal with intangibles, can have so much practical im-portance as our new position implies?

If it is not wrong to assume that social danger and social vitality spring from a common source, connected with the re-currence of certain characteristic personal (emotional, ethi-cal) involvements in a particular social structure; and if we may assume that a community's ceremonial life will sensitive reflect that pattern of involvements; then ritual-ceremoni procedures indicate areas of structural stress. In the Kach context, the balance of egalitarian and authoritarian ethics there to be seen in the procedures of sacrifice, and in the id of a spirit world which they imply. The spirits themselv are sharply ranked, and the corresponding ranking with the human world is expressed in the size and relative san tity of offerings on the different structural levels. But th ethic of *noblesse oblige,* the obligation falling on the priv leged few, is always maintained: if a pig is to be eaten, must be eaten by all. That appears very clearly in the thi day's ceremony of the September ceremonial cycle which wa described (p. 251). The condition under which the chiefl priestly officialdom is allowed to enjoy the seclusion of su perior status and sanctity is that the pig they sacrifice alon shall not be eaten at all, but buried. The sharing of sacrifici meat is a legitimate right of the people. The right *would nc exist* if the procedures of the sacrifice, in which the whol community solemnly takes part, allowed officialdom to ea alone: for that would be to state, in symbolic terms clearl understood by all, that the most important goods of the so ciety are reserved to the rich and powerful, not owed to th people.

Where does the constitution—the politically relevant socia structure—of a society reside? A constitution exists by virtu of a substantial agreement on procedures and on the prin ciples governing them. Ritual is rote-learned procedure; bu it may have vitality if its *raison d'être* is present to the per former, if he possesses the criteria by which at need th sequence of acts could be amended to acquire new meaning the difference is like that between the parrot's sentence an the child's. One consequence of Kachin ceremonialism i evidently to convince the people that their communities ar well structured, stable entities "having a very clear-cu authority system" (p. 263). But another consequence is actua vitality, mobility, structural versatility. No doubt, the languag of sacrifice is ancient in its origins; among the Kachins it is not a dead language but one through which the constitution of any community is and must be affirmed.

A ceremony is the celebration of particular values and their exhibition in particular arrangements of social structure. Why do we so often find ceremony connected with marriage? with death and burial? with inauguration to high office? What is the meaning of those elaborate rites of passage we sometimes find in connection with puberty, school graduation, and parturition/birth? Don't all such ceremonies refer to regularly recurrent crises, which may loom large in the lives of individuals, but which scarcely seem to "endanger the social structure"? And what, after all, is the significance of the fact that so much of that calendar of ceremony which characterized small-scale and traditional societies has been dropped from the structure of contemporary urban-industrial life? Clearly, ceremony is not restricted to the political life; and just as clearly, structure may be affirmed in other ways than through the idiom of ceremony. Our subject, then, is broader than politics; and we must examine phenomena other than ceremony.

Consider what we know of Kachin witchcraft. It is a sort of *tertium quid* between ceremonial procedures and those rather different procedures which are oriented to the handling of grievances and threats to the established tie network. Witchcraft among the Kachins is a half-sacred phenomenon: a witch will cause the same sort of illness or misfortune that a nat, a deity, may cause; a witch can be described as a sort of bad counterpart to a good nat (pp. 252–53). From societies where the actual procedures relating to "witch-ridding" are better known, we can surmise that the Kachins handled their witches without hysteria. Diviners are not agitators—they stay out of personal involvements with their customers, and in order to do that are restricted to making acceptable findings. Accusation of a person as a witch is generally hedged about so nicely with form and ceremonial that it could not in itself arouse the passions of a community—the passion would have to be there already. That is what E. R. Leach meant by saying, "Witchcraft becomes manifest when the moral constraints of the ideally correct social order lose their force (p. 254)." That is, witchcraft cases, with their half-sacred character, will be prominent when the ordinary operation of grievance procedures is not sufficient to maintain order. For when that happens, the constitutional premises on which the tie network has been evolved are in jeopardy. The "bad relationships of jealousy, malice and suspicion" which Leach associates with witchcraft are involvements falling into a pattern inimical to the principles by which the community is organized.

In all societies, private violence, carried to a certain pitch, becomes a matter of public concern. But in some of the communities we have considered in this book public concern does not mean official intervention. Feud in many societies is a legitimate condition: usually it is not very destructive, and is a preliminary to settlement, much as a labor strike may be a necessary step toward free negotiation of a new contractual agreement in an industrial setting. Where official intervention is possible and normal, we are dealing with a lower order of public concern than in the case where violence is able to upset the normal structural arrangements. The difference between a public disturbance and a riot is a matter of scale, to be sure; but a disturbance becomes a riot when it commands that higher order of public concern—at the point where a move must be made in defense of the structure itself. Again, within the household a child's misbehavior may become a matter of public concern; and if the child is successfully corrected we have to deal only with a lower order of concern. But if the correction doesn't work, so that the child produces a structural crisis—the family system can't continue as it was—and reorganization, the concern is of a higher order. The structure of the group has been endangered; and it may either fall apart or, with renewed vitality and ethnical consciousness of the group's nature, find a fresh form. When we seek to understand the regulative institutions of human societies it is not enough to consider only how the lower-order matters of public concern are handled; we must ask how the apparatus for handling them is itself maintained. Citizens of a highly bureaucratic nation may be possessed of the illusion of an infinite regression of officials, each one backed by another; but anthropology can help us to escape from that illusion.

Compare the two cases of Juw and Dimi, big men among the Kapauku Papuans (p. 224): Juw's execution was secular in style, but Dimi was killed by black magic. The sorcerers were the society's most powerful men; and the essential difference in the two cases was that the motive in Juw's killing was simple jealousy—he was rich and didn't share enough—while the motive in Dimi's half-sacred execution was more serious. He was dishonest and a troublemaker; and he is described as the leader of a political faction, anxious to become village headman. Juw had been setting a bad example, since his fellow villagers could not rely on him for the kind of dependency ties they expect to form with a rich man. Dimi, on the other hand, was attempting to unseat a headman who did exhibit the called-for virtues, though Dimi himself did not; and that would have upset the principles on which the scant-enough formal structure was based, which Kapauku culture had evolved. The procedures of the Kachins are more elaborate, but the place of magic and sorcery—between secular governance and sacred affirmation of the constitution itself—does not seem to have been different in principle. The execution of Juw was a serious, secular act. No community can survive in which it is possible for any five men to decide they will execute a sixth simply because they think they have cause. The Kapauku community is not protected by an elaborate procedure, but does have an effective constraint in its lineage-loyalty system. If Juw had not really been detestable, his nearest kin would not have agreed to the killing. If other persons than they had done the actual shooting, the kin would have been committed by lineage loyalty to taking revenge: it would have been not an execution but a murder. The procedure involved in such a handling of grievances is definite, and serves to isolate the resentments involved so that greater disruption of community doesn't result. But the procedure is a secular one. The danger which Juw's existence presented to his community was evidently not of an order which called for more than secular measures. The danger presented by Dimi, on the other hand, was apparently not felt as a secular matter. Involvements which lend themselves to sorcery and witchcraft have about them a style which borders on that of ritual-ceremonial procedure.

The seven-day cycle of sacrifice and "tabooed holiday" which was described for the Kachins is "perhaps the most sacred of all regular annual ceremonials: the time is one of anxiety; will the crop flourish or fail?" (p. 251) As a calendrically scheduled event, the ceremony is like a puberty rite, which focuses on the fertility of an individual person rather than that of the village fields. In a puberty rite, the community concerns itself with the fitness of a new generation of adults: will they flourish or will they fail? The two sorts of ceremony are similar in celebrating the values of the good life. Puberty rites also celebrate character values and their exhibition in the social structure: the docility of the individual in the face of a mastering group is implicit in such rites, whether of the sort which tends to mass initiates together in a school or the sort which isolates the adolescent—as in the vision-quest vigil of North America, or the widespread menstrual seclusion for girls. The Kachin calendrical ceremony centers on a pyramiding of sacrificial rites, from the level of the household to that of the village itself. In each case—the puberty rite and the agricultural ceremony—the values which are celebrated are the most general, and the ideal model of social relationships is similarly general, as if to exhibit only principles and not details, universals and not particulars. Ritual-ceremonial procedures focus on the office, not the incumbent temporarily taking up its mantle; on the male or female role, not the personality of the particular adolescent; on the constitution of the community, not the particular interpersonal and interdomestic network which at any given time manifests that constitution. Rite and ceremony are addressed not to clear and present dangers but to imponderable and chronic strains on the social order.

The recurrent involvements whose dangerous potential is contained by ritual-ceremonial procedures are therefore preeminently involvements "within the tie." A father—who, by reason of his status, alone is qualified to sacrifice, on behalf of his household, to his ancestors—is by that fact shown to be the key person of the house; and all his authority, with all the impassioned adjustments its requires in him and others, is in the balance. In the rite of ancestral sacrifice he celebrates and solemnizes his position; in partaking of the meat which was offered, members of the household subscribe to the structural statement which has been made. Involvements within intimate, maximal-claim ties have a residual sacredness about them, which is clearly related to their *constitutional* importance in human society. Patricide and incest are "unholy" crimes: in most societies, they would not be handled by courts at law but by apparently spontaneous and impassioned action—very often, by suicide. In contrast, adultery is in many societies the most frequent cause of litigation among neighbors. For the individuals concerned, involvement may be as intense in the adulterous relationship as in the other; but the implication upon public discovery is not the same. Irregular involvements within the context of ties with axiomatically given content are clearly threats to the fundamental social understandings by reason of which we can speak of such given content. Rite and ceremony, by affirming the acceptable content of the tie, serve to forestall irregular involvements by defining them anathema—mystically dangerous.

The effect of the myth and ceremony of divine kingship is to make it known that rebellion against the established political order is mystically, not just secularly, dangerous. A coronation ceremony is a statement, not about the person of the incumbent, but about the kingship itself—the nature and the ethics of the office, the scope of its authority and responsibility. Coronations, like induction ceremonies otherwise, speak as much to the office-taker as to the present public and official retinue. The office is a crucial one, and the occasion of succession to office by a new and untried person is clearly the proper time for a ceremonial affirmation of the ethical and structural principles embodied in it. If the actual political involvements of the king should exhibit antithetical principles, then the kingship itself is in danger. A king would have no power if he had not the power to disaffirm those common understandings on which his high throne is perched. For the power to affirm or disaffirm lies always in the same hands.

VITALITY OF STRUCTURES

Our study of the structure of human societies has brought us to the question of freedom and individuality. There's little comfort in the thought that everyone is both free and unfree; there is trouble with the logic involved. But the position we have reached does justify one small conclusion.

If we regarded the problem of governance in human affairs as really two problems, one of a lower and one of a higher order, the same should apply to the problem of freedom. On the one hand, my lot is to be cast in with a particular group, to become involved there, and to become in some measure knowingly aware of the social frame within which that involvement must be contained. To ask, with those considerations in mind, how far I am free is to ask the lower-order question. But, on the other hand, it is also my lot to affirm or disaffirm the principles on which that social frame is made; for the quality of my being lends substance and vitality to the structure of my group, or it drains them away. To ask about my freedom to affirm and disaffirm the structure of my social life is to raise the higher-order question. Do I freely determine the quality of my being? In his essay on social structure and culture, T. S. Eliot wrote:

T. S. Eliot
Notes Towards the Definition of Culture 1949, pp. 30–31

The reflection that what we believe is not merely what we formulate and subscribe to, but that behaviour is also belief, and that even the most conscious and developed of us live also at the level on which belief and behaviour cannot be distinguished, is one that may, once we allow our imagination to play upon it, be very disconcerting. It gives an importance to our most trivial pursuits, to the occupation of our every minute, which we cannot contemplate long without the horror of nightmare.

By arguing that character, well understood, resolved the "puzzle of motivation" (by committing us as persons to roles motivationally predefined), we established an idea of social structure bound to ethics. We have come now to the point of inquiring into the sources of vitality of social structures; and we have found that this is not distinguishable from an inquiry into their ethical depths.

As we move from a society with simple and informal arrangements to one pervaded by elaborate social forms—from Kiowa Indians or Kapauku Papuans (pp. 36, 224) to Hpalang or Totagadde (pp. 250, 264)—do we move from a context of less to one of more structure? from a context of more to one of less individual freedom? from one in which the individual looms large to one in which he is dwarfed by the clutter of forms among which he must find his way? If it is clear that some social systems have met the problem of ordering chaos better than others, what is the role of formality in achieving structural stability, and how far is a move toward formality a move away from vitality—how far does vitality spring from personal freedom of volition? If some structures will stand up better under stress than others, how casual can you make an institution without weakening it? How little constraining can you make the roles without vitiating the motivation of the persons who should take them up? What, in short, is the relation between structure in the special sense of form, and structure in the generic sense of order? between conformity to an ethical norm and affirmation of it?

Character and the ethical life come into being through actual involvement with others within the broad frame of that-which-was-structured-by-others-before-you. The structure includes, besides the established patterns for social ties, the patterns for recurrent involvement and the patterns of public procedure evolved about them. Social structure is not repressive in and of itself, although many structures provide for the repression of initiatives that others would allow;

and oppression may be real. No social structure can embody the ideal values of freedom, as they were once embodied in a mythical Golden Age or the Garden of Eden; human nature itself supplies us with no character at all—there is no way of life natural to human kind.

We began with the statement of Hobbes, that "a Person, is the same that an Actor is, both on the stage and in common Conversation." (p. 3) It is in the well-ordered society that we should look for Persons to be the most *convincing* Actors, at least off stage. Can we ever really understand the drama of Juw, the rich man who could not be brought around by moral persuasion but must be killed by his son and brothers? (p. 224) No, because neither Juw nor his cousins enjoyed any lucid understanding of the structure of their lives: if they had Juw would have been responsive—through normal sensitivity of character—to the demands others would have laid on him. Here is a case of deficiency of structure. We expect in the well-ordered society to find a moral nexus—a basis of intuitive mutual understanding and responsiveness—adequate to having saved Juw, or even to tolerating his eccentricity. Social structure and moral order are two aspects of the same thing; and some societies *do* have more and some less of that thing. The expressive life of man is intensified as truly as it is constrained by the social framework within which it must operate. The nearest approach we can make to a truly free society is the one in which the drama itself so fascinates and absorbs us that we can't be aware of its structure. We can't gain more than a spurious freedom *from* social structure: it was Juw, after all, who thought he could both gain the world and ignore his own good name.

PART FOUR

THE FUTURE OF EQUALITY

SECTION ONE

THREE KINDS OF SANCTION

POLITICS AND CEREMONY RECONSIDERED

There is no politics without ceremony, and ceremonial ehavior exhibits the political structure even where the spirit formality seems to have suppressed spontaneous feeling. he pageantry associated with the "rational" bureaucratic ate, as it must be one of the heaviest that men have de- sed, shouldn't be our measure. Anuak political enthusiasms e expressed in uninhibited dance whose mood plays upon e border of actual rebellion. The bureaucratic equivalent, y contrast, seems massive, wooden, and sanctimonious. atriotic speeches are not always dull, they may achieve lemnity, but they are seldom lively where their sentiments e unopposed. Open tension brings life to a public occasion; e possibility of tension renews the meaning of old symbols. he ceremonial atmosphere of a protest demonstration breaks own when there is violence, giving way to crowd behavior. he provocateur of the left or right is moved precisely to oil the symbolic effect of a politics he opposes. But even e most violent riot is fed by demonstrative behavior and so ares in the nature of dance as well as war. The Anuak ould need no subtle explanation of our inner-city up- sings.

The reason that officialdoms surround themselves with omp and use the language of ceremony to assert their privileged status is not hocus-pocus. An official who had establish his credibility through rational argument (as agai credentials) with every client in every case would not g his work done however sure his arguments. Rational thoug has made an essential contribution to the shaping of a workable social structure as it has to a physical building, b it takes more than thought to make a structure real.

If ceremony and politics are practically inseparable, th are analytically so distinct that we may fail to notice th actual interpenetration. We don't find it hard to distingui between what goes on in a church and what goes on in courtroom—they seem poles apart. The political alignments the mosque or the meetinghouse may be scandalous if th are furtive, but as "latent functions" of religion their structu weight will be hard to determine. The political functions worship which are manifest, such as disposing men to pea and brotherhood instead of war and strife, are genera taken for granted and often thought ineffective. Even wh churches in England and North America were found to part of the class system, few critics attributed *much* re influence to the churches. A comparable function of the cou of law would be maintaining ethnic discrimination: a cer monial function, relating to the allocation of privileges statuses, lurks behind the manifest political function of se ting conditions on the freedom of individuals. But the mo substantial link between church and courtroom lies in the claims to normative authority. In terms of a theory of soci sanctions, the church seems to deal in preventive sanctio the court in corrective or punitive sanction. The difference exhibited in a transparent manner by the juxtaposition taboo and law.

Taboo no more works by "emotion" than law works b "reason"; both have the character of negative sanctions, ope ating as deterrent threats. Both taboo and law can ha positive social value as well: a priest keeps taboos to pr serve his people, and a Babbitt or a Blimp will keep the la for the same reason. But where law is associated with *po facto* punishment, and hence with a philosophy of tran gression and guilt, taboo rests on ideas of supernatur danger and contagion. The virtues of law are much adve ised: legal norms can be discursively formulated and minutely odified, and lend themselves to political implementation: the ourt system is the backbone of state power everywhere. Taboo has the advantage of being much more direct as a leterrent, since the tabooed act is itself charged with danger, vhether the sanction is supposed to come suddenly or slowly. f you are an anarchist you will note as an advantage of aboo that it presupposes no authoritative institutions for its mplementation. But the fatal flaw of taboo as a system of anctions is that it depends on that deep consensus of values vhich is only associated with traditional cultures. The last ew millennia of human history have favored politics, and the ast few centuries have favored the breakup of tradition, substituting the new mysteries of utopian or other ameliorative deology. Taboo survives but furtively and has an understandably tarnished reputation; it is as obvious to *us* that aboos don't work as it was to the eighteenth-century Polyiesian that they do.

Taboo produces ritual avoidance, whereas penal law proluces prudential avoidance. The two systems of sanction are elated to social structure as sanitation and curing are related o health. Conditions for a healthy population are nutrition, reedom, and a favorable natural environment; and where heir opposites prevail, under modern or ancient civilization, he best of medicines won't give you health. The conditions or a viable social structure are those which make *diffuse* sanctions effective: that is, conditions which generate character sensitivity and the readiness of individuals to identify with the roles they must play. We sometimes speak of a person as having more or less "commitment" to a cause, and in like manner we observe that the commitment of a whole community to its espoused values can diminish or increase. In the political sphere we speak of "credibility" or "legitimacy." Where credibility and commitment levels are high, the viability of the social system is, too. The system of formal sanctions, whether based on taboo or on law, will operate smoothly. But when there is a general falling away from social values can we expect the regulative institutions to "fight" the trend, generating new commitment? A system of formal sanctions depending on its credibility can't create it. Superstructur have a regulative, not a mastering, function.

It is not hard to find cultures which exemplify the politi of minimal authority. Kiowa (p. 36) thinking about troub cases could scarcely be called legalistic, and the solutio have an *ad hoc* quality which it might be hard to find an urban boys' corner gang. There are rules, but no rule How are sanctions applied to transgressors? Evidently, the victim of violence has no kin group—no one who will sha the sense of outrage—there are likely to be no formal sanctio at all. People felt badly enough toward Twkoide to deny hi honor for killing his wife at what seemed to be a compromi ing tryst, but the balance of rights was doubtful, and her k were not prepared to be outraged. His second crime (p. 3 was against a kinless woman, a tribal stranger: his own sc would have been prepared to take her part but lacked autho ity to *sanction*—he could only have taken a personal veng ance, without organized support. But the Kiowa, like t Kapauku (p. 224), expect close kin to execute a person wh has outraged important segments of his society. When becomes a matter of keeping the public peace, an act vengeance or vindictiveness will cease to be private; it b comes a sanction.

The politics of minimal authority is not the politics of *n* authority, but of no *vested* authority. Public authority falls one party or another, in accordance with the situation. Sinc it is not enough to say that authority is situational, witho indicating how situations get their structure, I shall ca systems of sanction like those of the Kiowa or Kapauku *tran actional systems of social control.* Tangu (p. 56), Fula (p. 167), Dobu (p. 219), and Gumlao Kachin (p. 25 illustrate the principle involved: authority inheres in t act which can be shown to restore equilibrium in a bilater or polycentric social universe. The kind of act which is r garded as sanctionable in a transactional system is one whic seems to threaten the peace. Persons who are in position restore the peace have authority to do so. Social control transactional in the exact sense that the application of san tions is by lateral, not vertical, action. The motivation the sanctioning agent can be called sublimated self-intere and distinguished from the motivation of acts of vested authority, which are official acts. In the transactional system of social control there is no office and no official motivation to absolve the actor of personal responsibility. Rather, he must mobilize social support for action he undertakes on his own behalf. It is this social support which constitutes authority. No one is concerned with "victimless crimes," and no one plays the omniscient, disinterested punisher.

Any system of social control depends on the prior existence of structure, and structure is inseparably associated with a coherent spectrum of diffuse sanction. A transactional system will not bear a heavy load. It relies on the strength of the mores and is sufficient to meeting the occasional political emergency but is inherently risky. An alternative system of social control is the one which concentrates on risk-reduction—maintaining the political load at an artificially low level. The Andaman Islanders (p. 142) maintain the peace within their mobile villages of fifty or sixty persons without an "authority structure"; they depend on an elaborate system of deference, supported by ritual and ceremony. Among hunters, a system of deference to age is not likely to create a gerontocracy, since the important property—the ability to bring in the food—belongs naturally to the young. Among agriculturists, especially settled agriculturists whose land is at a premium, deference may create a secular power hierarchy. The classic examples are China, where the hierarchy is kept within the extended family, or clan, and India, where access to land is unevenly distributed among castes. But even where a system of deference does generate or maintain a structure of *power* it need not create a structure of *authority*. Authority is power exercised directly over the actions of others (by command); but the strategy of risk reduction avoids direct confrontation. Various kinds of property, especially the exercise of those ritual/ceremonial privileges which are sometimes called immaterial property, can serve an indirect system of power. Wherever a focus on form and precedence is the salient feature of a value system, we can expect to find that risk reduction is correspondingly important as a strategy of social control: as far as possible, trouble is not met but dodged.

Because the systems of social control which are dominate by this strategy are characterized by indirect mechanisms c sanction, I call them *mechanical systems of social control.* I the mechanical system, sanctions scarcely can be called re wards or punishments, for they are expressionless; they hav an external, not a psychological, necessity. Consider, for ex ample, "automatic excommunication" in the Roman Catholi Church. It is an agentless sanction, ordained by law to fa on anyone who ventures too far down a given path. Th men in authority can pretend not to sanction, only to recog nize a *fait accompli.* So when men shunned lepers it wasn to sanction them but to escape a mystical contagion. Th Havik *hoylu* (p. 264) illustrates the inner principle that i at work. Even in the direst need, an aggrieved person wi not seek justice directly by open confrontation but relies o his resort to an indirect, ritual mechanism which may mobiliz the diffuse sanctioning power of the caste community at large The action may take three generations.

Villagers in India sometimes took eagerly to the use o British courts, when they were introduced, for civil suits- not with the aim of getting justice, but rather of ruinin their opponents through the expense of a series of actions In the Totagadde cases Harper reviewed, the grievance itsel was never the effect of direct action but of the working of mechanical process such as foreclosure, in which the par played by an oppressor was veiled if not actually secretive One is trampled on not with malice but sanctimoniously in competitive societies which are not openly transactional opportunism may be masked behind elaborate structures o convention. Franz Kafka best describes such mechanisms o indirect manipulation as they operate in the institutional con text of the modern West. A strange turn of history has mad Adolf Eichmann their most prominent apologist in our time For him the machinery of government ought to be un complicated by human feelings or judgments. One of Eich mann's most characteristic defenses at his trial in Israel wa that he had hardly seen the apparatus of death to whicl he consigned his captives: and this is as if to admit that i he had *faced* what he was doing he would have felt re sponsible. Mechanical systems of social control rely on diffus sanction, the mask of propriety. Use of force is avoided or disguised. The sanctions themselves seem dissociated from the ordinary moral nexus of life, which comes to have secondary importance in men's minds. They are absorbed in a mechanical game which seems to control life chances.

A different alternative (where the transactional system will not bear the load of social control) is the development of institutionalized authority. Where the mask of propriety is featureless, saying nothing about what lies behind, the mask of authority is vibrant with messages about the power inhabiting it. The nature of authority is closely tied to the nature of politics. When we say that the ultimate sanction of politics is force we mean that political action can't shy away from direct confrontation. Like the transactional system, though, authority breaks down where it must rely on *actual* force: a system of equivalence like that of the Tangu (p. 56) has lost its nature when it becomes a feud to extermination, and a system of authority like that of the Anuak local settlement (p. 229) would fly apart if the village depended for its solidarity on the headman's ability to enforce unpopular decisions. The connection of authority with force is that no force shall stand up against authority. The connection of authority with the political state is that public authority, as long as it is intact, prevents the myth of the state's actual power from being tested. (Would the Army really fire on the People? Wherever such a question is seriously asked, the state's authority is being questioned. Authority is the cloak of a power which must never be seen naked.) But while the use of force to gain political ends is a certain sign of the insecurity of authority, force is a regular feature of the *authoritative system of social control.* Here authority is used to isolate a transgressor from the network of private loyalties which would be activated to support him in a transactional system. When Sandombu appears for trial in the *chota* (p. 43) it is he as an individual who is being held responsible for his alleged act of witchcraft, and he alone who stands to be sanctioned. When Anuak men quarrel at a "headman's dance" they are subject to authoritative intervention and the payment of damages though at the *agaanya* dance out in the bush even homicide could go (officially) unsanctioned. Authoritative systems of social cor trol center on the definition of crimes and the exaction c punishment. The guiding principle is neither reparation c damages nor reduction of social danger, but the transforma tion of a breach of the peace into an offense against officiall constituted authority. We can see the rudiments in the Anua case: if the headman should fail in quelling a disturbance o his dance ground he would *ipso facto* have a rebellion o his hands. The private delict is instantly submerged in th swelling sense of public–political–danger. Moral and politica matters belong together here almost as surely as in th transactional system of self-help. It is in a further stage c political evolution that law and morality become disjoinec when law comes to be conceived as a mechanical syster slaved to authority.

The three systems of social control I have outlined ar models representing alternative strategies for the sanctionin of order. All societies probably make some use of eac strategy, but the variation in emphasis is notable for differen ethnographic regions and periods.

REPARATION, INDIRECTION, PUNISHMENT

The universal human ideal is probably a system of socia control which requires no implementation–the ultimate hono system. Transgressions would be rare and their perpetrator seized with remorse in exact proportion to the gravity of thei offense. Here the controls are wholly internalized: they oper ate on the level of character and are so effective they neec no special institutional support. If there are any real socia groups which approach this ideal they would probably b found among families, communes, or folk societies; but w know enough about that kind of group to say real example are usually far from the ideal. It is a major function of family system to implement the internalization of behaviora onstraints: families must be manipulative, however subtle the process may be. Communes which have lasted have generally been as unambiguously authoritarian as benevolent, and the most successful have been monastic orders with a itual-ceremonial superstructure heavy enough to reduce the isk of trouble almost to nothing. Folk societies with minimal uperstructure, on the other hand, are not notable for restraint so much as for the jealousy with which individuals and groups will guard their rights and undertake such direct or indirect transactions as will restore an upset balance. The ultimate honor system is evidently for angels, not for us. Ethical restraint is a universal but universally insufficient curb on disorder.

Real systems of social control sacrifice the ideal in favor of the practical, but are not amoral or coldly utilitarian. Moral sentiments of approval and disapproval are universal and are never wholly suppressed. The role of a frankly ethical and popularly internalized code of values in any transactional system of social control should be evident. Equivalence couldn't be reached in a rivalry for sheer power, for in that case each added increment to one side or the other would give it a chance to pull away; the system would be in unstable equilibrium. A system of rivalry which tends toward equivalence will rather presuppose common acceptance of a normative state (a state of rest), to depart from which is morally degrading or dangerous (a state of dislocation) and confers the power of desperation. The chief element in the role motivation of a transactional system of social control is moral indignation; and the chief alternative to the *lex talionis* and continuing feud is the principle of reparation. The difference between exacting an eye for an eye and demanding reparation is the difference between a unilateral and a mutual moral concern. A system of mutual headhunting is not a system of social control, though it could become subject to transactional constraints and so generate such a system. The act of making reparation is an alternative to the act of resisting retaliation, and to make reparation for harm done is to express adherence to a moral law. Moral law in this sense operates in all societies at the level of private and interpersonal role relations. That is, the basic units of structure, whether households or individuals, are universally accorde the right to claim moral equivalence—justice—in relations wi peers.

The principle of reparation presupposes equality. Your op ponent is always your equal, whatever your relative stat otherwise—and your equal is always potentially your op ponent. Transgression is infringement of an opponent's righ in a transactional order, and equivalence is attained whe they have been vindicated. Haviks as Brahmins and Divar as Sudras, or commoners, occupy two nearly discrete realn of social control, presided over by priests or shamans, god or un-Sanskritic (and unpredictable) spirits, respectively. B within each realm the practice of the *hoylu* expresses th morality of equivalence and reparation. The Havik witho land can't believe that he has been brought to such a pass b the normal working of the social system, but insists on belie ing himself the victim of injustice to whom reparation mu eventually come, though it take three generations. The Divar who has been robbed can have satisfaction from a *hoy* which promises to devastate the robber, though he nev observe the result. Though a man be irretrievably ruined i the economic realm he can be pacified by a ritual procedu which restores his sense of equity in the moral realm. Th main ethical consequence of the *hoylu* is to make it reason able for a citizen of Totagadde to assert that wrongdoing sure to be requited.

When I insist on the universality of moral law I don't mea that the robber always feels remorse but that the same fello *when robbed himself* is stirred to moral indignation—that h feels he has a publishable grievance. The caste order of Tota gadde sanctions an overall structure of inequality which oth erwise would be hard to maintain in a village of five hundre persons; the Brahmins, controlling through land title the cas crop of arecanuts, control the wealth. The commoner caste such as the Divarus, are excluded from the valuable land an tend to be paddy farmers, self-employed but often in deb to a Havik money lender. Untouchables were traditionall the hereditary indentured servants of Havik families. Thes three strata do not comprise a system on the pattern of ruling middle, and lower classes: the Haviks make up 40 per cen of the village, somewhat outnumbering the Divarus and greatly outnumbering the Untouchables (p. 264). Intracaste *equality* is as strongly patterned as intercaste *inequality* and competitive privilege. The whole system is unthinkable without the internal complex of moral/ritual sanctions by which each caste, possessed of its own traditions, is set apart and maintained as an orderly community. Class systems, even where policing authority is most developed, are similarly dependent on the diffuse, internal sanctions which hold people more or less well to the orderly ideals of their class communities.

The principle of reparation, as an ethical basis for social sanctions, is universal, in that it is necessarily associated with the primary (granular) level of social structure wherever it is found. Transactional systems of social control represent a direct institutionalization of the principle of reparation, and are therefore the most simple of the three type systems—though they are likely to be the most dramatic as well. The archetypal transactional system might be one in which the largest corporate group was the domestic unit, and peace was maintained among households by institutionalized public palaver, each household advocating its case under the "moral law." Sometimes Kiowa cases were resolved in this manner (p. 36), and the endless discussions among Fulani herdowners must often provide the means for the restoration of moral equivalence, where a man has considered himself wronged or slighted. (p. 167) The Kapauku suffer a man to be powerful only so long as he offers them patronage: authority is on an openly *quid pro quo* basis. (p. 224) The political ethic which informs Kachin *gumlao* communitarianism prefers a similar directness. (p. 250) Tangu *br'ngun'guni* erects the principle of reparation to ceremonial and theatrical status, but the underlying strategy of sanctions is nonetheless directly understood by the lowliest member of the public. (p. 56) Another step toward indirection is exemplified by the Dobuans, who seem to keep moral equivalence by open wrangling, heavily supplemented by talk of sorcery. (p. 219) Generally, witchcraft and sorcery are substitutes for more direct action, giving rise to formal procedures of accusation and atonement, but in Dobu black magic remains a private affair, published only by gossip or the occasional dramatic encounter.

We can see in principle how societies move from transactional social controls to superstructural systems. Transactional systems are simpler because they are more direct. They are also risky and can't bear a heavy load of cases: the simpler they are, the more easily they will revert to raw self-help—coexistence in the absence of moral sanction. Superstructure is associated with indirection—the oblique sanctions of propriety, the displaced vengeance of punishment. Ultimately there are two avenues of development, leading either to the elaboration of a mechanical system of social control or to a hierarchy of authoritative offices; but most human societies seem to rely on a combination of direction and indirection, prevention and intervention, about equidistant from each of our three type systems. The Trobriand chief (p. 148) employed sorcery—which is to say, officially inspired rumors of danger—to have his way, rather than command. His office was ritually and ceremonially elevated by an elaborate protocol of taboo and deference; and his importance was otherwise made manifest by the number of his wives and the magnificence of his *urigubu* harvest; but he exercised an authority without hierarchy and without direct sanctions. The headman of an Iban longhouse-village (p. 130) received no title, wealth, or deference with his office. If he wanted to gain acclaim he would have to progress through the performance of a series of great rituals, *gawai,* which were far more important than politics in Iban estimation. If we have correctly understood the function of ritual and ceremony, the *gawai* represent the strategy of risk reduction. But the sense of longhouse solidarity which they serve to enhance and dramatize serves in turn to legitimate the headman's efforts at conflict resolution in accordance with the highly codified *adat* law of the Iban. If he can't reconcile the parties to a dispute informally, the headman will convene a panel of elders, whose authority will be binding: they collectively represent, though he alone cannot, the sanction of the community. Here we have both law and authoritative judgment, but again without hierarchy and personal/official command. The Iban, through their system of law and judgment, avoid the excesses of ritualism which beset the Brahmins of Totagadde (p. 264); and through their apolitical, ceremonial emphasis avoid also the chafing of authority, against which the Anuak or the Kachin are repeatedly led to rebel. (pp. 229, 250) Superstructures come in a variety of styles and sizes.

The ultimate in mechanical systems of social control would be a society so beset by formal rules and artificial infractions that no one ever became informal enough to be passionate, or raise another's passions. The game of formal dancing, in which we play at passion publicly but never really misbehave, has long served the Western bourgeoisies as an erotic coolant, helping to imbue relations between the sexes with the peculiar indirection which middle-class life requires. But Western formality is secular and prosaic. In comparison the Havik Brahmin's life is a minuet: he can't eat, drink, or defecate; dress or dry himself; walk out or talk to someone in his way without danger of pollution. Time itself will pollute his clothes, if he avoids all other dangers, and after childhood he will never be seen unclothed, even at his daily bath: bodily privacy and magical inviolacy are taken as the absolute conditions of his well-being. As the function of the bourgeois dance is to make sex a matter for showing off and courting rather than pairing off and conjugating, the Brahmins' purity regime also cultivates self-consciousness and narcissistic indirection at the expense of more active self-assertion. The reason a Havik will not plow his own land is not that he hates to think of hurting a worm, but because the worm's death would pollute him: he readily hires someone else to do the dirty work. The reason he will not make love to his hired girl is not that she is unattractive, nor that he knows he could not treat her well, but that she would spoil his purity and endanger his status with men of his caste. I don't suggest that every Brahmin is a hopeless narcissist, unable to feel for anyone but himself, but the *role* of Brahmin is as narcissistic a role as is that of the adolescent *femme fatale* at a bourgeois dance. The ultimate transgression for the Brahmin would be to act as though his caste were not his primary identity; for the girl, to act as though her sex and class were not the poles of her existence. Brahmins, after all, bathe no more often than some bourgeois maidens and make no more of modesty. Self-discipline and self-enhancement go hand in hand; this is the way of indirection. When Brahmins engage in crime it is devious; and white-collar crime in the bourgeois world is the same.

Narcissism is not the only way of cooling or deflecting passion. Sometimes formality becomes a value in itself. The Andaman Islanders refrain from interpersonal violence because it would bring group disruption, as their practices of deference and ceremonialism imply. (p. 142) But mechanical systems of social control operate on the level of role, not soul. The Brahmin may or may not be deeply religious, but he will keep up caste lines and refrain from stirring up caste disunity at least as well if he is not. What makes him safe is his outward practice, not his inward belief. The bourgeois banker may be a sadomasochist by night, but rumors of this could reach his board of directors without causing panic; we all have our foibles. What would signal an emergency would be the man's coming to a board meeting improperly dressed: why would a banker do *that*? It is the intrinsic meaninglessness of the rules of dress and demeanor which make them good vehicles of extrinsic meaning. The provost writes Radical but as long as he continues to talk Etonian the earth won't shake. That man with Mrs. Gage was not of her class; but as long as she wears her diamonds we know she hasn't forgotten who she is and we won't be perturbed. That we understand a thousand such subtleties, though we might find it hard to explain them to a stranger, is a credit to our training in the art of social control by indirection.

All mechanical systems of social control are ultimately backed up by "the reserve threat of force." The shameless Trobriander (p. 148) who faced out public exposure of his incestuous affairs seems to have enjoyed a precarious freedom which came of dodging attack from three directions: the resentment of injured parties, the power of the chief (muted by European supervision), and the diffuse sanction of the community. But even the last of these has a potential for violence, a threshold of provocation, though it may be only vaguely known. Often the threshold is stated explicitly for certain ritual transgressions, while the moral issues entailed are left formally undefined. A Havik Brahmin widow may become pregnant by a Sudra and doomed therefore to be outcasted; but this is styled not as a moral sanction for a moral act but as a ritually necessary measure: the sanction does not fall until she has delivered the child, bringing a non-Brahmin into her household. The child pollutes the kin group until mother and child are removed and the kin have been ritually purified again. Outcasting is an act of force, barring a person from access to goods and privileges, though it is the very opposite of direct action: everyone concerned is free to claim regret. But in another sense there is a threat of force and even violence just beneath the formal surface of any system of social control which depends on ritual prescription in lieu of a moral-legal code. When a Brahmin's buffalo dies, when a worker falls out of a tree or loses an eye, when men vomit blood or smallpox is about, the reason is that spirits have been angered by a breach of the ritual rules which men must keep to have peace in this life and honor in the next. The commandment of the caste village is not to be good but to be careful. To say that a developed ritualism precludes any need for a developed morality would be misleading. The "ultimate honor system" doesn't work. Filling a man's life with ritual procedures, which he voluntarily undertakes in order to keep himself out of trouble, fills him with fear of trouble. Morality then can be a private matter. The alternative to ritual mechanism is law and the spirit of punishment. This is also a kind of indirection and also works by inspiring men with the fear of trouble, but it masquerades as reparation.

The chief attribute of authority is its claim to represent *the community as plaintiff*. When Abba slays Baba in the transactional society the cathartic sequel depends on the initiative of Baba's vengeance group, and sometimes the neutral intervention of a third party as mediator, pact-holder, or (as with the Anuak headman) public peace-keeper. In a system of authority, the third party has taken on the structure of officialdom and asserted a monopoly of initiative. The fiction which makes this seem right is that (1) the interest of the community is embodied in the rights of the official establishment; (2) the establishment is threatened and the community wronged by Abba's act; and (3) Abba must therefore be required to atone for his act, not (by reparation of loss) to Baba's house but to the community's established authority. In Tangu, Kapauku, or Iban contexts (pp. 56, 224, 130) such a fiction would be blown apart by public opinion: the structure and the ethical devices of officialdom are lacking. The Iban have gone so far as to create an office of headman, but not to invest it with the authority to speak and act for the community; authority resides with the full council of elders which the headman may convene and which in a real sense he *serves.* The principle of the synod is characteristic of the politics of microcultures: true authority is invested only in the assembly, which when it disbands does not give over its powers to a standing officialdom. In such cases the fiction of the community as plaintiff does not arise. The philosophy of social control still centers on reparation, not repression.

Modern political parties, since they pretend to constitute communities of value, favor the synodic principle even where the party boss has national standing: public opinion is influenced and even manipulated but isn't subject to command. But actual government of the modern industrial state by assembly rule is unthinkable: the nearest approach is the parliamentary system, which makes its government directly responsible to a legislative body. This body is only symbolically reminiscent of a public assembly. The principle of hierarchy has long since triumphed over the communal principle expressed in the synod. The headman of the Iban or the Anuak has ceremonial prominence as symbol of the community's integrity but remains unambiguously a public servant: the public *can* band together and assume the role of master. In developed systems of authority, public sovereignty is commonly kept alive as a myth and witnessed through public identification with flag or monarch, though governmental hierarchies command a mass and force enormously greater than that any public could band together. Hence the rhetoric of the "public servant" in the modern urban context tastes about like the humility of Uriah Heep in *David Copperfield:* the mask of propriety alternates adventitiously with the mask of authority.

Transactional systems begin with bravado, mechanical systems with artificiality, and authority systems with hypocrisy of the this-hurts-me-worse-than-you variety. Authoritative sanctions are administered on persons but never *by* persons; the official hauteur intervenes, the language is that of a pompous proceduralism, the tone of finality. This is nowhere more apparent than in the cult of punishment to which authority has often found recourse: punishment comes to be valued as an end in itself and the system of punishment becomes a vital organ of government, which takes on a punitive character. The public servant becomes the grand inquisitor, the guardians of the people become the secret police. The zealot, four-square for ideological purity, becomes the indignant persecutor of all that seems impure.

The witch-hunt and the lynching illustrate the dilemma of authority which the cult of punishment resolves. In the witch-hunt, there is a popular movement to impugn the established authority for failure to keep the peace; secret crimes of a horrendous nature (the more mysterious the better) have been tolerated. To keep its monopoly of authority the official establishment must be prepared to punish these secret crimes. In the lynching, officialdom is even more directly challenged. The popular movement usurps authority for a token case to "show how justice should be done." The fully developed lynching pattern of the United States South involved the prominent use of ritual clothing, fiery crosses, and a shadow hierarchy pretending to higher-than-secular authority. It would be hard to conceive of a heavier form of popular drama, and its moving force is the spirit of punishment. When that spirit is abroad, established authority must take possession of it or lose control.

The logic of punishment is that of deterrence, and there is a popular belief that deterrence could be the *only* function of punishment. In the best of all possible hierarchic worlds official power would not need to be any wider than official authority. Secret police, propaganda, and public pomp would have no place. The credibility of an office would be reinforced by every act of the incumbent officeholder, or else he would be tossed out. Punishment would be used strictly as a deterrent, and the first function of authority would be to see that reparation was made for actual damages. A court could take responsibility for compensating an injured party out of public funds, assigning to government the job of collecting from the guilty party. Reparation could even take place before the perpetrator had been found, after a process to establish the validity of the claimed wrong, on the philosophy that the authorities are expected to prevent crime; it is *their* job to find the criminal, and the victim should not suffer if they fail. Such a system doesn't exist. Some modern states have assumed some responsibility for reparation, but what we must consider is whether punishment can be divorced from reparation in a systematic way. Suppose that the *first* concern of institutionalized justice were not vengeance but reparation. A court could consider what exactions seemed fair, beyond the payment of civil damages, to dissuade a rational offender against the peace from repeating his act: assessments on pocket and property would be proportional to a man's wealth and earning power; in short, the rationalistic and utilitarian assumptions which lie behind the idea of deterrence would be consistently recognized. And what of the offender who won't respond to these deterrent sanctions—shouldn't he be punished? This is the critical question for the authoritative system of social control: the logic of deterrence demands an escalation of sanctions, and escalation could only mean the legitimate use of cruelty. But it was long ago discovered in the West that the idea of a free society required the prohibition of state cruelty; and so corporal cruelty, which is comparatively easy to define, was formally forbidden. The alternative which was not closed was incarceration: surely not less cruel in ultimate consequence but capable of massive dilution. What prisoner would choose five years if he could get off with a flogging? Twenty years in prison does deter a man from crime (in the outside world) for twenty years; it hasn't been shown that it does more. The Arabian custom of cutting off a thief's hand is effective for exactly the same reason: the crime is physically prevented. But the dilemma of deterrence in a free society is not better resolved by the one expedient than by the other; in both cases, cruelty is made legitimate: authority claims a grievance against the offender and so justifies punishment. But in the incarcerating societies the cruelty of punishment is camouflaged.

The prevailing practice of social control in the urban-industrial world is the "correctional system" in which each trouble case must be handled as a "public example." Deterrence involves inspiring men *generally* with the fear of trouble; and particularly, fear of getting in trouble with the authorities. That is why the state masquerades as the injured party when an offense has been committed. The state then gains a demand right for reparation upon the offender, who can satisfy the demand only by doing penance. The prisoner while "paying for his crime" is supposed to be rehabilitated, but this is the philosophy of the prisons rather than of the public. When Abba slays Baba, the state destroys or incarcerates Abba even at the price of leaving two destitute wives with their children to fend for themselves. Rather than conforming to transactional ideals of justice, this is closer to the mechanical system, which creates an atmosphere of the inevitable by saturation with the arbitrary.

The theory of crime and punishment is *sui generis*. It is associated with developed systems of hierarchic authority, and the reason for its wide distribution is that the exercise of punishment demontrates and legitimates the power of the state over the individual. The state does not gain this power simply by declaring it, and it is a power which can be eroded if it is not continually reinforced. The specific function of punishment in this view is not to deter crime but to turn trouble to political use in the enhancement of constituted authority. By obversion, the penal system tends to stabilize the *value* of freedom from arbitrary rule. Unfortunately, this value in itself is no guarantee of democratic process; the fear of intervention can be used by a Hitler to cow a whole population, and similar but subtler forms of repression are endemic today. The psychology of punishment is an important force in making the mask of authority. The social structure of crime and punishment is comparable to that of war as a component of the power system comprising the state's rationale. Everyone agrees that private armies are intolerable, while the state's right to arms is unlimited. Everyone agrees that an unofficial jail would be a monstrous thing, but the official one is above the moral scruple. Punishment calls for cruelty, and the legitimate monopoly of cruelty is characteristic of the state. The mask of authority is godlike.

The modern state asserts exclusive right to handle trouble

cases above the level of the family. Certain corporate communities with a familistic ethical structure (colleges and religious communes) may sometimes be treated as beneath the law, exempt in the way that families are, and expected to handle ordinary trouble with familistic sanctions. On the other hand, elite organizations will be above the law: trouble within the army or the secret police doesn't get into the civil courts. That courts operate on the principle of public example—generalized rather than specific deterrence—is suggested in the tendency of magistrates to leniency in dealing with genteel crime, assigning penalties inversely proportionate to the social status of the offender. The rationale of this practice is that the genteel class is horrified so profoundly by the scandal of criminal prosecution that the mildest sentence can suffice as a public example. Embezzlement commonly requires elaborate planning and repeated acts of theft. The embezzler often presents himself to the court as a wastrel who has not intelligently hidden the money away but lost it foolishly—apparently a person insensitive to the subtler sanctions of the genteel life. To remotivate him specifically ought to require an especially heavy, not a light, punishment—that is, if you assume a philosophy of specific deterrence. But if you assume that an offender is viewed by the magistrate as representative of a class of potential offenders; and assume that the jurist regards his sanctions as having a *generally* deterrent effect upon that class, sufficient to keep the ordinary fellow out of court; then practice will be seen to accord with theory.

Can the theory of "generalized deterrence" really work? The high rates of recidivism in correctional systems the world around indicate that the philosophy of punishment is impractical for specific deterrence in the modern context. But how is one to say whether crime rates in the same societies are high or low? Practical tests of the general effect of any particular institutional complex on a culture are beyond the means of science. What is clear is that the topic of crime in modern society belongs to the sociology of danger—the study of shared fear orientations and their relation to fundamental beliefs. The architecture of authority as we know it would have to change considerably before the state would likely surrender the theory of punishment as a general deterrent to crime. As long as crime is defined as a threat to authority it will have to be dealt with by peremptory means, and the object will not be restitution or genuine prevention but the vindication of authority through the public example of punishment.

"SPONTANEOUS ORDER" AND MANIPULATION

In this age the most important task of a theory of social structure must be to penetrate the nature of authority and the vast social systems which seem so utterly to depend on its functioning. The salient character of the transactional system is that it is limited in the load it will bear: it lends itself easily to conflict and schism wherever the pattern of social alignments becomes complex. The salient character of the mechanical system is its inflexibility, the agency of social control being wholly diffuse. The old theocracies were systems of authority which grew up behind the façade of unpolitical, or mechanical, social control. But India's caste system is the greatest monument the world has seen to the architectonic potential of ritual sanctions. Indian communities and regions have never been without politics; but the stability of the civilization has never depended on its manipulative leadership. Indian tradition is sustained by the world's most decentralized elite. Everywhere, caste and the ritual order come first, practical-political judgment follows. Practical authority is derived from scriptural; high status depends on access to esoteric lore and practice, and no other basis for the legitimation of temporal authority has equivalent sanction. The analogy is that of an exoskeleton: the rigidity is in the surface form. By comparison, the endoskeleton of authority systems is far less precise in determining outward appearance; the character of life in the great urban-industrial societies is drastically altered with each new generation, though the inner structure of control and access to power remains.

An authority system is a superstructure which has not

wholly lost the capability of direct action on a significant scale of political coordination. Social control is not limited to the suppression of crime but is a condition for the coordination of positive action by groups. In the early hydraulic societies the problems of irrigation and defense were an impetus to the development of authority structures; in early capitalism transportation, fire control, and waste removal played a similar role. What followed in each case was an expansion and deepening of the nature of government until it is now in many ways identified with the total structure of the society. This is a process which culminates in such extravagances as the Persian, Napoleonic, or British Empires, in which the power of the state and the culture of the conquering people are mystically exalted by the subjugation of exotic populations. If the dilemma of the mechanical system of social control is the problem of ossification, the great problem of authority is its runaway tendency. This is particularly true where an authority system has presided over a period of radical structural change: government assumes responsibility for the change, and for the very shape of the new society. This Jovian complex has been tempered in historic societies by changes of regime and the rhetoric of loyal oppositions. But in the totalitarian government recent generations have seen an authority system which is committed to turning the myth of omniscient control into a living, squirming reality.

All regulative institutions must be regarded as secondary. The way a society replicates and connects its basic structural units, whether on several class levels or one, comprises its primary structure. Social control within the basic unit is personal, consistent with intense and enduring interpsychic involvement. Macrostructure begins with the connection of these units: kinship in one society, caste and kinship in another, class and community in a third. These relationships are certainly subject to political interference, but it would be another thing to try to subject them to political control. There is the dilemma here of the man who thought he could lift himself up by the bootstraps, combined perhaps with the problem of the child who would build a castle of dry sand. Unless there is a healthy and self-sustaining order of life "beneath the law" and outside of politics, there is no base on which authority can rest. We know that minorities can be persecuted by power which rests on majority support, and we are told that a disaffected majority may even be kept for a while with bread and circuses; but even those who think Nero could have put out the fire of elitist irresponsibility, which he has come to symbolize, don't suppose he could have put off for long the slow decline and fall. Decadence beset the Roman people in its several social classes, not just in its government. Solid superstructures presuppose solid foundations. Social control is a process which presupposes social structure, not a process which generates or motivates structures. The power for radical reconstruction has to come from the people: it arises from the infrastructure just as Anuak or Kachin upheavals do. Men who have great power in their hands can surely raise a storm, but a storm will go its own way. If a state gains terrible power to make war and brutalize men, we can't be content to blame either the tyrant or the masses who followed him. For an explanation we must look to the structure of their common life.

Perhaps the key to understanding this is distinguishing between spontaneous and manipulative order. The latter is the kind of order which only ceaseless vigil by qualified authority will keep. It features largely in the nightmares of ultra-reactionaries and nervous schoolmarms, who suppose that an unwatched world will revert to chaos. The simplest notion of spontaneous order is that of the beatific state of nature in which everyone gets along beautifully by minding his own business. Men, however, are not destined to stake out modest realms on limitless beaches and be content with them. Spontaneous order among men is not natural. If something like it exists it must be artificial in the sense of presupposing culture and social structure. The idea of the early capitalist theorists that competition could regulate the market better than authority is an example of a theory of spontaneous order; but orderly market competition depends on highly developed institutions and conventions. What we mean by "spontaneous order" is not something as complex as symbiosis (mutual exploitation by structurally different types) or complementary differentiation, but behavior associated with granular structure—in short, a stabilized form of competition among equals. But if this is so, then we must beware of associating this "spontaneity" with unsanctioned or uncontrolled behavior. What is meant rather is behavior "beneath politics," diffusely sanctioned and normally requiring no intervention by authority. Spontaneous order implies the social structure of freedom.

This is what the Greeks meant by "good laws"; they thought that if a political community was well enough designed it could administer itself, needing no planners and no police, presenting no problem of freedom. Except in the presence of authority, men can and do take freedom for granted. Before the British, the Andaman Islanders were free: when one speaks only of "internalized controls" it is silly to talk of constraint. The real stumbling block to understanding the idea of spontaneous order (or freedom) is the assumption that if it can't be found in a pure state it doesn't exist—that if there is no society with perfect laws and hence with perfect freedom it must follow that all order everywhere is manipulative order. It is more sensible to use the distinction analytically, recognizing that so far as any community is well structured we may speak of spontaneous order; but that all real societies require manipulative intervention as well, and sometimes on a very general level. It is where the manipulative order is the specialty of a recognized officialdom that we begin to speak of superstructure; while spontaneous order is preeminently a property of infrastructure.

This exploration of the nature of sanctions and their relation to structure and authority has been a prelude to discussing the future of equality. Most of the societies we have considered in detail were characterized by equality; and even in the case of Totagadde (p. 264) our focus has not been on the system of superordination but on relations within a caste whose adult male members are formally equal. When we come now to consider the massive inequality of urban class systems it will be important to keep in mind the distinction between direct and indirect forms of social control. Inequality certainly doesn't persist unkept; but it is not kept by a manipulative conspiracy of the upper classes to control the lower. Power and manipulative direction rest on a base of procedural and mechanical indirection.

SECTION TWO

SANCTIONS AND SOCIAL STRUCTURE

SANCTIONS IN THE PRIVATE DOMAIN

Sanctions are inescapable. The dream of sin without scorn, emancipation from moral constraints, is as naïve as its counterpart, caring nothing for good opinion. What distinguishes modern worlds from the microcultures in which human morality first evolved is the extent to which private and public forms of sanction have grown apart. Consider the campus revolt, in which all the passions which once were reserved for the family ("adolescent rebellion") break into the public, political arena. Is it any wonder these explosions are short-lived? Moral indignation, which is the essence of the sanctioning power a middle-class son may hold over his father, or a wife over her errant man, is strangely destructive in politics. Nazi indignation against the Bolsheviks switched 180 degrees to hatred for the shopkeeping Jew. Race riots and ghetto explosions in the United States generated a countermoralism within the governing institutions. Police and militia riots, with fascistic demagoguery, abetted a decline of law and order beyond the wildest dreams of Americans two generations before. We must learn the lessons of such phenomena; and one lesson is that order must be kept in different ways in the private and public domains of life.

Sanctions keep order *within* the framework we call the

social structure. In the public domain (churches, courts firms), titles and prerequisites mark out the structure of rank and function, and the rules for keeping persons in their places are explicit. Minor differences of reward within the basic pay scale can sanction the character values an institution wishes to affirm without shaking its structure perseverance here, ability there, connections or class in another case. In the private domain (families, friendships), structure is not less real but less apparent. It is easily dominated by personalities. Since genuine personal involvements effectively inhibit opportunistic manipulation but encourage tests of personal strength, the problem of keeping order is one of moderation, not regulation. Whereas in the public domain a series of specialized regulative institutions formally mete out sanctions according to procedures built on the file drawer and the memory drum, in the primary group reward and hurt are dimensions of a spontaneous emotional exchange. Where due process appears in the family, or emotional behavior on the bench, there is an anomaly—the same which the decent politician feels kissing babies or the gentle Brahmin having a high-status Christian at his board.

In the public sphere rationality is, or is supposed to be, supreme while in private the official mask is often laid aside with a vengeance, and the most pompous of lords may prove to be only too human; and it may be that modern society creates conditions of unbearable stress in its jacketed officialdoms. But a just picture is not given in the older sociological opposition of a competitive, male-oriented *Gesellschaft* (society) to a warm, therapeutic *Gemeinschaft* (community) centered in hearth, home, and the understanding woman. The primacy of persons in the family does not mean that its social life reduces to psychology; the primacy of office and role in government does not mean that activities in the Kremlin or the White House reduce to structure. There is a psychology of the public domain and a structural dimension of the private. Behind much present-day thinking lies the hunch that if we could solve the problem of domestic peace and harmony, the problem on a political level would solve itself. But the obverse is equally plausible: solve the politico-economic problems of society and families may begin to prosper as never before. Should middle-class families withdraw from the rat race? But competition at home, at school, and at work is the primal fact of middle-class existence around which its psychology, its structure, and its contribution to history have always been organized. Is a ghetto family disorganized? Where is the boundary between that fact and the disorganization of the ghetto world around it? What goes on in our heads is a reflection of what we see and hear from day to day. The problem of "the individual and society" is not the sum of the discrete problems of "personality" and "social structure." Structures are tightly woven with feeling, and role motivation is dogged by egoism, in the board room as surely as in the bedroom or the sandlot. That sandlot sanctions can or ought to run our societies, however, is not a necessary deduction.

SANCTIONS IN THE PUBLIC DOMAIN

What unifies the urban-industrial society today is competition. *E pluribus unum* could be the motto for Europe or Russia as well as for the United States. By struggling for a place in an expanding economy, individuals learn to identify with a common set of values. A study of the way positional sanctions operate should help to make clear how the process of homogenization works and where it can lead. The prizes for which man vie are not consumer goods.

We may distinguish three sorts of sanction which operate in the public domain:

(a) Explicit sanctions (freedom, wealth, life-style) are intentional, being knowingly claimed or imposed as social deserts, and highly visible. How they are allocated is a matter of public concern and generally subject to consensus.

(b) Implicit sanctions (rights, standing, identity) ar intentional but of an invisible or putative nature. How the are allocated is widely understood in principle, but th application to cases is not clear or open to examination.

(c) Indirect sanctions (life chances, power, strain) fa haphazardly, and the effect is unevenly visible. Since the are not objects of direct public awareness, indirect sanc tions may be characteristic of a society without being full legitimate.

The difference among the three sorts of sanctions may b suggested by sketching the social position and future of, say a successful gambler. His existence is facilitated by all man ner of positive *explicit* sanctions—mobility, big cars, fine food But *implicit* sanctions are less positive. He is excluded fron some clubs and banks by his bad repute, and treated witl diffidence in circles where others find ready acceptance The *indirect* consequence is a severe limitation of his prob able futures, including what a psychiatrist would reckon to be his chances for happiness.

The three sorts of sanction may be juxtaposed with the three types of social control—authority, transaction, and mechanism—by which sanctions are applied. This is made explicit in the matrix below, where the three-by-three juxta-position yields nine positional values. These values range from objective freedom to *Angst*—that apprehensive state of self-

SANCTIONS AND VALUES ATTACHING TO SOCIAL POSITIONS
CHARACTER OF SANCTION

Explicit	01	*Implicit*	02	*Indirect*	03	*Characteristic Mode of Allocation*
Freedom	11	Rights	12	Life-chances	13	10 Authority
Wealth	21	Standing	22	Power	23	20 Transaction
Style	31	Identity	32	*Angst*	33	30 Mechanism

(The matrix numbers will be used for reference to a cell by row and column.)

nd social awareness which corresponds to the stress and train inherent in the burden of maintaining any social role. 'or each value we must imagine both positive and negative ıtensities, motivating and demotivating experiences affecting he separate orientations of the millions of individuals comrising a nation. We can hope in this way to grasp how it is hat in our open societies, scrambling out of inequality, men erpetuate it.

Allocation by authority: The most explicit sanctions imosed by authority in the modern state are at the disposition f the police and the criminal courts. Police power stretches o total interference with a person's right to do as he pleases (11). A man's *freedom* is forfeit when he is deemed criminal. egal sanctions ought to refer only to the crime, not to the ocial position of the offender; yet the idea of equal rights for ll citizens is better established than the practice.

Regulative institutions allocate *rights* (12). Workers, vomen, immigrants, convicts, and children occupy legally lefined statuses to which specific rights are attached, over nd above (or in some cases, below) the common level acorded with citizenship. Though there is a fixed bundle of ights attached to your position, its actual value to you is ıot easily assessed. Milquetoast may have no rights at all because he is so easy to push around. Women may have the right to equal pay for equal work, but the law may not help them find equal work. Everyone—especially immigrants, youth, and the ill-educated—has rights of which he is unaware: such rights have at best a shadowy value. There are some rights which we sense, but which authority has failed to sanction: it is not just that you *can* get arrested for having the wrong color of skin or unkempt hair; there are also rights of a moral kind which the law does not heed. Should the young be considerate of the old or the crippled? help you when you're pregnant, frail, or hurt? Should nurses treat you decently though you are in no condition to demand it, and should politicians keep their promises? When we feel trampled on we don't always know whether we should take the case to court (12), stand on our dignity (22), or worry about our identity (32).

More elusive than the real value of rights is the meaning

we should attach to *life chances* (13). These are probab outcomes of moves in the competition for moral and materi goods. If I were to ask you why you aspire to a certa position or level on the structural grid of your world, I e pect you would have to answer in terms of the concre values (21, 31) and immunities (22) you would enjoy the If I should ask in turn why you thought you would enj this or that possession or privilege, I would *not* expect a so ological analysis in reply. In the class society, the motivati of mobility abounds in specific enthusiasms, and no o needs an ideology or a social theory to tell him which e of the society is up and which down.

Equally plain to all is the crucial role of politics determining how well off the cream will be and how po the dregs. In the twentieth century, through massive wa fare and a ponderous cycle of umemployment and affluenc the capitalist world has moved steadily from localism internationalism and from a philosophy of salvation throug religion to the expectation that all the important values a subject to management by the state. Since the great faile revolution of 1789–95, most of the movements in the We which could be called revolutionary have taken the form *demands upon* the state—which have the ultimate effect greatly increasing its power—rather than efforts to do awa with it. The demands for economic justice, civil rights, an responsibility to humane values have flown many banner carried by ideologues, true believers, fascist opportunists, an clowns. Whatever they may have intended to bring abou the net effect of every success has been to enhance the siz and scope of government—to strengthen the hold of stat authority on the allocation of important sanctions. But th nation-state's growing imperium even in the most fascisti interludes has been enormously cumbersome and indirect though the power of the state over each of our lives is no to be gainsaid, and though we may feel it in every dealin with the tax officials or city hall or the schools, the relatio of law to life chance remains inscrutably indirect. The stat figures in our lives as a sort of blind and generally distracted cyclops, whose potential power over us is incalculable, if we can't manage to stay out of harm's way. Most o us are drafted, arrested, or otherwise caught by the cyclops at least once in our lives, and we learn to be warier the next time. This may range from scaling down our aspirations to joining a political party or adopting an essentially furtive way of life. Whatever the response, it is a certain recognition of the sanctioning power of the state and an effort to achieve some immunity from it.

Transactional allocation: In an old-fashioned school two parallel systems of sanctions apply. In the classroom the teacher bestows rewards and penalties for right and wrong answers, good or bad conduct. But in the playground sanctions are not allocated by authority; they derive from one's equals. Despising or admiring another person openly is almost sure to sanction him; and transactions of this sort inhere in all social intercourse. The most conspicuous reward in urban-industrial societies is *wealth* (21), and its distribution in capitalist or socialist societies is competitive (transactional). In the case of the socialist meritocracy, competition is contained within a narrow set of institutions—the schools, the armed services, the industrial or governmental bureaucracies. Under capitalism the bag is only more mixed. Occupational promotions, for example, are for a majority the characteristic steps toward a better income. Like school promotions, these are administered from above and are made by a superior who knows you personally. The competition for promotion need not be intense and the style of the game need not be dirty; as long as there is a chance for failure there is a process of selection and there will be an atmosphere of candidacy. In the modern world, one qualifies or disqualifies oneself for school and job promotions and professional opportunities to which a raise is attached. There is room at the top, but most of the room is elsewhere.

The competition for money in the marketplace is still more explicit. The idol of the primitive market holds a balanced scale because the ideal of fair value on both sides of a bargain—equivalence—constitutes the unprofessional motivation to trade: if Abba has too much grain and Baba too much fruit both stand to gain by exchange. The outcome of the market game is determined by transactions in which the participants play independent if not equal hands. Wealth in the modern state is not distributed by fiat but by grabs, whether in the struggle for promotion or the chase after profit.

The distribution of wealth is obvious, and most men can (though few will) tell you what they are worth and where it came from. The distribution of status or social *standing* (22) is mysterious because it is rare for a person to be much concerned with it as an end in itself. Where estimates of a man vary, and none agree with his own, how shall we measure his standing? He will usually have arrived at it by pursuing something else—power (23), wealth (21), or choice elements of life-style (31). Although a man of high standing might betray no awareness of it in his manner of dealing with others, more often he will *claim* standing by his manner of dealing with them. Claims to standing are so effortlessly part of our normal demeanor—especially the little marks of deference or absentness by which we acknowledge the superior claims of another person—that we are able to define ourselves without thought. When we do have to think, having met a new situation, we revert as soon as may be to inattention. But obliviousness to standing is less true of Britain than America, France than Norway. It could hardly typify a society without mobility and without egalitarian mythos: novelists of an earlier age of the West suggest an explicit awareness of standing and its associated orders of precedence. In their time the competition for privilege (22) was as explicit as that for wealth today.

The distinction between privilege, which is attached to a particular standing (22), and *power* (23) is one of scope and degree of definition. A man's privileges may be many but will not be broad. "Power," on the other hand, is one of those words which shrink in the plural—the *powers* of an office may be detailed but its *power* not. The paths to power are rarely straight and they close behind the man who has found them. When we talk of power we do not mean exercising authority but controlling the money market, the arena of high politics, the kingmaker's circle in industry. These are the places of power, but how you will get there or how you will manage yourself when you do are not laid down.

Wealth, standing, and power (21–22–23) tend under capitalism to fall into the same hands, since by opportune transactions in an open society one may be transformed into another. Americans hardly remember the time when a "bourgeois gentleman" was a paradox, though it still takes a generation of public schooling to consolidate the transformation in Great Britain, and the left-over claims to "blood" aristocracy die hard everywhere. The shift toward the transactional allocation of sanctions has been characteristic of capitalism, being almost synonymous with the openness of which the "free world" boasts. Relics of the time when sanctions were supposed to be handed down from above are found in political as well as royal patronage: the parallel between an American city machine and the queen's court is not coincidence but reveals that, practically, openness has not always proved a solution to problems of order. In spite of that, eighteenth-century libertarians would probably be shocked by the "free world" of California today, where even religion has so often become the tool of private ambition. The recent emergence of a "new class" or consolidated elite in Western Communist nations suggests that the equation of wealth, standing, and power in less openly competitive industrial states will follow the familiar pattern, only without capitalism's emphasis on the central role of private wealth.

Mechanical allocation: Differences of outward *style* (31) are among the most obvious signs of inequality—so much so that when we fail to see such signs we can scarcely believe real inequalities exist. When the margarine prince goes about with bare feet and the janitor drives a sports car we do not suppose they both have the same credit at the bank, but we recognize that one important kind of inequality is in abeyance. *Are* the several sorts of inequality as easily separated as emancipated youth would have them? In the long run it may be impossible to maintain the difference at the bank if class should cease to exist on the level of style. Wealth and life-style have been bound together in class societies from Imperial China or Samurai Japan to the Italy of Lampedusa's *The Leopard* and the England of Galsworthy's *Forsyte Saga.* Sometimes, as in Faulkner's picturing of the old South in the United States, style may come to have more importance than money—better go poor than adopt a demeaning calling —and sometimes the old families are so encumbered by their style that they simply lose out to a cannier competition. The classic manual on the relation of class to style is Veblen's *Theory of the Leisure Class.* Its argument is that conspicuous consumption and leisure are what give point to the accumulation of wealth—a lavish style is the essence of "class." Such style, of course, calls for money, but only as a raw material. The rest lies in the realm of meanings, which are not to be gained in the same way.

There is a mystique of style in the class society which echoes the mystique of supernatural prerogative in the caste society. Style is not something one gets but something one emulates. The sanctions which are allocated by transactional process are in limited supply—Abba's gain is Baba's loss whether we are dealing with commodities, social standing, or power (21–22–23). Style transcends such limits. Men in the capitalist world regularly convert their cash or credit into perishable items, from cokes and recordings to drugs and motorcars, which they are said to consume—and which derive most of their market value from style. At its simplest level the mystique of style derives from the inscrutability of taste. The utility of a thing is the value it has regardless of taste; any excess value it may have for you is a matter of style. In the twentieth century, capitalism has come to be based on style rather than utility, in that to maximize profits a firm must offer not the most useful but the most stylish commodities. Once in a while an adman may succeed in promoting utility ("highest resale value of any import" *seems* to mean the object will hold up in use) but only if utility is currently in style. If selling were a rational process the hucksters would be out of work.

I have suggested by the way I placed style (31) in my paradigm that it is an explicit sanction mechanically allocated. Style exists only in public manifestation; and while we are often told that Soandso is an "arbiter of style" or a "leader of fashion" the claim does not really explain how styles are established. Yearly changes of fashion are decreed in the West by collusion of a vast marketing network; but the decisions have to be made by sensing which way the currents of style may go, and such decisions are not uniformly successful. Closer to the allocation of style sanctions by authority is the control of dress and demeanor by a totalitarian government—the Big Brother phenomenon. But this is more nearly a negation of style than mastery of it. Certain elements of the public code of manners are exempted from the free play of style. Men and women shall wear the same drab clothing, young and old, peasant and technician: this is a way of cancelling out class in the stylistic sense. The will to do so is a measure of the commitment of the people (as well as the governmental regime) to a set of values which can't coexist with those of class. We can't at this point of history predict that it will never be possible to organize a massive society without massive inequality, but a megapolitan utopia remains far away.

The meaning of stylistic distance is more stable and easier to grasp than the meaning of the particular styles contrasted. We respond to the distance between jazz and rock though we may have little sensitivity to either. So it is with styles reinforcing class and ethnic divisions: the more styles change, the more the distance between separate styles remains the same, corresponding to other structural facts. The upper class may change its clothes and quit going to church; the middle class may take on all the old togs and toys of its mentors; but the distance between them remains and is still expressed in style. As a new ethnic group moves in the language of the ghetto changes but not its address. The encysted minority can maintain its "own culture"—an idiosyncratic style—as long as it doesn't claim parity in the transactional system of the larger society. The significance of minority orthodoxies is not that they satisfy a need for changelessness; rather it is that they provide in the face of change the ritual (mechanical) basis for keeping up a separate ethnic identity. Members of a conspicuous minority, if their conspicuousness is a matter of style not race, are *asking* to be treated with discrimination—to be considered outside the regular competition. Where pariah occupations or other special niches are available, too risky or imbued with too much stress or too little glamour to appeal to the majority citizens, the minority can prosper while keeping its distance. When these conditions begin to fail and ethnic visibility no longer pays, the minority style will begin to fade as well: accent and ethnic demeanor will disappear, names will be respelled, occupations will be restyled. There occurs a change of social *identity* (32). Identity is both outward-looking and private. Its private aspect is its responsiveness to an inner sense of personal style. The fact that I wear a beard tends to set me apart from the clean-shaven, but my inner reason for wearing a beard remains private; the style is explicit, the identity is not. My identity is the meaning implicit in my total style of life.

Angst (33) is apprehensive self-awareness. There is an edge of anxiety attached to every social position which is in danger of being lost, and in a competitive society even the last man likes to think he has someone below him. Both humility and pride are fed by *Angst:* humility is not just feeling small but wanting to, pride is not just feeling big but being infatuated with the state of bigness and fearing to fall. What makes Sammy run? We can conceive the transactional struggle for position as an heroic battle of wits, verve, and fortune—the idea of the game of Monopoly. We can also see it as a rat race, pointlessly going in vicious circles. Or we can notice that some people seem to be running *from,* not *toward,* a position on the grid. More exactly, they are motivated more by discontent, alienation, a restlessness with life itself than by attraction to specific sanctioning values attached to high position. Although *Angst* may turn a man in almost any direction, it has a distinctive range of qualities for a given social identity (32). Who are the men who become missionaries, who soldiers of fortune, who disheartened storekeepers, who wheeler-dealers in oil and real estate, who respected senior executives? Understanding these motivations is an essential step toward understanding the social structure of the class society; the distribution of ennui and what may be called creative neurosis (33) is as much a part of the structure as the distribution of commodities (21) and life chances (13).

The distribution of sanction in an urban-industrial society at any given moment must be the tentative solution of nine—or ninety-nine—simultaneous equations. The parameters are often hard to give in exact terms, and even then the form in which we know the equation may be only approximate. But the effort to deal with structure as though it had no subjective dimension is a sociological detour like the psychologist's preoccupation with subjects (rats) who cannot communicate with him.

CLASS SEGREGATION

In a massive society characterized by gross inequality—and all urban-industrial societies are—class segregation has a mitigating function: it softens the *Angst.* Tolerantly viewed, a social class is a universe of style and outlook, sufficient and true to itself. What is confusing is that relative position in an economic power structure is so crucial to the *system* of classes in any society that we can't talk about that system without dark reference to power, privilege, and penury. For most of us, inequality has become synonymous with class. Freshly smarting from an encounter in the marketplace, we are apt to think that class is to be blamed for inequality—"they think they are better than we are." But much class behavior is a response to inequalities which are prior to it. Not that class "barriers" don't exist or that the terrible game of snobbery is never played for its own sake: but what corresponds most widely to the idea of social class is the tendency to exhibit a certain life-style and to act ethnocentrically about it. Statistical demonstrations that show everything of value correlating with "class" are only using the word to mean social level. It is true that privilege perpetuates itself not only through style and ceremony but by self-serving class institutions as well: segregated schools and job-sorting procedures. But privilege would presumably perpetuate itself with or without the aid of class, which is mainly a protective, not an offensive, mechanism.

Discussions of the class system in Marxist terms illuminate the subject of inequality in relation to economic power, though with insufficient attention to politics. In other discussions class is likely to get lost in the much more general problem of socioeconomic inequality or stratification. The guiding assumption of stratification studies has been that the significant variables which distinguish the top from the bottom people are continuously distributed among those in between. Since only a few values (such as income) generally are distributed in this way, these studies fail to explore many dimensions of inequality. They ignore social *class* as a phenomenon rooted in *dis*continuity and consciousness of kind. Only an ivory-towered type could believe that class societies do not dominate the world along with industry, money, and the market. The continuous curve in the distribution of goods in the most developed societies lends a new aspect to class but doesn't lessen its bite.

Class becomes real for us as we begin to recognize its constraints and values in ordinary life. For almost everyone this means discovering strangers above and below us. But the idea that boundaries must divide us from these strangers derives from the attempt to rationalize our feelings of difference, instead of recognizing that they must operate for everyone from a private vantage point. Consider the condition of the common crow in Europe. Two main varieties enjoy "class" rather than "caste" relations. The white-jackets of the north do not avoid the black-jackets of the south but have created a gray-jacket class between. Why has this situation stabilized in the interface zone without full merging of the two types? Preference for own kind seems to operate: the "class" balance does not depend on natural boundaries but on qualitative differences in white/gray/black mating dispositions. Much the same can be said for our social class systems. If the disposition to associate with one's own kind is pronounced, contact will produce a mix rather than a blend; and where a discontinuous structure is stratified there is a class society.

Classes have often been treated as subcultures and discussed as though each had an acknowledged center, a fixed code of values, and clear boundaries. We might call this the small-town attorney's view of class. Against it we may place the view of the academic dramaturge who can't think of class without hearing the music of destiny behind—and who eventually will have to be content to find himself labeled either radical or reactionary, depending on the destiny his intuition favors. On grand historical occasions the vague ethnocentrism of class can be woven into the rhetoric of collective action; but the idea that social structures predictably generate the cataclysms that befall them is a gratuitous assumption of the romantic/dialectic version of history. Neither romantic destiny nor dull equilibrium is a necessary feature of social structures; the norm lies between. Real structures don't conform to one-sided models: the recent evolution of a quite varied set of class societies in the West provides a vindication of that maxim. In this evolution, class action has scarcely played a clear role. Class consciousness there has been but it has been most notable for its un-Marxian character throughout the growth of urban-industrial civilization: to be a realistic term, *class* nust be used as referring to a different phenomenon today than it might have a century ago, when you could still distinguish the bourgeoisie as a propertied class and the workers as uneducated. There is at least as much inequality today, but less bold discontinuity. The distribution of values is less lumpy, and the objective correlates of class difference are less obvious.

Homogenization has been a result of the same deep change which accounts for the shift toward transactional (tit-for-tat) allocation of values. In the old North American West the six-gun became an "equalizer." In the New North America of suburb and freeway the same role is played by consumer capital goods—cars, kitchen machines, televisions, and the rest of the durable commodities which preside over middle-class life and seem almost magically to legitimate it. These commodities extend from the bottom of society to the top, offering subtly different degrees of utility and style to the keepers of the cold-water flat, the rural smallholders, and the lean or the overstuffed suburbanites. Chauffeurs and cooks still mediate with the machines for a few of the rich, and at the other end of society the style of life especially of ghetto youth may be almost untouched by the new kind of property tie; but mechanical possessions have put their charm upon most of us, even far beyond the boundaries of developed urbanism. The art of life for now and the foreseeable future is bound up with the enjoyment of gadgets and, through television and the new mobility, the vicarious enjoyment of other people's life-styles.

This is called consumerism, a thing-centered life. The readiest spenders in North America are unmarried men with a family-sized income and no personal dependents. They equip themselves with clothes, cars, and gadgets, as if to borrow from them the security a family later will offer. When the family does become the unit of consumption, the adult experience of class begins for most middle-class people. This experience centers in that opiate of the classes, budgetism: straining at the limits of the family income in order to build up consumer capital without loss of style. For the remainder of domestic life, if the marriage is successful, family-centeredness and thing-centeredness will be compatible. In North America over the last several generations the social class called the proletariat has tended to evaporate, leaving a hard core of urban (and rural) poverty. The process of homogenization is accelerated by an age of affluence and easy credit—an expanding economy—and retarded by economic troubles, large families, insistence on cheap labor, and limited educational facilities—in short, by conditions regarded as non-progressive. From the perspective of North America, if it is prepared to ignore its own hard core, some European capitalist societies seem to have followed along behind a wave of change led by American prosperity, and the most developed communist nations still show a woefully lean middle-class populace. Since materialism is the *de facto* philosophy of both communism and capitalism, it is hard to predict a sharp departure from consumerism as a way of life, or from a social structure polarized by Consumer *Angst*. The commitment to manufactured things is no simple matter of keeping up one's face in the neighborhood but has become the basis of a majority way of life, as surely as farming was for our fathers and hunting-gathering for our distant grandparents. How many of us would survive the real collapse of industry?

Consumer *Angst* is mitigated by class segregation and the ethnocentric social perspective that results. Our picture of social class and its meaning has perhaps been warped by the dramatic image of the striver—the importance of upward mobility and fear of the fall in the ethos of the progressive society. Upward striving is one response to inequality, class-consolidation is another and opposite one. The striver is restless with what he has, vibrating to a tune his compeers do not hear. The institutions of class ethnocentrism are designed to put him at peace. In North America these institutions have been downtown and country clubs, church sodalities, fraternal orders, Scouts and Little Leagues, and a host of commercial services from bars and bowling alleys to the eternal Beauty Parlor. Labor unions have played a special but uneven part: in most regions, having got the blue collar worker into the suburb, they have lost out to the other institutions on stylistic grounds. Class consolidation takes advantage of Consumer *Angst*. At the bridge club, women discover cheaper ways of achieving the same style. At the Knights of Columbus hall (or similar place for an alternate clientele), men have been put through a cathartic charade of making it: each degree is tougher and more grueling than the last, yet everybody makes it with only a little embarrassment, and solemn *Angst* is followed by beer, cards, and the rest that belongs with good fellowship. Gossip at bridge or the hairdresser's also plays upon the underlying anxieties proper to a woman's social position: it is sharp and comes close, but it never quite does touch home—a magical immunity is conferred on the participants, who can't be guilty of the faults they so freely discuss. The paradigm for understanding all class institutions is to be found here: by celebrating an explicit identity with others of comparable standing in society we achieve some immunity from concern with that which we are not. The oversimple identification of class with material satisfactions derives from ignoring the ceremonial aspect of civilized life.

A class society depends no less on segregation than a caste or plural society does, but each has its special qualities. Plural societies are those in which two or more culturally different peoples live under a common political roof without being assimilated. As the great Melting Pot, the United States assimilated European immigrant groups fairly readily by pulling away the younger generations, as individuals, into the competitive scramble for class position. But from the non-European (non-Christian) minorities which remain a century after the industrializing, urbanizing movement got under way, it is possible to imagine the plural society which might have developed if the pace of immigration and occupational explosio had been less hectic. Brazil and Argentina are more balance mixes of caste, class, and pluralism; they have shown greate cultural, combined with rather less political, stability.

The three kinds of segregation reflect different modes o sanctioning. Where class is a result of competitive scrambl and the merit system of advancement, sanctioned always i millions of separate transactions between freely contractin individuals, caste is quite inflexibly, mechanically sanctioned an offender against rules or taboos finds himself alone agains his world. Pluralism is never self-maintaining. In its more repressive forms (slavery, Bantustans, urban ghettos) it require elaborate policing; and even in milder forms (suburban segregation, religious pluralism) it needs the sanction of politica or ecclesiastic authorities. Caste should not be confused wit repressive pluralism, though both involve rigid segregatio and superordination. While it is hard to imagine the origination of caste except out of a less stable pluralism which woul have required repressive authorities, the mature arrangements of a caste society are maintained by scruples, not police. Which system interferes least with individual freedom On the surface class systems are less rigid and less arbitrary But the red man, black, or Jew who wants to keep his cultur must beware the lure of the mainstream. Regional and loca patriots who want to keep control of their environment mus fight industrial growth, which no longer respects even a national boundary.

In North America the end of slavery left a black minorit severely disadvantaged in relation to other (even the newl immigrant) minorities in the contest for position. If in th scramble between a black and a white the black is alway foredoomed the loser, there can be no scramble. The transactional system doesn't work without the conditions of freedom, equal rights, and open opportunity which a democrati constitution is supposed to provide. Collectivism in Americ scarcely offered an alternative ideology for mobility: the labo movement was itself too opportunistically led to provide effective shelter. The blacks became an unprivileged population: castelike in that the segregation was achieved by diffus sanction on the level of manners and belief, but unlike a cast in being systematically held down by the deliberate exercise of white authority in the political and economic domains. The segregation of American Indians during the same chapter of modern history conforms more classically to the type of repressive pluralism: military defeat was followed by location on bounded reservations. But North American society has been an unlikely context for the establishment of a static plural order: the civilization has regularly transformed itself from one generation to the next. The processes which homogenized the class structure, eliminating the classic barriers of property and education, was certain to erode other major structural compartments as well. In the absence of diffuse sanctions to prevent American Indians from shedding their minority identity off the reservation, that spurious system of repression became unreal; and in the relative absence of legal barriers to mobility for a Black outside the Deep South, his place in the social structure could become as ambiguous as that of a Greek intellectual in Imperial Rome.

Segregation by mechanical sanction is illuminated by consideration of dialect boundaries in Norway or England. A dialect is ambiguously voluntary. If you really don't want to be taken as countrified in Norway or as working-class in England it will take a very short while to lose your linguistic identity, though it may be harder to gain exactly the one you admire. On the other hand, if you do want to retain your original identity you will do so, though you live sixty years hardly hearing your native sounds from another man's lips: so with the southern priest in northern Norway, so with the expatriate Briton who one day will want to return to his own. Linguistic segregation and desegregation therefore is not simply a function of the quantity of interaction between two populations but is sensitive to the quality of contact as well. Men from certain tribes in East Africa are known for their facility with languages, while others claim to be unable to learn any but their own: the reason has not to do with linguistic ability as such, but the meaning of tribal identity in each case: the facile man enjoys the change of identity, the other emphatically would not. In England dialects are regional, but in Norway they would have to be called local: where a million families speak the same English, you are likely to find only a few hundred speaking the same Norwegian. Whatever makes an Englishman keep faith with his region seems to make a Norwegian want to keep faith with his local valley or fjord society; and language is part of the code of manners and style by which a man expresses such an identity.

Does a man put on his own identity or is it thrust upon him? Where the sanctioning process is by the diffuse mechanisms of style and ceremonial tradition the only choice is to move—if opportunity arises—from one set identity toward or to another. He can't invent his own idiom, though he may have to find his own compromise. The nearest he can come to shaping his own identity may be in joining the vanguard of a promising political movement or withdrawing to an ideal commune. An approach to this condition was enjoyed by some European colonists up to the first generations of this century, when they were able to encyst themselves as ruling elites in Asian or African settings; and something similar has motivated the proliferation of sects out of Protestantism since the seventeenth century in the English-speaking world; by withdrawing into a small, consensual community of brethren a man elects the qualities of his own social identity. But even where a small group of households takes authority to itself they will encounter that tide in human affairs which does not respond to command. This is the movement of style, meaning, and underlying concern which comprises the life of popularly shared values, and which has its regular expression in the diffuse sanctioning of behavior in which we all, perhaps inadvertently, participate. Class segregation, though it abounds with intention, is a product of tide rather than command. Changes in class position have to be achieved transactionally, but codes of class behavior, once arrived, may be as mechanical as any caste code: the dictates of fashion, or of decency, are not subject to negotiation.

In the final analysis, the phenomenon of class is the expression in mass society of the granular principle of order characteristic of the small-scaled society. If we suppose that men, women, and children are unable to work out a satisfactory life with each going his own way, and that sharing an ethic of domesticity with one's effective neighbors is a fairly ineluctable solution to the problem of order on the level of the private life, then it will appear that class is not an absurdity foisted upon us by the dark-enfolded demiurge of history but a normal result of structural process. We can expect that as long as inequality prevails, class will be continuously created. In the bare nature of class there is no special constraint put upon change: the class system is not the brittle thing Marx imagined, which would shatter under the building stress of socioeconomic growth. If class war is inherent in the nature of urban-industrial civilization, it is a chronic, guerrilla warfare characterized by situational strategies on both sides, and a constantly shifting ground. What has kept the matter so is, on the one hand, the sensitive nature of class identity as a reaction to inequality, functioning mainly to facilitate domestic order; and, on the other hand, the successful effort of the political state over the long run to maintain its monopoly of force by expanding its ability to mediate partisan demands. It may be the final irony of the twentieth century that the political power which was so constantly enhanced in the major capitals of the West in response to massive demands for social justice and security will utterly destroy the foundations of justice and security for men, through its untoward new prowess in the use of brute force.

SECTION THREE

THE LAST EMANCIPATION

REPRESSION AND SOCIAL STRUCTURE

The most difficult problem in the analysis of social structure is not social control but freedom. Regarded as a sanction, freedom is immunity from explicit authoritative constraint. But there can be no immunity without a powerful guarantor; and it follows that legally sanctioned freedoms will be subject to any condition deemed necessary to protect the authority from which they spring. But the question, How free is an Englishman? is not just a question about the design (or circularity) of the British system of legal sanctions; it is a question about the way that system actually works. To this issue, implicit and indirect sanctions are relevant, and transactional or mechanical modes of allocation: the way the law conceives itself to work is seldom affected by actual results, but an Englishman's freedom is affected by nothing else. It is to freedom in that phenomenological sense that structural analysis may be applicable. Effective freedom is sensitive to position in the social structure: objectively, since one position will offer more options than another at the same stage in the life cycle, and subjectively, since autonomy gives freedom its meaning. But apart from inequality, the idea of freedom is one of the important touchstones by which we *judge* social structures. It is a key to a major dimension of variability upon which any society can be located.

But when that is once said the trouble has begun. We may find it easy to rate Dobu (p. 219) less free than the Trobriands (p. 148) because Malinowski's folk seem less burdened with their *Angst* than Fortune's folk do. But where on the same continuum do we fit the Fulani (p. 167)? the Anuak (p. 229)? the Andamanese (p. 142)? or the Kachin village, either hierarchic in persuasion or "revolutionary" (p. 250)? It is no good, of course, to ask how free *we* would feel in this culture or that: the relativity of structure and character is embarrassingly obvious when we try. And while we may seem at first to fare a bit better by fitting abstractions to the puzzle—"rational" man or political man or the man of psychology books—we will find the societies don't arrange themselves nicely from free to unfree, while the arguments ramify and don't resolve. Freedom has almost as many faces as man. But then how is it that in common speech everyone seems to know what he means by the term?

The answer is that we share, directly and vicariously, experience of the specific constraints which urban-industrial life imposes, and we sense the very general movement in history which has favored a long series of specific emancipations. If you are urbanized but not "westernized," you will be understandably puzzled by Western talk of freedom, which assumes so much and examines so little; and if your Western heritage is filtered through Marxist hermeneutics you will make a point of refusing to follow un-Marxist talk. That is, if we know what freedom means it is because we share a common character and inhabit a common structural maze. Global migrations, international markets, and the colossal scale of modern imperialism and war have brought about a fusing of separate traditions and a knotting together of nations which make it possible to think about a single human future, even while appreciating the radical diversity of human pasts and the intensity of current divisions. But where as late as the nineteen-thirties One World was a phrase connoting earthly salvation, today it can suggest a colossal apparatus of power with many times the repressive potential of the modern state. The future of freedom can look gloomy: even if we should escape the current crescendo of international conflict and domestic violence, how can we be sure that the final trap will not then snap shut upon us all? We would all then mean the same thing when we spoke of freedom: we should be engaged in a common struggle, aimed at the last emancipation. But is all this at all likely?

The answer must be drawn from the experience of the more advanced urban-industrial societies; the appropriate frame of reference is structural. Specifically, the grand-scale movement is from oppression to repression, from the primacy of infrastructure to that of superstructure. Oppression is a matter of structure—one class oppresses another. In the idiom of certain European languages, members of an overclass are privileged to exploit in customary ways the members of an underclass. Whether this occurs in the context of class, caste, or pluralism (or a mix of all three) the element of conventionality and the attachment of privilege to social standing rather than office distinguishes oppression from repression, as I shall be using those terms. Oppression and repression are both considered in this context to be phenomena of panoramic scale, and "repression" is not supposed to have psychoanalytic overtones but means something more like "preventive punishment" or "arbitrary deprivation" or "rule by fear." The process which has homogenized the class systems of an urban-industrial society has dissociated the functions of ruling and of class, so that the concept of a ruling class no longer makes much sense. The importance of class has accordingly diminished, as has the restraint which convention formerly exercised upon the ruling function. This function, in turn, has been subsumed into what we may call the governing establishment, comprised mainly of professional officialdoms: the armed forces, the police networks, the bureaucracies, the party-political machines with the major public offices they control, and a number of more shadowy contingents which are usually to be found working through the public offices, as the old vizier used to work through an inattentive sultan. Though we may speak of a power elite in business and industry, it has always been the actual official machinery at their disposal which has constituted them a repressive force. The result of the shift from amateur and conventional to professional contingent rule has been to facilitate an enormous expansion of the sheer turnover in the business of government. The function of the overclass has been assumed by the state and has become a very big business.

How should we judge the main structural consequences of this shift? Though the demand for equality has colored all the major popular political movements, comprehensive leveling has taken place only in a few small states, notably in Scandinavia. However, in the larger industrial states the great bulge of population today is at least somewhat off the bottom strata, and the middle classes have been the most expansive, absorbing an upward movement. If the way between poor and rich hasn't shortened it has at least become more crowded. The most obvious trend in the major capitalist states has been homogenization. Again it is only in a few states, and probably those where the problems were least, that this movement has passed a point of no return; I should not like to predict when, if ever, racial and ethnic, linguistic and religious boundaries will cease to mark lines of conflict in the West. Emancipation from such cleavages, and the petty class oppressions they shelter, would have to precede any general shift in favor of limiting the repressive potential of the state. The last emancipation would be a movement not *to* the middle class but *of* it, and the prophet of that time will probably recognize that it has been religious and ethnic-racial particularism which for so long has been the bane of that class.

The resentment of oppression through inequality was a great engine of change in the West, spurring the great migrations and expansions of modern times, though every explicit manifestation of popular resentment might seem to have been suppressed with ease, or otherwise to have miscarried. The new resentment of manipulative repression, apparent in the massive disaffection of middle-class youth in the most homogenized states, may turn out to have the same quality of effectiveness over long periods of time, while consistently losing the immediate encounters. The demand for moral and material goods which is the basis of industrial prosperity is a function of the demand for equality: the emancipation from hunger, disease, and relative deprivation has motivated structural change in the West so far. But the form that change has taken is scarcely to be derived from its motives: the great complex of political, economic, and technical power we call the industrial stake is a weird stepchild of enlightenment and egalitarianism. What will the grandchild be?

Could repression be only an accidental attribute of the new social systems? Can we expect that a noncapitalist or a non-Western form of the industrial state may evolve which is not repressive? which would shape itself to meet the needs of a free people, instead of shaping the people to meet "needs of the state"? I am skeptical. There are no shortcuts to the last emancipation: the process of industrialization is an exceedingly demanding one, requiring a repressive superstructure and a steeply competitive occupational system. A stage of nationalistic expansion and repressive statism cannot be circumvented: if a nation wants industry, it will have to settle for being an urban industrial state; and there are no nations more powerful than the Pygmies of the Congo which are committed to remaining preindustrial forever. The rest of us, having made a god of industry and having become utterly dependent on its material dispensation, must be thinking of ways to tame or escape the power we have created.

A TURBULENCE MODEL OF THE SOCIAL SYSTEM

Discussion of the social structure of urban-industrial states ought to deal with class (infrastructure) and the regulative machinery (superstructure) which copes with that permanent state of crisis urbanism and industry create. In proposing a "turbulence model" I am taking an opposite position to that of the "equilibrium model," but I am not embracing a dialectical or evolutionary model of change which implies or assumes destination.

A fundamental methodological assumption is concealed in my preference for "dilemmas" over "switches." Equilibrium models are built on the assumption that social systems fall into set patterns, through a process like choice or chance, and having fallen into their patterns firmly hold them. The pattern will be unambiguous: each element is either "on" or "off." Picture a dozen dried peas in a roulette wheel: when it is jerked into motion they will bounce around, but long before the wheel stops they will have assumed positions, and the pattern will hold. The elemental movements of which this dance is composed can be called "choices from an arc of possibilities" and the analogy can be applied to "patterns of culture" in the manner of Benedict (p. 14). Supposing that only black and red positions are available on the wheel, each pea would have a choice between one or the other; and with each spin a new sequence of color choices around the rim would probably result: out of a series of binary choices, randomly variable patterns would emerge. In an equilibrium model social systems differ from one another in the same way as the color sequences do: each social system has the same arc of possibilities, but there are a sufficient number of variables to ensure that actual systems will be unique. History spins the wheel, and a different culture results each time. The people of that culture are bound to those one-way values which have crystallized out of their history, and this accounts for the equilibrium of their social system. History is external to the system itself. The example of the computer, which can resolve chaotic complexity into logical arrays, seems to lend credibility to the equilibrium model. Both are based on binary logic and brook no indeterminacy.

But what if your major variables do not operate like the switching elements in a computer but exhibit a continuous range of variance? Mathematically, this can be described by an equation or curve. A constant-product curve (graphing the equation $xy=k$) expresses the dilemma of the "minimax" strategist who can't gain a little x without losing a little y, and wants as much as he can get of both. David Hume suggested in the eighteenth century that freedom and equality were related in about that manner in a social system: if you maximized freedom you would lose equality, and in restoring equality you would be suppressing freedom. The major attributes of a social system are related to one another as the horns of such a dilemma more often than by a simple binary choice. Scarcity is as universal as choice, and two good things are often opposed: when you have an equal amount of both you have enough of neither; but to go after more of the one means giving up hope of having the other. As a very general attribute of the human condition this makes a reasonable first premise; and if you begin with "dilemmas" rather than "switches" you are less likely to finish with an equilibrium model.

In the diagram, the turbulence model is presented in a two-dimensional space, and vast movements seem to have gained a specious symmetry. This should not be taken as a claim that social structures have two dimensions or four poles. The function of mathematics here is to render clarity *in the model:* there is no presumption that history itself displays mathematical elegance, only that we may learn to perceive a little better the regularities which are to be found in the flux of human affairs, if we can be clear about what we are looking for. Equilibrium (or organic-homeostatic) models help to disclose real features of social systems. Dialectical models have stimulated scholarship in the East and West for many centuries. The construction of a turbulence model seemed to be particularly appropriate for this century.

The model is based on the distinction between infrastructure and superstructure, by which I do *not* mean the lower and higher regions of the structural grid. Infrastructure means that which is subject to the superstructure, and superstructure means the gamut of officialdoms grand and petty which comprise a society's regulative institutions. Hence the city boss's humble henchmen are figures, however dim, in the superstructure, though they eke out their lives in disreputable places and never attend an Hawaiian convention; and Mrs. Wrigley, lying in an endless coma which only her millions could have afforded her, enjoyed a lofty place in the infrastructure but no role at all in the exercise of official power. Everyone has a place in the infrastructure, and through the potential impact of dissidence, at least, everyone theoretically partakes in the superstructure; Nazism was not possible without broad consent, and empires crumble when their legitimacy fails among the masses of the common people. But the power of dissidence is the power of vulgar desperation,

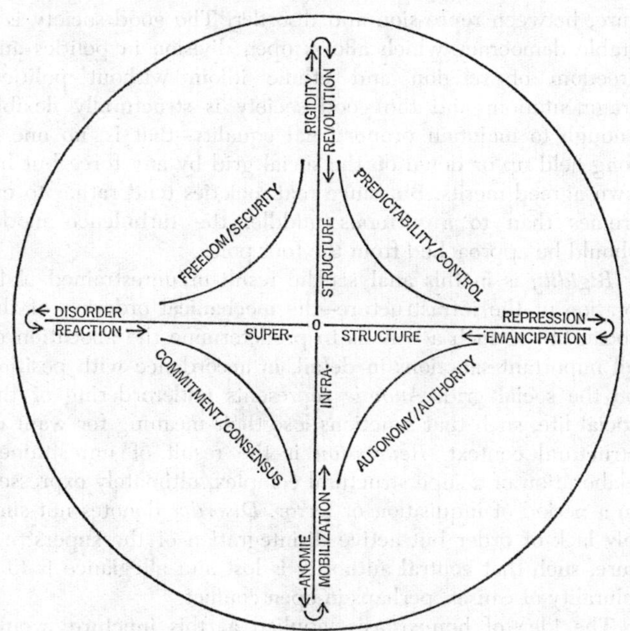

A TURBULENCE MODEL OF THE SOCIAL SYSTEM

just as the power of influence is the power of elite trepidation: the incumbents of office have the everyday, overweighing parts. In the half-industrial Western societies still marked by a ruling class, as in much of Latin America today, the power of officials to change the course of affairs is minimal: the infrastructure is developed to a point of great rigidity, and the superstructure undeveloped: which results in the paradox that a military coup with its charisma and its initial bit of leverage can sometimes offer relief of a sort from class oppression. The historic shift from oppression to repression is a shift from infrastructural to superstructural emphasis, scaled on each of the two axes of the model.

Let us assume, like Aristotle, that we know where virtue

lies. The point where the two axes cross is the point of optimal balance, or a golden mean between extremes: for the infrastructure, between rigidity and anomie; for the superstructure, between repression and disorder. The good society is a stable democracy which allows open division in politics and freedom of religion and ethnic idiom without political fragmentation; and the good society is structurally flexible enough to maintain proportional equality—that is, no one is long held up or down on the social grid by any force but his own agreed merits. But since real societies tend rather to extremes than to a virtuous middle, the turbulence model should be approached from the four poles.

Rigidity is in this analysis the result of unrestrained elaboration of the infrastructure—the mechanical ordering of the social life in such a way as to predetermine the allocation of all important sanctions in detail, in accordance with position on the social grid. *Anomie* represents underordering of the social life, such that sanctions lose their meaning for want of structural context. *Repression* is the result of unrestrained elaboration of a superstructural complex, ultimately expressed in a period of inquisition or terror. *Disorder* denotes not simply lack of order but active disintegration of the superstructure, such that central authority is lost and allegiance is to a plurality of causes, perhaps in open conflict.

The idea of homeostasis, applied at this juncture, would mean that societies tended to "return to the origin" representing the mean value on both axes of variability. But this could hardly be. No social system is so integral that it can be represented on the diagram by a single point. The concept of "the social structure of Spain" ignores the fact, which even an idle traveler comes to know, that there are many Spains. Further, history is never suspended: most movements are not movements of restoration but of irreversible change, and movement is never stilled. If a momentary balance is reached, it won't remain; that is the idea of a turbulence model. In fact, the place of "equilibrium" in this model is probably the pole of rigidity. Societies vary as to how well-centered or dispersed they would seem, if graphed upon our model of structural space. For example, there were periods in the history of Italy when in one way or another it was flying off the graph in all four directions: rigidity, repression, anomie, and disorder. Correspondingly, there were simultaneously movements of class revolution, liberal emancipation, ideological mobilization, and fascistic reaction. While such profligate dispersion of trends must be exceptional, I suspect it is closer to the historical norm than we are generally inclined to think.

Instead of an attraction to the center I assume some degree of repulsion from the extremes as the engine of turbulence in a social system. So *rigidity* may generate *revolutionary* movements, because a rigid structure can't be modified "by working from within"; an extraconstitutional force seems necessary. *Repression* by church or state hierarchies, on the other hand, can occur in the absence of an oppressive class system—for example, in spite of high mobility rates. Then the movement opposing repression might have the character of *emancipation* "from within"—a series of specific, constitutional reforms designed to enhance the rights and immunities of the people, and redistribute the sanctioning power of the officials. *Anomie* is not a condition of individual disorientation but of situational disturbance: psychologically sound individuals can be cast into an anomic situation and seem "disturbed." This is best discussed in the light of the distinction between motivation of the person and motivation of the role: the disturbance is psychological when it occurs on the level of personality, and anomic when it occurs on the level of role motivation. Anomie is sometimes regarded as an extreme "social pathology": it must be epidemic before it deserves to be named. In small doses we could refer to the same phenomenon as "low morale" —analytically, a sort of opposite number to role-strain which occurs where the demands of the situation are highly specific and overtax the resources of the persons. In the role disturbance characteristic of anomie, the person has more to offer than the role will absorb and give form to: joblessness and rootlessness may generate such situations. I have labeled the movement in reversion from anomie *mobilization* because that word points to a popular state of readiness for new commitments. In contrast, *reaction* from a state of disorder is reversion to old commitments—or at least to commitments so rationalized.

The *revolutions* which the model points to are not narrowly political but more deeply structural events, bound up with renewal of the infrastructure itself. Though they respond to extreme rigidity, this is to be distinguished from stability (obviously *not* a cause of turbulence). But diametric change is a lot easier to intend, as part of a utopian movement, than to achieve. Could the two great revolutions of this century, in Russia and China, have occurred if the old regimes had not first been weakened and the peoples shaken by disastrous foreign wars? An extreme of rigidity must be judged on evidence of the system's inability to still basic sources of turbulence—generally, an inability to meet elemental economic needs or to protect life. Rigidity, then, does not imply strength.

Revolution will not directly produce anomic crisis. A tightly woven social structure can't be laid in fragments overnight; the conditions of anomie, unless imposed from without, are more likely to result from a gradual disintegration over several generations. Some civil wars, especially disturbances of the peasant-industrial transition, are the culmination of just such a process of disintegration. These wars should be classed as "wars of mobilization" for our purposes. The formula for revolution applies only to the breaking up of a rigidly oppressive system—a monolith. It is hard to conceive the historic contingency that would produce a revolution with *moderating* results, unless we allow the possibility of a modest revolution against modest oppression. In the immoderate case, revolution having broken up the monolith, a new and well-knit infrastructure will not rapidly evolve; there will be a period in which the unity or disunity of the society will be expressed in the organization of the superstructure: a revolutionists' government, a counterrevolutionary government, or disorder. If the turbulence produces a new extreme it will be of the political sort represented by the horizontal axis of the model.

Similarly *emancipation from within* assumes conditions that would not lead directly from one pole of the model to its opposite. The bourgeois demand for rights has sometimes miscarried to the point of establishing a rigid class system, maintaining a regimented and uneducated working class, but it has also miscarried in the other direction, producing an unviable structure, incapable of maintaining an efficient and well-motivated culture of work. This is the case with some European, Latin American, and Asian societies which have become stalemated at a half-industrial stage, without the indigenous basis for industrialization of the capitalist variety, but so far immune from any further process of emancipation from within which might lead to socialist industrialization. In some cases, anomie is sufficiently widespread that a period of peasant mobilization has begun, which should initiate a new phase of national history.

Mobilization movements result from opposite conditions to those which produce revolution. A full reversal of structural conditions would not directly result from the processes which anomie produced. Ideological mobilization can be religious or political. The former in urban-industrial societies has not been associated with movements of national scale; but in the preindustrial world there have been ages of pan-national religious movement, leading when successful to political consolidation and armed conflict. Labor-union movements have taken on the character of mobilizations, with an idiom somewhere between the political and the religious. Sometimes they have hastened the advent of fascism or produced irreconcilable political factionalism; but they have usually not so far miscarried as to produce lasting repression or major disorders. Political mobilization movements, however, may *aim* to produce disorder—and, miscarrying, have hastened the triumph of a repressive regime. In the confused situation exploited by Mussolini after World War I in Italy, a popular mobilization movement *became* a repressive regime, and this act was repeated in a somewhat different situation a decade later by Hitler in Germany.

The roots of fascism are in anomie rather than in factional disorder. My formula for disorder and the *reactionary movements* it may inspire should not be taken to suggest that mobilization movements in reversion from anomie can't trade on reactionary ideological themes. On the contrary, the distinction of mobilization movements is precisely their ideological character, whether radical, reactionary, or otherworldly. My formula for reaction to disorder applies to movements of the official establishment, not popular mobilizations. Usually a military junta, if it is going to be successful, must take over a divided government *before* there is popular involvement in the crisis. But establishment reaction seldom puts an end to turbulence; it is a holding operation out of which a new direction may emerge, whether it be popular retrenchment or further demoralization or both. The reaction of the Southern states to the disorder of the period of the Reconstruction after the American Civil War led to a far more rigid social structure than the antebellum one. On the other hand, the increasingly reactionary character of the Weimar regime in Germany brought only anomie and the communist/fascist mobilizations which led to submergence of Weimar in Nazism. The *disorder* with which I am concerned is disarray of the regulative institutions of the society, not disarray of the populace as such; the first, if left to work itself out through conflict in a complex society, would lead to the second—and to a period of accelerating turbulence. The function of regulative institutions is the maintenance of order through control of infrastructural organization; and when the regulative function fails in a society lacking conventional controls, popular disarray occurs.

I now want to offer an alternative conceptualization of the main implications of the turbulence model—not in terms of social movements but in terms of "rationalizing" or "strategic" dilemmas. This approach could hardly be more abstract, in the sense of its generality, than the foregoing; but the dilemmas are also abstract in the sense of being mental. That hardly would make them less real, but it probably makes them harder to pin down to a time and place. They are certainly easier to discuss without meeting the embarrassing paradox of theoretical application—that history doesn't provide pure cases. I am concerned with states of mind which in a myriad forms must be endemic in urban-industrial societies. The dilemmas I discuss seem to me inherent in the nature of the complex structure, and connected with its inherent turbulence. Perhaps the way to conceive them most directly is to imagine that you are somehow in position to rationalize the structure of a developing state, and that you want to maximize its viable features. You are concerned with the logic of ends, not means.

The *predictability-control* dilemma is this: As you seek to increase your control of a social system you lose the ability to make objective predictions about it; and to regain the predictability you must give up your control. Predictability in human affairs depends on "spontaneous order"; the law of averages doesn't apply to a manipulated universe. Life in a mechanically sanctioned society runs endlessly on in worn channels and is substantially more predictable than life in an efficient authoritarian system, though the authoritarian is likely to find the unmanipulable society cluttered up intolerably with "inefficient" ceremonialism and indirection. To maximize the superstructural control of events, if you had the power, you would loosen up the structural weave of the society, subjecting both contracts and conventions to review and manipulation. But as you do this you frustrate your ability to plan on the basis of objective statistical projections: planning decisions which you can't now predict will continue to be made at an expanding rate. Though "spontaneous order" is misnamed because it presupposes structure, you can deal with it *as if* it were a natural phenomenon; infrastructure is lawful in a way that superstructure is not.

The predictability-control dilemma comes into being as totalitarianism (on local, regional, or national level) becomes possible: there is no dilemma until the authority is strong enough to exert over time a radical effect upon the infrastructure. The active force is not a single mind but the entire officialdom: in attempting to maximize their control, the officials lose their ability to control because they open the structure to other forces of manipulation than their own. If in response to the dilemma they revert to genuine conservatism, they may come to comprise a conventional ruling class. If they try to stay always ahead of the problems of planning, they will be taking the road of totalitarian government. I don't suggest that there is any inherent tendency to go as far as the extremes of rigidity and repression—only that there is no stable resting point along the curve between the two poles.

The *autonomy-authority* dilemma is another source of turbulence in societies subject to rationalizing processes. To maximize autonomy in a population is to make every man his own authority—the radical decentralization of initiative. The result is a considerable dependence on "spontaneous order," which presupposes a diffusely sanctioned (traditional) social structure. In open societies the disappearance of authority means the depolarization of values—anomie. What is to be gained in achieving popular autonomy? The gain is that values should be built in—ingrained in individual character. But if you were really in position to rationalize your society as a viable urban-industrial system, could you afford to have an *individual* set of values built into each character? In maximizing the gains of popular autonomy, where the infrastructure weighs lightly on the individual, you will defeat your purpose. Similarly, the regime which wants to maximize authority will risk defeating its own purpose. The classic realization of this dilemma is the problem of stopping the buck in a hierarchy of authority. As local autonomy breaks down in a centralizing system all the decisions even slightly out of the routine are passed in for central processing, and the central authority becomes encumbered with red tape; theoretically, the chief is responsible for all decisions, but practically, they must be farmed out. The more you seek to maximize the gains of centralized authority, the more you find yourself obliged to create new forms of decentralized autonomy. Again there is no stable resting point where the opposition is resolved.

The *commitment-consensus* dilemma occurs on the level of taste as well as that of ethical values. The turbulence of fashions in the modern West is the innocent surface of a much deeper and chronic disturbance which is the moral dilemma of the open society: what we can freely agree upon we can't really believe, and the things we do put our faith in seem to set us at odds, group against group. In the world of fashion the dilemma centers on the value of novelty: the value of a style is a function of its freshness and its popularity, but as the latter grows it extinguishes the former, and the search for something fresh leads again to diversity. The result is not a simple cycle or "oscillating equilibrium"; it is turbulence. In the case of fashion it is easy to see why consensus is empty and enthusiasm not to be trusted. The West is prone to fashions in ideas as well as the arts, but if all values were merely popular there would be an end to civilization altogether. Consider the law, the church, and the school: each institution enshrines certain values and responds only ponderously to the specific pressures of the times. When there is a response, the social effects are often long delayed; felt at another time, they are perhaps understood in other terms. The "basic values" are so built into the structure that to change them radically would require much more than a mass conversion; it would mean breaking up the structure of right and obligation, mutual identity and involvement which were built on the old values. But if some values are safe from the corruption of fashion because they are built into the structure, the structure which lodges them is vulnerable to the cumulative effects of fashion: nothing is quite so Western as *aggiornamento,* cleaning out the ecclesiastical attic or rewriting the bylaws of the club. The course of history toward ethical and ideological modernity (whatever may comprise the "modern" at any given time and place) is inevitably a turbulent one. The true believer probably has more power to change men's minds than the skeptic; and the conventional wisdom has never had the field to itself, even in the most repressive state.

The *commitment-consensus* dilemma is peculiarly characteristic of the West and of the more competitive nation-states within the Western group. Religious and political divisiveness have tended to go together; it is not hard to name men of various nations who were zealous reformers in both fields. Politically, the heart of the dilemma is that as you compromise in order to have the consensual basis for practical political action, you lose the idealists; and they in turn are incapable of that necessary compromise. In religion, perhaps because practical action is not so demanding, compromise has usually been something of an embarrassment all around—not so squarely faced as in politics. The theological dilemma therefore begins at the other end, with idealism: as a person moves toward the fullest commitment of faith he moves into the realm of the private and incommunicable. Most of the great saints have been irrelevant to their times, or else they were martyred. Evangelists whose ideas are not difficult seem to be able to fold their tents and leave nothing behind. The overwhelming commitment of the West, and especially certain nation-states, to scientific-technological revolution has owed little to those who were content with easy ideas, and a great deal to those who could turn a private invention into a public value. The technical inventiveness of the West, at least, is unexampled. It was stimulated by a tension between idealism and pragmatism, peculiar to the Western tradition, and illustrated in the turbulent history of its religious and political movements.

The *freedom-security* dilemma is the one, of the four which the model suggests, most frequently discussed in relation to social structure. The upwardly mobile person glories in his freedom even while he fears for his security. Political value systems swing between liberalization and collectivization. The central tendency in the West is toward welfare, which is a kind of median between the two, and not toward either extreme; but on the level of ideas the turbulence doesn't settle. The maximum security is of course offered not in the most planned but in the most rigid society; the unpredictability of planners has been discussed. Security can even be defined in terms of freedom: freedom from poverty, disease, and interference. The dilemma is that these freedoms must be bought at the sacrifice of others—specifically, of the one which must be central to all human experience, the freedom to be and do as one pleases.

TEMERITY AND TERROR

In the distant past, in the simplest societies, men knew equality but not peace. In the distant future, in the most complex societies, men conceive they may know both—if not, the human future itself is in doubt. Our task in this age is to get through the foreseeable future, so that the distance might be gained. The study of social structure is one of the means at hand—academic but scarcely irrelevant. For our safety we must learn to tranquilize our superstructures. The most advanced societies will not be safe from terror until they have taken *off* a great deal of the load they now put on their regulative institutions—or at least until the load is distributed much more broadly. I think the issues of equality and peace are closely related. So far, the industrial world has pursued equality with some success, while peace is lost to sight. The specter haunts us of a society held together by nothing but the power of the state, and that power committed to war.

In *War and Peace* Tolstoy argued that it is the people that rise to conflict, not their political states; the emperors and generals only ride the tide of human affairs as best they can. For the sake of our sanity in the age of overkill we must hope he was wrong. I propose, in place of his tidal view, the idea of social structure: great events arise from the whole situation, in which mass and elite partake, and whose central motives are not historical or natural accidents but systematic. To accept the Tolstoyan view today is to accept that the future of the world is radically predestined and presumably short, as history is directly exposed to what treatment human nature may bestow. The idea of social structure suggests, however, that the exposure is less direct, and the independent variable need not be so vacillating as the huge range of possible human behavior suggests. There are impressive regularities in institutional conformation from one society to another, and we can better hope to understand the limits imposed on us by our social than by our biopsychic structures. One of these limits is that the greater reliance for order must be on the infrastructure and not on centralized authority.

Part of the argument is very old: for Plato it was a matter of reliance on laws not men, but he saw little hope of getting from bad laws to good without the help of a virtuous tyrant. Translated into our terms this is to say that the goal is the good society—neither too rigid nor too loose, neither over- nor undergoverned—but that to get there we have to go through a period of benevolent repression, as only a powerful superstructure could act upon the infrastructure with enough force to bring about wholesale change. I will not defend such nonsense. The Marxist version of this salvation *ex machina*, the dictatorship of the proletariat, has had a number of trials —enough to afford a rough reckoning of the odds. Benevolent repression as a culmination of current trends in the most developed societies, where equality really seems almost within reach, has been considered by such writers of the grotesque as Kafka and George Orwell; hardly anyone would want to take bets as to when we might come out the end of *that* tunnel. Let us hope rather that it won't come to that—that a viable infrastructure for the new kind of society will evolve out of the long-term popular movements for equality and emancipation, turning now to the demand for freedom from the overgrown superstructures themselves.

The conclusion to be drawn from a comparison of life in the microcultures and life in the urban-industrial setting is that for the immediate future sanity and social order will depend on a balanced rhythm of public and private involvement. Conventional forms of the domestic life provide most adults with an unquestioned, and unquestionably moral, identity with an intimate group: an identity which can provide a motivational base apart from the marketplace or the political arena. The future of the family has often enough been called into question: since that is happening again, we will once more see the domestic institution adapt itself to a new situation. On sheerly political grounds, massive desertion of domesticity is unlikely. True privacy—privacy in the life of the mind—is the basis of any free public opinion and would be imperiled by any shift away from a structural pattern which favors enduring intimacy in small groups united by maximal-claim ties. But in the long run domestic autonomy is guaranteed not by the good will but by the self-interest of the state: the superstructure still is built on the foundation of "spontaneous order" among the people—that is, the infrastructure. Without the bourgeois family the bourgeois state is not possible; and nonbourgeois states have discovered the same truth. It is only because we incessantly meet and somehow resolve the problem of order in the microcosm that we don't enter the marketplace with quite the untamed egoism which Hobbes (p. 3) presupposed. The cult of the individual has its place in the myth life of the transactional order, but the really volatile individual remains a Peer Gynt —more than one of a kind would be a load upon the system, and there is a limit to the load it will bear. Before we go ahead in our enthusiasm for a new emancipation and remove the family entirely from our scheme for the future we should consider the possibility that alternatives would be worse.

I am less sanguine than Plato about finding a good politician, but no less prone to speculating how men might arrange their public affairs for the better. I doubt that saviors will be pulled out of a black box called politics. Instead I turn to one called possibilities. There are two recurrent postures of man which I find remarkable—two opposite responses to terror: docility and violence. The mass graves of six million Jews are a monument to the one, still perplexing, though not without nobility. There are more recent monuments to terror. Our nature allows each of us to make either of these responses to overwhelming power; the question is how the response is decided. My answer is that our response is a direct expression of the character we are given in our intimate life with others, whether family or peers. The docility of European Jews and of the British working classes well past mid-century reflects the self-sufficiency of a family system which in each case has been *the* reference group monopolizing individual members. As families cease to have that significance, public violence in the name of one or another extravagant utopia becomes more likely. As the temerity of the people, particularly of youth, increases, the techniques of state repression will escalate as well; and police escalation must be rated a necessary evil at best, even by those who defend the politics of punishment.

It would be better if the terror could be avoided. It is unlikely that the open, competitive, enormously unselfsufficient middle-class family of the United States could produce a larger crop of docile youths in the future; the trend seems the other way, toward the primacy of the peers and the questioning of public values: toward readiness for mobilization in whatever sort of fashionable movement or cause. Police suppression of these movements probably would not succeed. There must be an expansion of the private domain of youth in such a way as to institutionalize not fashions or causes but new values: that is, old values with new looks. Since the family is in abeyance there is a massive need for that honesty in private life which, at an earlier and a later stage of life, the family will provide. It is foolish to expect much of politicians, and hard to see what the academics or the clergy can do. Plato is still waiting for his virtuous tyrant. I have more hope for the building up of fresh patterns of spontaneous order: new structures emerging from below, finding their viable forms, and multiplying.

BIBLIOGRAPHICAL NOTE

Neither of the lists which follow is meant to be a measure of what this work owes to others—no short list could be such. But many of the anthropologists and others cited have had a formative influence on my thinking, and rather more have taught me through my disagreeing with them. Since I also have learned eristically from a host of teachers, colleagues, and students over the years, I can only offer my thanks here, knowing they will know who they are. The list of REFERENCES gives only works actually cited in the text; and I have indicated [in brackets] the pages extracted. The list of GENERAL WORKS is short and intended to suggest first steps outward or onward from this book. In composing the list I have also been aware of expressing in each case special ties of descent or affinity; but we have no proper terms for more narrowly defining such intellectual kinship.

REFERENCES

Beattie, J. H. M. "Matiyo and his Two Wives." *Africa,* XXXV:3 (July 1965) 252–63. [P. 259.]

Benedict, Ruth. *Patterns of Culture.* (First edition 1934.) New York: Mentor, 1946. [Pp. 219–21, 234–35.]

Berndt, R. M. and C. H. *The World of the First Australians.* Chicago: University of Chicago Press, 1964. [P. 324.]

Burridge, Kenelm O. L. "Disputing in Tangu," 1952. *American Anthropologist,* 59:5 (October 1957) 763–80.

Eliot, T. S. *Notes Towards the Definition of Culture.* New York: Harcourt, Brace & Co., 1959. [Pp. 30–31.]

Fortes, Meyer. "Introduction" to Jack Goody (ed.), *The Developmental Cycle in Domestic Groups* (Cambridge Papers in Social Anthropology No. 1). Cambridge: The University Press, 1958. [Pp. 12–13.]

Fortune, Reo F. *Sorcerers of Dobu.* (First edition 1932.) New York: Dutton, 1963. [Pp. 57, 61–2.]

Freeman, J. D. "The Family System of the Iban of Borneo" in Jack Goody (ed.), *The Developmental Cycle in Domestic Groups,* Pp. 15–52. Cambridge: The University Press, 1958. [Pp. 16–18.]

Harper, Edward B. "Hoylu: A Belief Relating Justice and the Supernatural," *American Anthropologist,* 59:5 (October 1957), 801–15.

Henry, Jules. *Jungle People.* (First edition 1941.) New York, Vintage, 1964. [Pp. 194–97.]

Hobbes, Thomas. *Leviathan.* New York: Dutton, 1950. [Pp. 133–34.]

James, Henry. "The Beast in the Jungle," *Henry James: Selected Short Stories.* New York: Pyramid Books, 1961 (copyright 1903). [Pp. 277–78.]

Kroeber, Theodora. *The Inland Whale.* University of California Press, 1963. [Pp. 148–49.]

Leach, E. R. *Political Systems of Highland Burma.* Cambridge, Mass.: Harvard University Press, 1954. [Pp. 172–95.]

Lienhardt, Godfrey. "Anuak Village Headmen," *Africa,* XXVII:4 (October 1957) 341–54.

Malinowski, Bronislaw. *The Sexual Life of Savages in Nort[h]western Melanesia.* London, 1929. [Pp. 114–15, 122–24, 13[0]-31, 144–46.]

———. *Coral Gardens and Their Magic.* American Book Com[-]pany, 1935. [Vol. I. Pp. 198–211.]

———. *Argonauts of the Western Pacific.* (First edition 1922. New York: Dutton, 1953. [Pp. 62–65.]

Pospisil, Leopold. *Kapauku Papuans and Their Law,* 1954–5[5] (Yale University Publications in Anthropology, No. 54, 1958. Human Relations Area Files Press, 1964. Pp. 80, 109–10, 244-45.

Radcliffe-Brown, A. R. *The Andaman Islanders,* 1906–8. Glencoe The Free Press, 1948. (First edition 1922.) Pp. 34, 35, 50, 5[3]-56.

Richardson, Jane. *Law and Status Among the Kiowa Indian[s]* c. 1865. (Monographs of the American Ethnological Society N[o] 1.) New York: J. J. Augustin, 1940. Pp. 35, 44, 45–7, 48–4[9] 50, 112.

Stenning, Derrick J. "Household viability among the pastora[l] Fulani," in Jack Goody (ed.), *The Developmental Cycle i[n] Domestic Groups* Pp. 92–119. Cambridge, The University Pres[s] 1958.

———. *Savannah Nomads.* London, Oxford University Pres[s] 1959. [Pp. 173, 181–82, 183–84.]

Turner, V. W. *Schism and Continuity in an African Society: [A] study of Ndembu Village Life,* 1953. Manchester: The Uni[-]versity Press, 1957. Pp. 95, 98, 116, 118–20, 138, 144–45, 154-57, 159–61, 162–64.

GENERAL WORKS

Dumont, Louis. *Homo Hierarchicus: an Essay on the Caste System.* Chicago: University of Chicago Press, 1970.

Fortes, Meyer. *Kinship and the Social Order.* Chicago: Aldine, 1969.

Fried, Morton H. *The Evolution of Political Society.* New York: Random House, 1967.

Gerth, Hans, and C. Wright Mills. *Character and Social Structure: The Psychology of Social Institutions.* New York: Harcourt, Brace and World, 1953.

Gluckman, Max. *Politics, Law, and Ritual in Tribal Society.* Chicago: Aldine, 1965.

Goody, Jack. *Comparative Studies in Kinship.* Stanford: Stanford University Press, 1969.

Malinowski Bronislaw. *The Family Among the Australian Aborigines.* London: University of London, 1913.

Murdock, George Peter. *Social Structure.* New York: Macmillan, 1949.

Nadel, Siegfried. *The Theory of Social Structure.* London: Cohen and West, 1957.

Redfield, Robert. *The Little Community.* Chicago: University of Chicago Press, 1955.

INDEX